Planning Regional Futures

Planning Regional Futures is an intellectual call to engage planners to critically explore what planning is, and should be, in how cities and regions are planned.

This is in a context where planning is seen to face powerful challenges – professionally, intellectually and practically – in ways arguably not seen before: planning is no longer solely the domain of professional planners but opened-up to a diverse group of actors; the link between the study of cities and regions, which traditionally had a disciplinary home in planning schools and the like, steadily eroded as research increasingly takes place in interdisciplinary research institutes; the advent of real-time modelling posing fundamental challenges for the type of long-term perspective that planning has traditionally afforded; 'regional planning' and its mixed record of achievement; and, the link between 'region' and 'planning' becoming decoupled as alternative regional (and other spatial) approaches to planning have emerged.

This book takes up the intellectual and practical challenge of planning regional futures, moving beyond the narrow confines of existing debate and providing a forum for debating what planning is, and should be, for in how we plan cities and regions.

The chapters in this book were originally published as a special issue of *Regional Studies.*

John Harrison is Reader in Human Geography at Loughborough University, UK.

Daniel Galland is Associate Professor of Urban and Regional Planning at Aalborg University Copenhagen, Denmark.

Mark Tewdwr-Jones is Bartlett Professor of Cities and Regions at the Centre for Advanced Spatial Analysis, University College London, UK.

Regions and Cities
Series Editor in Chief
Joan Fitzgerald, *Northeastern University, USA*
Editors
Roberta Capello, *Politecnico di Milano, Italy*
Rob Kitchin, *Maynooth University, Ireland*
Jörg Knieling, *HafenCity University Hamburg, Germany*
Nichola Lowe, *University of North Carolina at Chapel Hill, USA*

Routledge
Taylor & Francis Group
LONDON AND NEW YORK

Regional Studies Association

A leading & impactful community

In today's globalised, knowledge-driven and networked world, regions and cities have assumed heightened significance as the interconnected nodes of economic, social and cultural production, and as sites of new modes of economic and territorial governance and policy experimentation. This book series brings together incisive and critically engaged international and interdisciplinary research on this resurgence of regions and cities, and should be of interest to geographers, economists, sociologists, political scientists and cultural scholars, as well as to policy-makers involved in regional and urban development.

About the Regional Studies Association (RSA)
The Regions and Cities Book Series is a series of the Regional Studies Association (RSA). The RSA is a global and interdisciplinary network for regional and urban research, policy and development. The RSA is a registered not-for-profit organisation, a learned society and membership body that aims to advance regional studies and science. The RSA's publishing portfolio includes five academic journals, two-book series, a Blog and an online magazine. For more information on the Regional Studies Association, visit www.regionalstudies.org

There is a **30% discount** available to RSA members on books in the *Regions and Cities* series, and other subject-related Taylor and Francis books and e-books including Routledge titles. To order, simply email Luke Mc-Nicholas (Luke.McNicholas@tandf.co.uk), or phone +44 (0)20 701 77545 and declare your RSA membership. You can also visit the series page at www.routledge.com/Regions-and-Cities/book-series/RSA and use the discount code: **RSA225**

Latest books in the series

139 **Regional Economic Development and History**
Edited by Marijn Molema and Sara Svensson

140 **Rural Development in the Digital Age**
Exploring Neo-Productivist EU Rural Policy
Edited by Martin Pělucha and Edward Kasabov

141 **Smart Cities and Connected Intelligence**
Platforms, Ecosystems and Network Effects
Nicos Komninos

142 **Industry 4.0 and Regional Transformations**
Edited by Lisa De Propris and David Bailey

143 **Smart Development for Rural Areas**
Edited by André Torre, Stefano Corsi, Michael Steiner,
Fred Wallet and Hans Westlund

144 **Creative Cluster Development**
Governance, Place-Making and Entrepreneurship
Edited by Marlen Komorowski and Ike Picone

145 **Urban Competitiveness in Developing Economies**
Edited by Peter Karl Kresl

146 **The Confines of Territory**
Edited by John Agnew

147 **The Randstad**
A Polycentric Metropolis
Edited by Wil Zonneveld and Vincent Nadin

148 **Planning Regional Futures**
Edited by John Harrison, Daniel Galland and
Mark Tewdwr-Jones

149 **Border Cities and Territorial Development**
Edited by Eduardo Medeiros

For more information about this series,
please visit: www.routledge.com/Regions-and-Cities/book-series/RSA

Planning Regional Futures

Edited by
**John Harrison, Daniel Galland
and Mark Tewdwr-Jones**

Routledge
Taylor & Francis Group

LONDON AND NEW YORK

First published 2022
by Routledge
2 Park Square, Milton Park, Abingdon, Oxon, OX14 4RN

and by Routledge
605 Third Avenue, New York, NY 10158

Routledge is an imprint of the Taylor & Francis Group, an informa business

British Library Cataloguing-in-Publication Data
A catalogue record for this book is available from the British Library

ISBN: 978-0-367-70575-6 (hbk)
ISBN: 978-0-367-70576-3 (pbk)
ISBN: 978-1-003-14700-8 (ebk)

DOI: 10.4324/9781003147008

Typeset in Times New Roman
by codeMantra

Publisher's Note
The publisher accepts responsibility for any inconsistencies that may have arisen during the conversion of this book from journal articles to book chapters, namely the inclusion of journal terminology.

Disclaimer
Every effort has been made to contact copyright holders for their permission to reprint material in this book. The publishers would be grateful to hear from any copyright holder who is not here acknowledged and will undertake to rectify any errors or omissions in future editions of this book.

Contents

Citation Information   *ix*
Notes on Contributors   *xiii*

Introduction: whither regional planning?   1

John Harrison, Daniel Galland and Mark Tewdwr-Jones

1 **Regional planning is dead: long live planning regional futures**   10

John Harrison, Daniel Galland and Mark Tewdwr-Jones

2 **The return of the city-region in the new urban agenda:**
   is this relevant in the Global South?   34

Vanessa Watson

3 **Planning, temporary urbanism and citizen-led**
   alternative-substitute place-making in the Global South   53

Lauren Andres, Hakeem Bakare, John R. Bryson,
Winnie Khaemba, Lorena Melgaço and George R. Mwaniki

4 **Getting the territory right: infrastructure-led development**
   and the re-emergence of spatial planning strategies   75

Seth Schindler and J. Miguel Kanai

5 **City-regional imaginaries and politics of rescaling**   99

Simin Davoudi and Elizabeth Brooks

6 **Two logics of regionalism: the development of a regional**
   imaginary in the Toronto–Waterloo Innovation Corridor   121

David Wachsmuth and Patrick Kilfoil

7 **Planning megaregional futures: spatial imaginaries and**
   megaregion formation in China   148

John Harrison and Hao Gu

8 Understanding heterogeneous spatial production externalities
as a missing link between land-use planning and urban
economic futures 172

*Haozhi Pan, Tianren Yang, Ying Jin, Sandy Dall'Erba
and Geoffrey Hewings*

9 Spatial planning, nationalism and territorial politics in Europe 193

Claire Colomb and John Tomaney

10 Towards a sustainable, negotiated mode of strategic
regional planning: a political economy perspective 220

Ian Gordon and Tony Champion

11 Regional planning as cultural criticism: reclaiming the
radical wholes of interwar regional thinkers 244

Garrett Dash Nelson

12 Future-proof cities through governance experiments?
Insights from the Resilient Melbourne Strategy (RMS) 265

Sebastian Fastenrath and Lars Coenen

13 The new normative: synergistic scenario planning for
carbon-neutral cities and regions 288

Joe Ravetz, Aleksi Neuvonen and Raine Mäntysalo

Index *315*

Citation Information

The chapters in this book were originally published in *Regional Studies*, volume 55, issue 1 (2021). When citing this material, please use the original page numbering for each article, as follows:

Introduction

Whither regional planning?
John Harrison, Daniel Galland and Mark Tewdwr-Jones
Regional Studies, volume 55, issue 1 (2021) pp. 1–5

Chapter 1

Regional planning is dead: long live planning regional futures
John Harrison, Daniel Galland and Mark Tewdwr-Jones
Regional Studies, volume 55, issue 1 (2021) pp. 6–18

Chapter 2

The return of the city-region in the new urban agenda: is this relevant in the Global South?
Vanessa Watson
Regional Studies, volume 55, issue 1 (2021) pp. 19–28

Chapter 3

Planning, temporary urbanism and citizen-led alternative-substitute place-making in the Global South
Lauren Andres, Hakeem Bakare, John R. Bryson, Winnie Khaemba, Lorena Melgaço and George R. Mwaniki
Regional Studies, volume 55, issue 1 (2021) pp. 29–39

Chapter 4

Getting the territory right: infrastructure-led development and the re-emergence of spatial planning strategies
Seth Schindler and J. Miguel Kanai
Regional Studies, volume 55, issue 1 (2021) pp. 40–51

Chapter 5

City-regional imaginaries and politics of rescaling
Simin Davoudi and Elizabeth Brooks
Regional Studies, volume 55, issue 1 (2021) pp. 52–62

Chapter 6

Two logics of regionalism: the development of a regional imaginary in the Toronto–Waterloo Innovation Corridor
David Wachsmuth and Patrick Kilfoil
Regional Studies, volume 55, issue 1 (2021) pp. 63–76

Chapter 7

Planning megaregional futures: spatial imaginaries and megaregion formation in China
John Harrison and Hao Gu
Regional Studies, volume 55, issue 1 (2021) pp. 77–89

Chapter 8

Understanding heterogeneous spatial production externalities as a missing link between land-use planning and urban economic futures
Haozhi Pan, Tianren Yang, Ying Jin, Sandy Dall'Erba and Geoffrey Hewings
Regional Studies, volume 55, issue 1 (2021) pp. 90–100

Chapter 9

Spatial planning, nationalism and territorial politics in Europe
Claire Colomb and John Tomaney
Regional Studies, volume 55, issue 1 (2021) pp. 101–114

Chapter 10

Towards a sustainable, negotiated mode of strategic regional planning: a political economy perspective
Ian Gordon and Tony Champion
Regional Studies, volume 55, issue 1 (2021) pp. 115–126

Chapter 11

Regional planning as cultural criticism: reclaiming the radical wholes of interwar regional thinkers
Garrett Dash Nelson
Regional Studies, volume 55, issue 1 (2021) pp. 127–137

Chapter 12

Future-proof cities through governance experiments? Insights from the Resilient Melbourne Strategy (RMS)
Sebastian Fastenrath and Lars Coenen
Regional Studies, volume 55, issue 1 (2021) pp. 138–149

Chapter 13

The new normative: synergistic scenario planning for carbon-neutral cities and regions
Joe Ravetz, Aleksi Neuvonen and Raine Mäntysalo
Regional Studies, volume 55, issue 1 (2021) pp. 150–163

For any permission-related enquiries please visit:
http://www.tandfonline.com/page/help/permissions

Notes on Contributors

Lauren Andres
School of Geography, Earth and Environmental Sciences, The University of Birmingham, Birmingham, UK.
Bartlett School of Planning, UCL, London, UK.

Hakeem Bakare
City-Region Economic Development Institute, Birmingham Business School, The University of Birmingham, Birmingham, UK.

Elizabeth Brooks
School of Architecture, Planning and Landscape, Newcastle University, Newcastle upon Tyne, UK.

John R. Bryson
City-Region Economic Development Institute, Department of Strategy and International Business, Birmingham Business School, The University of Birmingham, Birmingham, UK.

Tony Champion
Centre for Urban and Regional Development Studies, Newcastle University, Newcastle upon Tyne, UK.

Lars Coenen
Mohn Centre for Innovation and Regional Development, Western Norway University of Applied Sciences, Bergen, Norway.
Melbourne Sustainable Society Institute, The University of Melbourne, Melbourne, VIC, Australia.

Claire Colomb
The Bartlett School of Planning, University College London, London, UK.

Sandy Dall'Erba
Regional Economics Applications Laboratory, University of Illinois at Urbana-Champaign, Urbana, IL, USA.

Garrett Dash Nelson
Dartmouth College – Geography, Hanover, NH, USA. Present affiliation: Leventhal Map & Education Center, Boston Public Library, Boston, MA, USA.

Simin Davoudi
Global Urban Research Unit, School of Architecture, Planning and Landscape, Newcastle University, Newcastle upon Tyne, UK.

Sebastian Fastenrath
Melbourne Sustainable Society Institute, The University of Melbourne, Melbourne, VIC, Australia.

Daniel Galland
Department of Planning, Aalborg University Copenhagen, Copenhagen, Denmark.

Ian Gordon
Department of Geography and Environment, London School of Economics, London, UK.

Hao Gu
School of Public Administration, Hunan University, Changsha, China.

John Harrison
Geography and Environment, Loughborough University, Loughborough, UK.

Geoffrey Hewings
Regional Economics Applications Laboratory, University of Illinois at Urbana-Champaign, Urbana, IL, USA.

Ying Jin
Martin Centre for Architectural and Urban Studies, Department of Architecture, University of Cambridge, Cambridge, UK.

J. Miguel Kanai
Geography Department, University of Sheffield, Sheffield, UK.

Winnie Khaemba
African Center for Technology Studies, ICIPE Duduville Campus, Kasarani, Nairobi, Kenya.

Patrick Kilfoil
School of Urban Planning, McGill University, Montreal, QC, Canada.

Raine Mäntysalo
Department of Built Environment, Aalto University, Aalto, Finland.

Lorena Melgaço
School of Geography, Earth and Environmental Sciences, The University of Birmingham, Birmingham, UK.

George R. Mwaniki
National Environment Trust Fund, Nairobi, Kenya; and African Center for Technology Studies, ICIPE Duduville Campus, Kasarani, Nairobi, Kenya.

Aleksi Neuvonen
DEMOS Helsinki, Helsinki, Finland.

Haozhi Pan
School of Design, Shanghai Jiao Tong University, Shanghai, China.

Joe Ravetz
Manchester Urban Institute, University of Manchester, Manchester, UK.

Seth Schindler
Global Development Institute and Manchester Urban Institute, University of Manchester, Manchester, UK.

Mark Tewdwr-Jones
Centre for Advanced Spatial Analysis, University College London, London, UK.

John Tomaney
The Bartlett School of Planning, University College London, London, UK.

David Wachsmuth
School of Urban Planning, McGill University, Montreal, QC, Canada.

Vanessa Watson
School of Architecture, Planning and Geomatics, University of Cape Town, Cape Town, South Africa.

Tianren Yang
Martin Centre for Architectural and Urban Studies, Department of Architecture, University of Cambridge, Cambridge, UK.

Introduction

Whither regional planning?

John Harrison ⓘ, Daniel Galland ⓘ
and Mark Tewdwr-Jones ⓘ

Introduction

Since *Regional Studies* was founded in 1967, planning and planners have been central to understanding cities and regions. Lest we forget that in the first ever issue of the journal, the opening papers all contained 're-gional plan' or 'regional planning' in their title (Figure 1). 'Regional plan-ning' was the first concept mentioned and the first purposeful argument proclaimed the need 'to ask and analyse some questions about the future of regional planning in the light of recent events' (Self, 1967, p. 3). Yet, fast forward to the present and it is striking how a journal synonymous with regions and planning contained no mention of regional planning in its 50th anniversary special issue (Turok et al, 2017).[1] This raises an important question: Have we witnessed the withering away of regional planning?

Recent developments and trends raise fundamental questions about the 'p' word (planning) in academic and policy circles.

We can point to how planning is no longer solely the domain of profes-sional planners but open to a diverse group of actors involved in place-making and place-shaping. In 1967, planning at various spatial scales was generally accepted as a function of the state. Over the last 40 years, plan-ning has been subject to ongoing ideological attacks from right-wing and populist governments globally for its perceived thwarting of growth and development, ostensibly neoliberal, agendas; in this sense, not only has planning been kicked in the shins and gone out of fashion, it has been un-dermined by the changing role and expectations of the state versus market interests.

We can observe how the study of cities and regions has traditionally had a disciplinary home in planning schools (geography departments, and the like, certainly since the early 20th century and more prominently since the 1940s), but this link with place and space disciplines is steadily eroding as research increasingly takes place in and through interdisciplinary research institutes.

We can identify the advent of real-time modelling of cities and regions (and the rise of so-called 'smart cities' set within 'smarter regions') and the challenges this poses for the type of long-term perspective that planning has traditionally afforded at a time, and in a society, where immediacy and short-termism are the watchwords. For citizens and communities increasingly leading and shaping their lives through smart technologies and social media, taking responsibility to shape their geographies themselves rather than rely on the state and government to operate on their behalf appears arguably to be both the present and the future. In 2020, 3.5 billion people own or have access to a smart phone, representing 44.87% of the world population, and the numbers that will own mobile devices are forecast to increase to 7.33 billion by 2023.

We can reflect on 'regional planning', based historically on arduous geographical surveys and analytical paper exercises undertaken by professional planners, and its mixed record of achievement. And we can recognize how the link between 'region' and 'planning' is decoupling as alternative regional (and other spatial) approaches to planning emerge in conjunction with more networked and relational forms of place-making, and the wider reimagination of the urban and the region.

Planning Regional Futures is an intellectual call-to-arms to engage planners (and those who engage with planning) to critically explore research agendas at the intersection of planning and regional studies. Our aim is to move beyond the narrow confines of existing debate, providing a forum for debating what planning is, and should be, for in regional studies. Let us be clear from the outset what this is not. It is not a narrowly focused discussion about the future of regional planning.[2] Neither is it an attempt to comprehensively document the depth and breadth of current work. And, despite the tide, it is not designed to be

Figure 1 Regional Studies, 7(1) (1967).

pessimistic. This special issue has quite the opposite purpose. The aim is to re-energize and provoke planning debates in regional studies by forging new ways of 'planning regional futures'. Our optimism comes from approaching this task as firm believers in the function of regional planning, if not the institutionalized form that regional planning typically takes. For us, this is about recovering the essence, purpose and values of planning suitable for a 21st-century context and bringing these to bear on wicked regional problems. It is here that we would argue planning's future in regional studies should be debated (Harrison et al., 2020, in this issue).

Debating planning regional futures

What kind of planning?

How we answer the question: What kind of planning? depends largely on whether we take 'planning and institutions' or 'place and problems' as the starting point. Contributors to this issue take as their starting point place-specific needs and wicked regional problems (cf. Purkarthofer et al., 2021). In this way we return to planning history, where regional planning occurred in an ad hoc, place-specific way, to address specific regional problems. It is sometimes easy to forget that the prehistory of institutionalized regional planning emerged in this way, rather than because there was a regional government or set of nationally determined institutions to perform it.[3] The implication of taking 'place and problems' as a starting point is that answering the question of what kind of planning becomes one of asking which planning style and approach is most appropriate for framing the problem at hand (Harrison et al., 2020, in this issue). Across the papers in this issue we see this in action as the focus of attention moves from one wicked regional problem to another – be it population dynamics and the impact of migration processes (Gordon & Champion, 2020, in this issue), increased nationalist, regionalist, separatist forces (Colomb & Tomaney, 2020, in this issue), the need for climate-compatible growth and environmental sustainability (Ravetz et al., 2020, in this issue), and managing competing demands on land use and their spatial externalities (Pan et al., 2020, in this issue).

A common theme is the weakness of traditional planning institutions and how they are not sufficiently agile to adjust to the new drivers of change (Tewdwr-Jones & Galland, 2020). While preparing this issue we have been able to observe the responses to the COVID-19 pandemic, critical questions about planning's role in facilitating racial inequality across US cities and regions, alongside many other issues which when looked at together emphasize the centrality of change and the need for planning to change with the times. It is here that we can see how approaches focusing attention on multiculturalism, decolonization and informality are leading to ever more diverse perspectives on what planning is and should be (Barry & Thompson-Fawcett, 2020; Bhan et al., 2017; Huq & Miraftab, 2020; Williams, 2020; Yiftachel, 2020). At one level this calls for reforms to the planning system. However, this does not solve the longer standing issue: How do we make the planning system adjust to, and accommodate, change?

Constantly subjected to shifting political ideologies and institutional reforms of the governing framework around planning (Davoudi et al., 2020), the regional tier of planning administration has always lacked the necessary agility to efficiently adjust to the multiple drivers of change constantly affecting territorialization. Operating within more fluid governance structures, planning regional futures will require more agile forms of planning activity. Developing the idea of 'alternative substitute place-making', Andres et al. (2020, in this issue) show how contemporary planning processes require embedding informal and temporary dynamics acting as surrogates in places where formal planning is hindered. Drawing on both lay and expert judgment, the resulting malleable planning style is shown to effectively grasp the complex interaction between place-making processes at different scales, allowing cities and regions to respond better to different temporalities. In a similar vein, Watson (2019, in this issue) argues for a more widespread recognition of place diversity and regional difference. Exposing the many parochial assumptions and limitations of the New Urban Agenda (NUA), Watson takes issue with the NUA's framing of cities and regions as well as the proposed managerial style of top-down, hierarchical state implementation. Across these contributions, we see that the kind of planning required is not old-style regional planning but new styles of planning regional futures capable of effectively addressing wicked regional problems. Or more accurately, an emphasis must be placed on how wicked regional problems are being, and will potentially be, dealt with by emerging styles of planning regional futures.

What kind of regions?

Planners and planning are having to adapt to a world comprising an increasingly unplanned and messy configuration of regional, and other spatial, imaginaries. Wachsmuth and Kilfoil (2020, in this issue) see the transition from the 'structured coherence' of the Fordist-Keynesian era to 'structured incoherence' as presenting multiple challenges for navigating today's regional planning landscape. Such is the fluidity and rapidity of change that discerning what new regional imaginaries mean for regional planning is a formidable task, especially when these 'imaginaries are performed to fix that which is fluid and unsettle that which is long conceived of as fixed' (Davoudi & Brooks, 2020, in this issue, p. 52).

Incoherence brings confusion, but coherence can just as easily lead to confusion. We should not forget that regional planning always takes on (sub)nationally specific forms (Bhan et al., 2017; Nadin et al., 2020). Yet, as Watson (2019, in this issue) argues, for all that the NUA is reviving international interest in planning, it is guilty of promoting a one-size-fits-all concept of city-regions which is neither appropriate nor even possible to use across much of the Global South. In the current period, growing international interest in regions and planning is a significant development because regional planning has traditionally been caught between the two main elected tiers of government national and local unable in many instances to sets its own definitive agenda. Contrast that with today where you have international organizations (such as UN-Habitat; Watson, 2016), global financial firms and international developers (Raco et al., 2019), and philanthropic organizations (such as the Rockefeller Foundation; Fastenrath & Coenen, 2020, in this issue; Taylor et al., 2020) as increasingly powerful actors, the ability for regional planning to be adaptive and agile to the needs of individual regions, sensitive to individual places and trends, and responsive to the multiple agencies operating in any one region becomes key. Agility also requires those doing the planning to be adept at juggling different skills, knowing when, where and how to deploy them (Harrison et al., 2020, in this issue).

Perhaps the biggest concern to emerge is the growing gap between the ambition and the reality of what regional planning can achieve. Exploring the re-emergence of spatial planning strategies connected to large-scale infrastructure-led developments, Schindler and Kanai (2019, in this issue, p. 48, original emphasis) argue that although 'ambitious *territorial forms* may be realized ... their *content* may escape the control of (inter-)national planners'. This sense of detachment comes through strongly in Harrison and Gu's (2020, in this issue) distinction between planning mega-regions (as discursive and imagined) and megaregional planning (as concrete and actual). They argue that while both connect regions and planning, directing attention to the former is a worrying distraction from the actual practice of planning. Across all papers, the message coming through loud and clear is that the current form of regional planning is problematic; however, optimism rests in recovering the essence, values and purpose of planning as it was always intended. This requires reconnection to place, addressing regional needs and capitalizing on regional opportunities – the very hallmarks of regional planning.

What kind of futures?

Shifting the horizons for planning in regional studies cannot involve business-as-usual approaches. Equally it cannot involve throwing the baby out with the bathwater by attempting to press a fictional reset button and wishing for a return to the halcyon days of institutionalized regional planning. Rather, planning regional futures necessitates going back to recover the essence, purpose and values of regional planning so that it continues to serve its fundamental wider purpose of addressing regional specific place needs.

For Nelson (2020, in this issue) reclaiming the reform-minded planning of interwar regional thinkers such as Benton MacKaye and Lewis Mumford is essential to break free from the administrative rationality of present-day institutionalized regional planning. Similarly, Gordon and Champion (2020, in this issue) return to a classic spatial planning case study in regional studies – London and the South East region of England (Hall, 1967; John et al., 2002) – to make the case for going back to first principles with strategic spatial planning. Arguing against the practice of adhering to the centrality of any singular 'strategic' plan of the conventional professional kind, they argue how:

> the role of a socially licensed professional represents a tamer, more institutionalized but politically defensible, counterpart to his [Rein's 1969 original taxonomy of available sources of legitimation for planning practice] 'guerrilla' role which has planners striving to enhance governmental competence and responsiveness by any means available. If not specifically one for 'planners', his guerrilla role does ... have something in common with the view of strategic planning (as practice) for which we are arguing.
>
> (Gordon & Champion, 2020, in this issue, p. 125)

Going back to move forward is also integral to Ravetz et al.'s (2020, in this issue, p. 157) futures claim that achieving carbon neutrality targets in metropolitan regions requires a synergistic-collaborative planning style that facilitates practical pathways which are capable of 'linking future goals with present-day actions'.

When considering planning regional futures (and planning's future in regional studies) a stark warning is offered by Fastenrath and Coenen (2020, in this issue) when examining the future-proofing of cities via the adoption of resilience frameworks. Set against the context of claims that 'governance experiments' promise new ways of collaborating and innovating, capable of breaking down bureaucratic silos and fostering transformative change, they question how much of this planning actually amounts to transformative change or 'simply camouflages business as usual' (p. 147).

Opening a debate on regions and planning

Planning has not disappeared from regional studies. Indeed, and perhaps curiously, despite the ideological coshing of planning by state entities over some decades, planning is still alive and well in most nations, even if it is subject to continual reform narratives amidst complaints from some politicians and business leaders that it is not fit for purpose. This said, other themes have emerged over the past 50 years such that 'regional studies' is no longer a byword for regional planning and development. Regional studies has matured into an increasingly pluralist forum encouraging diversity of perspectives and approaches over any single paradigm, interpretation or approach. Our argument is that planning remains integral to the future of regional studies, but not in the form it once took. Stated bluntly, we do not need regional planning, but we do need planning in regional studies.

Our view is that planning in regional studies will always have an important connection to formal structures and frameworks of government/governance. This is essential to provide a democratic legitimacy and give form to planning activities. As Wray (2015), drawing on the work of the aforementioned Peter Self, notes, 'planning exists not simply to anticipate the future but to actively shape it – and sometimes to change, rather than accommodate, current trends'.

Planning regional futures will increasingly centre on consortia of willing actors bringing their skills, competencies and resources to bear on trying to actively address those wicked problems affecting cities and regions. Planning and planners can have a key role to play in this and it is one they must be ready to grasp. Planning's origins lay there. Why not its future too?

Disclosure statement

No potential conflict of interest was reported by the authors.

Notes

1 Across 13 articles, Paasi and Metzger (2017) fleetingly mention 'regional planning' once, while Chen and Vickerman (2017, p. 156) do likewise, but only to say 'there is no administrative body and statutory planning power to consider the wider effects of HSR [high-speed rail] at the city-regional level'.
2 Given our starting point (see the first paragraph), the original title for this special issue was going to be 'Regional Planning Futures'. However, we found this limiting, and in the spirit of opening up debates over the future of planning in regional studies, we wanted to leave nothing off the table – including the future of regional planning itself.
3 In the opening paragraph of *Regional Studies'* first editorial, we are struck by the wording that differentiates other professionals (economists, engineers, geographers, agronomists and sociologists) from 'those who would describe themselves as planners' (Sharman, 1967, p. 1). This highlights how despite the emphasis on 'regional planning', planning itself was still in the process of becoming institutionalized.

ORCID

John Harrison ⓘ http://orcid.org/0000-0002-6434-5142
Daniel Galland ⓘ http://orcid.org/0000-0003-2648-806X
Mark Tewdwr-Jones ⓘ http://orcid.org/0000-0002-8786-6434

References

Andres, L., Bryson, J., Bakara, H., Khaemba, W., Melgaço, L., & Mwaniki, G. (2020). Planning, temporary urbanism and citizen-led alternative—substitute place-making in the Global South. *Regional Studies*. https://doi.org/10.1080/00343404.2019.1665645

Barry, J., & Thompson-Fawcett, M. (2020). Decolonizing the boundaries between the 'planner' and the 'planned': Implications of indigenous property development. *Planning Theory and Practice, 21*(3), 410–425. https://doi.org/10.1080/14649357.2020.1775874

Bhan, G., Srinivas, S., & Watson, V. (Eds.). (2017). *The Routledge companion to planning in the Global South*. Routledge.

Chen, C., & Vickerman, R. (2017). Can transport infrastructure change regions' economic fortunes? Some evidence from Europe and China. *Regional Studies, 51*(1), 144–160. https://doi.org/10.1080/00343404.2016.1262017

Colomb, C., & Tomaney, J. (2020). Spatial planning, nationalism and territorial politics in Europe. *Regional Studies*. https://doi.org/10.1080/00343404.2020.1744552

Davoudi, S., & Brooks, E. (2020). City regional imaginaries and the politics of rescaling. *Regional Studies*. https://doi.org/10.1080/00343404.2020.1762856

Davoudi, S., Galland, D., & Stead, D. (2020). Reinventing planning and planners: Ideological decontestations and rhetorical appeals. *Planning Theory, 19*(1), 17–37. https://doi.org/10.1177/1473095219869386

Fastenrath, S., & Coenen, L. (2020). Future-proof cities through governance experiments? Insights from the Resilient Melbourne Strategy. *Regional Studies*. https://doi.org/10.1080/00343404.2020.1744551

Gordon, I., & Champion, T. (2020). Towards a sustainable, negotiated mode of strategic regional planning: A political economy perspective. *Regional Studies*. https://doi.org/10.1080/00343404.2020.1759795

Hall, P. (1967). Planning for urban growth: Metropolitan area plans and their implications for south-east England. *Regional Studies, 1*(2), 101–134. https://doi.org/10.1080/09595236700185131

Harrison, J., Galland, D., & Tewdwr-Jones, M. (2020). Regional planning is dead: Long live planning regional futures. *Regional Studies*. https://doi.org/10.1080/00343404.2020.1750580

Harrison, J., & Gu, H. (2020). Planning megaregional futures: Spatial imaginaries and megaregion formation in China. *Regional Studies*. https://doi.org/10.1080/00343404.2019.1679362

Huq, E., & Miraftab, F. (2020). 'We are all refugees': Camps and informal settlements as converging spaces of global displacements. *Planning Theory and Practice, 21*(3), 351–370. https://doi.org/10.1080/14649357.2020.1776376

John, P., Musson, S., & Tickell, A. (2002). England's problem region: Regionalism in the South East. *Regional Studies, 36*(7), 733–741. https://doi.org/10.1080/0034340022000006051

Nadin, V., Stead, D., Dąbrowski, M., & Fernandez-Maldonado, A. M. (2020). Integrated, adaptive and participatory spatial planning: Trends across Europe. *Regional Studies*. https://doi.org/10.1080/00343404.2020.1817363

Nelson, G. (2020). Regional planning as cultural criticism: Reclaiming the radical wholes of interwar regional thinkers. Regional Studies. https://doi.org/10.1080/00343404.2020.1737664

Paasi, A., ScMetzger, J. (2017). Foregrounding the region. *Regional Studies, 51*(1), 19–30. https://doi.org/10.1080/00343404.2016.1239818

Pan, H., Yang, T., Dall'erba, S., Jin, Y., & Hewings, G. (2020). Understanding heterogenous spatial production externalities as a missing link between land-use planning and urban economic futures. *Regional Studies.* https://doi.org/10.1080/00343404.2019.1701186

Purkarthofer, E., Humer, A., & Mäntysalo, R. (Forthcoming 2021). Regional planning: An arena of interests, institutions and relations. *Regional Studies.*

Raco, M., Livingstone, N., & Durrant, D. (2019). Seeing like an investor: Urban development planning, fmancialisation, and investors' perceptions of London as an investment space. *European Planning Studies, 27*(6), 1064–1082. https://doi.org/10.1080/09654313.2019.1598019

Ravetz, J., Neuvonen, A., ScMantysalo, R. (2020). The new normative: Synergistic scenario planning for carbon-neutral cities and regions. *Regional Studies.* https://doi.org/10.1080/00343404.2020.1813881

Schindler, S., & Kanai, J.-M. (2019). Getting the territory right: Infrastructure-led development and its spatial planning strategies. *Regional Studies.* https://doi.org/10.1080/00343404.2019.1661984

Self, P. (1967). Regional planning in Britain: Analysis and evaluation. *Regional Studies, 1*(1), 3–10. https://doi.org/10.1080/09595236700185021

Sharman, F. A. (1967). The Regional Studies Association — Origins and opportunities. *Regional Studies, 1*(1), 1–2. https://doi.org/10.1080/09595236700185011

Taylor, Z., Fitzgibbons, J., & Mitchell, C. (2020). Finding the future in policy discourse: An analysis of city resilience plans. *Regional Studies.* https://doi.org/10.1080/00343404.2020.1760235

Tewdwr-Jones, M., & Galland, D. (2020). Planning metropolitan futures, the future of metropolitan planning: In what sense planning agile? In K. Zimmermann, D. Galland, & J. Harrison (Eds.), *Metropolitan regions, planning and governance* (pp. 225–234). Springer.

Turok, L, Bailey, D., Clark, J., Du, J., Fratesi, U., Fritsch, M., Harrison, J., Kemeny, T., Kogler, D., Lagendijk, A., Mickiewicz, T., Miguelez, E., Usai, S., & Wishlade, F. (2017). 50th anniversary special issue. *Regional Studies, 51*(1), 1–8. https://doi.org/10.1080/00343404.2016.1255720

Wachsmuth, D., & Kilfoil, P. (2020). Two logics of regionalism: The development of a regional imaginary in the Toronto- Waterloo Innovation Corridor. *Regional Studies.* https://doi.org/10.1080/00343404.2020.1817362

Watson, V. (2016). Locating planning in the New Urban Agenda of the urban sustainable development goal. *Planning Theory, 15*(4), 435–448. https://doi.org/10.1177/1473095216660786

Watson, V. (2019). The return of the city-region in the New Urban Agenda: Is this relevant in the Global South? *Regional Studies.* https://doi.org/10.1080/00343404.2019.1664734

Williams, R. A. (2020). From racial to reparative planning: Confronting the white side of planning. *Journal of Planning Education and Research.* https://doi.org/10.1177/0739456X20946416

Wray, I. (2015). *Great British plans: Who made them and how they worked.* Routledge.

Yiftachel, O. (2020). From displacement to displaceability: A southeastern perspective on the new metropolis. *City, 24*(1–2), 151–165. https://doi.org/10.1080/13604813.2020.1739933

Regional planning is dead: long live planning regional futures

John Harrison ⓘ, Daniel Galland ⓘ
and Mark Tewdwr-Jones ⓘ

Introduction: it's the end of regional planning as we know it (and we feel fine)

The aim in this paper is to re-energize planning debates in regional studies. This is despite our somewhat less optimistic starting point, which is a contention that regional planning as we know it is now defunct and something we need to get used to. However, let us be clear from the outset. This is not as it may first appear a one-way critique of regional planning and by implication the history of planning within regional studies, one written with all the benefits of hindsight. What it is instead is a provocation of a different sort. It is a provocation that amounts to a first step towards forecasting a more positive future for planning in regional studies, albeit one which is very different in style, approach and purpose. Rather than defend or try to reclaim that which has been lost with the decline of institutionalized forms of regional planning, our motivations centre on forging new ways of planning regional futures. For us, this is about recovering the very essence, purpose and values of planning. It is about bringing these to bear on the wicked problems affecting regional futures. It is to say that regional planning was of its time, but that time is not now. It is to claim that much of what we associate with this era – the all-encompassing geographically fixed grand plan, uniformal approaches, formally institutionalized planning, planners as kingmakers – is best remembered as a relic of an age which is passing or has already passed. What interests us is what is relevant to today's needs and those which lay ahead. It is here that planning's future in regional studies should be debated.

The paper is structured as follows. To shift the horizons for planning in regional studies, we start by identifying those disruptive elements that have undermined traditional forms of institutionalized regional planning, developing an argument that contemporary planning debates have become too obsessed with the institutional planning frame and distracted from the changing content of the real-world picture (the second section). For our part, we seek to reassert the purpose and values of planning by rediscovering the content, conceptualize multiple and fluid forms of planning frames, repositioning the planner as an orchestrator and enabler of planning regional futures (the third section). In the conclusions (the fourth section), we reflect on how our vision challenges conventional understandings for the future of planning cities and regions.

Why planning? Why regions? Why now?

Planning

The hallmark of planning is that it is:

> a professional and highly politically contentious process attempting to make sense of the drivers of change that have land use effects geographically, against short-, medium and long-term trends, within changing governing structures, and individual and collective expectations that have social, economic and environmental implications that change over time.
>
> (Tewdwr-Jones, 2012, p. 4)

If this is the hallmark of planning per se, the adjectives that precede 'planning' alert us to multiple understandings that emerge from different *planning traditions* (most notably, positivist planning with the statutory land-use plan as the yardstick and regulation as the model of implementation versus interpretative approaches, which are less about the plan and implementation, focusing instead on place-making strategies, relational processes and spatial governance) and *planning styles* (1950s' 'rational', 1960s' 'advocacy' and 1970s' 'radical' from the United States; 'communicative', 'collaborative' and 'deliberative' from Europe and North America since the 1990s; 'post-political' and 'agonistic' emerging in the 2000s) (Allmendinger, 2017; Davoudi, 2012; Fainstein & DeFilippis, 2016). Each emerges from its own context, generates its own definition and meaning of what planning is, and then the spatial scales at which this mode of planning occurs, the role of the planner and the plan therein, and the methods and skills required to do planning. Today, and looking ahead, approaches focusing attention on multiculturalism, decolonization and informality are leading to ever more diverse perspectives on what planning is and should be (Gunder et al., 2018).

With planning being an activity of the public, private and third sectors, different aspects of planning occur at different geographical scales, formulated, regulated or implemented by different governance actors. Let us not forget that in the early 20th century, planning in Western countries was characterized by informality and very localized arrangements, often operationalized by individual architects or local governments, acting where there was a justifiable need for intervention (Hall, 2014). Only as time progressed, and people understood growing relationships between adjacent places, did ideas about regional planning begin to emerge (Geddes, 1915). In an array of contexts in the Global North, it was only in the mid-to-latter half of the 20th century that planning became an institutionalized activity of the state in its various guises, shaped by statute and associated with the conferment of legal rights and responsibilities to defined, geographically fixed administrative or government units.

What was an activity of the central state in the mid-20th century soon became an activity of multiple levels of government, shared between the central and local state. As the decades passed, so the governing framework of planning changed and adapted to suit political ideological preferences. Nations have flirted with these changing scales and revised institutional forms of government (and therefore with planning) throughout the last century, as different governments prioritized different scales of policy- and decision-making, not linearly but often moving forward then doubling back to previous older forms and recognizable governing structures, depending on global economic changes, ideological preferences on the part of the governing political party, and the needs of individual nations and regions.

Governments may pursue planning through national action and policy through subnational mechanisms or, in the case of federal nations, through separate legal and policy arrangements (Knaap et al., 2015). What may be regarded as national and regional planning issues may be matters of national and regional significance (such as the provision of infrastructure), but it may also refer to nationally and regionally important issues that are delegated to subnational government (such as the operation of the planning system of development regulation). Equally, regional planning is not a static or single entity: it largely depends on the nation being considered, the constitutional settlement in each country, the style of planning present, and the relationship to both national forms of planning and local planning conditions. As conditions and times change, so do successive reforms of the governing framework around planning, with historical roles of some governing scales retaining a legacy for newly emerging forms of planning tiers. Since the late 1990s this picture has been clouded by the emergence of governance and the market, alongside government, initiating policies, developing strategies, and taking decisions on issues and in areas that perhaps had been undertaken previously by the state (Harrison, 2020; Raco & Savini, 2019).

At first glance, it is easy to believe that as time marches on, some ideas brought to bear in planning are new, whereas others have sometimes been tried before but are recycled in new times, in new guises and given new labels. The fact that planning has endured through all these changes is a remarkable testament to its resilience. An alternative perspective is that maybe planning is a useful political tool because it has become sufficiently adaptable to take on new agendas and preferences. Regional planning is therefore a much more dynamically changing activity than is sometimes recognized, susceptible to changing political preferences and institutional reform even in individual nation states, as well as the consequence of changing regional needs.

Planning and regions

During the second half of the 20th century, the regional dimension to planning appeared self-evident: after all, there were regional plans, regional planners and regional planning. Integral to this was knowing what 'the region' was that was being planned, but there are two fundamental problems with this assumption. The first is *spatial* because, as any student of regional studies can state, there are no regions out there waiting to be planned (Allen et al., 1998). Regions are constantly in a state of flux, and yet much 20th-century planning was fixated with the ideal of all encompassing, geographically fixed grand plans. In our fast-paced and volatile globalizing world, regions increasingly take on multiple forms such that asking What is a region?' has never been so redundant. Far more important is understanding how regions are being constructed, who or what is mobilizing them, and most critically, to what end (Paasi et al., 2018).[1] Planning is no different. Planners cannot assume the region in which, through which, or over which planning happens because the landscape is far more complex than ever before (Healey, 2007). Those traditional forms of longer term planning with fixed plans that required time to prepare and adopt are also likely to be a relic of regional planning, not relevant to today's needs (Friedmann, 1993). To survive, planners and planning must adapt to a world comprising the unplanned – and decidedly messy – configuration of multiple, overlapping, competing and contradictory spatial imaginaries (Paasi & Zimmerbauer, 2016).

The second problem is *scalar,* because a hallmark of regional planning is that it has always been at the mercy of the two main elected tiers of government – national and local – as opposed to setting its own definitive agenda (Friedmann & Weaver, 1979). Regional planning was always caught between national government, for whom regional planning is the vehicle for implementing projects which have national and interregional significance, and local government, for whom regional planning is a way to address intraregional issues that have localized implications. In post-war welfare states, different styles of regional planning emerged in response to a dual *problematique* – indicative planning styles in response to increasing inequalities between regions (Friedmann, 1963) and land-use control to mitigate the environmental consequences of urban sprawl in the automobile age (Glasson, 1978). The story of regional planning, therefore, owes much to where the power lies between national and local because this determines what can happen at the regional level (Kuklinski, 1970). More problematic than this, however, has been the constant challenge for regional planning effusing two fundamentally different rationales (national – top-down – interregional vis-à-vis local – bottom-up – intraregional) for its existence, both of which appear contradictory (Haughton & Counsell, 2004). The upshot is regional planning always took on nationally specific forms such that there is, and never was, one 'regional planning' so to speak. In a federal system, such as Germany or the United States, regional planning was always less at the whims of local and national government than in a non-federal system (e.g., the UK), while in more centralized authoritarian states such as China, regional planning is key to promoting growth, whereas in Britain the opposite discourse exists (Wu, 2015).

Context is important, but our argument is that while the window dressing is, and will always be, different in different contexts (sprawl, metropolitan regionalism, zoning in the United States; greenbelts and new towns in the UK; natural resources in Venezuela and Chile, for example) the essential purpose of regional planning remains the same: capitalizing on regional opportunities, dealing with regional problems. In other words, while the endpoint (the outcomes) and midpoints (the means, styles, mechanisms and focus) of regional planning are always going to be different, the starting point is the same, and that is place. A further important point is that our contention that regional planning is dead is not just limited to those contexts where fixation with administrative and institutionalized forms of 'regional planning' has been eroded (e.g., the UK, Denmark and the Netherlands) (Roodbol-Mekkes & van den Brink, 2015). Regional planning may still exist in its institutionalized form across many countries, and indeed still soldiering on preparing regional plans, but the practice of regional planning is dead (at best on life support) because while it might exist in name it is powerless as a shaper of regional spatial change (Galland, 2012). We say powerless because it is insufficiently agile to deal with constant change and complexity, too susceptible to long periods of governmental preparation in a fast-paced modern world, undermined by administrative containment in a world of increased connection and flow, and a small player vis-à-vis more powerful arms of the state and market forces which can and will instantaneously undermine any instrument of regional planning, however, well legally fixed it is in those countries constitution.

Planning, regions and futures

Former, current and future institutionalized forms of regional planning have been, are being and will continue to be undermined by disruptive elements. Oftentimes perceived beyond the grasp of planning, the 'wicked' character of these disruptive issues is essentially reified as external, paradigmatic, ideological-motivated forces holding an intrinsic capacity to subvert, destabilize and ultimately erode regional planning. While it might be a truism that any unsettling of the essence and values of regional planning takes place within the scope of a larger political domain, we must similarly acknowledge the influence of three other parallel domains: economic (e.g., firm strategies, investment decisions, technological developments, labour dynamics), socio-spatial (e.g., rising inequality and differentiation, increased population and migration) and socio-environmental (e.g., pressures around climate-energy-water, food supply, aging, security) (Galland et al., 2020).

Against this backdrop, changing institutional and policy landscapes have triggered the increasing use of ad hoc, incremental or project-led approaches in planning, oftentimes denoted by a confusing range of styles and the struggle to align actors continually. The scope and time elements of planning have respectively transitioned from comprehensive, spatial and long-termed approaches towards siloed, less spatial (or even spaceless) and shorttermed perspectives. Planning policies articulated as forms of single policy interventions have gradually become cancelled out by other external interventions frequently lacking synoptic and systems thinking. Planning has consequently and steadily become subservient to other narrow interests and, in doing so, has unreflectively cut and pasted policy ideas from other territories – adamant to take institutional and spatial histories into account (Stead, 2012). At the same time, there has been a progressive fragmentation of those doing 'actual' planning (Raco & Savini, 2019).

As the fortunes of institutions and policies ebb and flow, so does the fate of formalized regional planning. Characterized by the primacy of the global market and its flows of investment, accelerated regional change is mobilized through the close alignment between real-estate markets and global financial capital (Savini & Aalbers, 2016). Neoliberal reforms, policy interventions and readjustments increasingly allow for changes in legislation related to agricultural land and planning, facilitating the incorporation of public and communal land into real-estate markets. Through these mechanisms, the commercialization of low-priced rural land enables the dispersed expansion of residential suburban, industrial and commercial, and infrastructural lands (Murat Güney et al., 2019), as well as service-oriented uses in large city-regions and increasingly intermediate ones in Global North and South contexts (Schindler & Kanai, 2019).

Mobilized and honed through the logic of global financial capitalism, financial real-estate development is facilitated through a myriad of instruments where only specific actors (banks, hedge funds and institutional investors) get to participate, pragmatically and swiftly materialized in the form of industrial and logistical parks, commercial centres, residential areas, gated communities and transport infrastructure. Given their size and shape, these physical interventions deeply affect urban-regional dynamics through processes of accelerated dispersed expansion at the expense of the sustainability of smaller city-regions. This increasingly results in the congestion of regional spaces as well as other socio-spatial and environmental externalities. Surely we should all be concerned that many now hold the view that 'planning is [only] good for some basic tasks of economic management, such as building big infrastructures, but is inferior to markets in seeing the future' (Storper, 2016, p. 247).

Adding to this, the crisis of representative democracy and the rise of alternative forms of democracy have further undermined the legitimacy of planning and fragmented the means through which these multiple agencies affecting and effecting regional change are held responsible for their actions (Allmendinger & Haughton, 2019). If we recognize and accept that accountability operates along multiple dimensions, uses various mechanisms of performance, and requires various levels of organizational response, then planning is clearly facing an accountability crisis.

Regions and planning at the crossroads: from institutionalized regional planning to multiple forms of planning regional futures

Twentieth-century regional planning is dead and the form that planning took expired with it as the pillars upon which it was constructed (structurally, ideologically, spatially) have been removed or severely weakened. As noted above, this may be uncomfortable for those in places where institutional regional planning remains, or those who crave for its return. Moreover, it will present a challenge to those looking to the New Urban Agenda as a framework for shaping urban and regional futures, particularly across the Global South:

> §49 We commit ourselves to support territorial systems that integrate urban and rural functions into the national and subnational spatial frameworks
>
> §72 We commit ourselves to long-term urban and territorial planning processes and spatial development practices.
>
> (UN-Habitat, 2017)

A new urban agenda it may be, but old regional planning it is – territorial, top-down, long-term. So where next?

Regional planning is at a crossroads. One option is to carry straight on, adopt a stoic business-as-usual mentality, and try to ignore how regional planning is dead (or dying) in places which have actually done regional planning. Another option is to turn off and head in the direction adopted by the New Urban Agenda, presenting old-style regional planning as some-how 'new', but this path will quickly become bumpy and reach another dead end (Watson, 2019). The third option is to turn off in a different direction altogether – what we present here as 'planning regional futures'.

We may have reached the end of regional planning as we know it but rather than feel sorrow or nostalgic about this, we have a renewed sense of hope that the multiple forms regional planning now takes offer a far more optimistic outlook for planning regional futures. We are optimistic because we see planning becoming more, not less, important. This rests on seeing planning as an entity, not all of which is – or should be – professionalized and institutionalized as 'planning'.

The proposition is simple: we need to recognize the world for what it is, not as it once was, and to plan accordingly. To do this we must direct our attention back toward the content of the picture rather than the institutional frame which we have become increasingly fixated with.

For a new planning of regions

Reasserting the purpose and values of planning

The case for initiating any form of regional planning stems from a desire to deal with major externalities associated with the growth or decline of places, most often urban areas. That has always been the hallmark of re-gional planning. Alongside rapid urbanization, a requirement to analyse changing social, economic, environmental and technological changes, spa-tial connectivity and differentials between neighbouring places, and a need to propose phased and resourced essential infrastructure, have all necessi-tated a more-than-local, regional, response. The task of relying on regional planning to analyse trends and create a political and resourced programme of action is the very essence of planning. Or at least it should be.

Let us not forget that the Garden City Movement that emerged in the UK and the City Beautiful Movement in the United States came about pre-cisely because of a desire to address how we live, the need to address social plights of the most vulnerable in society, and the externalities of industrial development (Howard, 1902). Moreover, Patrick Geddes, who influenced planning with its working method of survey the region, analyse and finally – and only then – plan, was premised on the idea of place-to-place interre-lationships, connectivity and infrastructure links (Geddes, 1915). Geddes' evolutionary urbanism was part developmental, part evolutionary and part environmental, linking social processes to physical forms, but that cities should be studied in the context of the region. What this reminds us is the development of regional plans, more commonly referred to as regional re-ports, in the 1910s and 1920s occurred in an ad hoc, place-specific way, to address economic decline and unemployment. Not one of these pivotal mo-ments in the emergence of regional planning occurred because there was a regional government or set of nationally determined institutions to perform it. And yet, in the second half of the 20th century, as soon as regional planning gradually institutionalized through standardized nationally imposed frameworks and forms covering larger administrative areas, planners lost some of the raison d'être for having regional planning. Planning forgot that regional planning was meant to be there to serve a wider purpose, rather than to see it as just another administrative tier of institutional forms and one-size-all responses (Rydin, 2011).

It is little wonder that constant arguments have materialized since this time between national and subnational actors – centred around differentials in top-down funding allocations, infrastructure spending, new housing development numbers – and within national governments. Against this constant game of regional political football, politicians have resorted to seeing the means – the tools and forms of regional planning – in all their flawed glory, as the real problem at hand. It is an easy if somewhat lazy response to make. Planners, too, have tended to resort to arguing over the institutional and political forms of regional planning, lamenting their loss, or loss of status and reformulation, rather than address regional specific place needs (Watson, 2009). The result is the regional has often been seen as a convenient, if troublesome, tier of administration, drawing constantly on national funding resources and operating at arm's length of government (Allmendinger & Haughton, 2007; Brenner, 2003).

And so we come full circle: planners and planning advocates aided and abetted by national government welfarist policies accelerated regional planning from a spatially selective activity where it was needed, into an institutionalized and standardized bureaucratic machine that became divorced from place needs and increasingly resented (Hall & Tewdwr-Jones, 2020). Over a century after Geddes, we can still identify a range of social, economic, environmental and technological problems that places are experiencing, and we recognize that those problems take on different degrees of importance or relevance in different places, affected by circumstances of place and history and policy intervention. We also recognize that places change as much due to relational changes outwith a place as the drivers of change internal to and affecting the place itself. Some of the problems might be different today compared with the 1920s, but they remain issues that require a form of regional response. The regional is a vital and convenient tier of strategic planning and will remain so, even if identifying an appropriate spatially fixed administrative and democratic fit between the national and the local is often an unobtainable task.

In the 21st century, the case for regional planning is set against a backdrop of politically unfavourable large units of subnational government, weak democratic accountability and legitimacy, subnational plans that take an eternity to prepare, and the bypassing of subnational strategies in practice by more immediate ad hoc spatially selective national responses. Having a regional plan might now be seen as something of a luxury. And so, a critical question remains: Can the region ever be planned and, if so, what future form should regional planning take?

Recognizing the fragmented and multiple agency landscape of planning

Cities and regions are becoming increasingly complex, technologically driven, and difficult to plan for with any degree of certainty. The world faces an array of crises, from economic uncertainty, demographic change, climate change and extreme weather events, to greater social polarization, spread of infections and diseases, and political turbulence. The impact of these changes will be difficult to ascertain and the resultant disruption these will have on places in the immediate future and longer term. However, we do know the changes will have geographical implications for different settlements in the same region. We will need to address the spatial implications of climate change, flooding and the loss of habitat. We will continue to address the economic fate of places as global trade patterns affect business relocation, failure and growth, and nation-states financial stability fluctuate. We remain appalled at harrowing stories of social exclusion, poverty levels, the left behind, the fate of migrants and populist attitudes towards different groups in society. We marvel at the availability of technology to compress time and space, instantly at our fingertips. We can celebrate all that is unique about places that make them attractive, or historic, or worth protecting or visiting.

It goes without saying that researchers and practitioners with advanced knowledge and understanding of urban and regional change recognize that all of these trends affect spatial change in different ways, within the same country, within a city, between cities, between urban and rural, and how different sectoral changes affect other sectors. How often do we lament also at the continuing failings of government to address issues, in a timely way, even when evidence is presented. We become frustrated at the misalignment between different public and private agencies responsible for service or policy delivery in different places. We criticize political institutions and multinationals for their lack of transparency in how they make decisions that affect cities and regions in the present and long term. And we become agitated with the arrogance of government bodies in how they exclude the subjects to which they are supposedly answerable.

In place of larger units of subnational government, that are either being abolished or at least subjugated, an array of agencies now jostle to perform tasks that might otherwise have lay at the door of regional planners and regional government. Utility companies responsible for energy and water are often privatized companies, controlled by multinationals; transport services are in the hands of a multitude of state and business interests, with a lack of integration between transport infrastructure sunk costs and the provision of different modes of public transport services; health services and education provision are shaped by more localized governance forms; economic development policy might be instigated by more-than-local agencies in an era of inter-place competition; and development itself is increasingly determined by real estate market interests where meeting demand will generate the best financial returns (Pike et al., 2019; Raco & Savini, 2019). An individual region in the 2020s might have dozens of different types of agencies public, private, public-private, governance, government taking critical decisions that shape the future spatial form of the regional area. This is a recognition of how difficult it now is to have any form of regional coordination and regional alignment of strategic investment decisions across a myriad of vested interests.

Not only have we forgotten about the original 20th-century intention of having regional planning (i.e., it exists only where it is needed), we have ended up with a lamentable substitute for it in the 21st century. Addressing regional problems is not only resolved by new nationally determined infrastructure spending. Nor is it addressed by simply having a regional plan. Technology and climate change, global trade and world social mobility, occurring rapidly and disruptively, have all made the task of institutionalized and siloed regional planning a difficult endeavour. The result has been for regional planning exercises, where they still exist, to retrench into focusing on narrow growth and infrastructure matters but with little political force over the real agencies of change. The 20th-century tools we once relied upon cannot be used today to address such critical issues as interregional differences, the relationships between capital cities and second-tier urban regions, and the vulnerability of parts of a region to rising sea levels or drought or wildfires. Some may use that as an argument to abandon planning altogether, an approach some politicians have used to justify the removal of those institutionalized and bureaucratic standard regional forms. However, rhetorically, do we still not need to identify what is happening at a regional scale, by analysing changes, coordinating responses, mapping vulnerabilities and opportunities, and delivering political programmes of action?

Embracing and promoting the unique qualities and attributes of planning

Not having regional planning apparatus does not equate to not having regional planning. Here we need to think less of late 20th-century regional planning as regional plans and regional institutions. Rather, we need to think of regional planning as an enduring set of attributes and qualities, a toolkit of perspectives, knowledges, skills and methods that are still available to address regional issues and problems. The world has moved on; there is little point at lamenting about past forms of regional planning that are probably no longer fit for purpose to address the changing and changeable forms of both subnational and more-than-local spatial and economic trends.

To be effective and relevant to the 21st century, regional planning does not need to be constrained within past institutional shackles. Planners are still likely to have to identify and manage a whole host of economic, environmental and infrastructural issues that affect large geographical areas with or without regional-wide government and regional plans.

The future impact of new forms of design, technology, the impact of new infrastructure, new patterns of living and working, and the digital dynamics that affect every aspect of our world will need assessing and monitoring. Regional impacts will still accrue from the growth of megalopolis sprawling outwards and pointing skywards, and future changes in transportation will impact upon commuting times, work-home and liveability patterns, and logistic flows and trading routes between places. Thinking in the context of the next decade or more, these trends might not cause the development of new ideal planned cities, imposed in a top-down way politically and professionally, but rather the acceleration of urban agglomerations over much greater physical distances at the megapolitan or megaregion scale (Brenner, 2019; Friedmann & Sorensen, 2019). The regional externalities are likely to be significant.

The 21st-century smart cities debate, for example, and the development of an Internet of Things that embeds digital technology in the life and design of cities, is but the latest series of inventions that will have far reaching consequences for the way we plan, manage, and govern future regions and cities (Batty, 2013). How this will happen is more uncertain. We know technologists are advancing innovations that can benefit the future management of regions at a bewildering pace; we also know that social scientists can be sceptical of the advancement of digitization and the impact it has on political accountability, democratic transparency and social inclusion. In 2017, for example, Sidewalk Labs started undertaking a planning experiment to redevelop part of the Toronto Waterfront as a testbed for developing future planning ideas based on the smart city model and the notion of 'building a city from the internet up'; however, it has drawn criticism over concerns relating to data privacy and how embedding a technical product in a government system leaves the state ever more dependent on a corporation – in this case Alphabet Inc., the parent company of Google. Meanwhile, cities such as Hangzhou and Suzhou are using Chinese retail giant Alibaba's Urban Cloud City Brain to coordinate traffic light signalling to reduce overall congestion and give emergency response vehicles priority passage from the point of dispatch to the site of emergency, but accompanying this are concerns about data privacy breaches, increased surveillance and dependence on a single centralized system were it to fail or be hacked.[2] This means places are likely to be increasingly difficult to manage and regulate in traditional ways, at least using tools and processes that were designed in another era with set institutions and defined roles and attributes that are all increasingly uncertain. In this context, it is not the future form of regional planning that we should be concerned about, but rather how cities within regions will become the intersections of a host of global and local flows and the physical embodiment of continual spatial churn (Batty, 2020).

Forging multiple and fluid planning frames

In the future, who will take responsibility for assessing these trends, analysing their impact, monitoring spatial differentials, modelling dynamic change, establishing the case for intervention, communicating options, and presenting the intelligence to politicians and others? There is a role here for regional planning; not regional planning as we witnessed in the last century, but regional planning as a suite of methods, data and processes, interlinked and aligned, and undertaken by a range of organizations. There will remain an even greater need to create processes of legitimation and regulation to deal with the impacts and costs of externalities, allowing individuals, communities and businesses voices in dynamic regional change, and communicating spatial change through visual and verbal means. Previous forms of regional planning, even using simple territorial maps, are not going to be adequate for this task. Even 20th-century forms of governance and democracy are not necessarily fit for purpose.

Data on everything, from transport usage, air pollution and flood risk, to pedestrian footfall and energy usage, are produced from sensors placed in urban and regional locations, generated by the second, and immediately accessible to anyone who wishes and is able to see that data. Long gone are the days when such survey data would only be available to and analysed periodically by the professional planner, creating options and published through successive drafts of a plan before their official release to everyone else some years down the line. New technology, coupled with the different digital ways people interact with agencies, makes the case for a different style of regional planning. Future forms of regional planning are required that are responsive to development opportunities, but also ones that are capable taking on board a myriad of intelligence and data flows, multiple forms of citizen and business interaction, and a plurality of planning organizations beyond elected government (Raco & Savini, 2019).

The early 20th-century guise of regional planning focused on the picture of economic disadvantage in distinct places. The focus was very much on the perspective: identifying the causes of the problem and bringing about an agreed plan of action. In the mid-20th century, as the case for regional planning to address spatial unevenness in individual nations became a cause celebre, so the focus began to consider not only the content but also the frame of the picture, to give it a robust political and institutional status. By the latter 20th century, continual academic and governmental attention focused overtly on the pictures frame – finding the right regional institutional fix – so much so that the real reasons for having regional planning – to address significant regional sector problems – were relegated. In the first two decades of this century, not only has the frame for the regional planning picture been largely abandoned, so too has any effective national political commitment to address regional differentials and unevenness (Allmendinger, 2016). We have, in essence, the worst of all worlds, fragmented agencies working to different agendas, duplicating responsibilities and tasks, growing social and economic disparities both within and between regions, the rise of a data-driven world recording urban and regional trends, but lacking any coherent way to assess and analyse the dynamic changes as they are occurring, absence of a platform for regional dialogue and debate. Not only is the regional planning frame being eroded, the regional picture is becoming increasingly pixelated and fuzzy.

The content of the regional picture needs to be captured systematically, and presented visually and accessibly to wider audiences. The data and digital tools increasingly available need to be harnessed as a continuous and enduring set of accessible and interpreted spatial analysis, not only led and controlled by technologists, but used by spatial strategists and social scientists and available to all. Regional planning would not take on a static form, but rather become a fluid and changeable process, a continual cycle of regional study, that brings focus to the regional picture. The frame remains important politically and legitimately to further selective intervention and project development, allocate future resources, provide accountability for action, and communicate change to foster greater understanding, but the frame may take on multiple forms by a range of actors through checks and balances (Valler & Phelps, 2018). This would give rise to a 'pragmatic' form of regional planning (cf. Healey, 2009), adaptive and agile to the needs of individual regions, sensitive to individual places and trends, and responsive to the various agencies operating in any one region. It is also one that is suitable for a more complex and fast-paced world (Friedmann, 2019).

Repositioning the planner as an orchestrator and enabler of planning regional futures

A future form of regional planning will need to attach less importance to a plan as a physical, all-encompassing entity and more to the need to align different types of spatial intelligence across various organizations (Batty, 2018). Regional planning's future could well be centred on achieving spatial alignment in a fragmented and highly diffuse landscape, performed with agility according to need and opportunity, but also adaptive to place distinctiveness and audience. How that would be achieved, by necessity, would be different in different regions, and possibly different within different parts of a region. However, it is important to reiterate here that these tasks are, and always have been, essentially *planning skills,* irrespective of what sort of organization any one planner works within.

The traditional regional planning process, as we see it, still exists. This is the one that identifies the problem or trend, gathers data and analyses it, understands it, proposes a solution or solutions, manages delivery on the agreed one, and finally evaluates. The problem for planning is that while in the mid-20th-century heyday of regional planning it was a single group of professional planners taking it all the way through, the first parts of the process have now been lost with the advent of real-time modelling. The result is that planners have ended up focusing on the delivery, all the time becoming increasingly detached from engaging with the new actors in a continual dialogue.

Our strong contention is that planning regional futures lay firmly in the latter. Traditional planning skills appeared linear in Geddes' inspired model of Survey Before Plan, taken forward by Abercrombie (1933) and a theme for planning in the interwar years (Figure 1a), through to a more circular but still linear model of Identify → Gather → Analyse → Deliver → Evaluate by the mid-to-late 20th century (Figure 1b), where planning became focused on the need to prepare and implement a blueprint for some desired end state. Indeed, this linear approach still remains prevalent today with Beauregard (2020), for instance, proposing Knowing → Engaging → Prescribing → Executing as the foundations of planning. We take a different approach, suggesting a suite of planning skills which, as time marched on and cities and regions became more complex, have increasingly required planners (professional or otherwise) to be adept at juggling:

- *Asset assessment*: the ability to understand how places and territories are changing, identifying the unique circumstances that have shaped spatial change over time and their legacy for the present and the future, and the challenges and opportunities that individual territories possess. The legacy issue, combined with present circumstances, creates a unique place make-up that may lead to the identification of territorial or place assets. This is an early planning skill most neglected, focusing on place need rather than institutional need, and might cover, for example, regional resilience (Christopherson et al., 2010) or the potential for regions of high-speed rail routes (Vickerman, 2015).
- *Synopsis and political astuteness*: the need to take different sectors as they are driving regional change and relate them to each other, beyond single policy and agency perspectives, by taking a synoptic perspective of how regions are changing over time (Cejudo & Michel, 2017). This need for this planning skill has been exacerbated over the last 40 years by increasing governance fragmentation and multiple agency involvement in regional change. This includes identifying the cumulative spatial effects of multiple drivers of change over, and in, specific territories, and assessing the possible domino spatial effects caused by a sequence of events over time – both unforeseen or foreseeable, such as global financial shocks – and how they might be brought to bear on a single place. It also includes the need for political astuteness (Tewdwr-Jones & Goddard, 2014).
- *Analysis and synthesis*: the ability to undertake and commission spatial data and trends relating to how places change over time, through

backcasting to the previous period of time and through scenario planning by projecting forward how changes may accrue in the future and relate these to specific geographical areas. This might involve, for example, demographic and migration trends (Giannakouris, 2010) and regional skills development (Glaeser et al., 2014). The planning skill here is to analyse and combine different data sets and intelligence, often from different sources, through synthesis for the same region, leading to a suite of options for discussion and decision-making.

- *Alignment and integration*: the need to bring together all necessary agencies from different sectors to prepare a jointly agreed project plan for a region or subregion, or deliver a programme of spatial development change. This new planning skill is required to align different agencies, through programme management, and requires an understanding of the agencies' different remits and expectations, but also an enduring search for common ground to achieve results. Typical needs revolve around, for example, delivering low carbon transport (Gray et al., 2016) or linking water supply with housing growth (Hanak & Browne, 2006). Integration implies abonding between agencies that might, in turn, compromise the independence of a participating agency; alignment implies a temporal or enduring ability to 'making sense together' (Healey, 1992) without transformational change of participating agencies.
- *Phasing and temporality*: a requirement to recognize the spatial, territorial and developmental sequencing of discussion, analysis, implementation across and between relevant agencies in order to manage change and delivery expectations. In planning terms, this may involve progressing results for x and y before z can be achieved, and is common for large-scale infrastructure projects, landownership and land assembly overcoming legal obstacles, or even financing. Examples could include the phasing out of internal combustion engine vehicles in cities and regions (Glazebrook & Newman, 2018), or meeting the needs of age-friendly cities (Buffel & Phillipson, 2016). Skill requirements involve a recognition of the importance of phasing and time sequencing in long-term programme planning.
- *Mediation*: the need to align different agencies to reach a relatively common position to deliver an outcome or position; mediation may be an enduring process of negotiation and compromise or a one-off process for a specific project. This is a planning skill that has developed in need and importance over time as the number of relevant agencies that contribute to, deliver or shape spatial change has increased. An example might be the need to deliver logistic services around port and airport in the context of urban expansion plans, property investment and global trade deals (Hesse, 2016).
- *Communication*: the requirement to explain and disseminate aspects of urban and regional change to interested agencies and organizations as they affect places. Traditionally, regional planning communication has

occurred through a regional spatial plan or policy framework, accompanied by a spatial schematic or map highlighting principal geographical features and possible changes. More lately, communication can be achieved through social media and digital form or representation, and can be much more instantaneous. Communication also refers to the skill of achieving communicable interaction between different actors within a regional space that have a vested interest in regional change (Wilson & Tewdwr-Jones, 2019), tasks that planners themselves may find challenging.

• *Visualization*: whereas planning has traditionally relied on preparing and disseminating a two-dimensional map or schematic that identifies physical places by the plan-making agencies, visualization may refer to any form of media – by recovering illustration, film and animation, and embracing dashboards, virtual reality and cyberspace – that can represent and communicate spatial change and analysis and employed as a device by any interested organization (Stehle & Kitchin, 2020). This includes recent examples in developing digital twins for metropolitan regions (Mohammadi & Taylor, 2017), and these skills are not necessarily held by professional planners but rather by computer scientists.

This is by no means an exhaustive or even definitive list of skills, but it does present a different way of envisaging planning in and for the 21st century, with the planner assuming the role of orchestrator and enabler of planning regional futures[3] – a notable contrast with the 'planners as leaders' rhetoric to which we have grown accustomed (Neuman, 2019).

We could look at these as being new planning skills, necessity skills for (securing planning's and a planner's role in) planning regional futures. Yet, what is clear, from our perspective, is that some of these skills have not necessarily changed, but have been freed from institutionalized regional planning, evolving quickly such that traditional approaches to these skills are being left behind, and with it planners and planning as we have to come to identify them. Another way is to view them as the unique planning skills, a modern take on the essence of planning as it was always envisaged and conceived to be all those years ago, and which today provides the pillar on which to reassert the key role of planning in regional futures. Yet, what is clear, again from our perspective, is that these skills are not unique to planning. There is no reason why some of the individual skills cannot be done – indeed are already being done – by actors other than planners. What we are clear on is that *the ability to understand all these skills simultaneously and to deploy them when required is a unique planning skill* (Figure 1c). For us this is the fundamental pillar on which planning regional futures can, and should, be centred. The ways these skills interact and are brought to bear with each other in territories and places are unique, with the skill of the planner to know tacitly when to use which specific skill(s). Why this is important for regional studies is because it differentiates regional planning skills and knowledge as a unique set when compared to more generic planning skills,

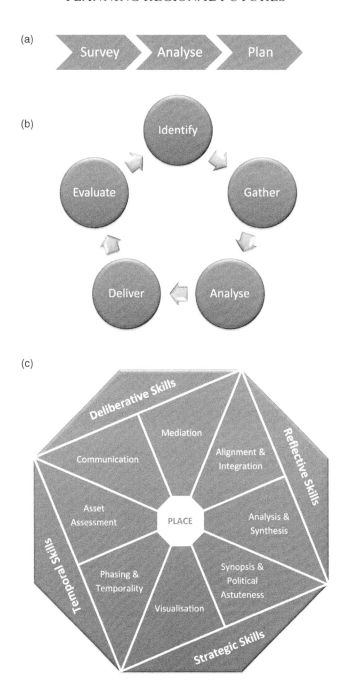

Figure 1 Evolving approaches to regional planning and professional planning skills: (a) regional planning in the interwar years; (b) regional planning in the post-war years; and (c) skills for planning regional futures.

something which has implications for the study skills we teach as well as practice professionally (cf. American Planning Association, 2020; Green Leigh et al., 2019; Sandercock, 1997). Allied to this, other accounts of planning skills are determined by theorizing planning differently, leading to a different emphasis on the role of the planner and by implication a different taken on the planning skills required (cf. Alexander, 2001; Ozawa & Seltzer, 1999), whereas our primary focus is thinking more generally about planning and regions per se.

The final point here is that these skills are not directly dependent on and subservient to governance forms. Although they may become functions of government agencies, they can exist and be pursued outside of bounded institutions or government. Recognizing the rise and fall, ebb and flow, of traditional regional planning was to all intents and purposes dictated by the whims of local and national government, securing a future for regional planning which is dependent on and subservient to governance forms is increasingly risky, especially in these turbulent political and economic times. Our proposition here is that the regional planning will always have important connection to formal structures and frameworks of government, but planning regional futures will increasingly centre on consortia of willing actors bringing their skills, competencies and resources to bear on trying to address those wicked problems affecting cities and regions. Planning and planners can have a key role to play in this new landscape, but it is one they must grasp. Planning's origins lay here, so why not its future?

Conclusions: an introduction to a debate on planning regional futures

The aim of this paper is to re-energize planning debates in regional studies. For our part we approach this as firm believers in the function of regional planning, but not the form that regional planning generally takes. In this paper we make the case for recovering the purpose of regional planning as an approach and skillset for addressing regional needs in a place-specific way. This stands in opposition to the type of standardized institutionalized forms and one-size-fits-all solutions that have become the hallmark of regional planning, but increasingly resented for undermining place distinctiveness and divorced from addressing regional needs. The role of planning in addressing regional place-specific needs, rather than the future form of regional planning, is the terrain on which planning regional futures should be debated.

So why do some nations still persist with 'old-style' regional planning? Or, for nations that have abolished regional plans, why do some crave their return? We can identify several reasons:

- Asserting higher level control: through requirement from higher tiers of the state that might include the allocation of central resources on

a regional scale; devolving responsibility (and therefore blame) to sub-national government to shape more localized spatial arrangements particularly on contentious matters; to fulfil international goals (e.g., Sustainable Development Goal 11), requirements (e.g., administering European funds) and agendas (e.g., New Urban Agenda).
- Nostalgia: a longing for stability and certainty through neatly defined regional planning forms, situated within clear administrative hier-archies, delivering (at least on paper) territorial synchronicity, and yearning for legitimating planning, planners and plans, irrespective of whether or not they actually deliver.
- Filling the void: a desire or requirement to redress a perceived or ac-tual democratic, accountability or transparency deficit of policy-and decision-making below the level of the nation-state and above locali-ties, with an attraction to administratively and politically determined arrangements.

The problem is that this amounts to fiddling (with the planning 'frame') while Rome (the 'picture' of who and where is being planned for) burns.

We do not need old solutions to new problems, but new approaches for addressing wicked regional problems (both old and new). As firm believers in the purpose and values (but not the current form) of regional planning and the need to recover its raison d'etre, we must first see regional problems for what they are – heterogeneous. Wicked problems never go away, and it is the essence of planning to deal with them. However, besides recogniz-ing the heterogeneity and wickedness underlying these problems, planning regional futures needs to roll out in accordance with certain parameters characterized by adaptability and flexibility, not one-size-fits-all parame-ters. Many geographical contexts are already witness to this, with a grow-ing nexus between community activists and businesses with or without the local authorities interfering or mediating. Our argument is that the future (and indeed the present) rests in multiple forms of planning – one of which *may* in certain circumstances and contexts be something akin to 'old-style' regional planning, but are more likely to include a diverse range of increas-ingly ad hoc and agile planning measures, delivering change, and shaping future cities and regions – which implies multiple forms of legitimacy, ac-countability and democratic transparency. In short, the question we pose for anyone reading this is: Are we prepared to acknowledge and engage? If not, can planning (as both a profession and discipline) remain legitimate if we fail to respond?

Acknowledgements

The paper benefitted from feedback received at various international con-ferences, research seminars, as well as very constructive feedback from the external reviewers and editors of the journal.

Disclosure statement

No potential conflict of interest was reported by the authors.

Notes

1 Of note is how Paasi, among others, is commonly referring to slow long-term processes of region-building, something which increasingly runs counter to the dynamic short-term churn of present-day regional planning imaginaries.
2 At the time of writing, Alibaba's City Brain is operating in 23 cities (22 in China plus Kuala Lumpur in Malaysia), serving customers in 48 different specific application scenarios across 11 major areas of city life, including transportation, urban government, cultural tourism and health.
3 This list results from ongoing discussion between the authors, drawing in particular on: the findings of major research projects examining digital means of planning urban and regional futures (Tewdwr-Jones), international comparative planning (Galland) and private actors in planning (Harrison); roles as Director of a Future Cities Urban Living Partnership 2015–19 working across public, private and voluntary sectors to deliver projects in Newcastle-Gateshead (Tewdwr-Jones) and Chair of the Association of European Schools of Planning (AESOP) Excellence in Education Board (Galland); and collective participation in a three-year international working group examining the planning and governance of metropolitan regions (2016–19, all authors).

ORCID

John Harrison ⓘ http://orcid.org/0000-0002-6434-5142
Daniel Galland ⓘ http://orcid.org/0000-0003-2648-806X
Mark Tewdwr-Jones ⓘ http://orcid.org/0000-0002-8786-6434

References

Abercrombie, P. (1933). *Town and country planning.* Thornton Butterworth.
Alexander, E. (2001). What do planners need to know? *Journal of Planning Education and Research, 20(3),* 376–380. https://doi.org/10.1177/0739456X0102000309
Allen, J., Cochrane, A., & Massey, D. (1998). *Rethinking the region.* Routledge.
Allmendinger, P. (2016). *Neoliberal spatial governance.* Routledge.
Allmendinger, P. (2017). *Planning theory.* Palgrave Macmillan.
Allmendinger, P., & Haughton, G. (2007). The fluid scales and scope of UK spatial planning. *Environment and Planning A: Economy and Space, 39(6),* 1478–1496. https://doi.org/10.1068/a38230
Allmendinger, P., & Haughton, G. (2019). Opening up planning? Planning reform in an era of 'open government'. *Planning Practice and Research, 34(4),* 438–453. https://doi.org/10.1080/02697459.2019.1630973
American Planning Association. (2020). *What skills do planners need?* Retrieved from https://www.planning.org/choosingplanning/skills/
Batty, M. (2013). Big data, smart cities and city planning. *Dialogues in Human Geography, 3(3),* 274–279. https://doi.org/10.1177/2043820613513390
Batty, M. (2018). *Inventing future cities.* MIT Press.

Batty, M. (2020). How disruptive are new urban technologies? *Environment and Planning B, 47(1),* 3–6. https://doi.org/10.1177/2399808320902574

Beauregard, R. (2020). *Advanced introduction to planning theory.* Edward Elgar.

Brenner, N. (2003). Metropolitan institutional reform and the rescaling of state space in contemporary Western Europe. *European Urban and Regional Studies, 10(4),* 297–324. https://doi.org/10.1177/09697764030104002

Brenner, N. (2019). *New urban spaces.* Oxford University Press.

Buffel, T., & Phillipson, C. (2016). Can global cities be 'age-friendly cities'? Urban development and ageing populations. *Cities,* 55, 94–100. https://doi.org/10.1016/j.cities.2016.03.016

Cejudo, G., & Michel, C. (2017). Addressing fragmented government action: Coordination, coherence, and integration. *Policy Sciences,* 50(4), 745–767. https://doi.org/10.1007/sll077-017-9281-5

Christopherson, S., Michie, J., & Tyler, P. (2010). Regional resilience: Theoretical and empirical perspectives. *Cambridge Journal* of Regions, Economy and Society, 3(1), 3–10. https://doi.org/10.1093/cjres/rsq004

Davoudi, S. (2012). The legacy of positivism and the emergence of interpretive tradition in spatial planning. *Regional Studies, 46* (4), 429–441. https://doi.org/10.1080/00343404.2011.618120

Fainstein, S., & DeFilippis, J. (Eds.). (2016). *Readings in planning* theory. Wiley-Blackwell.

Friedmann, J. (1963). Regional planning as a field *of study. Journal of the American Institute of Planners, 29(3),* 168–175. https://doi.org/10.1080/01944366308978061

Friedmann, J. (1993). Toward a non-Euclidian mode of planning. *Journal of the American Planning Association,* 59(4), 482–485. https://doi.org/10.1080/01944369308975902

Friedmann, J. (2019). Thinking about complexity and planning. *International Planning Studies, 24(1),* 13–22. https://doi.org/10.1080/13563475.2018.1517594

Friedmann, J., & Sorensen, A. (2019). City unbound: Emerging megaconurbations in Asia. *International Planning Studies, 24(1),* 1–12. https://doi.org/10.1080/13563475.2019.1555314

Friedmann, J., & Weaver, C. (1979). *Territory and function: The evolution of regional planning.* University of California Press.

Galland, D. (2012). Is regional planning dead or just coping? The transformation of a state sociospatial project into growth-oriented strategies. *Environment and Planning C, 30(3),* 536–552. https://doi.org/10.1068/clll50

Galland, D., Harrison, J., & Tewdwr-Jones, M. (2020). What is metropolitan planning and governance for? In K. Zimmermann, D. Galland, &J. Harrison (Eds.), *Metropolitan regions, planning and governance* (pp. 237–256). Springer.

Geddes, P. (1915). *Cities in evolution.* Williams & Norgate.

Giannakouris, K. (2010). *Population and social conditions: Eurostat statistics in focus 1/2010.* Eurostat. Retrieved from https://ec.europa.eu/eurostat/documents/3433488/5564440/KS-SF-10-001-EN.PDF/d5b8bf54–6979-4834–998a-f7dla6laa82d

Glaeser, E. L., Ponzetto, G. A. M., &Tobio, K. (2014). Cities, skills and regional change. *Regional Studies, 48(1),* 7–43. https://doi.org/10.1080/00343404.2012.674637

Glasson, J. (1978). *An introduction to regional planning: Concepts, theory and practice.* Hutchinson.

Glazebrook, G., & Newman, P. (2018). The city of the future. *Urban Planning, 3(2),* 1–20. https://doi.org/10.17645/up.v3i2.1247

Gray, D., Laing, R., & Docherty, I. (2016). Delivering low carbon urban transport choices: European ambition meets the reality of institutional (mis)alignment. *Environment and Planning A, 49* (1), 226–242. https://doi.org/10.1177/0308518X16662272

Green Leigh, N., French, S., Guhathakurta, S., & Stiftel, B. (Eds.). (2019). *The Routledge handbook of international planning education.* Routledge.

Gunder, M., Madanipour, A., & Watson, V. (Eds.). (2018). *The Routledge handbook of planning theory.* Routledge.

Hall, P. (2014). *Cities of tomorrow* (4th ed.). Blackwell.

Hall, P., & Tewdwr-Jones, M. (2020). *Urban and regional planning* (6th ed.). Routledge.

Hanak, E., & Browne, M. (2006). Linking housing growth to water supply: New planning frontiers in the American West. *Journal of the American Planning Association, 72(2),* 154–166. https://doi.org/10.1080/01944360608976736

Harrison, J. (2020). Seeing like a business: Rethinking the role of business in regional development, planning and governance. *Territory, Politics, Governance.* https://doi.org/10.1080/21622671.2020.1743201

Haughton, G., & Counsell, D. (2004). *Regions, spatial strategies and sustainable development.* Routledge.

Healey, P. (1992). Planning through debate: The communicative turn in planning theory. *Town Planning Review, 63(2),* 143–162. https://doi.org/10.3828/tpr.63.2.422x602303814821

Healey, P. (2007). *Urban complexity and spatial strategies.* Routledge.

Healey, P. (2009). The pragmatic tradition in planning thought. *Journal of Planning Education and Research, 28(3),* 277–292. https://doi.org/10.1177/0739456X08325175

Hesse, M. (2016). *The city as a terminal: The urban contexts of logistics and freight transport.* Routledge.

Howard, E. (1902). *Garden cities of tomorrow.* Faber & Faber.

Knaap, G. J., Nedovic-Budic, Z., & Carbonell, A. (2015). *Planning for states and nation states in the US and Europe.* Lincoln Institute of Land Policy.

Kuklinski, A. R. (1970). Regional development, regional policies and regional planning: Problems and issues. *Regional Studies, 4* (3), 269–278. https://doi.org/10.1080/09595237000185291

Mohammadi, N., & Taylor, J. (2017). Smart city digital twins. Paper presented at the 2017 IEEE Symposium Series on Computational Intelligence (SSCI). Honolulu, HI, USA, pp. 1–5.

Murat Guney, K., Keil, R., & Ucoglu, M. (Eds.). (2019). *Massive suburbanization: (Re)building the global periphery.* University of Toronto Press.

Neuman, M. (2019). Leadership. In N. Green Leigh, S. French, S. Guhathakurta, & B. Stiftel (Eds.), *The Routledge handbook of* international planning education (pp. 174–183). Routledge.

Ozawa, C., & Seltzer, E. (1999). Taking our bearings: Mapping a relationship among planning practice, theory, and education. *Journal of Planning Education and Research, 18(3),* 257–266. https://doi.org/10.1177/0739456X9901800307

Paasi, A., Harrison, J., & Jones, M. (2018). New consolidated regional geographies. In A. Paasi, J. Harrison, & M. Jones (Eds.), *Handbook on the geographies of regions and territories* (pp. 1–20). Edward Elgar.

Paasi, A., & Zimmerbauer, K. (2016). Penumbral borders and planning paradoxes: Relational thinking and the question of borders in spatial planning. *Environment and Planning A, 48(1),* 75–93. https://doi.org/10.1177/0308518X15594805

Pike, A., O'Brien, P., Strickland, T., & Tomaney, J. (2019). *Financialising city state-craft and infrastructure.* Edward Elgar.

Raco, M., & Savini, F. (Eds.). (2019). *Planning and knowledge: How new forms of technocracy are shaping contemporary cities.* Policy Press.

Roodbol-Mekkes, P. H., Sevan den Brink, A. (2015). Rescaling spatial planning: Spatial planning reforms in Denmark, England, and the Netherlands. *Environment and Planning C: Government and Policy, 33(1)*, 184–198. https://doi.org/10.1068/c12134

Rydin, Y. (2011). *The purpose of planning.* Policy Press.

Sandercock, L. (1997). The planner tamed: Preparing planners for the twenty first century. *Australian Planner, 34(2)*, 90–95. https://doi.org/10.1080/07293682.1997.9657754

Savini, F., & Aalbers, M. (2016). The de-contextualisation of land use planning through financialisation: Urban redevelopment in Milan. *European Urban and Regional Studies, 23(4)*, 878–894. https://doi.org/10.1177/0969776415585887

Schindler, S., & Kanai, J.-M. (2019). Getting the territory right: Infrastructure-led development and the re-emergence of spatial planning strategies. *Regional Studies.* https://doi.org/10.1080/00343404.2019.1661984

Stead, D. (2012). Best practices and policy transfer in spatial planning. *Planning Practice and Research, 27*(1), 103–116. https://doi.org/10.1080/02697459.2011.644084

Stehle, S., & Kitchin, R. (2020). Real-time and archival data visualisation techniques in city dashboards. *International Journal of Geographical Information Science*, 34(2), 344–366. https://doi.org/10.1080/13658816.2019.1594823

Storper, M. (2016). The neo-liberal city as idea and reality. *Territory, Politics, Governance*, 4(2), 241–263. https://doi.org/10.1080/21622671.2016.1158662

Tewdwr-Jones, M. (2012). *Spatial planning and governance.* Palgrave Macmillan.

Tewdwr-Jones,M., & Goddard, J. (2014). A future for cities? Building new methodologies and systems for urban foresight. *Town Planning Review*, 85(6), 773–794. https://doi.org/10.3828/tpr.2014.46

UN-Habitat. (2017). *New urban agenda.* UN-Habitat.

Valler, D., & Phelps, N. (2018). Framing the future: On local planning cultures and legacies. *Planning Theory and Practice*, 19(5), 698–716. https://doi.org/10.1080/14649357.2018.1537448

Vickerman, R. (2015). High speed rail and regional development: The case of intermediate stations. *Journal of Transport Geography*, 42, 157–165. https://doi.org/10.1016/j.jtrangeo.2014.06.008

Watson, V. (2009). Seeing from the South: Refocusing urban planning on the globe's central urban issues. *Urban Studies*, 46(11), 2259–2275. https://doi.org/10.1177/0042098009342598

Watson, V. (2019). The return of the city-region in the new urban agenda: Is this relevant in the Global South? *Regional Studies.* https://doi.org/10.1080/00343404.2019.1664734

Wilson, A., & Tewdwr-Jones, M. (2019). Let's draw and talk about urban change: Deploying digital technology to encourage citizen participation in urban planning. *Environment and Planning B.* https://doi.org/10.1177/2399808319831290

Wu, F. (2015). *Planning for growth: Urban and regional planning in China.* Routledge.

The return of the city-region in the new urban agenda: is this relevant in the Global South?

Vanessa Watson ⓘ

Introduction

The adoption in 2015 of the United Nations' 2030 Agenda for Sustainable Development and its linked Sustainable Development Goals (SDGs) opened the way for a new focus on the planning and development of urban settlements. SDG 11 (Cities) was elaborated in the New Urban Agenda (NUA) adopted by the United Nations Conference on Housing and Sustainable Urban Development (Habitat III) in Quito, Ecuador, in 2016. Responding to several global policy frameworks in addition to SDG 11, the NUA (2016, p. 4) states:

> The implementation of the New Urban Agenda contributes to the implementation and localization of the 2030 Agenda for Sustainable Development in an integrated manner, and to the achievement of the Sustainable Development Goals and targets, including Goal 11, of making cities and human settlements inclusive, safe, resilient and sustainable.

Significantly, this document shifts a long-held position across many parts of the world that urbanization is negative and needs to be controlled. Instead it proposes that well-planned urbanization can be a powerful tool of sustainable development.

The need for well-planned urban growth finds expression in the NUA through a revived emphasis on 'urban and territorial planning', recommending various spatial (or 'territorial') planning concepts to guide both urban and regional development. Three planning guideline documents (United Nations Human Settlements Programme (UN-Habitat), 2015, 2017; United Nations Human Settlements Programme (UNHSP), 2018) linked to SDG 11 and the NUA spell out the details of these concepts. This paper focuses on one of these spatial planning concepts – the city-region – from both analytical and normative perspectives. There are two problems with how city-regions are presented. The first is that it echoes much older ideas in the planning literature without taking into account major global shifts and an extensive literature on regional change and city-regions in the last several decades. The second is that it suggests a 'one-size-fits-all' approach to city-regions across the world and misses more recent emphasis in the literature on 'place' or 'locality', as well as networks, in shaping how cities and regions grow and change. This paper argues that while there is clearly diversity across all parts of the world, significant difference is likely to be found between economically advanced regions of the world and economically emerging and resource-poor territories. The terms 'Global North' and 'Global South' are frequently used to capture this distinction but can suggest an oversimplified, territorial and binary view of the world. The present paper uses Dados and Connell's (2012, p. 13) definition of Global South, which stands for more than a metaphor for underdevelopment: 'It references an entire history of colonialism, neo-imperialism, and differential economic and social change through which large inequalities in living standards, life expectancy and access to resources are maintained ... .' In this sense understanding the implications of acknowledging differences in locality (or place) calls to attention the need to look across a set of places and locate them within shifting global cores and peripheries (Bhan, 2019). The overall purpose of the paper is to draw attention to the problematic conceptualization of the city-region in these NUA-linked documents and the implications this has for intervention.

The paper is structured as follows. The next section explains how the concept of the city-region has been formulated in the NUA, and its related planning guidelines, along with its strong 'territorial' orientation. The third section explores the origins of the city-region idea and the critiques and debates that have unfolded over the last several decades. The fourth section refers to the 'southern turn' in urban studies and planning thought. It considers the relevance of the city-region concept in the Global South based on two published case studies that show the kinds of challenges faced when implementing the idea in very different localities. The fifth section asks if the approach to city-region planning set out in the NUA planning guidelines is likely to meet the goals and targets of SDG 11, in all parts of the world. The final section argues that identifying and responding to the key urban issues in a particular context is the starting point for planning, and applying a city-region concept or framing action in the ways implied in the guideline documents may well not be the best way forward. This paper has relied on accessing published and online material on the city-region. The conceptualization of the city-region in UN-Habitat planning guideline documents linked to the NUA has been assessed in the light of a literature review of theory and practice on city-regions and how this thinking has evolved over time.

Concept of the city-region in the NUA and related planning guidelines

The introduction for the first time of an urban goal (SDG 11) in the global development goals raises the centrality of the urban process in securing sustainable futures across other goals which focus on sectoral issues such as climate, health, economy and poverty. Barnett and Parnell (2016) suggest that this introduces into the SDGs a city-centric concept of development which is also place based, scalar and focused on the local.

A further shift in SDG 11 and the NUA[1] is a renewed emphasis on spatial planning, but this time a more inclusive and participatory form of planning encompassing issues wider than just land-use (Barnett & Parnell, 2018). The approach to planning in the NUA is multi-scalar and assumes state-led intervention at national, regional, city-regional and local levels, with an emphasis on subnational government. There is a strong spatial emphasis, although it also incorporates and integrates social, economic and environmental aspects to address the full range of global 'challenges'. Further, it shifts from an earlier approach to cities and/or 'the urban' as a site of developmental problems, which must be planned better, to cities as 'hubs', 'drivers' or 'nodes' which can be used to address much wider development issues (Barnett & Parnell, 2018).

The foreword of the NUA (2016) states:

> we have reached a critical point in understanding that cities can be the source of solutions to, rather than the cause of, the challenges that our world is facing today. If well-planned and well-managed, urbanization can be a powerful tool for sustainable development for both developing and developed countries.
>
> (p. iv)

Paragraph 15 indicates the expectation that spatial planning will once again play an important role in this, using the term 'reinvigorating' to suggest that planning was at some point in the past an important and effective mechanism of urban management and can be so again. This section of the NUA commits to an urban paradigm shift which involves '(iii) Reinvigorating long-term and integrated urban and territorial planning and design in order to optimize the spatial dimension of the urban form and deliver the positive outcomes of urbanization' (p. 8).

Paragraph 96 is the only reference in the NUA to planning at the scale of the city-region: 'We will encourage the implementation of sustainable urban and territorial planning, including city-region and metropolitan plans, to encourage synergies and interactions among urban areas of all sizes and their peri-urban and rural surroundings ...' (p. 25). This is a shift from an earlier use of the term 'city-region' in UN-Habitat policy documents (UN-Habitat, 2009) where it was used more descriptively to refer to large and polycentric metropolitan areas in developed countries where governmental coordination would be required. In the NUA the definition suggests that city-region plans (now in both developed and developing countries) for towns of all sizes can initiate new linkages and processes of development across the wider urban system and between towns and their rural hinterlands.

The NUA is supported by three key planning guideline documents: *International Guidelines on Urban and Territorial Planning* (UN-Habitat, 2015) approved in 2015 by the 25th UN-Habitat's Governing Council as a global framework for improving policies, plans, design and implementation processes that will lead to more compact, socially inclusive, better integrated and connected cities and territories that foster sustainable urban development and are resilient to climate change;[2] *Implementing the New Urban Agenda by Strengthening Urban—Rural Linkages* (UN-Habitat, 2017); and *Leading Change: Delivering the New Urban Agenda through Urban and Territorial Planning* (UNHSP, 2018), which draws as well on the 2015 Guidelines document. All three documents attempt to both conceptualize and define a city-region (an analytical step) and suggest directions (through planning) to promote what they regard as better functioning city-regions (a normative step). The documents tend to hold back from very specific planning proposals or strategies and mostly put forward planning principles, guidelines and objectives, but the particular concept or definition of a city-region has direct implications for planning. Definitions differ somewhat across the three reports.

In UN-Habitat (2017):

> The term city-region refers to the concept of an urban core or cores, linked to peri-urban and rural hinterlands by functional linkages. The city-region approach shifts away from administrative boundaries and sectorial development strategies towards territorial strategies, characterized by vertical and horizontal structures of governance and sectors and focuses on the interconnectivity of an urban agglomeration and its hinterland.
>
> (p. vii)

UNHSP (2018) provides a definition of the city-region as:

> The area within which the connections between one or more cities and the surrounding rural land are intense and functionally (economically, socially, politically and geographically) connected. These areas are typically 80–100 km across and occupy up to 10,000 km^2.
>
> (p. iv)

These definitions are concerned with an urban core and its proximate rural hinterland, and the linkages between them. They offer the concept of the city-region as territorially defined, with the 2018 report being explicit about the bounded geographical nature of the city-region, and even its expected spatial extent. Both align with the NUA in terms of foregrounding the role of spatial planning in this scale of action, but whereas the NUA reference to city-regions emphasises linkage across systems of towns and cities, the policy documents discussed here suggest a more local and geographically defined perspective of a city and its identifiable surrounding hinterland. This geographical (or spatial) perspective comes through strongly in the use of the term 'territorial planning' which is defined in UN-Habitat (2015, p. 2) as a decision-making process taking place 'through the development of spatial visions, strategies and plans...'.

These approaches and definitions of the city-region can be inserted into a long history of academic debate, analysis and planning to locate and frame their development and sources of influence. Situating them in this way then lays the ground for assessing the extent to which this objective in the NUA of planning city-regions is likely to be realized across the globe.

Debates on the city-region: shifting positions

The concept of the city-region has a long history in urban and regional planning. The idea can be traced back to planning 'founders' Patrick Geddes (Geddes, 1915) and Lewis Mumford (Mumford, 1925) who were concerned about rapidly growing and expanding cities in England and the United States and their impact on surrounding natural environments. Mumford argued for a national plan with 'regions delimited on the basis of natural geographic entities' and a 'minimum of interregional exchanges based only on such products as the home region cannot economically produce' (quoted in Hall, 1988, p. 151). The city-region idea of this time was geographically defined by the linkages between a settlement and its rural hinterland, and was relatively autonomous in an economic sense.

However, during the 1950s' attempts to analyse and measure the city-region shifted conceptions of it away from the 'Fabian socialist' inspiration of Geddes and Mumford (Hall, 1988) and towards more economic definitions. Davoudi (2008) argued that despite the potential complexity of relations between a city and its region, definitions focused on economic relationships and more narrowly on labour market areas using journey-to-work data. Concepts of the city-region in the mid-20th century and beyond were dominated by an 'urban-centred and economically driven' view (Davoudi, 2008), which focused on defining and explaining the extent of larger metropolitan areas, or conurbations, where larger and smaller towns had grown together. This is the sense in which the term is used in the UN-Habitat (2009) policy document.

From a planning and policy perspective the concept of city-region plans developed by national governments shaped the emergence of regional planning in the United States, the UK and Europe, aligning with organized, state-centred Keynesian capitalism of the post-Second World War period. However, the adoption of the city-region for strategic planning purposes varied across Global North territories, with some countries not using it at all, while in others it has shaped discussions on regionalism, or been used as a basis to qualify for national or European aid (Davoudi, 2008). Nonetheless, Healey (2009) suggests that the concept of the city-region was deeply embedded in European spatial planning consciousness, along with attempts to align 'functional realities' with administrative jurisdictions to create planning areas at city-region, metropolitan and urban scales. Later, Healey (2015, p. 266) was to argue that following the 'tradition of contained towns and cities where the city core commands the surrounding territory...', planning in Europe is still influenced by this vision of cities and their regions. It will be argued below that this essentially European concept of the city-region has been an important influence on the form of the concept which has found its way into the recent planning guidelines linked to the NUA. This will lead to the question: To what extent have these planning documents taken into account the now-extensive analysis and critique of the city-region?

New-regionalism

Since the start of the 1990s, both analytical and policy-related ideas of the city-region have experienced a resurgence of interest and debate, and these debates have shifted as well over the period up until the present. The following sections review these evolving arguments which turn particularly on what has been called the network versus territory debate (Jessop, Brenner, & Jones, 2008; Painter, 2010). A key issue in this literature has been the extent to which it is valid to define a city-region geographically as an entity with high levels of economic, social and institutional intra-linkage and some degree of autonomy, and the extent to which a city and its hinterland is likely to have wider local and even global economic and other linkages which make attempts at boundary definition problematic.

Particularly in the field of regional economic development, a new literature that emerged in the 1990s focused on the economic linkages of cities and their regions in an increasingly global economic system. The idea of the city-region as a discrete and bounded set of economic relations between a city and its hinterland was challenged (Scott, 2001; Scott & Storper, 2003; Storper, 1997) from perspectives that pointed to the growing dominance of economic linkages between a city and its city-region and urban economic centres elsewhere in the nation or world. This has significantly changed the role and function of certain city-regions:

> The most striking forms of agglomeration in evidence today are the super-agglomerations or city-regions that have come into being all over

the world in the last few decades. ... These city-regions are locomotives of the national economies within which they are situated.

(Scott & Storper, 2003, p. 581)

In the same line of argument, Scott and Storper (2003) argued that city-regionalism is a phase in capitalist territorial development in a new post-Fordist and post-national era where the political and regulatory authority of the nation-state is challenged by newly emerging and global connected city-regions. In this new 'post-national' age, the region could no longer be considered as a territorially fixed and bounded unit amenable to top-down state planning and management. Moreover, the recognition of a city-region's multi-scalar economic networks and their ability to achieve international economic competitiveness required policy to consider relationally networked space rather than territorial and administrative geographies. Hence, urban hierarchy and bounded territories were pitted against cities as hubs of economic networks in what Harrison and Growe (2014) called the territorial/relational divide.

Countering the network-centrism of early newregionalism

By the early 2000s a critique of this economy-centred and network-oriented position on city-regions began to emerge. There were two lines of critique. The first countered the view that the state had been 'hollowed out' by globalization, arguing that the state has not disappeared and neither has the importance of space, place or territory and the institutions that manage them. Painter (2010) accepts the need to move on from post-war concepts of territory (evident in Geddes' city-region concept) that saw it as a 'bounded' and possibly 'homogenous' portion of geographical space, with fixed borders, and taking on an expression of state power. He argues instead that territory is relevant but exists as 'the product of networked socio-technical processes...' (Painter, 2010, p. 1114). Hence, territory and network are not rival principles of spatial organization but are closely connected, and while the role of the state may have shifted it is no less important. For example, McGuirk (2007) shows how Sydney in Australia was transformed to a 'national champion' city-region through national strategic strategies of economic-territorial management. However, this process also required 'discursive production, political mediation and institutional formation "from below"' (McGuirk, 2007, p. 181), dependent in turn on the particular nature of policy and discursive communities in Sydney at the time.

There is now a rich literature that conveys a more nuanced interpretation of the concept of city-regions. It recognizes that territory and network can be complementary, or overlapping or competing, in different configurations of state/space (Harrison & Growe, 2014). In a key publication, Jessop et al. (2008, p. 391) pointed to the 'one-dimensionalism' that had characterized previous socio-spatial theorizing of regions: 'methodological territorial-ism', which subsumes all socio-spatial relations under 'territoriality' as in state-centric and territorialist understandings of cities, states and the world economy; 'place-centrism', which treats places as self-contained ensembles of social-ecological interactions; 'scale-centrism', which sees scale as the basis around which other socio-spatial relations are organized; and 'net-work centrism', with its one-sided focus on networks, flows and mobilities. They caution particularly against 'scale-centrism', which had been promi-nent in previous theorizing of socio-spatial relations. Instead Jessop et al. offer a 'territory-place-scale-network' understanding of socio-spatial rela-tions which takes into account 'historically specific geographies of social relations... and explores contextual and historical variation in the structural coupling, strategic coordination, and forms of inter-connection among the different dimensions of the latter' (p. 392).

The second line of critique questioned the locality-blind nature of the economy-centred and network-oriented position on city-regions. Jessop et al. (2008) emphasize the importance of 'historically specific geographies' as one entry point to understanding socio-spatial relations, while avoiding 'place-centrism', which treats places as discrete, selfcontained entities. Jonas and Ward (2007, p. 170) suggest that while the 'new-regionalism' movement of the previous decade had much to admire, there has been an underempha-sis in the literature on 'how new territorial forms are constructed politically and reproduced through everyday acts and struggles around consumption and social reproduction'. City-regions are shaped in part by their wider eco-nomic connections to other parts of the nation or world (the globalization thesis of new-regionalism), but much has to be attributed, in any particu-lar city-region, to changing politics of governance and state reterritoriali-zation, the role of democracy and citizenship, and tensions around social reproduction and sustainability. In sum, 'city-regional territories are always produced through material politics and struggles framed at diverse scales' (p. 172). Jonas and Ward are here drawing attention to the importance of 'place' and to the problem of the tendency to universalize a concept such as the city-region, as well as attribute agency to a particular scale of function-ing. They also acknowledge the 'tendency to infer general processes of eco-nomic change and state re-territorialization from a few select places (usually global city-regions) in the global north...' (p. 170) and accept that these pro-cesses will play themselves out very differently not only beyond their case studies but also in the Global South.

Reinforcing this critique, Healey (2009) notes that the concept of city-region emerged in Europe in response to particular institutional reconfigu-rations, but these may manifest very differently elsewhere. It is not 'a well-developed package which can be inserted into a government system to fix and reconfigure sub-national government...' (p. 839). Cochrane and Ward (2012) similarly suggest that specific developments across European space in the Fordist-Keynesian era were highly influential in shaping concepts of the city-region, and recognizing the role of both place and time in assessing the relevance of concepts is important.

Finally, it is possible to consider the city-region approach drawing on literature that questions the reification of scale, referred to as 'scale-centrism' by Jessop et al. (2008), in which scale is seen as determining other sociospatial relations and particularly the prioritizing of the local scale. While these writers have not made reference to the city-region explicitly, their arguments are highly pertinent in this regard. Born and Purcell (2006) refer to the 'local trap' as the assumption that the local (or regional; Purcell, 2007) territorial scale is inherently 'good' for achieving outcomes such as sustainability or justice, and this can obscure other scalar options that might be more effective in achieving certain goals. They argue it is impossible to justify that there is anything inherently better or worse in any scale of action.

The assumption that the local is inherently better has been also been criticized from the perspective of the development studies field. Zoomers (2018) points to the implications of globalization for new and changing development trajectories and livelihoods such that 'the local' can no longer be viewed as a separate and delineated entity. Zoomers and Van Westen (2011) offer the interesting perspective that globalization has resulted in 'translocal' patterns of development: hence, intervention requires linking 'the local' to 'the local elsewhere', rather than scalar integration through levels of the nation-state. Their empirical studies show that local development opportunities, even in places with little global connectivity, are very much determined by what happens elsewhere and people often shift between several localities to secure a livelihood, rather than connecting in 'transnational space'. Positive impacts in one locality may have negative impacts in others, and hence there is 'a need to move away from traditional space-bound assessments of "local" development...' (Zoomers, 2018, p. 8).

In sum, it appears that the concept of, and guiding principles for, city-regions in the NUA planning guideline documents, while admittedly brief, have not taken into account shifts and debates on the subject since its earliest Geddensian formulation. As problematically, a one-sizefits-all approach ignores now extensive recognition of place-diversity and particularly differences between Global North and Global South cities and regions. The following section draws attention to the significance of Global South difference in considering the city-region approach.

Why the city-region approach should take into account regional difference

In recent years the fields of urban and regional studies, and planning, have undertaken a 'southern turn'. A growing body of scholars has been questioning the dominant and persistent assumptions of many theorists that differences between Global North and South regions of the world (or perhaps territorial difference per se) are no more than empirical variation and not significant enough to warrant different and separate concepts for different cities or regions of the world. The positions of Roy (2016) and Storper and Scott (2016) are examples of this now extended debate in urban studies, with the latter taking issue with postcolonial (and, by implication, southern) urban theory for what they refer to as its particularism and insistence on the provincialization of knowledge. The claim by Scott and Storper (2015) that all cities can be understood through a single conceptual model of the dynamics of agglomeration and the unfolding of an associated nexus of locations, land uses and human interactions is not too distant from the assumptions that appear to underlie the concept of cities in the NUA and its related planning documents.

In the field of planning, constructing a 'southern planning theory project' (*inter alia* Bhan, 2019; Bhan, Srinivas, & Watson, 2018; Watson, 2016; Yiftachel, 2016), with its implications for both planning theory and practice, has been underway for a while. Planning draws on concepts from the field of urban studies and other disciplines but requires further understanding of context in order to intervene and implement plans. A core argument in southern planning theory is that globally dominant planning theories and practice have mostly emerged from Global North (and economically advanced) regions of the world and have been applied unquestioningly everywhere else, and in localities which are significantly different from where they emerged. Hence, many of these dominant planning ideas are based on assumptions (regarding, for example, economy, governance, environment, society and culture, the nature of settlement, and so on), which simply do not hold (or hold in very different ways) in many other parts of the world. Herein lies an explanation for the frequent and profound disconnect between planning systems and practices and the urban and regional contexts in which they are applied (Healey, 2012).

The form of the city-region offered in the NUA planning guidelines may then be yet another example of a Global North-inspired planning idea (in this case shaped by early 20th-century Europe), which is now to be used in all parts of the world to implement aspects of SDG 11 and the NUA. For this reason, these concepts and their underlying assumptions demand close scrutiny. There are relatively few studies of attempts to create city-regions in the Global South, but they do highlight how very different patterns of urban growth and change, as well as historically different administrative and governance systems, make it difficult to translate European or US-style city-regions into very different parts of the world. For example, Roy (2009) has argued that much of the theoretical work on city-regions is located in the urban experience of EuroAmerica and new ideas and concepts need to emerge from the very different metropolises of the Global South.

All NUA planning guideline documents deal with the need to initiate linkages and connections between towns and their hinterlands, and the UN-Habitat (2017) document is specifically on this issue. The assumption in these documents is that in all parts of the world increases in urban-rural linkages (within a city-region) are a positive development strategy. However, an extensive 2014 research report on urban-rural linkages in selected Global South regions of the world points to the complex and place-specific nature of these linkages:

> the nature of rural—urban linkages and their growth and distributional effects are contextual, underpinned by: (a) the idiosyncratic character-istics of the specific urban and the specific rural, and (b) the position of the country and the subnational regions in the urbanization process.
>
> (Berdegue, Proctor, & Cazzuffi, 2014, p. 6)

These authors found that there is still a strong tendency in policy and prac-tice to treat urban and rural as distinct categories, when in fact they are frequently interlinked and overlapping.

Elaborating on this they point to extensive intermediate rural-urban functional areas or territories that encompass rural areas, small towns and medium cities, and these cannot be treated as either urban or rural. Further, stronger urban-rural linkages can be beneficial for poorer people, but not equally so: 'Relations with urban centres can be predatory. It takes more than having a link with an urban centre to have inclusive rural development' (Berdegue et al., 2014, p. 6). Urban-rural linkage can increase farm and non-farm jobs, which are mostly informal, but these activities can also increase income inequality due to access barriers, which differently affect poorer households. Linkage can increase rural to urban migration, but this impacts differently on rural households of origin as often richer rural households migrate before poorer ones – much depends on the stage of urban transition in which a country finds itself. And much will depend on the nature of gov-ernance at the urban-rural interface: frequently development in these areas is hindered by multiple coordination failures between levels of government, between public and private agents and between social actors, and difficul-ties are more likely to arise where governments are responsible for rural areas and small towns. Zoomers and Westen's (2011) work reinforces this point, rejecting the commonly held assumption that the key to development is changing local conditions (with strengthened urban-rural linkage featur-ing strongly here) and rather taking into account translocal forces and new forms of multi-locality.

UN-Habitat (2017) recognizes the importance of urban-rural linkages and the idea of a rural-urban continuum, but less so the great diversity of these linkages and how they can affect households and people in both positive and negative ways, depending on locality. It is also important to recognize that rather than considering local development to mean access to local resources, more relevant at this point in time is to understand the relationship between local development and translocal linkages: 'Local de-velopment opportunities are very much determined by translocal linkages – what is happening in other places, sometimes directly, as a result of flows of capital, goods, people and information' (Zoomers, 2018, p. 1). Territorial policies applied to delineated spaces need to be complemented with the management of flows (Zoomers & Van Westen, 2011). The highly localized definitions of city-region in the UN-Habitat guideline documents, and especially in UNHSP (2018), which identifies it as an area of some 80–100 km *within which* linkages need to be considered, tends to ignore the impact of globalization and translocalism.

Other assumptions embedded in the UN-Habitat city-region concept can also be brought into question. Both the nature of towns and cities, and institutions of governance vary significantly across the globe and may be very different from the prevailing situation in Europe and the United States which appears to have informed this concept. Case studies from Africa and China illustrate these aspects.

Agyemang, Amedzro, and Silva (2017) assess the city-region idea in relation to Accra, the capital of Ghana. They ask how assumptions of spatial governance in the city-region concept might work in situations where cities are very rapidly growing and spatially changing. With Accra expanding five-and-a-half times between 1991 and 2014, or by 6% per annum, there is a major spatial mismatch between spatial governance frameworks and the actual spatial extent of the metropolitan area, even though a level of regional government (regional coordinating councils) was introduced. Accra now extends across and beyond three different regional councils, each with its own different spatial development framework, and with no mechanism for coordinating them. Major transformations in national, regional and local government would be required to create governance structures or mechanisms able to coordinate development for the whole of metropolitan Accra and its hinterland, that is, to create a city-region. Even if not taking the form of an administrative tier with rigid boundaries, any mechanism would have to consider how to respond to ongoing expansion and change in the metropolitan area and its hinterland. Rapid urban expansion and change is a defining feature of much of the Global South; almost any city-region that fitted planning guidelines of 80–100 km across and occupying up to 10,000 km^2 (UNHSP, 2018, p. iv) might not do so for long.

In China, the city-region approach was enthusiastically adopted by the national government in the post-1980s' reform period as a way of promoting coordination and collaboration between adjacent cities. A strong and hierarchical state planning system was potentially a sound precondition for implementation. Yet, case study assessments of attempts to implement the approach show it has been less than successful. Li and Wu (2018) point to the difference between the Western liberal-democratic states in Europe and the United States, where the city-region concept can align with existing (if varied) administrative systems, and China's political-economic system which is hierarchical in nature and supervised by administrative authorities. In the former, the city-region relies on continual negotiation between central state and the region, as well as bottom-up processes of regional partnerships and horizontal linkages. The Chinese political and administrative system does not fit well into this model. There has been significant devolution to city-level government with these governments now playing a strong role in their own economic development but being less amenable to regional level coordination (Li & Wu, 2018).

Luo and Shen (2008) discuss the first approved city-region plan in 2002 that aimed to coordinate the three cities of Suzhou, Wuxi and Changzhou. They show the difficulty of achieving consensus on the regional plan between the three cities as it worked against their separate ambitions to achieve economic competitiveness and there were few complementarities between the cities as a basis for cooperation. In China city-region plans are formulated and approved by provincial governments, yet provinces lack the financial capacity and legal power to implement them. This process found itself at odds with existing city-level government which had benefitted from earlier decentralization programmes and had gained strong administrative and financial powers. These city administrations found little benefit from the regional plan and preferred to promote their own economic growth, often in competition with neighbouring cities (Luo & Shen, 2008).

Li and Wu (2018) assess attempts at city-region-building in the Yangtze River Delta (YRD), a trans-provincial mega-city-region with a history of region-building attempts. Here there were deliberate national government attempts to encourage horizontal collaboration, yet these were resisted by cities attempting to compete with Shanghai to be the lead city of the region. Also, as elsewhere in China, official appointment and promotion systems encourage local cadres to prioritize their own jurisdictions rather than promoting regional interests. As a result, the YRD city-region illustrates 'the constitutive role of the localspecific context and territorial politics. Rather than outcomes driven by external economic development, regionmaking under Chinese circumstances is closely tied with the internal challenges posed by territorial administrative divisions' (p. 317). More recently, these authors suggest there have been signs in China of bottom-up regional practices, but these are mostly around cross-border transportation systems. There has been no attempt to establish a level of government at the city-region level and 'on-the-ground city-regionalism turns out to be ad hoc, without a coherent governing mechanism' (p. 320). This, they suggest, is not unique to China, and other post-Communist countries such as those in Central and Eastern Europe have had difficulties in building regional governance within inherited legacies of state-centric administration and management.

These case findings should not suggest that the city-region concept can only be used in those parts of the world where the idea was formulated. Regional collaboration anywhere may be important for a range of possible reasons, from interregional coordination on infrastructure to developing particular kinds of linkages between a city and its hinterland. However, place and history (Jessop et al., 2008) will be fundamental to whether or not the city-region model as set out in the NUA and related planning guidelines is appropriate or even possible. Depending on locality and the aims of planning and policy intervention, the city-region scale may or may not be the appropriate level at which to intervene, and this could depend as well on the way in which relations within and across a city-region have been socially constituted (Jonas & Ward, 2007).

Problems with the city-region in the NUA

This paper has argued that the concepts of the city-region, as presented in the planning guidelines linked to the NUA, may not be the best ones on which to base strategies to promote the new role for cities and towns as drivers or hubs of development, or achieve sustainable and equitable settlements and regions. This is not to suggest, however, that the city-region concept per se does not have merit as the basis for a development strategy under certain conditions and in certain localities (as the success of Sydney, above, suggests). The paper recognizes that the NUA and the three planning guideline documents have somewhat different emphases in the way they present the city-region idea: this paper draws out the common threads from these documents.

There seems to be little recognition of the temporal and locational origins of the idea (Europe and the United States in the early part of the last century) and the subsequent extensive debate and critique of it, in the theoretical literature but also in published assessments, of attempts to promote city-region strategies. This debate has moved well away from early Geddesian presentations of the concept, and now recognizes both the influence of globalization as well as local characteristics of space and place, which interact in very different ways with each other across the globe. The literature is also increasingly recognizing the nature of difference between Global North and South territories, and hence how city-regions would need to be approached differently, if this strategy were adopted.

Despite this wealth of publications, the planning guidelines offer a city-region concept that in parts appears very close to the early origins of the idea. The definition of a city-region in the most recent guideline document (UNHSP, 2018) comes closest to this. Generally the documents present a concept that focuses on the local scale (a city or town and its hinterland), in which building relationships and integration between towns and their regional hinterland is paramount. As those who criticize the reification of 'the local' argue, whether or not this strategy will produce the outcomes intended will depend very much on an understanding of particular conditions in different places: in some situations it may produce negative ones. The approach could also be accused of spatial reification: the assumption of relative social and economic homogeneity within a geographically defined area. Yet, local and global economic and social change is giving rise to new and more extreme inequalities within both cities and their regions, and planning interventions (e.g., to promote transport links between a city and its region) will benefit some households and further marginalize others.

The guideline documents also make several assumptions regarding governance and the role of the state in achieving the aims of the NUA, and these assumptions shape the city-region idea as well. The assumptions largely reflect forms of governance evident (to varying degrees) in much of the Global North: relatively strong and wellresourced systems of state and planning; high degrees of decentralization or devolution where devolved powers are also matched by resources and professional skills; a relatively law-abiding citizenry that conforms (to a degree) to land management and other planning regulations; welldeveloped civil society networks and organization that can be called on to support city-region partnerships and initiatives; clear tiers and hierarchies of spatial planning emanating from the state (far more in Europe than in the United States) within which fitting a city-region scale of action (through either a tier of governance or the creation of partnerships) is less problematic than in other parts of the world; and processes of urban and rural growth and change that are slower and more predictable, and thus more amenable to spatial and institutional planning, than they are in many of the regions of the Global South. Urban centres, especially in Asia and Africa, are growing very rapidly. UN-Habitat (2012, p. 28) has pointed out that in the last decade 'the urban population in the developing world grew an average 1.2 million people per *week,* or slightly less than one full *year's* demographic growth in Europe's urban areas'. Moreover, much of this growth takes place in urban peripheries, leading to spreading urban agglomerations with multiple cores and fragmented administrative arrangements (as in the case of Accra).[3]

There are also assumptions regarding the power of the state relative to economic forces, and hence state planning's ability to direct and control development which is largely the outcome of private sector and household actions. Overall the guideline documents take little account of how economic forces (formal and informal) impact on cities and regions, and how these forces need to be taken into account when considering development strategies. This older assumption of state dominance is probably now questionable in all parts of the world other than perhaps in post-Communist countries such as China where strong state-centrism prevails.

Conclusions

Rather than debating the best form or approach to the city-region concept to achieve the goals of the NUA, this paper suggests a move away from the city-region as a starting point, along with its suggestion of cities and regions as 'containers' within which state-led planning can manage development. Policies, plans and strategies rather need to start from the particular urban developmental issues faced by cities in different parts of the world. For example, the key issue in most African cities is a chronic lack of basic infrastructure (clean water, sanitation, shelter, transport) under conditions of rapid expansion, extreme poverty and inequality. Moreover, the establishment of strong and well-capacitated systems of government and finance (and dealing with the state-owned enterprises which control much infrastructure) is a precondition for addressing these infrastructure issues. These problems will demand very different plans and strategies from, for example, Chinese cities that have good infrastructure and relatively strong government, although it is hierarchical and top-down, and lacking in the ability to form governance collaborations (Li & Wu, 2018). Major planning concerns in the largest cities in this region are more likely to be serious pollution, climate risk and natural resource issues, and growing urban inequality.

Plans to promote NUA objectives also need to prioritize the role of the economy (formal and informal) in shaping flows of capital and associated flows of people, and hence urban change (Zoomers, 2018). Economic factors are now primary drivers of urban change, although occurring differently in various parts of the world, but city-region framed, territorial and state-led planning does not acknowledge this or suggest how it should be addressed to achieve NUA goals. Two issues are a priority here: first, where the informal economy is a current and probably future dominant aspect of cities, as in many Global South regions, this needs careful analysis (linkages can be local, national and international) and planning interventions to create supportive infrastructure, spaces and regulations; and second, in rapidly growing cities the issue is that of urban land grabs through the real estate sector, often in collusion with the state, leading to land commodification and speculation which place major obstacles in the way of achieving NUA goals.

In sum, this paper has argued that based on somewhat parochial assumptions the NUA planning guideline documents offer a concept of city-regions which they suggest can be applied in all parts of the world to achieve the goals of the NUA. However, a growing body of literature on urban and regional development is pointing to the importance of understanding difference in making any kind of city-region strategy possible. It is therefore not clear if the planning guideline documents can deliver on the hope of cities acting as hubs or drivers of development rather than territorially bounded sites with development problems which need to be addressed (Barnett & Parnell, 2018).

Disclosure statement

No potential conflict of interest was reported by the author.

Notes

1 It is recognized that the NUA was responding to several global policy frameworks in addition to SDG 11. The NUA states: 'The implementation of the New Urban Agenda contributes to the implementation and localization of the 2030 Agenda for Sustainable Development in an integrated manner, and to the achievement of the Sustainable Development Goals and targets, including Goal 11....'

2 This was produced before the NUA, but was subsequently recognized as a means of implementing it.
3 Spreading urban agglomerations incorporating multiple cores and fragmented administrations is true of some Global North city-regions as well.

ORCID

Vanessa Watson ⓘ http://orcid.org/0000-0001-9965-6891

References

Agyemang, F., Amedzro, K., & Silva, E. (2017). The emergence of city-regions and their implications for contemporary spatial governance: Evidence from Ghana. *Cities (London), 71,* 70–79. doi:10.1016/j.cities.2017.07.009

Barnett, C., & Parnell, S. (2016). Ideas, implementation and indicators: Epistemologies of the post-2015 urban agenda. *Environment and Urbanization, 28,* 87–98. doi:10.1177/ 0956247815621473

Barnett, C., & Parnell, S. (2018). Spatial rationalities and the challenges for planners in the new urban agenda for sustainable development. In G. Bhan, S. Srinivas, & V. Watson (Eds.), *The Routledge companion to planning in the Global South* (pp. 25–36). Abingdon: Routledge.

Berdegué, J. A., Proctor, F. J., & Cazzuffi, C. (2014). *Inclusive ruralurban linkages* (Working Paper Series No. 123). Santiago: Working Group: Development with Territorial Cohesion, Territorial Cohesion for Development Program, Rimisp.

Bhan, G., Srinivas, S., & Watson, V. (Eds.). (2018). *Routledge companion to planning in the Global South.* London: Routledge.

Bhan, G. (2019). Notes on a southern urban practice. *Environment and Urbanization,* 1–16. doi:10.1177/0956247818815792

Born, B., & Purcell, M. (2006). Avoiding the local trap. Scale and food systems in planning research. *Journal of Planning Education and Research, 26,* 195–207. doi:10.1177/ 0739456X06291389

Cochrane, A., & Ward, K. (2012). Researching the geographies of policy mobility: Confronting the methodological challenges. *Environment and Planning A: Economy and Space, 44,* 5–12. doi:10.1068/a44176

Dados, N., & Connell, R. (2012). The Global South. *Contexts, 11*(1), 12–13. doi:10.1177/1536504212436479

Davoudi, S. (2008). Conceptions of the city-region: A critical review. *Proceedings of the Institution of Civil Engineers — Urban Design and Planning, 161,* 51–60. doi:10.1680/udap.2008.161.2.51

Geddes, P. (1915). *Cities in evolution.* London: Williams & Norgate.

Hall, P. (1988). *Cities of tomorrow.* Oxford: Blackwell.

Harrison, J., & Growe, A. (2014). When regions collide: In what sense a new 'regional problem? *Environment and Planning A: Economy and Space, 46,* 2332–2352. doi:10.1068/a130341p

Healey, P. (2009). City-regions and place development. *Regional Studies, 43,* 831–843. doi:10.1080/00343400701861336

Healey, P. (2012). The universal and the contingent: Some reflections on the transnational flow of planning ideas and practices. Planning *Theory, 11*(2), 188–207. doi:10.1177/1473095211419333

Healey, P. (2015). Spatial imaginaries, urban dynamics and political community. *Planning Theory and Practice: Interface, 16,* 266–268.

Jessop, B., Brenner, N., & Jones, M. (2008). Theorizing sociospatial relations. *Environment and Planning D: Society and Space,* 26, 389–401. doi:10.1068/d9107

Jonas, A., & Ward, K. (2007). Introduction to a debate on cityregions: New geographies of governance, democracy and social reproduction. *International Journal of Urban and Regional Research, 31*(1), 169–178. doi:10.1111/j.1468–2427.2007.00711.x

Li, Y., & Wu, F. (2018). Understanding city-regionalism in China: Regional cooperation in the Yangtze River Delta. *Regional Studies,* 52(3), 313–324. doi:10.1080/00343404.2017.1307953

Luo, X., & Shen, J. (2008). Why city-region planning does not work well in China: The case of Suzhou–Wuxi—Changzhou. *Cities (London),* 25, 207–217. doi:10.1016/j.cities.2008.04.003

McGuirk, P. (2007). The political construction of the city-region: Notes from Sydney. *International Journal of Urban and Regional Research, 31*(1), 179–187. doi:10.1111/j.1468–2427.2007.00712.x

Mumford, L. (1925). The fourth migration and regions — To live in. *Survey, 54.*

New Urban Agenda (NUA). (2016). *United Nations Conference on Housing and Sustainable Urban Development (Habitat III).* Quito: United Nations.

Painter, J. (2010). Rethinking territory. *Antipode, 42,* 1090–1118. doi:10.1111/j.1467–8330.2010.00795.x

Purcell, M. (2007). City-regions, neoliberal globalization and democracy: A research agenda. *International Journal of Urban and Regional Research, 31*(1), 197–206. doi:10.1111/j.1468–2427.2007.00714.x

Roy, A. (2009). The 21st-century metropolis: New geographies of theory. *Regional Studies, 43,* 819–830. doi:10.1080/00343400701809665

Roy, A. (2016). Who's afraid of postcolonial theory? *International Journal of Urban and Regional Research, 40*(1), 200–209. doi:10.1111/1468–2427.12274

Scott, A. (2001). Globalization and the rise of city-regions. *European Planning Studies, 9,* 813–826. doi:10.1080/09654310120079788

Scott, A., & Storper, M. (2003). Regions, globalization, development. *Regional Studies, 37,* 579–593. doi:10.1080/0034340032000108697a

Scott, A., & Storper, M. (2015). The nature of cities: The scope and limits of urban theory. *International Journal of Urban and Regional Research, 39*(1), 1–15. doi:10.1111/1468–2427.12134

Storper, M. (1997). *The regional world: Territorial development in a global economy.* New York: Guilford.

Storper, M., & Scott, A. (2016). Current debates in urban theory: A critical assessment. *Urban Studies, 53*(6), 1114–1136. doi:10.1177/0042098016634002

United Nations Human Settlements Programme (UN-Habitat). (2009). *Planning sustainable cities: Global report on human settlements.* Nairobi: UN-Habitat and Earthscan.

United Nations Human Settlements Programme (UN-Habitat). (2012) *State of the world's cities 2012/2013: Prosperity of cities.* Nairobi: UN-Habitat.

United Nations Human Settlements Programme (UN-Habitat). (2015) *International guidelines on urban and territorial planning.* Nairobi: UN-Habitat.

United Nations Human Settlements Programme (UN-Habitat). (2017) *Implementing the new urban agenda by strengthening urban—rural linkages.* Nairobi: UN-Habitat.

United Nations Human Settlements Programme (UNHSP). (2018). *Leading change: Delivering the new urban agenda through urban and territorial planning.* Kuala Lumpur: UNHSP.

Watson, V. (2016). Shifting approaches to planning theory: Global North and South. *Urban Planning, 1*(4), 32–41. doi:10.17645/up.vli4.727

Yiftachel, O. (2016). The Aleph—Jerusalem as critical learning. *City, 20*(3), 483–494. doi:10.1080/13604813.2016.1166702

Zoomers, A., & Van Westen, G. (2011). Introduction: Translocal development, development corridors and development chains. *International Development Planning Review, 33*(4), 377–388. doi:10.3828/idpr.2011.19

Zoomers, A. (2018). Development at the crossroads of capital flows and migration: Leaving no one behind? *Sustainability, 10,* 4807. doi:10.3390/su10124807

Planning, temporary urbanism and citizen-led alternative-substitute place-making in the Global South

Lauren Andres⊙, Hakeem Bakare⊙,
John R. Bryson⊙, Winnie Khaemba⊙,
Lorena Melgaço⊙ and George R. Mwaniki⊙

Introduction

Cities in the Global South face major intractable challenges from infor-mal settlements, housing provision and transport to environment deg-radation (including air pollution). Nevertheless, these challenges are intensified through limited planning capacity and resource constraints. At the start of this millennium, Hall and Pfeiffer (2000) called for a new global agenda for 21st-century cities under the tide Urban Future 21. They emphasized the importance of liveability identifying three types of cities (p. 139): those coping with informal hyper growth; those coping with dy-namic growth; and weakening mature cities coping with ageing. Creating liveable cities involves a process of both planning at macro-scales *and* of micro-scale place-making. This reflects a combination of bottom-up, citizen-led, unplanned, and informal actions and processes that are poorly accounted for in formal planning decision-making processes. In this paper, we propose a new way of understanding urban futures for Global South cities, focusing on South Africa, Kenya, Uganda and Ethio-pia, where planning plays a key role in transforming city-regions, despite major challenges. We recognize the diversity of these four countries and the African continent, specifically differences in planning systems and governance. The purpose here is to extract some overarching considera-tions that will facilitate planning regional futures, including alternative planning approaches, rather than attempting to generalize without ap-preciating diversity.

The argument is constructed upon two pillars: first, to address the com-plexity and diversity of urban environments, a system of systems approach is required to account holistically for the different connected components underpinning social, economic and environmental wellbeing; and second, such an approach goes beyond 'planning' and includes a significant element of place-making. This includes temporary and informal dynamics acting as alternative substitutes in places experiencing real difficulties in creating, implementing and enforcing formal planning processes. These approaches embed citizens or voluntary-sector organizations engaging in activities that alter their immediate surroundings through processes of localized place-making. Cities are the outcome of a layering of different types of interventions with very different geographies and time scales: from comprehensive city-region plans to what is often considered to be impermanent forms of temporary urbanism.

We recognize that our argument is provocative and not without risks of misinterpretation. Having said this, it complements existing research that has explored planning in the Global South accounting for both formal and informal processes as part of a critique of the inability of traditional planning processes to respond to urban challenges in such diverse, complex and unequal urban contexts (Harrison, 2006; Miraftab, 2009; Watson, 2014). This led to debates into the meaning and use of participation for planning with recent calls for a move towards understanding 'participation *as* planning' for research conducted in the Global South (Apsan Frediani & Cocina, 2019). The present paper complements these approaches but shifts the debate beyond planning to place-making.

The analysis draws upon two distinct but complementary research projects. First, research in South Africa, which undertook the largest survey to date of planning practitioner attitudes toward the state of the profession (June-August 2017), comprising 212 questionnaire responses and 89 in-depth qualitative interviews. Second, research developing a systems approach to exploring environmental challenges and place-making based on 54 interviews with national, regional and local governments, nongovernmental institutions (NGIs), researchers, nonprofit (government) organizations (NGOs) and community-based organizations (CBOs) in Kenya, Uganda and Ethiopia. Primary data were coded in NVivo using a combination of deductive (theoretically led) and inductive (data-led) approaches. The analysis highlights the importance of new forms of context-specific approaches to place-making, including combining alternative citizen and community processes with planning. Blending these approaches is a pathway towards more balanced, sustainable and resilient urban futures (e.g., the United Nations' New Urban Agenda). These arguments contribute to ongoing debates about how best to approach and analyse cities and planning in the Global South, engaging with the calls to search for new ideas, methodologies and strategies across north-south contexts. This includes identifying new insights and innovative planning ideas (Watson, 2013, p. 96) whilst building upon 'policy-generated or applied knowledge' that 'can feed a revival in theoretical reflections on the city' (Parnell & Robinson, 2012, p. 603).

The paper is structured as follows. The next section reviews existing approaches to understanding planning and place-making focusing on formal planning, reading cities, shadow place-making and temporary urbanism. The third section identifies three pillars that contribute to a new planning and place-making approach (PPA) to understanding the evolution of African cities. The final section engages further with limitations arising from the alternative approach while reinforcing this paper's primary contribution and its argument that African cities and Global South cities should be conceptualized as the outcome of layers of planned interventions combined with alternativesubstitute place-making that represents different forms of 'permanent impermanence'.

From planning cities in the Global South to place-making

Formal planning in the Global South

Many cities of the Global South are characterized by dichotomic though contrasting dynamics. On the one hand, from the mid-1970s, many countries started applying master and development plans informed by planning approaches developed in the Global North (Okpala, 2009; Watson, 2013). By 1990, 196 Nigerian cities had town and settlement plans, while another 197 towns planned to develop master plans (Okpala, 2009). Master plans were developed by Addis Ababa, Dodoma, Lilongwe and Nairobi (Okpala, 2009), which included challenging visions (Watson, 2013) targeted at investors through forms of speculative urbanism (Goldman, 2011) as well as the upper and rising middle classes along with international expats, while ignoring the majority of the population. On the other hand, uncontrolled informal settlements are spreading on the outskirts of cities and where integrated planning solutions cannot be implemented (see Apsan Frediani & Cocina, 2019, for a recent overview). For Uganda, this results in political bargaining which then takes precedence over planning procedures, weakening formal planning processes encouraging the growth of informal settlements (Goodfellow, 2010). Those peri-urban areas where land is available, inexpensive and outside the control of urban land regulation are sites for localized citizen-led place-making practices.

Africa's informal urban population is recognized as a key contributor to urban growth (Lund & Skinner, 2004), but informal settlements are initially excluded from formal planning processes (Baffour Awuah & Hammond, 2014). Calls to recognize the importance of informality, the need to rethink planning processes to embrace the informal, have been made (de Satgé & Watson, 2018; Roy, 2009; Watson, 2003). The literature on sustainable urban development highlights the need for congruency between planners and end users of planning outcomes to achieve 'best for all' results (Miescher, 2012, p. 1; Ross, 2018). Despite consistent evidence of current planning failures and suggestions on future strategies, planning and the redesign of urban peripheries continues to benefit urban elites and informal place-making continues to persist (Adam, 2014; Allen, 2003). Nevertheless, informality is not appropriately addressed by mainstream planning.

The planning challenges experienced by African cities and the recognition of their role as engines of growth amidst informalities represents a planning paradox in which areas experiencing rapid urbanization are excluded from the formal planning process (Alemayehu, 2008; Sihlongonyane, 2015). In this context, the urban periphery is marginalized in formal planning processes with urban residents either being displaced to benefit urban elites or their socioeconomic challenges ignored in planning or place-making processes. A significant gap exists between planning and the end users of planning outputs; Africa's problem is a need for a more inclusive planning system combined with implementation.

It is timely to consider what type of planning combined with localized and contextualized place-making is required for African cities that have different histories, lifestyles, environments and planning systems. Everyday living in hyper-growth cities is supported by blending citizen-led interventions with continual chronic and acute shocks. These persistent shocks result in continual citizen and household adaptation. The outcome is survival, but this is an inequitable process based on household location, capacities, capabilities and access to resources. Planning and place-making needs to be embedded within a more complex and systemic framework of city-region functions and transformations, whilst also advocating for and incorporating informal and temporary dynamics. This is critical and resonates with ongoing debates including Harrison's (2006) call for new models and the importance of focusing:

> on how Africa, and its many different parts, is – through the resourceful responses of its residents to conditions of vulnerability – in the process of becoming something new that is both part of and separate from Western modernity. This new imaginary may provide a conceptual opening that would allow us to think about Africa in ways that are more hopeful and positive; that acknowledge the success of Africans in constructing productive lives at a micro-scale, and economies and societies at a macro-scale, that work despite major structural constraints.
>
> (p. 323)

Part of this new imaginary is to explore the differences and interdependencies between top-down approaches to planning versus bottom-up micro-scale approaches to placemaking. This is to highlight alternative processes of place-making and also of reading cities.

Reading and understanding cities

Alternative perspectives to exploring cities have emerged that include an emphasis on trying to 'look through a city' (Amin & Thrift, 2017), to try to 'make sense of cities' (Badcock, 2002) or to 'reading cities' (Bryson, Andres, & Mulhall, 2018). These approaches try to interpret the complexity of urban living, livelihoods and lifestyles by understanding the 'mangle of machines, infrastructures, humans, nonhumans, institutions, networks, metabolisms, matter and nature – where the coming together is itself constitutive of urbanity and its radiated effects' (Amin & Thrift, 2017, p. 10). This 'coming together' is complex: cities are never homogeneous but rather consist of many different types of place. Urban theory has appreciated the diversity of urban life, but there is still a tendency to 'generalise from prevalent phenomena' (Amin & Thrift, 2002, p. 8). This is unfortunate. There are many different forms of urban experience including important differences between global or extraordinary cities (Taylor, 2013) compared with more ordinary cities (Salder & Bryson, 2019).

City-regions are complex, dynamic and evolving systems. Evolutionary economic geography highlights the importance of the impacts of an accumulation of incremental decision-making producing path dependency or path creation (Boschma & Martin, 2010; Martin, 2012). Path dependency comes from accumulations of incremental decision-making that can be traced back centuries. These decisions take many forms including those made by governments, private sector firms, individuals and households. The many interconnected systems that support city-living must not be conceptualized as reflecting the outcome of a logical process that provides some form of functionality. This is to overlook perverse consequences and also the relationships between the provision of infrastructure-enabled services and their use. An alternative approach is to recognize that city systems are systematizing networks that may initially provide some shape to urban living (Latour, 1988). For cities in the Global South, the presence of alternative and informal structures and networks created in the absence of institutional interventions calls for exploring new approaches to planning regional futures (Simone, 2016).

Reading cities of the Global South and developing an alternative approach to planning regional futures requires understanding the complex interplay between microand macro-scale place-making processes. There is a tendency, inherited from colonialism, to control urban dynamics, uses and practices artificially through strict regulations and plans that in practice cannot be enforced. These are 'bad' plans and 'bad' regulations. This highlights three different processes. First, people-and household-based decisions may result in substitution interventions for structures and processes that currently do not exist in a city. This results in various forms of 'temporary urbanism'. These forms of individual and collective adaptation may result in physical transformation or in processes that encourage interactions between people and place. Second are flows of people, ideas, raw materials and products. A city is a complex concatenation of flows with different households and places having different forms of connectivity. At a household level, different individuals will engage with the city in very different ways by developing their own temporal and spatial rhythms. Third, spatial planning acts as the primary mechanism by which the local and national state engages in plan-making and place regulation. Spatial planning is about the formal and proactive management of the urban environment. Planning by essence is about foresight, designed futures and does not allow for an appreciation of flexibility, especially short-term and everyday adaptability. Here there is a gap in dealing with temporary and fluctuant rhythms of the everyday and associated place-making dynamics.

Temporary urbanisms and shadow placemaking

Temporary urbanisms are the outcome of processes and practices contributing to spatial and social adaptability, allowing places to be purposely used and activated responding to specific economic and social needs. This concept emerged to explore temporary solutions for housing, or social needs mainly in the Global North (Bishop & Williams, 2012; Oswalt, Overmeyer, & Misselwitz, 2013), but it resonates with research conducted on the realities and challenges of Global South cities where informal and formal interventions shape place (Miraftab, 2009, 2017; Watson, 2013, 2016). Global South and planning theory debates have begun to explore insurgent planning (Miraftab, 2009, 2016, 2017), informed by radical planning approaches initially explored by Friedmann (1973, 2002) and Sandercock (1998a, 1998b) recognizing citizens' practices as forms of planning (Miraftab, 2016).

Temporary urbanisms are forms of insurgent planning or 'an alternate planning as it happens among subordinate communities, be it informal settlements and townships in the ex-colonies or the disadvantaged communities in the belly of the beast – North America and Western Europe' (Miraftab, 2016, p. 3). It sits separately from traditional planning, theoretically distancing itself from traditional approaches focusing on practices rather than actors. This approach 'ontologically departs from liberal traditions of so-called inclusive planning that have held the inclusion of disadvantaged groups as an objective of professional intervention' (Miraftab, 2017, p. 276). 'Temporary urbanism' concerns places and areas that are left aside and neglected by the state, the private sector and planning (Oswalt et al., 2013, p. 11). It goes beyond neglection reflecting evolution rather than permanence. To thrive, cities and their inhabitants need to adapt and have opportunities for other choices to emerge from specific needs and contexts. These choices can occur if 'alternatives' are sought or as substitutes or coping mechanisms. Temporary urbanism is embedded within everyday, informal practices rather than long-term visions (Madanipour, 2017). Unpacking these temporalities within the built environment and in the process of place-making highlights the importance of physical 'grey spaces', informal settlements (Yiftachel, 2009), which remain in a state of 'permanent temporariness' or, as we shall argue, should be conceptualized as being in a state of 'permanent impermanence'.

Forms of temporary urbanism in developing cities are strongly connected to public and private sector failures in tackling key urban challenges and delivering adequate formal planning. Three literatures can be identified that explore these dynamics. First, Katz's (2004, p. 242) work on social resilience highlights how individuals and groups engage in autonomous initiatives reflecting strategies to get by through various forms of mutual support. This emphasizes the importance of family and friendship networks as one element of a survival strategy. Second, recent research, informed by the alterity debate, has explored the provision of local infrastructure by blending non-capitalist with capitalist activities. In other words, the provision of local infrastructure-enabled services using an 'alternative' approach that attempts to address infrastructure exclusion by the development of citizen-led alternative infrastructure business models (Bryson et al., 2018). This highlights the role that citizens and communities play in shaping cities through alternatives to conventional forms of infrastructure provision. Third, during the late 1980s, Wolch (1989) realized that the scale and scope of voluntary or third-sector activities had increased as one compensatory mechanism for the ongoing restructuring of the welfare state in developed market economies. This led to the identification by Wolch of the *shadow state* as 'a parastate apparatus comprised of multiple voluntary sector organisations, administered outside of traditional democratic politics and charged with major collective service responsibilities previously shouldered by the public sector, yet remaining within the purvey of state control' (Wolch, 1990, p. xvi). This parastate apparatus undertakes many of the functions that were provided by the welfare state: it is independent of the state, but is 'enabled, regulated, and subsidised' by the state (p. 41). This account of the shadow state did not engage with the neo-liberalism debate (Mitchell, 2001), but these are closely connected debates.

More recently, 'after a period of disengagement, ... critical attention is once more being directed towards the shadow state concept' (Deverteuil, 2016, p. 43). In this more recent debate, the voluntary sector is not seen as inherently progressive or completely co-opted by the state (p. 41). One role the shadow state can play is as a translation mechanism for state policies that results in on-the-ground service delivery (Trudeau & Veronis, 2009). In the Global South, shadow governance has been equated with extortion, corruption and patronage (Olver, 2017) and marginalization (Alpa, 2010). The present argument is that the shadow state provides one entry point for considering place-making in the Global South, but in the context of moving beyond neo-liberalism approaches (Parnell & Robinson, 2012). This is to distinguish between shadow place-making by and for the people compared with placemaking that is imposed on places by the para-state apparatus. This form of people-centric place-making fills gaps in provision given the absence of robust accountable institutions and transparent planning processes and frameworks. It is part of a process by which the marginalized can take ownership of places transforming informal settlements into liveable places. The key challenge is that, on the one hand, this type of temporary urbanism fills gaps left by the absence of formal planning. On the other hand, temporary urbanism will develop solutions for particular places reflecting the capacity and capabilities of people, but this will never result in a coordinated citywide approach to place-making.

Combining these three debates on alternatives to state-based solutions with forms of temporary urbanisms characterized by their 'permanent impermanence', which we will farther refer to as a process of 'alternative substitute place-making', provides a set of building blocks that inform the development of a new conceptual framework for considering planning regional futures in the Global South focusing on Africa. This concept differentiates our approach from the shadow-state literature given our focus on people-centric approaches to place-making. This framework must include the activities of the state, the shadow state, but also individuals and households. The ongoing evolution of Global South cities has a different balance between the actors involved in place-making processes. Planning has a role to play, but there are whole areas of these cities that have emerged as a direct result of individual and household micro-scale interventions as immediate solutions to housing provision and everyday living through different forms of alternative substitute place-making.

African urban futures: a planning and place-making approach

The present review of these three processes involved in planning as a macro-scale intervention and place-making as a micro-scale practice highlights the importance of developing a new planning and place-making approach (PPA) to conceptualizing planning in the African context. We here specifically consider South Africa, Kenya, Uganda and Ethiopia. This approach can be localized and contextualized to address the diversity of urban places accounting for the role individuals play in transforming cities in the Global South (Apsan Frediani & Cocina, 2019). This new framework begins by identifying a set of challenges facing African cities reflecting the 17 UN Sustainable Development Goals (Figure 1). Although we recognize that Africa is very diverse, we also acknowledge the importance of international frameworks, typically the New Urban Agenda highlighting that 'particular attention should be given to addressing the unique and emerging urban development challenges facing all countries, in particular developing countries, including African countries' (UN-Habitat, 2017, p. 9). Agents of change, both formal and informal, are then identified including state-and citizen-led approaches to planning versus place-making. Our framework recognizes that formal planning has struggled to account for informal settlements and their residents tending to exclude and marginalize them (Miraftab, 2009, 2016; Roy, 2009; Watson, 2003). Collective and individual forms of place-making, building upon informal and formal regulations, are responses to the limitation of planning in such contexts (Apsan Frediani & Cocina, 2019, p. 145). The challenge is how to combine informal place-making with formal planning. The new approach combines formal and informal planning outcomes acknowledging alternative-substitute place making as a citizen-led permanent impermanent form of urbanism. Our contribution is to show how planning can embrace informal place-making to develop a more integrated approach to planning in the Global South. This calls for a planning approach facilitating informal place-making, but in the context of an integrated approach to city planning. We now explore the key elements of this new approach.

Formal planning and permanent impermanence

Formal planning in Kenya, Uganda, Ethiopia and South Africa has evolved since the colonial period. In South Africa, since the end of apartheid in 1994, a succession of key planning Acts established planning frameworks aligned with new political directions, including removing spatial racial segregation and rights to housing. In 1995, the Development Facilitation Act 67 first positioned formal planning as key to transforming cities. The 2013 Spatial Planning and Land Use Management Act (SPLUMA) aimed to achieve social and economic inclusion in planning and land-use management practices. In Ethiopia, the government deployed integrated development master plans (e.g., the 2013 Addis Ababa and Surrounding Oromia Special Zone Integrated Development Plan).

Planners face a series of challenges, including difficulties of implementing master plans (Watson, 2013), coping with political change, corruption, and problems with data availability and resources. A South African planner noted that 'People meant to manage planning have such limited knowledge about the profession, making it difficult for planners to perform their duties' ((survey), planner, South Africa, 14 June 2017). Another respondent argued that:

> Africa though vast in extent, lacks the purse to support planning activities as a result the planning sphere fails to effect change which is its

raison d'être. Over and above, the planning sphere is heavily eclectic and tends to be infiltrated by other disciplines or professionals without the absolute skills and technocratic sensibilities to deliver effective solutions. The political landscape is equally at fault, ... a point in case is the proliferation of informal settlements versus legislative instruments and policies that impede development control.

(planner, South Africa, 13 July 2017)

Formal planning has failed to address the complexity of diverse cities, and particularly their informal and unplanned nature, leading to a proliferation of informal settlements with limited or no social services and public utilities (Okalebo, 2011; Rukwaro, 2009). Thus,

> Kampala has developed faster than the plan. Many things are unplanned and because of that, you know, you find things being in place, before others being done, and that causes lots of challenges around pollution, around use of resources and the effectiveness of those resources.
> (NGI NGO consultant, Uganda, 18 October 2018)

This rests upon the essence of formal planning which is about attempting to shape city-region futures guided by long-term visions based on often unrealistic scenarios and ambitions. Formal planning leaves very little space for informality. For South Africa, 'national building regulations and standards are just there for formal structures and comply with health and safety and structural requirements and nothing else. You know, it doesn't recognise informality, and sees informality as a contravention of the law' (planner, South Africa, 8 February 2018).

This is the case for East African cities. Plagued by land tenure, housing upgrading and infrastructure deficiencies (UN-Habitat, 2006), Kampala city's increasing informal activities have been described as a new 'normality' (Richmond, Myers, & Namuli, 2018, p. 3); in the present PPA this is characterized as a new form of permanent impermanence, in other words, a more, adaptable, dynamic and temporary place-making process. Permanent impermanence reflects different types of temporary urbanisms in such contexts from the transitory features based on social resilience to the impermanence of temporary structures. In the Bum Bum estate, Nairobi, Kenya, building regulations conflicted with residents' needs resulting in a call to rewrite the regulations (Rukwaro, 2009) recognizing this settlement as a form of permanent impermanence. This highlights the requirement to combine planning approaches with an appreciation of the role of informal processes including adaptability in formal planning processes and regulations. This includes formally allowing unplanned and uncertainty in urban-making

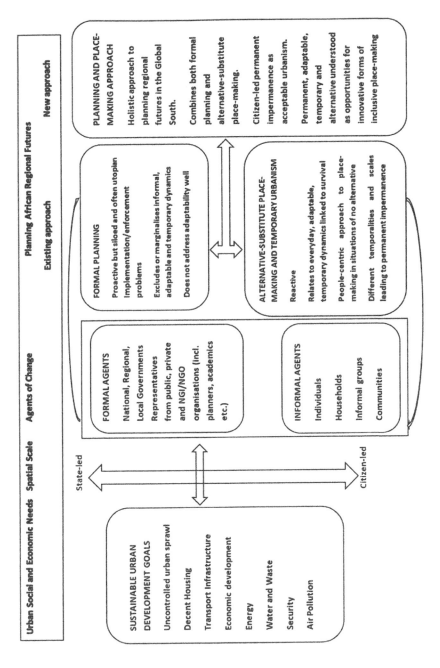

Figure 1 Planning and place-making approach (PPA).

processes and accepting the informal as a core, though mutable component of policy and place-making strategies.

The informal and unplanned nature of cities is complex as it includes access to housing and basic networks with limited adaptability but also wider societal issues including everyday coping tactics that shape communities' survival (Odendaal, 2012; Watson, 2009). Planning in such contexts too often fails to develop a systematic approach given the difficulties faced by planners combined with capacity problems and perceptions that such forms of place-making are not acceptable forms of urbanism. Amongst other factors, those difficulties arise from the dynamic nature of informal activities (Harrison, Todes, & Watson, 2007; Watson, 2009). 'Do-it-yourself practices grounded in survival mechanisms are common including access to water and electricity. The Hope for Communities aerial water project in Kibeira, Kenya, one of largest informal settlements in the world, is an excellent example of an alternative solution to water provision. This highlights the role of adaptable, temporary processes of 'alternativesubstitute place-making' through which individuals, households and collectives engage with place-based transformation.

Alternative-substitute place-making

Such forms of alternative-substitute place-making constitute a form of permanent impermanence characterized as an individual and collective shadow state mechanism emphasizing citizen practices as forms of planning. Alternative-substitute place-making attempts to develop local and immediate solutions to the distractions of the challenges of everyday living. These include shelter and temporary 'investments' in local infrastructures (e.g., transport, roofs) or services (e.g., water). The raw reality of survival involves an accumulation of discrete and mundane initiatives undertaken by individuals and households as relatively micro-scale attempts to enhance the quality of everyday living. Alternative-substitute place-making is a local process, but the accumulation of many local and often relatively minor informal interventions has the potential to transform city living. It is the accumulation of these initiatives and survival mechanisms that plays an important role in transforming cities impacting on more formal approaches to city-region planning. Alternative-substitute place-making is a substitute for what is not yet provided by the state and by planning processes; it is 'alternative' as it represents a people-centric approach to place-making, but in situations in which there is no alternative. This includes two contrasting dynamics: regulatory and foresight dynamics, on the one hand, and the everyday, adaptable and informal, on the other. One of the interviewees emphasized that:

> In Kenya, what we've been experiencing ... urban planning infrastructure or service delivery issues ... has led to a mushrooming in forms of

settlement and slums leading to inadequate and unaffordable housing amongst urban residents and poor solid waste management.

(government representative, Kenya, 29 August 2018)

Alternative-substitute place-making is a partial substitute for planning. The outcome is a diversity of different types of alternative-substitute place-making reflecting different needs, temporalities and scales towards which planning professionals in the field struggle to understand and to manage. This creates paradoxes and tensions regarding how to include, account for and deal with contrasting realities. Thus:

> We did an interesting study in Marikana… . Residents made their own water channels and water systems because of the failure of authorities to provide for their needs. It's an informal settlement that is very much for-malised, but they can't be formalised because of policy restrictions. So, yes, these people are located there and they are living there and they've got basically all the services that they need, but it's still informal. ... In practice it's real and it's happening, but in policies it's not allowed.
>
> (planning academic, South Africa, 6 April 2018)

Some forms of alternative-substitute place-making may be ignored initially and eventually removed, but some elements of this place-making should be conceptualized as a form of permanent impermanence in which the application of planning processes will enhance this form of place-making rather than remove it. Absorbing this form of temporary urbanism into the planning process raises new challenges of how to decide which forms are acceptable for adaptation and which or not.

Understanding the ongoing evolution of African cities is a process based on understanding alternative-substitute place-makings' contribution to formal planning. This is to highlight the multisided nature of place-making that blends alternative-substitute place-making processes with formal planning. These two approaches have different geographies and temporalities. On the one hand, the alternatives may be the dominant form of place-making in an area, and a resistance 'to Western models of planning and urban development' (Miraftab, 2009, p. 45). On the other, alternatives may develop in 'planned' parts of a city addressing individual and community needs. Upgrading alternative-substitute place-making has too often led to demolition under a credo of creating better living conditions (8 February 2018, planner, South Africa).

Alternative-substitute place-making – combined with planned interventions – will continue to alter places, including investments in infrastructure. These should be 'investments' in places that are incorporated into the city rather than ignored or removed. The accumulation of many alternative-substitute place-making activities contributes to transforming a city-region. Flexible and adaptable approaches, combining planning with place-making, enable cities to respond to contrasting dynamics and temporalities by drawing on expert and lay planning interventions. This highlights the importance of planning cities based on combinational knowledge with professional planners working alongside residents.

Citizens as end-user innovators in alternative-substitute place-making

Alternative-substitute place-making, as insurgent planning, places individuals as key change agents as an everyday coping and survival strategy. The recognition of this role, and support mechanisms, requires a shift in how these individuals are recognized as participating in place-making processes. Urban residents should no longer be conceptualized as passive receivers of services planned and provided by government, but as possible end-user innovators. Innovation used to be conceptualized as an activity undertaken by the private and public sector rather than by citizens. Von Hippel (2005) challenged this account of innovation by revealing that innovation was also undertaken by individuals motivated by personal needs or frustrations with existing products or services (Nielsen, Reisch, & Thogersen, 2014). The end-user innovation literature has not yet been applied to public services or to place-making. Conceptualizing citizens as end-user innovators, directly and indirectly involved in alternative-substitute place-making, alters the ways in which the relationship between planning, communities and individuals is conceptualized. This is to shift the focus away from citizen consultation processes to include citizens as place-shapers, place-makers and place-innovators.

This type of end-user place-making is important as new solutions can be developed to everyday challenges and, in some cases, these solutions can be scaled-up. One challenge facing planners is:

> Not providing what communities want or not understanding what different communities require for their well-being. I think a lot of our Town Planners are situated in offices, come from a wealthy background and we don't really understand what the lower income communities need. And I think that's the difficulty that we face is to plan for them and to understand what they would need and to keep them happy.
>
> (planner, South Africa, 23 March 2018)

This is a knowledge asymmetry problem; planners may not fully appreciate the place-making needs of residents and residents fail to understand planning processes. Incorporating alternative-substitute place-making into planning processes comes with a communications challenge in that 'most of these documents are prepared by experts and not for lay people, who are not conversant with policy requirements' (government representative, Kenya, 29 August 2018). One resident noted:

> That is why it is important that once the government puts a policy in place, they should go a step further to provide a simplified version of

that policy for the purpose of educating the populace ... in a language understood by people.

(residents' representative, Kenya, 22 February 2018)

Alternative-substitute place-making rests on the ability and capacity of individuals to organize, develop and create services to address everyday needs. This is an autonomous co-creation process where individuals become end-user innovators (von Hippel, 2005). There are many types of transformation across Africa. For example:

[An informal settlement from Mitchell's plan] was formalized, it was an informal settlement and then they organised and eventually it was formalised. ... The community was very mobilized, very organized, very orderly with its own street committee's and hierarchies around control in informal settlements. When it was formalized, they lost that, and it was each to their own.

(planner, South Africa, 8 February 2018)

Recognizing alternative-substitute place-making requires alterations in planning legislation, planning credos and training. If combined with formal planning, it would enable the development of more immediate local solutions while formally, and legally, empowering residents to engage in such activities. This should only occur with guidelines ensuring that citizen solutions are eventually incorporated into integrated solutions. This is about accepting non-permanence and hence adaptability as a feature of both planning and place-making responding to the challenge that 'planners don't know how to plan with more flexible standards' (planner, South Africa, 16 March 2018). It is not just about developing visions and strategies but about letting creative ideas emerge. Part of this includes 'asking communities to be organized, getting communities to come to us with a proposal and how we can help them?' (planner, South Africa, 8 February 2018). In addition, it addresses responsibilities and mandates regarding 'who is supposed to do what and where is the money coming from, arguments about if the people in the informal settlements need these services, are they actually paying for them, are they willing to pay for them' (NGI, NGO consultant, Kenya, 26 October 2018).

Advocating for change is part of the essence of planning. This means acknowledging the complexity of the urban system including alternatives and informal structures and networks. This includes appreciating the importance of alternative-substitute place-making and temporary urbanism in reading and understanding African cities. This form of place-making rests upon a more holistic understanding of the valorization of space. 'Value' should not be solely equated with price or monetarization; 'Value' is not just an economic concept but is a social and cultural construct (Tonkiss, 2013). To Slater and Tonkiss (2001, p. 49), economics has much to say about price but nothing to say about value. This is unfortunate; value involves trust, sharing, community and is performative, disparate and conflictual (Boltanski & Esquerre, 2015; Mazzucato, 2018). Place-making individuals and collectives can substitute non-monetized inputs for the absence of investment in local infrastructure. Such interventions are about survival and a process of place-based embeddedness rather than financial investments. Thus:

> I think for any planning to make sense, it has to take into consideration the reality that is existing and, in our case, we have people who will always be only able to afford housing in informal areas. So, when we are talking about planning and doing plans for our city we cannot do that without taking into consideration that there will be people who can only live in those kinds of area. So they have to be part of the planning and you must be able to ensure that we put in place mechanisms to make sure that much as it is informal people are still able to live with dignity.
> (residents' representative, Kenya, 22 February 2019)

Such place-making processes reflect a place-based accumulation of different forms of investments including planning and finance provided by the state combined with the layering onto a place of many different individual and collective alternative-substitute initiatives. Value will differ between individuals depending on their perceptions and use of space potentially leading to tensions between formal and alternative-substitute place-making processes.

Conclusions

This paper explores new approaches to planning regional futures focusing on East and South Africa, but with wider implications for reading and understanding African and Global South cities characterized by complex dynamics between formal and informal processes, both inclusionary and exclusionary. This fits with the call for reassessing planning regional futures. Planning needs to be embedded within a more complex and systemic framework of regional understanding of city-region functions and transformations, at both local and regional levels, whilst also advocating for and incorporating informal and temporary dynamics, here insisting on the importance of adaptability as a central pillar of all planning processes. This methodological and conceptual shift acknowledges that planning often remains an under-resourced activity despite playing an important role in determining urban and regional futures. This explains the importance of developing new ways of thinking to tackle local, regional and national challenges enhancing sustainable local development.

The starting point for this analysis is an appreciation that cities are complex system of systems underpinning social, economic and environmental well-being. It is important to distinguish between planning as a formal process, which tends to ignore and reject informality, and the more informal processes of alternative-substitute place-making, which enable individuals and communities to shape their living environment. African cities are the outcome of a complex interplay between different layers of planned and alternative-substitute place-making. Alternative-substitute place-making emerged out of our review of the ongoing debate on the shadow state, but the present analysis extends this theory by engaging with the literature on temporary urbanism. The emergence of a shadow state is part of a neo-liberalism agenda that does not apply to many cities of the Global South. Cities of the Global South instead are places and spaces of citizen-led micro-scale alternative-substitute placemaking processes. For many urban residents in African cities there is no alternative to alternative-substitute place-making.

Under-resourced cities have left people and places on the margins. These marginalized people and places, within and on the edge of cities, experience different forms of public and private sector failure including planning and the provision of infrastructure-enabled services. An accumulation of incremental individual/household and collective activities in these places on the margins results in ongoing processes of place-making. This type of alternative-substitute place-making is also found in more planned parts of the city. There is an issue of scale here. The key driver behind alternative actions is necessity and the distraction of the immediate needs to survive through place-based localized initiatives. Cities of the Global South need to be conceptualized as a mosaic of different types of formal, informal, individual/ household and highly localized collective place-making. There is a danger that the diversity of alternative-substitute place-making approaches are ignored by retaining a very traditional approach to planning, governance and power dynamics. The greater danger is to ignore the role and the voice local citizens have in shaping everyday living producing better outcomes for people.

The development of a more holistic approach to planning regional futures requires new approaches to planning recognizing the contribution made by alternative-substitute place-making. This PPA has important implications for the training and positionality of planners and for the relationships between formal planning processes and alternative-substitute place-making in current and future policy. Planning training practices, strategies and policy must include an appreciation of alternativesubstitute place-making's contribution to urban transformation and approaches to management and adaptation strategies. Citizen-led place-making should not be marginalized but be facilitated by formal planning processes. The outcome of the accumulation of many processes of citizen-led alternative-substitute place-making is too often considered as an unacceptable form of urbanism. Our argument is that this type of place-making should be considered as a form of permanent impermanence. This is to argue that cities evolve and that alternative interventions should be incorporated into a city through processes of inclusion, enhancing connectivity, service provision and structures.

The impermanent, adaptable, temporary and the alternative then become opportunities for innovative novel forms of inclusive place-making.

Acknowledgements

The authors thank the two rounds of reviewers for their constructive comments, as well as the editors, John Harrison, Daniel Galland and Mark Tewdwr-Jones, for developing the special issue and for their encouragement. This paper was first presented at the 2018 Regional Studies Association (RSA) Winter Conference and the authors are grateful for those who attended their session and provided stimulating questions and comments. The authors also acknowledge and thank their two colleagues, Stuart Denoon-Stevens (University of Bloemfontein, South Africa), National Research Foundation (NRF) principal investigator of the Economic and Social Research Council (ESRC)/NRF SAFER (South African Planning Education Research) project, and Francis Pope, lead of the Department for International Development (DFID) ASAP East Africa (A systems approach to Air Pollution in East Africa) project (University of Birmingham, UK).

Disclosure statement

No potential conflict of interest was reported by the authors.

Funding

The data collected from this paper draw upon two research projects: SAPER (South African Planning Education Research), funded by the Economic and Social Research Council (ESRC) [grant numbers ES/P00198X/1 and EP/P002021/1]; and ASAP-East Africa, funded by the Department for International Development.

ORCID

Lauren Andres ⃝ http://orcid.org/0000-0002-0039-3989
Hakeem Bakare ⃝ http://orcid.org/0000-0002-6174-6223
John R. Bryson ⃝ http://orcid.org/0000-0002-6435-8402
Winnie Khaemba ⃝ http://orcid.org/0000-0003-0326-0943
Lorena Melgaço ⃝ http://orcid.org/0000-0003-1363-8014
George R. Mwaniki ⃝ http://orcid.org/0000-0001-5013-0012

References

Adam, A. G. (2014). Peri-urban land rights in the era of urbanisation in Ethiopia: A property rights approach. *African Review of Economics and Finance, 6*(1), 120–138.

Alemayehu, E. Y. (2008). Revisiting 'slums', revealing responses: Urban upgrading in tenant-dominated inner-city settlements, in Addis Ababa, Ethiopia. *Fakultet for arkitektur og billedkunst*. Retrieved from https://brage.bibsys.no/xmlui//handle/11250/231000

Allen, A. (2003). Environmental planning and management of the peri-urban interface: Perspectives on an emerging field. *Environment and Urbanization, 15*(1), 135–148. doi:10.1630/095624703101286402

Alpa, S. (2010). *In the shadows of the state indigenous politics, environmentalism, and insurgency in Jharkhand, India*. Durham: Duke University Press.

Amin, A., & Thrift, N. (2002). *Cities: Reimaging the urban*. Cambridge: Polity.

Amin, A., & Thrift, N. (2017). *Seeing like a city*. Cambridge: Polity.

Apsan Frediani, A., & Cocina, C. (2019). 'Participation *as* planning': Strategies from the south to challenge the limits of planning. *Built Environment, 45*, 143–161. doi:10.2148/benv.45.2.143

Badcock, B. (2002). *Making sense of cities: A geographical survey*. London: Arnold.

Baffour Awuah, K. G., & Hammond, F. N. (2014). Determinants of low land use planning regulation compliance rate in Ghana. *Habitat International, 41*, 17–23. doi:10.1016/j.habitatint.2013.06.002

Bishop, P., & Williams, L. (2012). *The temporary city*. London: Routledge.

Boltanski, L., & Esquerre, A. (2015). Grappling with the economy of enrichment. *Valuation Studies, 3*(1), 75–83. doi:10.3384/VS.2001-5592.153175

Boschma, R., & Martin, R. (Eds.). (2010). *The handbook of evolutionary economic geography*. Cheltenham: Edward Elgar.

Bryson, J. R., Andres, L., & Mulhall, R. (2018). People, place, space and city-regions: Towards an integrated or systemic approach to reading city-region regeneration economies. In J. R. Bryson, L. Andres, & R. Mulhall (Eds.), *A research agenda for regeneration economies: Reading city-regions* (pp. 162–173). Cheltenham: Edward Elgar.

Bryson, J. R., Mulhall, R. A., Song, M., Loo, B. P. Y., Dawson, R. J., & Rogers, C. (2018). Alternative-substitute business models and the provision of local infrastructure: Alterity as a solution to financialization and public-sector failure. *Geoforum; Journal of Physical, Human, and Regional Geosciences, 95*, 25–34. doi:10.1016/j.geoforum.2018.06.022

de Satgé, R., & Watson, V. (2018). *Urban planning in the Global South: Conflicting rationalities in contested urban space*. Cham: Palgrave Macmillan.

Deverteuil, G. (2016). Resilience in the post-welfare inner city. Bristol: Policy Press.

Friedmann, J. (1973). *Retracking America: A theory of transactive planning*. New York: Anchor.

Friedmann, J. (2002). *The prospect of cities*. Minneapolis: University of Minnesota Press.

Goldman, M. (2011). Speculative urbanism and the making of the next world city. *International Journal of Urban and Regional Research, 35*, 555–581. doi:10.1111/j.1468-2427.2010.01001.x

Goodfellow, T. (2010). *'The bastard child of nobody?': Anti-planning and the institutional crisis in contemporary Kampala* (Working Paper No. 2, 67). London: Crisis States Research Centre, London School of Economics and Political Science (LSE). Retrieved from http://eprints.lse.ac.uk/28474/

Hall, P., & Pfeiffer, U. (2000). *Urban Future 21: A Global agenda for twenty-first century cities*. London: Routledge.

Harrison, P. (2006). On the edge of reason: Planning and urban futures in Africa. *Urban Studies, 43,* 319–335. doi:10.1080/00420980500418368

Harrison, P., Todes, A., & Watson, V. (2007). *Planning and transformation: Learning from the post-apartheid experience.* London: Routledge.

Katz, C. (2004). *Growing up global: Economic restructuring and children's everyday lives.* Minneapolis: University of Minnesota Press.

Latour, B. (1988). The politics of explanation: An alternative. In S. Woolgar (Ed.), *Knowledge and reflexivity* (pp. 155–176). London: Sage.

Lund, F., & Skinner, C. (2004). Integrating the informal economy in urban planning and governance: A case study of the process of policy development in Durban, South Africa. *International Development Planning Review, 26,* 431–456. doi:10.3828/idpr.26.4.5

Madanipour, A. (2017). *Cities in time: Temporary urbanism and the future of the city.* London: Bloomsbury.

Martin, R. (2012). (Re)placing path dependence: A response to the debate. *International Journal of Urban and Regional Research, 36,* 179–192. doi:10.1111/j.1468-2427.2011.01091.x

Mazzucato, M. (2018). *The value of everything.* London: Allen Lane.

Miescher, S. F. (2012). Building the city of the future: Visions and experiences of modernity in Ghana's Akosombo Township. *Journal of African History, 53*(3), 367–390. doi:10.1017/S0021853712000679

Miraftab, F. (2009). Insurgent planning: Situating radical planning in the Global South. *Planning Theory, 8,* 32–50. doi:10.1177/1473095208099297

Miraftab, F. (2016). Insurgency, planning and the prospect of a humane urbanism. Keynote Speech at the World Congress of Planning Schools, 'Global Crisis, Planning and Challenges to Spatial Justice', Rio de Janeiro, Brazil, 3–7 July 2016. Retrieved from https://www.academia.edu/5009516/Displacement_Framing_the_global_relationally

Miraftab, F. (2017). Insurgent practices and decolonization of future (s). In M. Gunder, A. Madanipour, & V. Watson (Eds.), *The Routledge handbook of planning theory* (pp. 276–288). London: Routledge.

Mitchell, K. (2001). Transnationalism, neo-liberalism, and the rise of the shadow state. *Economy and Society, 30,*165–189. doi:10.1080/03085140120042262

Nielsen, K. R., Reisch, L., & Thogersen, J. (2014). *Users, innovation and sustainability. The role of end-users and policy makers in sustainable innovation.* Retrieved from https://www.researchgate.net/publication/303823582_Users_Innovation_and_Sustainability_The_Role_of_End-users_and_Policy_Makers_in_Sustainable_Innovation

Odendaal, N. (2012). Reality check: Planning education in the African urban century. *Cities (London), 29,* 174–182. doi:10.1016/j.cities.2011.10.001

Okalebo, F. (2011). *The evolution of town planning ideas, plans and their implementation in Kampala City 1903–2004.* Retrieved from https://www.diva-portal.org/smash/get/diva2:466031/ FULLTEXT02.pdf

Okpala, D. (2009). *Regional overview of the status of urban planning and planning practice in Anglophone (Sub-Saharan) African countries.* Retrieved from http://www.unhabitat.org/ grhs/2009

Olver, C. (2017). *How to steal a city.* Cape Town: Jonathan Ball.

Oswalt, P., Overmeyer, K., & Misselwitz, P. (2013). *Urban catalyst: The power of temporary use.* Berlin: DOM.

Parnell, S., & Robinson, J. (2012). (Re)theorizing cities from the Global South: Looking beyond neoliberalism. *Urban Geography, 33,* 593–617. doi:10.2747/0272-3638.33.4.593

Richmond, A., Myers, I., & Namuli, H. (2018). Urban informality and vulnerability: A case study in Kampala, Uganda. *Urban Science, 2*(1), 22. doi:10.3390/urbansci2010022

Ross, A. (2018). *Cities are a growth engine of the global economy, but they must become sustainable.* Retrieved from https://www.information-age.com/smart-cities-become-sustainable-123473974/

Roy, A. (2009). Why India cannot plan its cities: Informality, insurgence and the idiom of urbanization. *Planning Theory, 8*(1), 76– 87. doi:10.1177/1473095208099299

Rukwaro, R. W. (2009). The owner occupier democracy and violation of building by-laws. *Habitat International, 33*(4), 485–498. doi:10.1016/j.habitatint.2009.03.004

Salder, J., & Bryson, J. R. (2019). Placing entrepreneurship and firming small town economies: Manufacturing firms, adaptative embeddedness, survival and linked enterprise structures. *Entrepreneurship and Regional Development.* doi:10.1080/08985626.2019.1600238

Sandercock, L. (1998a). Framing insurgent historiographies for planning. In L. Sandercock (Ed.), Making the invisible visible: A multicultural planning history (pp. 1–33). Berkeley: University of California Press.

Sandercock, L. (1998b). *Towards cosmopolis.* New York: Wiley.

Sihlongonyane, M. F. (2015). Empty signifiers of transformation in participatory planning and the marginalization of black people in South Africa. *Planning Practice and Research, 30*(1), 83–100. doi:10.1080/02697459.2015.1008803

Simone, A. (2016). City of potentialities: An introduction. *Theory, Culture and Society, 33,* 5–29. doi:10.1177/0263276416666915

Slater, D., & Tonkiss, F. (2001). *Market society.* Cambridge: Polity.

Taylor, P. J. (2013). *Extraordinary cities.* Cheltenham: Edward Elgar.

Tonkiss, F. (2013). Austerity urbanism and the makeshift city. *City, 17*(3), 312–324. doi:10.1080/13604813.2013.795332

Trudeau, D., & Veronis, L. (2009). Enacting state restructuring: NGOs as translation mechanisms. *Environment and Planning D: Society and Space, 27*(6), 1117–1134. doi:10.1068/d0906

UN-Habitat. (2006). *Situation analysis of informal settlements in Kampala.* Nairobi: UN-Habitat.

UN-Habitat. (2017). *New urban agenda.* Quito: UN-Habitat.

Von Hippel, E. (2005). Democratizing innovation: The evolving phenomenon of user innovation. *Journal fur Betriebswirtschaft, 55*(1), 63–78. doi:10.1007/s1301-004-0002-8

Watson, V. (2003). Conflicting rationalities: Implications for planning theory and ethics. *Planning Theory and Practice, 4,* 395– 407. doi:10.1080/1464935032000146318

Watson, V. (2009). The planned city sweeps the poor away...: Urban planning and 21st century urbanisation. *Progress in Planning, T2,* 151–193. doi:10.1016/j.progress.2009.06.002

Watson, V. (2013). Planning and the 'stubborn realities' of Global South-east cities: Some emerging ideas. *Planning Theory, 12,* 81–100. doi:10.1177/1473095212446301

Watson, V. (2014). African urban fantasies: Dreams or nightmares? *Environment and Urbanization, 26,* 215–231. doi:10.1177/0956247813513705

Watson, V. (2016). Shifting approaches to planning theory: Global North and South. *Urban Planning, 1*(4), 32–41. doi:10.17645/up.vli4.727

Wolch, J. R. (1989). The shadow state: Transformations in the voluntary sector. In J. Wolch, &M. Dear (Eds.), *The power of geography* (pp. 197–221). Boston: Unwin Hyman.

Wolch, J. R. (1990). *The shadow state: Government and voluntary sector in transition.* New York: The Foundation Centre.

Yiftachel, O. (2009). Theoretical notes on 'gray cities': The coming of urban apartheid? *Planning Theory, 8,* 88–100. doi:10.1177/1473095208099300

Getting the territory right: infrastructure-led development and the re-emergence of spatial planning strategies

Seth Schindler◉ and J. Miguel Kanai◉

Introduction

Saudi Crown Prince Mohammed bin Salman announced the development of Neom in the Kingdom's north-west on the Red Sea coast in 2017. Not only is it expected to diversify the national economy but the glossy materials produced by Saudi Arabia's Public Investment Fund also promise that Neom will also become the most exciting place to live and work on the planet.[1] While media reports focused on how the proposed 'megacity' will dwarf New York and London, Neom is actually a territory slightly smaller than Belgium that will incorporate parts of Jordan and Egypt. It will supposedly enjoy semi-autonomous status, a rather liberal governance regime and have world-class infrastructure to attract firms in strategic high-tech sectors. Ambitious projects such as Neom are emblematic of an emergent development paradigm whose aim is to create and integrate dynamic subnational urban systems into transnational territories through networked mega-infrastructure projects. While Saudi Arabia seeks to cultivate high-tech sectors, many of these transnational schemes integrate resource frontiers, agribusiness and production nodes with large-scale connective logistics infrastructure. There is a bewildering number of examples of such initiatives and some of the most illustrative include the Programme for Infrastructure Development in Africa, the Lamu Port–South Sudan–Ethiopia Transport Corridor, the Initiative for the Integration of the Regional Infrastructure of South America, the Abidjan–Lagos Transport Corridor Project, the China–Pakistan Economic Corridor, the New International Land–Sea Trade Corridor between Chongqing and Singapore, the Greater Mekong Subregion, India's five demarcated development corridors, and China's signature Belt and Road Initiative (BRI).

The present paper advances the argument that these initiatives constitute an emergent regime of infrastructure-led development whose ultimate objective is to produce functional transnational territories that can be 'plugged in' to global networks of production and trade. Large-scale infrastructure projects such as railways, highways, dams, ports and regional power grids underpin comprehensive territorial development plans geared toward extracting resources, producing commodities, and moving goods to manufacturing facilities and finally to market. These initiatives include strategies reminiscent of regional planning programmes and practices from the mid-20th century, such as river basin developments, development corridors, new towns and metropolitan master plans. However, in contrast to the post-war period in which many newly independent countries employed 'spatial Keynesianism' in pursuit of the creation of an integrated national space economy that could foster import substitution industrialization, the contemporary regime privileges cross-border connections and integration with global value chains (GVCs). The imperative of this emergent regime, as demonstrated by policy discourse and investment priorities, is to 'get the territory right' in order to attract foreign investment, foster industrial upgrading and export-oriented growth. By mobilizing spatial planning strategies from the post-war era in pursuit of neoliberal objectives, infrastructure-led development offers an increasingly hegemonic rationale for spatial planning and development policy in the Global South.

Infrastructure-led development highlights the durability of globalization and the ongoing expansion of GVCs to emerging and frontier economies (Horner, Schindler, Haberly, & Aoyama, 2018). It was borne out of the 2008 economic crisis that served to discredit earlier aspatial varieties of neoliberalism. In response to the crisis, the World Bank (2009) embraced state-led spatial planning under the leadership of Chief Economist Justin Yifu Lin who advocated a 'global Marshall Plan' (Yifu Lin & Wang, 2013). Meanwhile, China sought to stabilize its economy by funding infrastructure projects, while a decade of low interest rates in the United States encouraged investment in infrastructure worldwide (Tooze, 2018). Infrastructure-led development is currently driven by a 'global growth coalition' that includes multilateral development banks, multinational corporations, multilateral governmental institutions, consultancies and some of the most powerful governments in the world such as China and the United States.

The paper is structured as follows. The next section situates the emergent regime of infrastructure-led development historically. It identifies its origins in the consensus surrounding regional planning in the post-war era, which unravelled with the rise of neoliberalism. It then recounts the imperatives and spatial manifestations of successive rounds of neoliberal reform. The third section shows how the current regime of infrastructure-led development emerged as a result of the 2008 economic crisis and is driven by a global growth coalition whose primary imperative is to 'get the territory right'. Quantitative data is provided that illustrates how spending on large-scale connective infrastructure increased tremendously in the past decade, and three mini-case studies of contemporary infrastructure-led development initiatives are introduced. The fourth section concludes by introducing a series of questions surrounding the emergence of infrastructure-led development regarding its developmental outcomes and impacts.

The rise and fall (and re-emergence) of regional planning

In the decades following the Second World War, the creation of a well-integrated national urban system and balanced space economy was considered a necessary precursor to the structural transformation and modernization of newly independent countries. Planners in many newly independent countries sought to address regional imbalances in national economies that were a legacy of colonialism (Horton & McNulty, 1974, p. 178; Logan, 1972). These efforts included river basin development schemes, new towns, development corridors and comprehensive metropolitan plans, which, when taken together, amounted to 'spatial Keynesianism' (Brenner, 2004, ch. 4). Many of these projects were components of competing American and Soviet development aid and technical assistance programmes, which constituted a second wave of regional planning that was applied to what was then known as the 'Third World' (Berliner, 1958; Lippman, 1959). The Soviet Union's aid programme drew on its domestic experience building industrial new towns in its vast hinterland and its 'hydraulic mission' in Central Asia (Shkvarikov, Haucke, & Smirnova, 1964; Suyarkulova, 2014), while American assistance programmes were modelled on the early 20th-century first wave of regional planning epitomized by the Tennessee Valley Authority (TVA) (Ekbladh, 2002; Sneddon, 2015). The TVA's director celebrated the democratic incorporation of labourers, who he euphemistically referred to as 'dreamers with shovels' (Lilienthal, 1944), while the Soviets celebrated the selfless worker willing to sacrifice for the realization of five-year plans and a Utopian society (Kotkin, 1995). In practice, American and Soviet foreign aid programmes sought to implement similar spatial planning strategies as the superpowers competed for the loyalty of client states (Adas, 2006).

The United Nations Human Settlements Programme's (UN-Habitat) first Urban Agenda passed in 1976 (UN-Habitat, 1976, pp. 3, 7) is illustrative of the consensus surrounding spatial planning that had formed in the postwar era. It states that a national human settlements policy should be 'led by public sector action' and promote 'balanced development for all regions'. In order to ensure balanced regional growth, the UN-Habitat advocated the development of 'a system of intermediate settlements' and 'growth poles for relatively undeveloped regions' (p. 11). The World Bank (1979, p. 33) endorsed 'integrated rural development' plans and argued that 'the advantages of a coordinated effort, focused on a national plan or programme for rural development, are almost self-evident' (p. 33). In a similar vein, it urged governments to steer investment to second-tier cities and achieve balanced regional growth. Leading regional planners Friedmann and Weaver (1979, p. 1) were understandably self-congratulatory when they noted that regional planning had become 'part of the established machinery of government' and that there was 'a growing consensus about theory and doctrine'. Unbeknownst to them the world was on the cusp of political upheaval, and the electoral successes of Margaret Thatcher and Ronald Reagan catapulted proponents of supply-side neoclassical economics from obscure think tanks to positions of power.

The rapid rise of neoliberalism shattered the post-war consensus surrounding regional planning, and the role of the state in newly independent nation-states more generally. The remainder of this section traces the evolution of the objectives, policies and spatial manifestations of successive rounds of neoliberal reform. It applies the framework of adaptive neoliberalism developed by Peck and Tickell (2002), which periodizes neoliberalism's constant iterations into an initial roll-back of post-war institutions followed by a subsequent roll-out of 'neoliberalized state forms, modes of governance, and regulatory relations' (p. 384).

Neoliberal roll-back: 'get the prices right'

Proponents of neoliberal policies were steadfastly opposed to state-led regional planning for ideological reasons, but it was a series of events in the Middle East and the North Atlantic that sent shockwaves through the global economy and forced newly independent countries to abandon spatial planning initiatives abruptly. The successive oil crises in the 1970s forced many developing countries to increase their borrowing levels dramatically (Krueger, 1987a). This was sustainable because of high inflation, which meant that 'the real rate of interest was negative for several years' and there 'were even some years in which developing countries' real debt outstanding declined despite significant borrowing' (Krueger, 1987b, p. 180). This changed when the United States and the UK began pursuing anti-inflationary monetary policy in an effort to combat persistent stagflation, that is, high inflation coupled with unemployment. The US Federal Reserve raised interest rates from 10.5% in April 1979 to a whopping 20% in 1980 (Trading Economics, 2018), and this led to significant capital flight from developing countries as investors chased higher returns in the Organisation for Economic Cooperation and Development (OECD). Many developing countries struggled to service existing debt payments and ongoing infrastructure development projects were abandoned (Krueger, 1987a, 1987b). The first full-blown economic crisis triggered by neoliberal reforms began in 1982 when Mexico defaulted on its sovereign debt, and it was quickly followed by a host of other countries.

International financial institutions responded to the debt crisis with the ostensible objective of achieving macroeconomic stability, and they subsequently imposed 'structural adjustment' as a condition on countries that received emergency financial assistance. Structural adjustment loans (SALs) were established by the World Bank in 1980 and typically imposed a series of roll-back reforms that represented a repudiation of the post-war consensus surrounding spatial planning, such as 'fiscal adjustment, getting the prices right, trade liberalization, and, in general, a movement towards free markets and away from state intervention' (Easterly, 2005, p. 3). In a remarkable about-face from its *World Development Report* (1979), the World Bank – and the Washington Consensus in general – suddenly prioritized 'getting the prices right' over balanced regional development.

The development strategy endorsed by the Washington Consensus was aspatial (Williamson, 1990), but it impacted the spatial distribution of settlements. Agglomeration tendencies were reinforced by policies that relied on market forces to distribute goods and services (Anyinam, 1994; Mattos, 1999; Grant & Nijman, 2004). By isolating regions that policy-makers had previously sought to integrate into national space economies (Mkandawire & Soludo, 1998), the introduction of neoliberal reforms had 'an inherent bias towards the reinforcement of the colonial pattern of intra-national spatial disparities' (Owusu, 1998, p. 19). The rollback of post-war development strategies was accompanied by the devolution of power to more local levels of government (Faguet, 2014), while civil society organizations were empowered vis-à-vis the state (Edwards & Hulme, 1996).

By the late 1980s, state-led development strategies had been so thoroughly rolled back that, according to Leys (1996, p. 24), 'the only development pol-icy that was officially approved was not to have one'. However, it became increasingly apparent that weak local governments were not the best guar-antors of free markets. In an effort to establish the conditions in which 'free' markets could be realized, the Washington Consensus began to roll out a series of market-oriented institutional reforms.

Neoliberal roll-out: 'get the institutions right'

The World Bank's report *Sub-Saharan Africa from Crisis to Sustainable Growth* (1989) began by acknowledging the durability of the prolonged eco-nomic crisis in many African countries. While it insisted that '[t]he countries that have persisted with [structural adjustment] reforms since the mid-1980s are showing the first signs of improvement' (p. 1), it also noted that '[i]t is not sufficient for African governments merely to consolidate the progress made in their adjustment programs' (p. 1). The report asserted that in addition they must foster an 'enabling environment' for private enterprise: 'Africa needs not just less government but better government – government that concentrates its efforts less on direct interventions and more on enabling others to be productive' (p. 5). Thus, the World Bank became a staunch supporter of the 'good governance' agenda (Woods, 2000), whose imperative to 'get the institutions right' (Rodrik, 2007) became a further conditionality of SALs. While the basket of reforms varied from country to country, they typically included measures to reduce corruption, ensure transparency, enhance private property rights and foster an investor-friendly regulatory environment (McCarney, 2000).

The 'good governance' agenda became the lens through which all development issues were understood, including the growing awareness that infrastructure had entered a general state of decline during the neoliberal roll-back period. The World Bank devoted the *World Development Report: Infrastructure for Development* (1994) to infrastructure, whose 'poor performance' was cited as a factor that could inhibit economic growth. The report concluded that 'the performance of infrastructure derives not from general conditions of economic growth and development but from the institutional environment' (p. 6). It stated that 'a consensus is emerging on a larger role for the private sector in infrastructure provision' (p. 7) and in instances where state-led involvement in infrastructure was necessary, the World Bank advocated 'applying commercial principals of operation' (p. 20). Thus, the role of the state was to establish an institutional environment that would encourage private investment in infrastructure, and if this were not possible, the World Bank advocated that states assume the guise of an enterprise. This refrain was repeated two years later in *World Development Report: From Plan to Market* (1996), which targeted formerly planned economies. Again, the World Bank advocated privatizing stateowned enterprises and assets, but commercialization was considered a second-best option that 'involves creating enterprises that, although still public, are similar in structure and operation to private enterprises. Enterprises should be removed from the control of ministries and converted into joint-stock companies reporting to a board of directors' (p. 57). The articulation of the good governance agenda culminated with the *World Development Report 2002: Building Institutions for Markets* (2002), and it maintained the position that the role of the state is to introduce 'competition as much as possible in those infrastructure sectors where it can substitute for regulation' (p. 152).

The good governance agenda resulted in the privatization of public infrastructure across the Global South throughout the 1990s. The World Bank (2002, p. 151) noted that although 'private sector provision of infrastructure rose tremendously during the 1990s in all sectors in all regions', the growth in private investment in infrastructure 'has been smaller than might be possible' due to incomplete regulatory reform. There was scant contingency planning to address the shortfall of private investment in infrastructure because most national institutional reforms lacked a spatial component (Barca, McCann, & Rodríguez-Pose, 2012). Impatient with the slow pace of regulatory reforms and lack of investment at the national scale, policymakers established zones with particular regulatory regimes designed to counter the country-specific barriers that inhibited foreign direct investment (FDI). Indeed, the spatial manifestation of neoliberalism's roll-out period is the proliferation of demarcated territories within which market-supportive institutions were established (e.g., special economic zones (SEZs), free trade zones and export processing zones) (Ong, 2006). One study published by the World Bank notes that 'in 1986, the International Labour Organization's (ILO's) database reported 176 zones in 47 countries; by 2006, it reported 3,500 zones in 130 countries' (Farole, 2011, p. 17). The quantitative proliferation of zones was accompanied by a qualitative shift in which zones progressively incorporated more and more aspects of economy and society (Easterling, 2014; Murray, 2017; Shatkin, 2017).

The establishment of zones largely failed to meet the ambitious economic expectations of planners. A recent global survey of SEZs found that 'on the whole [SEZs] cannot be considered as a growth catalyst in emerging countries', and that typically 'their overall economic dynamism does not exceed that of the countries where they are located' (Frick, Rodríguez-Pose, ScWong, 2018, p. 26). A study on African SEZs notes that they 'are not yet contributing to any significant dynamic benefits to their [national] economies', and they 'may shift permanently and prematurely to a low-growth path' (Farole, 2011, p. 62). Similarly, the vast majority of India's SEZs contribute little to export-oriented industrialization and 'SEZs occupying 10 per cent of the land are responsible for 90 per cent of the total exports' (Jenkins, Kennedy, Mukhopadhyay, & Pradhan, 2015, p. 3). Thus, even relatively modest attempts to get the institutions right within demarcated enclaves largely failed to result in industrial upgrading or export-oriented growth.

In addition to the establishment of zones, other innovative approaches to territorial planning were piloted as part of the good governance reforms. Their focus was on fostering endogenous growth factors and locally embedded forms of institutionalized cooperation, and they were a reaction to the deepening of uneven development engendered by decentralization and the creation of strategically designated export-processing zones (Pike, Rodriguez-Pose, & Tomaney, 2017). These approaches constitute a 'third wave' of regional planning – sometimes referred to as 'new regionalism', global city-regions and the growth-with-equity movement (Scott, 2001). This new regionalism was particularly influential with activist local governments, and progressive academic promoters have theorized its possibilities in both Northern and Southern contexts. They argue it holds potential to improve conditions of rural development as well as metropolitan management (Boisier, 2000). Important contributions to this third wave of regionalism have come from Latin America, a region where neoliberal reforms occurred alongside, and may have been buffered by, a wave of democratization and the deepening of social and economic rights over the past several decades (Chappie, Montero, & Sosa, 2012). However, even within this context of institutional innovation and political empowerment, spatial strategies reminiscent of secondwave regional planning, and predicated on large-scale

Table 1 Infrastructure-led development in historical perspective.

	Imperative	*Strategy*	*Spatial manifestation*
Post-war consensus	Create an integrated and balanced national space economy	Spatial Keynesianism and state-led planning	Enhanced integration of national economic space and balanced regional growth
Neoliberal roll-back	Get the prices right	Market liberalization, privatization, deregulation	Reinforcement of colonial-era spatial patterns
Neoliberal roll-out	Get the institutions right	Good governance reforms, devolution and empowerment of civil society	Proliferation of zones with particular legal regimes
Infrastructure-led development	Get the territory right	Transnational spatial planning and inter-city infrastructure projects	Transnationally networked territories designed to extract resources, move and make commodities

infrastructure investments and connectivity upgrades for logistics, have made a remarkable comeback in the 21st century. As demonstrated by the example of the Initiative for the Integration of the Regional Infrastructure of South America (IIRSA) that is introduced below, infrastructure-led development is largely embraced by national governments, promoted by supranational institutions that remain extremely influential in the region, as well as consultancies, financiers and new global actors such as Chinese state-owned enterprises and new centres of finance.

In conclusion, the neoliberal period witnessed the expansion of global trade, but economic activity that was offshored from the OECD became highly concentrated in a small number of developing countries (Baldwin, 2016). While these countries attracted FDI, many other developing countries experienced deindustrialization (Rodrik, 2016). This led to a backlash against the Washington Consensus (Behuria, 2018; England, 2018; Grugel & Riggirozzi, 2012; Svampa, 2015), and the 2008 economic crisis created a political opportunity for those who favoured a renewed role for the state in planning and governance (Table 1).

Infrastructure-led development goes global

There is a growing global consensus among national governments and supranational institutions surrounding the merits of large-scale networked infrastructure such as roads, bridges, pipelines, regional energy grids, railways, ports, airports and zones dedicated to production and transportation. This section demonstrates that this consensus is animated by a global growth coalition whose hegemony is shaping an emergent regime of infrastructure-led development. Largescale infrastructure projects underpin coordinated spatial planning initiatives reminiscent of strategies from the postwar era, and their primary objective is to 'get the territory right'. Centralized spatial planning is meant to constitute functional territories that can be 'plugged in' to GVCs in order to foster industrial upgrading and export-oriented growth. We conceptualize this regime and show how the 2008 economic crisis created the conditions for development policy to be respatialized. We will identify its primary objectives, planning strategies and the key actors responsible for its hegemony. We then present quantitative data that demonstrate a dramatic surge in spending on large-scale connective infrastructure initiatives in the past decade, and present three mini-case studies of contemporary infrastructure-led development initiatives.

From the 2008 financial crisis to infrastructure-led development

The rediscovery of space and uneven development within neoclassical economics was pioneered by Paul Krugman, whose research explained, among other things, how imperfect competition and increasing returns could result in uneven development rather than lead to a convergence of factor prices (Krugman, 1991, 1993). While Krugman's research confirmed what geographers had long known, his influence on economics doctrine should not be underestimated. By awarding Krugman the Nobel Prize in 2008, the discipline's elite establishment signalled its approval of the spatialization of neoclassical economics.

The spatial turn in neoclassical economics was translated into development policy by Justin Yifu Lin, who was in the unenviable position of becoming the World Bank's Chief Economist just three months before the dramatic collapse of Lehman Brothers and the onset of the 2008 financial crisis. Born in Taiwan and educated in China, Lin was the World Bank's first non-Western Chief Economist. While well trained in neoclassical economics orthodoxy, his understanding of development was informed by China's rapid transformation. He refined a theory of 'new structural economies' whereby proactive governments augment comparative advantage through deliberate investment in hard and soft infrastructure (Yifu Lin, 2012). In this context, Lin argues that it is helpful to think of infrastructure 'as one more component of an economy's [factor] endowments', and purposeful investment in infrastructure reduces transaction costs and 'allow[s] the economy to reach its new production-possibility frontier' (pp. 111–112). The ideas of Krugman and Lin contributed to the *World Development Report 2009: Reshaping Economic Geography* (2009), in which spatial planning was reintroduced in development policy-making. The report began 'by elevating space and place from mere undercurrents in policy to a major focus' (p. 3). It stated that 'spatial disparities in income and production are inevitable' (p. 6), so rather than an instrument designed to deliver balanced regional growth, it embraced spatial planning as a complement to market-oriented institutions. Thus, while the World Bank maintained that 'the bedrock of integration policies should be spatially blind institutions' (p. 23), it advocated spatial planning in some instances: '[A] foundation of institutions must be universal and come first, investments in connective infrastructure should be both timed and located well and come second, and spatially targeted interventions should be used least and last' (p. 25). Spatial planning was thus presented by the World Bank as a last resort, when getting the prices and institutions right failed to have the desired effect.

Policy-makers turned to this last resort in response to the 2008 financial crisis. The US Treasury Department embraced loose monetary and fiscal policy, and offered 14 central banks near-unlimited access to US dollars (Tooze, 2018). The availability of cheap capital and low interest rates fuelled a global rush of investment in infrastructure – particularly in 'emerging markets' – which was bolstered by assessments of financial institutions and intermediaries (e.g., sovereign wealth funds and pension funds) that infrastructure is a sensible investment (Clark, 2017; Torrance, 2007, 2009). Meanwhile, as the world reeled from the financial crisis, China experienced a dramatic decline in demand for its exports. The Chinese government responded swiftly and with conviction, and launched an unprecedented spending programme that 'was the first truly large-scale fiscal response to the crisis worldwide' (Tooze, 2018, p. 243). Much of this stimulus was initially channelled into domestic infrastructure, such as an extensive high-speed rail network, and according to Tooze (2018, p. 251), 'for the first time in the modern era, it was the movement of the Chinese economy that carried the entire world economy'. The Chinese stimulus took on a global dimension in 2013 under the leadership of Xi Jinping with the inauguration of the Belt and Road Initiative (BRI) whose objective is to establish Sino-centric global production and trade networks (see below).

Infrastructure deficits remain in many developing countries despite America's monetary and fiscal policies and China's unprecedented programme to build infrastructure globally. The United Nations (2015, p. 8) estimates that between US$1 and US$1.5 trillion is needed annually to 'bridge the infrastructure gap', and the signatories of the Addis Ababa Action Agenda committed to 'facilitate development of sustainable, accessible and resilient quality infrastructure in developing countries through enhanced financial and technical support' (UN, 2015, p. 8). This provided an impetus to the ongoing activities of international institutions and governments to invest directly in infrastructure. The World Economic Forum (WEF) (2013), Asian Development Bank (ADB) (Bhattacharyay, Kawai, & Nag, 2012; Mitra et al., 2016), the African Union (AU) (2015) and the African Development Bank (AfDB) (2019) have prioritized large-scale infrastructure investment that promises to enhance connectivity and economic integration. Furthermore, a host of institutions situated at various scales seek to encourage private-sector investment through the implementation of regulatory mechanisms designed to generate revenue streams from privately owned infrastructure (O'Neill, 2013). The Institute for International Finance (IIF) established an Infrastructure Working Group that 'represents an important step towards bringing together key stakeholders, with the goal of finding and promoting practical solutions to financing the infrastructure gap'.[2] The G20 established the Global Infrastructure Hub (GIH) in 2014 to coordinate infrastructure initiatives and facilitate private investment. It operates a database of existing infrastructure projects in eight stages from 'initial government announcement' to 'operations phase/construction phase',[3] which serves to match potential investors with opportunities. The G20 subsequently established the Global Infrastructure Connectivity Alliance in 2016, which is headquartered at the World Bank Hub for Infrastructure and Urban Development, and whose mission is to 'work across regions and disciplines to promote cooperation, knowledge exchange, and meaningful progress in the field of global interconnectivity'.[4] The Asian Infrastructure Investment Bank (AIIB) (2018, p. 1) – a global multilateral development bank essentially under Chinese leadership – announced that one of its long-term aims is to 'develop emerging market infrastructure as an asset class'. Finally, key stakeholders in the private sector complement the efforts of international institutions and powerful nation-states (Dodson, 2017; Torrance, 2009). Most illustrative is the global consultancy McKinsey & Co., which established the Global Infrastructure Initiative (GII) in 2012 to identify 'ways to improve the delivery of new infrastructure and to get more out of existing assets' (McKinsey, 2016, p. 3).

The international institutions, multilateral development banks, powerful nations-states and key stakeholders in the private sector that are financing and financializing infrastructure constitute a global growth coalition. Policymakers at the forefront of this emergent dirigisme reject unbridled markets characteristic of the neoliberal era whilst remaining committed to its objectives, namely the pursuit of industrial upgrading and export-oriented growth through ever-enhanced global economic integration. Spatial planning – and infrastructure development in particular – is identified as the missing ingredient in earlier rounds of neoliberal reform. The World Bank Group's (n.d.) consultancy service portrays spatial planning as an antidote that can correct market and governance failures:

> In recent years, a number of countries have experimented with various strategies to correct market and governance failures within and across industries. One approach is to work with spatial strategies such as growth poles, growth corridors, and special economic zones (SEZs).

Spatial planning is thus represented as a turnkey component of contemporary development policy, and World Bank consultants offer to 'help countries custom-design spatial growth strategies' by 'identifying the spatial

growth tools available; and selecting the best tool and optimizing implementation of the chosen approaches' (World Bank, n.d.).

The aim of contemporary spatial plans is to 'get the territory right'
through internationally coordinated investments in networked infrastructures, and to produce territories that can be 'plugged in' to competitive
global networks of production and trade. Territorial designs resurrect regional planning strategies from the developmentalist era, such as the creation of development corridors (Athukorala & Narayanan, 2018; Enns, 2018),
growth poles (WEF, 2013) and new towns (Côté-Roy & Moser, 2018; Lynch,
2018). In contrast with the post-war era in which these strategies were deployed to create or enhance national economic space, spatial planning is
increasingly geared toward the production of transnational territories.

Infrastructure-led development is first and foremost an industrial strategy
that integrates production processes across expansive geographies stitched
together with extensive logistics networks (Cowen, 2014; Danyluk, 2018). Indeed, signatories of the Addis Ababa Declaration (UN, 2015, p. 9) affirm
a commitment to advancing 'the linkages between infrastructure development, inclusive and sustainable industrialization and innovation'. Similarly,
the AfDB (2018, p. 64) asserts that 'African countries can jump directly into
the global economy by building well-targeted infrastructure to support competitive industries'. These initiatives integrate extended rural landscapes
(Zoomers, van Noorloos, Otsuki, Steel, & van Westen, 2017) with a network
of urban nodes geared toward specific value-addition activity. Ultimately
the infrastructure-led development regime is giving rise to functional territories that constitute a globally oriented geography of resource extraction,
production, urbanization and integrated logistic networks.

Despite consensus surrounding the practice of infrastructure-led development, infrastructure construction and spatial planning is increasingly a
field of great power rivalry. The primary protagonists are China and the
United States, and they are engaged in a race to connect isolated places
through the expansion of infrastructure networks. Although the United
States and China are in competition to integrate far-flung territories into
their respective spheres of influence, they are largely in agreement on the
practice of infrastructure-led development. China's involvement in the
global infrastructure sector is well known, and the BRI is explored below.
In contrast, the United States had forsaken the global infrastructure sector until recently. A bipartisan initiative signed into law by US President
Donald Trump in October 2018 established the International Development
Finance Corporation (IDFC), whose mandate is to provide affordable loans
for infrastructure projects to lowincome countries that are American allies.
The IDFC's objective is to 'provide countries a robust alternative to state-
directed investments by authoritarian governments and [the] United States [']
strategic competitors' (US Congress, 2018). This thinly veiled reference
to China was echoed in a more explicit fashion by the US Department of

Defense (DoD) (2018, p. 2), which argues that the BRI is 'indicative of [China's] intention to use economic means to advance its interests and enhance its global role by integrating hard infrastructure development with trade and financial architecture'.

In summary, superpower rivalry is enhancing connectivity and shaping how places are connected to the global economy.

A decade of enhanced connectivity

The implementation of infrastructure-led development presupposes continuous flows of investment capital to support the construction of connective infrastructure projects in emerging and frontier economies. Data from the World Bank's Public Participation in Infrastructure Database[5] demonstrates that there was a decisive shift from a focus on the privatization of city-based infrastructure in the 1990s to the current emphasis on the construction of inter-city infrastructure. Over the past decade, infrastructure projects have been concentrated in connectivity-oriented sectors in the Global South. In low-income and 'low middle income' countries, the largest sector of investment was electricity. Approximately 80% of initiatives were greenfield projects, about 40% of which were in excess of US$1 billion. The case of Sub-Saharan Africa is illustrative. Privatization of the existing infrastructure accounted for approximately 40% of projects in low and low-middle income countries in Sub-Saharan Africa in the 1900s, and information and communication technology (ICT)-related projects were the most numerous. In the past decade privatization represented a fraction of total investment in the same countries, and the two leading sectors in terms of investment and number of projects were electricity and ports. The cost of individual projects, on average, has also increased significantly.

Such investments are part of the global proliferation of infrastructure space (Easterling, 2014) and while they are reconfiguring geographies of inter-city and transnational connectivity, many initiatives fail to get off the ground, are perpetually unfinished or have unintended consequences. This paper began with the example of Neom, which was thrown into jeopardy as a result of the statesponsored murder of journalist Jamal Khashoggi. In contrast, many projects never materialize for mundane reasons. Indeed, large-scale infrastructure projects have historically faced challenges because many firms deliberately underestimate costs and risk in order to secure contracts (Flyvbjerg, 2007). Furthermore, according to Swiss Re and the Institute of International Finance (2014), there are several particular challenges in developing countries including underdeveloped capital and bond markets, a lack of domestic institutional investors and outdated legal and regulatory frameworks. Existing risks are amplified when infrastructure is transnational, but they are offset by the potential for transnational infrastructure to generate lucrative returns. The Global Infrastructure

Hub highlights the advantages of investing in cross-border infrastructure projects:

> including access to a bigger market and potentially reduced demand risk. Multiple studies have shown that there are many opportunities to be gained in upgrading cross-border infrastructure, including benefits for trade and economic growth, which will trigger further demand for better connectivity, and hence, more opportunities for investment.[6]

Finally, according to a recent AIIB (2019) report, some infrastructure investments are only viable if they are transnational in scope. '[M]any connectivity infrastructure projects would only make economic sense if linked up as a network to other countries and regions' (p. I). Thus, transnational infrastructure projects involve heightened risks that inhibit investment, while they continue to be embraced by policy-makers and planners given their potential returns. Multilateral institutions such as the AIIB are increasingly preoccupied by the challenges of coordinating transnational infrastructure networks and securing privatesector investment. Nevertheless, the grandiose visions and rhetoric surrounding large-scale projects tend to outpace their actual construction and connectivity. In these instances the conceptualization of seamlessly integrated regions is often not realized in practice, and instead there is a patchwork of selective connectivity (Kanai & Schindler, 2019; Liu, 2018; Macrorie & Marvin, 2019). The remainder of this section presents three mini-case studies that are illustrative examples of infrastructure-led development that demonstrate its global scope.

Belt and Road Initiative (BRI)

China's BRI is by far the most ambitious and geographically expansive example of infrastructure-led development. Its immediate objective is to cultivate Sino-centric global production and trade networks through the development of inter-city and logistics infrastructure. It was inaugurated by Xi Jinping in 2013 and its initial geographical scope on a Eurasian 'belt' and maritime 'road' in the Indian Ocean has been expanded significantly and it now incorporates European and Latin American countries.[7] This has required China to increase its state-directed outward investment (Collier, 2018), which eclipsed inward FBI in 2015 (England, 2018). Many multilateral development banks and other institutional lenders have committed to supporting the BRI by undertaking or financing large-scale infrastructure projects (Dunford & Liu, 2019). The result of China's outward pivot and its inexorable influence on global capital has led to a bewildering array of spatial planning schemes that integrate development corridors, SEZs and an extensive network of ports (Melecky, Roberts, & Sharma, 2019; Song, Liu, Liu, & Wuzhati, 2018; Wei, Sheng, & Lee, 2018).

In many ways the BRI represents continuity with regard to the central government's reversal of market-oriented reforms from the 1980s in favour of the state-led urbanbased strategic sectors of the economy (e.g., construction and steel) (Huang, 2008). Its international focus is novel, however, and according to Xi Jinping the BRI represents an inclusive variant of globalization and addresses global deficits of peace, development and governance (Dunford & Liu, 2019; Liu, Dunford, & Gao, 2018). However, it remains unclear whether the BRI will facilitate a rebalancing of the global economy and accelerate its reorientation toward East Asia. While a host of BRI projects are indeed underway and Chinese state-owned enterprises have proven resilient in uncertain economic times (Kwan Lee, 2018), the transfer of policy, standards and spatial planning models represent significant challenges (Song et al., 2018; Wiig & Silver, 2019). Furthermore, it is also too early to determine the impact of the BRI on partner countries. While poverty rates have decreased and urbanization has accelerated in Eurasian countries incorporated into the BRI (Chen, Sui, Liu, Liu, & Huang, 2019), it is unclear if the BRI was a catalyst for these changes. Certain places and sectors are ultimately likely to benefit from their deepened integration with the Chinese market, while places with competing manufacturing sectors may experience industrial decline (Bastos, 2018).

Initiative for the Integration of the Regional Infrastructure of South America (IIRSA)

Launched in 2000, the IIRSA constitutes an unprecedented effort to link South American infrastructure networks across national borders. Initiated by Brazil's Fernando Henrique Cardoso administration, the scheme received broad support from virtually every country in the region. It initially aimed to coordinate infrastructure investments in the transportation, telecommunications and energy sectors, thereby strengthening continental-scale axes of integration and development. During the first decade, the IIRSA was an effective institutional vehicle for the realization of modest cross-border roadway projects, and the consolidation of bi-oceanic corridors that cut across erstwhile remote Amazonian and peri-Andean regions (Théry, 2005). The scheme evinced a strong emphasis on corporate logistics seeking to reduce intra-regional transportation costs and improve the global competitiveness of South American exports through faster, more reliable and cheaper access to coastal ports servicing global markets. Under the political leadership of Brazil's federal government and influence of related investment institutions, the IIRSA served to export Brazilian capital and corporate construction capacity to nearby countries (Hochstetler, 2014). Despite major opposition in the local communities where infrastructure projects bore a direct impact, the IIRSA survived South America's so-called 'left turn' and was incorporated to the South American Union's Infrastructure and Planning Council. The new discourse on social integration espoused in the 2010s came with few if any revisions to the territorial designs planned in the neoliberal era (Kanai, 2016). While continental integration may be disrupted by Brazil's political crisis and Argentina's impending economic crisis, extensive investment in extractive industries and a diversification of global investment sources give reason to expect further infrastructure projects designed to integrate subnational systems across international boundaries.

Lamu Port-South Sudan-Ethiopia-Transport Corridor

As the tide suggests, this ambitious project links subnational urban systems in Kenya, South Sudan and Ethiopia via rail and road networks. It also includes nodes geared toward oil extraction and a pipeline for its shipment, as well as an airport, a port and three 'resort cities'. Components of the initiative date back to the 1970s and were planned under the post-war consensus, but never realized (Brown, 2015). The project is now more comprehensive and has been repurposed to complement Kenya's national development strategy Kenya Vision 2030. Indeed, the Kenyan government boasts that this 'is the first single Gigantic, Integrated, Transformative and Game-Changer infrastructure Project the Government has initiated and prepared under Vision 2030' (LAPSSET Corridor Development Authority (LCDA), 2015, p. 5). It is also integrated with other spatial development schemes, such as the Equatorial Land Bridge, which links East and West Africa, and the East African Community's Road Network Programme Japan Port Consultants, 2011; LCDA, 2015). Thus, the project is designed to foster an integrated transnational territory oriented around Kenya's dynamic economy by 'enhance[ing] efficient, seamless inter-modalism in the country's transport and logistics operations throughout the country and linkage to neighbouring countries' (LCDA, 2015, p. 2). Kenyan President Uhuru Kenyatta stated that this project 'will strengthen Kenya's regional hub status as the originator of trans-boundary transport projects, SEZs and free trade areas' (p. 1). The overall project is divided into seven components, each of which requires significant private-sector investment, that are at various stages of completion and face unique challenges such as resistance from local communities and civil unrest (Enns, 2019).

Conclusions: impacts and consequences of infrastructureled development

Infrastructure-led development is geared toward the design and production of comprehensive cross-border territories that integrate resource frontiers and industrial hubs with the global economy via large-scale networked infrastructure. This regime employs spatial planning strategies from the mid-20th century and its proponents hope that by 'getting the territory right' they will achieve the neoliberal objectives of attracting FDI, industrial upgrading and enabling export-oriented growth. To this end, infrastructure-led development integrates resource frontiers, agribusiness and production nodes with logistics networks. This represents a reversal of decades of decentralization, as national and international policy-makers are once again asserting authority over the domain of spatial planning.

We demonstrated how the infrastructure-led development regime was born out of the 2008 economic crisis. A decade of loose monetary policy and low interest rates in the United States, combined with China's unprecedented economic stimulus, allowed for massive investment in ambitious infrastructure projects. This precipitated a shift among investors from a focus on the privatization of city-based infrastructure systems to the construction of transnational inter-city infrastructure. Although China and the United States compete to connectplaces and expand their respective spheres of influence, this paper presented three case studies that demonstrated the global scope of infrastructure-led development. Thus, there is competition to connect specific places, but there is consensus surrounding the merits of connectivity and infrastructure-led development is increasingly hegemonic. Nevertheless, research has shown that the promises of large-scale connective infrastructure projects often remain unfulfilled, and the remainder of this section raises questions surrounding developmental outcomes and impacts of infrastructure-led development that can serve as a starting point for future research.

The most obvious question is whether the transformation of territory will have the *developmental outcomes* that its proponents anticipate. If we assume for a moment that in some instances planners will be able actually to 'get the territory right' and attract investment to historically isolated and poor regions, it does not necessarily follow that these territories will indeed be 'plugged in' to global networks of production and trade in ways that foster exportoriented industrialization and upgrading. According to Baldwin (2016), the fundamental factor underlying the success of developing countries that were able to attract industrial activity that was offshored from the OECD in the 1990s and 2000s was their combination of high-tech production methods with low-cost labour. Furthermore, in some cases – particularly Poland, South Korea and Mexico – industrialization was partly determined by access to large markets. Infrastructure-led development will not alter these dynamics, so the real question is whether the enhanced connectivity of hitherto rather isolated places will offset their comparative and locational disadvantages.

We speculate that the centralization of planning has the potential to influence outcomes at the regional or national scales. Indeed, national-scale spatial planning may serve to protect biodiversity hotspots and ensure that the most productive agricultural land remains under cultivation (Schindler, Mitlin, & Marvin, 2018). However, we consider it likely that this centralized regime of top-down spatial planning will be unable to coordinate events and actors at scalar and spatial distance. Indeed, (inter-)national planners will most likely struggle to come to terms with the dense thicket of street-level politics that determine how and by whom urban space is used on an everyday basis in most cities in the Global South (Bayat, 2000). Similarly, even well-meaning civil servants may struggle to manage – and contain – the social and ecological impacts of investment in remote areas. Corporate-run, transnationally oriented regional economies tend to subsume local economic activity and ways of life (Li, 2018; Perrault, 2018), and as shown by collapsed dams in Laos and Brazil in recent years, poor oversight of shoddy infrastructure can have deadly consequences. Thus, ambitious *territorial forms* may be realized, but their *content* may escape the control of (inter-)national planners given their scalar and spatial distance from neighbourhoods and remote areas.

This paper has sought to situate the origins of infrastructure-led development in a longer history of spatial planning, and interpret its emergence as an outcome of the 2008 financial crisis. It concluded by questioning its developmental outcomes and impacts. And although newly constructed rail lines, bridges, ports and airports may indeed link new towns with resource frontiers along extended corridors, it is difficult to anticipate the urban or rural worlds that these territories will incubate beyond this very rudimentary description of infrastructural connectivity. Future research should document the evolution of infrastructure-led development and undertake situated case studies in order to analyse critically its developmental outcomes, unintended consequences and impacts.

Acknowledgements

Seth Schindler has presented parts of this paper at the Regional Studies Annual Conference 2018. Earlier versions of this paper received supportive comments from three anonymous reviewers as well as from Vincent Béal, Max Rousseau, Mark Usher, David Hulme, Niki Banks, Cristina Temenos, Mike Hodson, Tom Gillespie, Mustafa Bayirbağ, Connie Smith and Łukasz Stanek. The usual disclaimers apply.

Disclosure statement

No potential conflict of interest was reported by the authors.

Funding

Seth Schindler acknowledges generous funding from the British Academy's Tackling the UK's International Challenges Programme, 2017 [Megaprojects and the Reshaping of Urban Futures and Regional Studies Association [Early Career Grant, 2015].

Notes

1 See https://www.neom.com/.
2 See https://www.iif.com/content/infrastructure-working-group.
3 See https://pipeline.gihub.org/.
4 See https://www.gica.global/about-us/what-global-infrastructure-connectivity-alliance.

5 See https://ppi.worldbank.org/.
6 See https://www.gihub.org/blog/financing-cross-border-infrastructure-projects-bankability/.
7 See https://eng.yidaiyilu.gov.cn/.

ORCID

Seth Schindler ⓘ http://orcid.org/0000-0003-2233-0628
J. MiguelKanai ⓘ http://orcid.org/0000-0002-4347-5175

References

Adas, M. (2006). *Dominance by design: Technological imperatives and America's civilizing mission.* Cambridge, MA: Harvard University Press.

African Development Bank (AfDB). (2018). *African economic outlook 2018.* Abidjan: AfDB.

African Development Bank (AfDB). (2019). *Cross-border road corridors: The quest to integrate Africa.* Abidjan: Infrastructure and Urban Development Department, AfDB.

African Union (AU). (2015). *Agenda 2063: The Africa we want: First ten-year implementation plan 2014–2023.* Addis Ababa: AU.

Anyinam, C. (1994). Spatial implications of structural adjustment programmes in Ghana. *Tijdschrift voor Economsche en Sociale Geografie, 85*(5), 446–460. doi:10.1111/j.1467–9663.1994.tb00703.x

Asian Infrastructure Investment Bank (AIIB). (2018). *Strategy on mobilizing private capital for infrastructure.* Beijing: AIIB.

Asian Infrastructure Investment Bank (AIIB). (2019). *Bridging borders: Infrastructure to connect Asia and beyond.* Beijing: AIIB.

Athukorala, P.-C., & Narayanan, S. (2018). Economic corridors and regional development: The Malaysian experience. *World Development, 106,* 1–14. doi:10.1016/j.worlddev.2018.01.009

Baldwin, R. (2016). *The great convergence: Information technology and the new globalization.* Cambridge, MA: Belknap/Harvard University Press.

Barca, F., McCann, P., & Rodríguez-Pose, A. (2012). The case for regional development intervention: Place-based versus placeneutral approaches. *Journal of Regional Science, 52*(1), 134–152. doi:10.1111/j.1467–9787.2011.00756.x

Bastos, P. (2018) *Exposure of belt and road economies to China trade shocks* (Policy Research Working Paper No. 8503). Washington, DC: World Bank Group.

Bayat, A. (2000). From 'dangerous classes to 'quiet rebels': Politics of the urban subaltern in the Global South. *International Sociology, 15*(3), 533–557. doi:10.1177/026858000015003005

Behuria, P. (2018). Learning from role models in Rwanda: Incoherent emulation in the construction of a neoliberal developmental state. *New Political Economy, 23*(4), 422–440. doi:10.1080/13563467.2017.1371123

Berliner, J. S. (1958). *Soviet economic aid: The new aid trade policy in underdeveloped countries.* New York: Council on Foreign Relations (CFR).

Bhattacharyay, B. N., Kawai, M., &Nag, R. M. (2012). *Infrastructure for Asian connectivity.* Cheltenham: Asian Development Bank (ADB) and Edward Elgar.

Boisier, S. (2000). El desarrollo territorial a partir de la construction de capital sinergetico. *Revista Brasileira de Estudos Urbanos e Regionais, 2*, 39–53. doi:10.22296/2317-1529.2000n2p39

Brenner, N. (2004). *New state spaces: Urban governance and the rescaling of statehood.* Oxford: Oxford University Press.

Brown, A. (2015). *LAPSSET: The history and politics of an Eastern African megaproject.* Nairobi: Rift Valley Institute.

Chappie, K., Montero, S., & Sosa, O. (2012). Evolving *Regionalismos:* Latin American regions in the twenty-first century. *Regional Development Dialogue, 33*(1), iii–xii.

Chen, M., Sui, Y., Liu, W., Liu, H., & Huang, Y. (2019). Urbanization patterns and poverty reduction: A new perspective to explore the countries along the Belt and Road. *Habitat International, 84*, 1–14. doi:10.1016/j.habitatint.2018.12.001

Clark, G. L. (2017). *The new era of global economic growth and urban infrastructure investment: Financial intermediation, institutions and markets.* Available at SSRN: https://ssrn.com/ abstract=2954616

Collier, A. (2018). *China buys the world: Analyzing China's overseas investments.* Singapore: Palgrave Macmillan.

Côté-Roy, L., & Moser, S. (2018). 'Does Africa not deserve shiny new cities?' The power of seductive rhetoric around new cities in Africa. *Urban Studies, 56*(12), 2391–2407. doi.org/10.1177/0042098018793032

Cowen, D. (2014). *The deadly life of logistics: Mapping violence in global trade.* Minneapolis: University of Minnesota Press.

Danyluk, M. (2018). Capital's logistical fix: Accumulation, globalization, and the survival of capitalism. *Environment and Planning D: Society and Space, 36*(4), 630–647.

Dodson, J. (2017). The global infrastructure turn and urban practice. *Urban Policy and Research, 35*(1), 87–92. doi:10.1080/08111146.2017.1284036

Dunford, M., & Liu, W. (2019). Chinese perspectives on the Belt and Road. *Cambridge Journal of Regions, Economy and Society, 12*(5), 145–167.

Easterling, K. (2014). *Extrastatecraft: The power of infrastructure space.* London: Verso.

Easterly, W. (2005). What did structural adjustment *adjust? Journal of Development Economics, 76*(1), 1–22.

Edwards, M., & Hulme, D. (1996). Too dose for comfort?: The impact of official aid on nongovernmental organizations. *World Development, 24*(6), 961–973. doi:10.1016/0305-750X(96)00019-8

Ekbladh, D. (2002). 'Mr. TVA': Grass-roots development, David Lilienthal, and the rise and fall of the Tennessee Valley Authority as a symbol for U.S. overseas development, 1933–1973. *Diplomatic History, 26*(3), 335–374. doi:10.1111/14677709.00315

England, E. C. (2018). *The third revolution: Xijinping and the new Chinese state.* New York: Oxford University Press.

Enns, C. (2018). Mobilizing research on Africa's development corridors. *Geoforum; Journal of Physical, Human, and Regional Geosciences, 88*, 105–108. doi:10.1016/j.geoforum.2017.11.017

Enns, C. (2019). Infrastructure projects and rural politics in northern Kenya: The use of divergent expertise to negotiate the terms of land deals for transport infrastructure. *Journal of Peasant Studies, 46*(2), 358–376. doi:10.1080/03066150.2017.1377185

Faguet, J.-P. (2014). Decentralization and governance. *World Development, 53*, 2–13. doi:10.1016/j.worlddev.2013.01.002

Farole, T. (2011). *Special economic zones in Africa: Comparing performance and learning from global experience.* Washington, DC: The World Bank.

Flyvbjerg, B. (2007). Policy and planning for large-infrastructure projects: Problems, causes, cures. *Environment and Planning B: Planning and Design, 34,* 578–597. doi:10.1068/b32111

Frick, S., Rodriguez-Pose, A., & Wong, M. D. (2018). Toward economically dynamic special economic zones in emerging countries. *Economic Geography, 95*(1), 30–64. doi:10.1080/00130095.2018.1467732

Friedmann, J., & Weaver, C. (1979). *Territory and function: The evolution of regional planning.* London: Edward Arnold.

Grant, R., &Nijman, J. (2004). The rescaling of uneven development in Ghana and India. *Tijdschrift voor Economische en Sociale Geografie, 95*(5), 467–481. doi:10.1111/j.0040–747X2004.00333.x

Grugel, J., & Riggirozzi, P. (2012). Post-neoliberalism in Latin America: Rebuilding and reclaiming the state after crisis. *Development and Change, 43*(1), 1–21. doi:10.1111/j.1467-7660.2011.01746.x

Hochstetler, K. (2014). The Brazilian national development bank goes international: Innovations and limitations of BNDES' internationalization. *Global Policy, 5*(3), 360–365. doi:10.1111/1758-5899.12131

Horner, R., & hindler, S., Haberly, D., & Aoyama, Y. (2018). Globalisation, uneven development and the North–South 'big switch'. *Cambridge Journal of Regions, Economy and Society, 11* (1), 17–33. doi:10.1093/cjres/rsx026

Horton, F., & McNulty, M. (1974). Lagos-Ibadan Corridor. In S. ElShakhs & R. Obudho (Eds.), *(1974) Urbanization, national development and regional planning in Africa* (ch. 12). New York Praeger.

Huang, Y. (2008). *Capitalism with Chinese characteristics: Entrepreneurship and the state.* Cambridge: Cambridge University Press.

Japan Port Consultants. (2011). *LAPSSET Corridor and New Lamu Port feasibility study and master plan.* Retrieved from http://www.lapsset.go.ke/reports/

Jenkins, R., Kennedy, L., Mukhopadhyay & Pradhan, K.C. (2015). Special economic zones in India: Interrogating the nexus of land, development and urbanization. *Environment and Urbanization Asia, 6*(1), 1–17. doi:10.1177/0975425315585426

Kanai, J. M. (2016). The pervasiveness of neoliberal territorial design: Cross-border infrastructure planning in South America since the introduction of IIRSA. *Geoforum; Journal of Physical, Human, and Regional Geosciences, 69,* 160–170. doi:10.1016/j.geoforum.2015.10.002

Kanai, J. M., & Schindler, S. (2019). Peri-urban processes of connectivity: Linking project-led polycentrism to the infrastructure scramble. *Environment and Planning A: Economy and Space, 51* (2), 302–322. doi:10.1177/0308518X18763370

Kotkin, S. (1995). *Magnetic mountain: Stalinism as a civilization.* Berkeley: University of California Press.

Krueger, A. (1987a). Debt, capital flows, and LDC growth. *American Economic Review, 77*(2), 159–164.

Krueger, A. (1987b). Origins of the developing countries' debt crisis 1970 to 1982. *Journal of Development Economics, 27,* 165–187. doi:10.1016/0304–3878(87)90013-7

Krugman, P. (1991). Increasing returns and economic geography. *Journal of Political Economy, 99*(3), 483–499. doi:10.1086/261763

Krugman, P. (1993). *Geography and trade.* Cambridge, MA: MIT Press.

Kwan Lee, C. (2018). *The spectre of global China: Politics, labour, and foreign investment in Africa*. Chicago: University of Chicago Press.

LAPSSET Corridor Development Authority (LCDA). (2015). *Investment prospectus*. Nairobi: The Presidency and LCDA.

Leys, C. (1996). *The rise and fall of development theory*. Bloomington: Indiana University Press.

Li, T. M. (2018). After the land grab: Infrastructural violence and the 'mafia system' in Indonesia's oil palm plantation zones. *Geoforum; Journal of Physical, Human, and Regional Geosciences, 96*, 328–337. doi:10.1016/j.geoforum.2017.10.012

Lilienthal, D. (1944). *TVA: Democracy on the march*. New York: Penguin.

Lippman, W. (1959). *The communist world and ours*. New York: Hamish Hamilton

Liu, W., Dunford, M., &Gao, B. (2018). A discursive construction of the Belt and Road Initiative: From neo-liberal to inclusive gloalization. *Journal of Geographical Science, 28*(9), 1–17.

Liu, X. (2018). Characterizing broken links on national and local expressways in Chinese city-regions. *Regional Studies, 55*(8), 1137–1148. doi.org/10.1080/00343404.2018.1555371

Logan, M. I. (1972). The spatial system and planning strategies in developing countries. *Geographical Review, 62*(2), 229–244. doi:10.2307/213214

Lynch, C. R. (2018). Representations of Utopian urbanism and the feminist geopolitics of 'new city' development. *Urban Geography*, doi.org/10.1080/02723638.2018.1561110

Macrorie, R., & Marvin, S. (2019). Bifurcated urban integration: The selective disand re-assembly of infrastructures. *Urban Studies, 56*(11), 2207–2224. doi.org/10.1177/0042098018812728

Mattos, C. A. (1999). Santiago de Chile, globalization y Expansion metropolitana: Lo que existia sigue existiendo. *EURE (Santiago), 25*(76), 29–56. doi:10.4067/S0250-71611999007600002

McCarney, P. (2000). Thinking about governance in global and local perspective: Considerations on resonance and dissonance between two discourses. *Urban Forum, 11*(1), 1–30. doi:10.1007/BF03036829

McKinsey. (2016). *Voices on infrastructure: Novel solutions* (Spring Edn.). Global Infrastructure Initiative, McKinsey & Co. Retrieved from https://www.mckinsey.com/industries/capital-projects-and-infrastructure/our-insights/voices-on-infrastructure/voices-on-infrastructure-novel-solutions

Melecky, M., Roberts, M. & Sharma, S. (2019). The wider economic benefits of transport corridors: A policy framework and illustrative application to the China–Pakistan Economic Corridor. *Cambridge Journal of Regions, Economy and Society, 12*(1), 17–44.

Mitra, S., Hasan, R., Sharma, M., Yun Jeong, H., Sharma, M., & Guha, A. (2016). *Scaling new heights: Vizag–Chennai Industrial Corridor India's first coastal corridor*. Manila: Asian Development Bank (ADB).

Mkandawire, T., & Soludo, C. (1998). *Our continent, our future: African perspectives on structural adjustment*. Dakar: Council for the Development of Social Science Research in Africa.

Murray, M. J. (2017). *The urbanism of exception: The dynamics of global city building in the twenty-first century*. Cambridge: Cambridge University Press.

O'Neill, P. M. (2013). The financialisation of infrastructure: The role of categorisation and property relations. *Cambridge Journal of Regions, Economy and Society, 6*(3), 441–454.

Ong, A. (2006). *Neoliberalism as exception: Mutations in citizenship and sovereignty.* Durham: Duke University Press.

Owusu, J. H. (1998). Adjustment, industrial locational incentives and structural transformation in Ghana. *East African Geographical Review, 20*(2), 1–24. doi:10. 1080/00707961.1998.9756264

Peck, J., & Tickell, A. (2002). Neoliberalizing space. *Antifode, 34*(3), 380–404. doi:10.1111/1467-8330.00247

Perrault, T. (2018). The plantation and the mine: Comment on 'After the land grab: Infrastructural violence and the "mafia system" in Indonesia's oil palm plantation zone' by Tania Li. *Geoforum; Journal of Physical, Human, and Regional Geosciences, 96*, 354–347.

Pike, A., Rodríguez-Pose, A., & Tomaney, J. (2017). Shifting horizons in local and regional development. *Regional Studies, 51*(1), 46–57. doi:10.1080/00343404.2016. 1158802

Rodrik, D. (2007). *One economics, many recipes: Globalization, institutions and economic growth.* Princeton: Princeton University Press.

Rodrik, D. (2016). Premature *demdustnaiization. Journal of Economic Growth, 21*(1), 1–33. doi:10.1007/s10887-015-9122-3

Schindler, S., Mitlin, D., & Marvin, S. (2018). National urban policy making and its potential for sustainable urbanism. *Current Opinion in Environmental Sustainability, 34*, 48–53. doi:10.1016/j.cosust.2018.11.006

Scott, A. (Ed.). (2001). *Global city-regions: Trends, theory, policy.* London: Oxford University Press.

Shatkin, G. (2017). *Cities for profit: The real estate turn in Asia's urban politics.* Ithaca: Cornell University Press.

Shkvarikov, V., Haucke, M., & Smirnova, O. (1964). The building of new towns in the USSR. *Ekistics; Reviews on the Problems and Science of Human Settlements, 18(108)*, 307–319.

Sneddon, C. (2015). *Concrete revolution: Large dams, Cold War geopolitics, and the US Bureau of Reclamation.* Chicago: Chicago University Press.

Song, T., Liu, W., Liu, Z., & Wuzhati, Y. (2018). Chinese overseas industrial parks in Southeast Asia: An examination of policy mobility from the perspective of embeddedness. *Journal of Geographical Science, 28*(9), 1288–1306. doi:10.1007/ s11442-018-1526-5

Suyarkulova, M. (2014). Between national idea and international conflict: The Roghun HHP as an anti-colonial endeavour, body of the nation, and national wealth. *Water History, 6*, 367–383. doi:10.1007/s12685-014-0113-7

Svampa, M. S. (2015). Commodities consensus: Neoextractivism and enclosure of the commons in Latin America. *South Atlantic Quarterly, 114*(1), 65–82. doi:10.1215/00382876-2831290

Swiss Re and Institute of International Finance. (2014). *Infrastructure investing: It matters.* Zurich: Swiss Re.

Théry, H. (2005). Situações da Amazônia no Brasil e no continente. *Estudos Avançados, 19*(53), 37–49. doi:10.1590/S0103-40142005000100003

Tooze, A. (2018). *How a decade of financial crises changed the world.* New York: Allen Lane.

Torrance, M. I. (2007). The power of governance in financial relationships: Governing tensions in exotic infrastructure territory. *Growth and Change, 38*(4), 671–695.

Torrance, M. (2009). The rise of a global infrastructure market through relational investing. *Economic Geography, 5*(1), 75–97. doi:10.1111/j.1944-8287.2008.01004.x

Trading Economics. (2018). *United States Fed funds rate, 1971–2018*. Retrieved August 5, 2018, from https://tradingeconomics.com/ united-states/interest-rate

United Nations. (2015). *Addis Ababa action agenda of the Third International Conference on Financing for Development*. New York: United Nations.

United Nations Human Settlements Programme (UN-Habitat). (1976). *The Vancouver Declaration on Human Settlements*. New York: United Nations.

US Congress. (2018). *FAA Reauthorization Act of 2018*.

US Department of Defense (DoD). *(2018). Assessment on US Defense implications of China's expanding global access*. Washington, DC: US DoD.

Wei, H., Sheng, Z., & Lee, P. T.-W. (2018). The role of dry port in hub-and-spoke networks under Belt and Road Initiative. *Maritime Policy and Management, 45*(3), 370–387. doi:10.1080/03088839.2017.1396505

Wiig, A., & Silver, J. (2019). Turbulent presents, precarious futures: Urbanization and the deployment of global infrastructure. *Regional Studies, 53*(6), 912–923. doi.org/10.1080/00343404.2019.1566703

Williamson, J. (1990). *Latin American adjustment: How much has happened?* Washington, DC: Institute for International Economics (IIE).

Woods, N. (2000). The challenge of good governance for the IMF and the World Bank themselves. *World Development, 28*(5), 823–841. doi:10.1016/S0305-750X(99)00156-4

World Bank. (1979). *World development report*. Washington, DC: World Bank.

World Bank. (1989). *Sub-Saharan Africa from crisis to sustainable growth: A long-term perspective study*. Washington, DC: World Bank.

World Bank. (1994). *World development report: Infrastructure for development*. Washington, DC: World Bank.

World Bank. (1996). *World development report: From plan to market*. Washington, DC: World Bank.

World Bank. (2002). *World development report 2002: Building institutions for markets*. Washington, DC: World Bank.

World Bank. (2009). *World development report 2009: Reshaping economic geography*. Washington, DC: World Bank.

World Bank. (n.d.). *Spatial growth strategies: Realizing the benefits of geographically-targeted approaches*. Retrieved from http://www.worldbank.org/content/danVWorldbank/document/Trade/ CompSector_SpatialGrowth.pdf

World Economic Forum (WEF). (2013). *The African competitiveness report 2013*. Geneva: WEF.

Yifu Lin, J. (2012). *The quest for prosperity: How developing economies can take off*. Princeton: Princeton University Press.

Yifu Lin, J., & Wang, Y. (2013). *Beyond the Marshall Plan: A global structural transformation fund* (Background Research Paper submitted to the High Level Panel on the Post-2015 Development Agenda) Retrieved from https://www. post2015hlp.org/ wp-content/uploads/docs/Lin-Wang_Beyond-the-Marshall-Plan-A-Global-Structural-Transformation-Fund.pdf.

Zoomers, A., van Noorloos, F., Otsuki, K., Steel, G., Sevan Westen, G. (2017). The rush for land in an urbanizing world: From land grabbing toward developing safe, resilient, and sustainable cities and landscapes. *World Development, 92*, 242–252. doi:10.1016/ j.worlddev.2016.11.016

City-regional imaginaries and politics of rescaling

Simin Davoudi⦿ and Elizabeth Brooks⦿

Introduction

> There is no such thing as a single, uniquely defined 'region' that mani-fests a full spectrum of city-regional relationships.
>
> (Duncan, 1960, p. 402)

The above statement speaks to the relational understanding of scale and space. It is an early recognition of the coexistence of multiple views of 'regions' and 'city-regions' as: functional spaces of economic flows, bi-ophysical spaces of ecological relations, cultural spaces of shared mem-ories, social spaces of experiences and encounters, or political spaces of struggle for justice and citizens' rights – all of which compete for the position of dominance in the politics of rescaling of governance and plan-ning. Building on early insights such as this, theorization of scale, as one of the core geographical concepts, has gained momentum since the 1980s and led to a binary division between materialist and idealist schools of thought. Accounts of the politics of rescaling have followed a related di-vide between a structuralist focus on political economic factors and the role of the state, and a poststructuralist emphasis on cultural factors and the role of discourse.

The aim of this paper is to forge productive linkages between these mod-ernist binaries by deploying the concept of imaginary. While as a term im-aginary is sometimes mentioned in the literature on scale (Harvey et al, 2011; Jones & MacLeod, 2004; Paasi, 2004), as a concept, it is rarely en-gaged with.

The paper is structured as follows. The next two sections bring together two, otherwise separate, bodies of literature on scale and imaginary to offer a first step towards conceptualizing scale not just as an entity (a materialist approach), nor just as an episteme (an idealist approach), but as an imagi-nary. We argue that such a perspective provides a better understanding of how scales are called into being through the entangling of both discursive and material practices, and how the tensions between the ontological fluidity of relational scale and the rigidifying tendencies of socio-spatial practices are played out. We argue that, in the politics of rescaling, imaginaries are performed to fix that which is fluid and unsettle that which is long conceived of as fixed.

The fourth section uses 40 years of experimentations with scalar fixing in England as an illustrative example to explore how the invocation of a distinct imaginary of the city-region as an *economic-* and *city-centric* (ECC) space has been integral to the rescaling experiments, and how the normalization and sedimentation of this imaginary has been bound up with the politics of scalar fixing. We argue that the co-alignment of the enacted scale, the scalar imaginary and the political projects that they serve is a necessary, but not sufficient condition for successful institutionalization of a particular scale. We call these the *what,* the *how* and the *why* questions of scalar fixing and use them to organize the subsections in this part of the paper. In discussing the *how,* we focus particularly on the role of two distinct forms of knowledge in driving the ECC city-regional rescaling project: economic geography and its rationalization of the vertical ordering of *scale,* and cartographical mapping and its demarcation of the horizontal ordering of *space.* The aim is to show how their mutually reinforcing effects have sedimented the ECC city-regional imaginary. Our analysis of the interactions between *scalar* (vertical) and *spatial* (horizontal) ordering is also a response to Brenner's (2001) call for a *plural* understanding of the politics of scaling, in which production of scale and space become inescapably entwined.

The fifth section argues that despite the alignment between the what, the how and the why, institutionalization of the ECC city-regional imaginary has led to variable geometries of subnational governance in England because of multiple sources of resistance which are discussed in the concluding part of the paper.

Scale and politics of scalar fixing

The last 40 years have seen numerous scholarly attempts to develop deeper understandings of socio-spatial relations by focusing particularly on four key geographical concepts: territory, place, scale and network (Jessop et al., 2008). Conceptualizing scale, in particular, has attracted a growing debate that began with the traditional views of scale as a neutral, Euclidian, Cartesian and territorially bounded container, before advancing into deeper theoretical engagements in the 1980s. Lefebvre's insight about space being a social product became the touchstone for conceptualization of 'the scale question' (Lefebvre, [1976] 1991) and the development of social constructivist approaches to scale. Although it is now widely agreed that scale is socially produced and historically contingent, disagreements over the ontological status of scale continue to generate lively debate between two schools of thought (MacKinnon, 2011). One, rooted in Karl Marx's materialist philosophy, adopts a structuralist, political economic approach to scale. The other, rooted in Immanuel Kant's idealist philosophy, embraces post-structuralist perspectives. For the former, scale is a material social entity; it is the 'materialization of contested social forces' (Smith, 1993, p. 101). For the latter, scale does not exist; it is a 'fundamentally epistemological construct that presents specific sociospatial ordering' (Moore, 2008, p. 204).

The Marxist-oriented, political economic understanding of scale is founded on three central tenets (Marston, 2000): first, scalar differentiations are socially produced; second, how scale is constructed has material impacts; and third, the production of scale is a political process infused with tensions and contradictions with uncertain and potentially transformative outcomes. Much of the theoretical and empirical work on scale within this tradition focuses on the interactions between capital, state, and nonstate political actors, especially in the context of globalization. Attention is focused on, in Smith's (1993) coinage, 'the politics of scale' and political struggles over the production of 'scalar fixes'.

The concept of the scalar fix builds on Harvey's (2000, p. 54) provocation that, 'capitalism cannot do without its spatial fixes'. Using the term to bring space into the understanding of capital over-accumulation and its endemic crises, he suggests that such crisis tendencies are temporarily arrested not only by pinning down surplus value in particular locations through physical developments (literally fixing), but also through reconfiguring space to allow expanded production and consumption and rescaling governance structures (metaphorical fixing). Harvey's thesis, as is further developed by regulation theorists and particularly in Brenner's (2001) 'scalar structuration theory', suggests that the rescaling of governance powers and responsibilities offers a contingent 'spatio-temporal fix' to capitalism's inherent crises (Jessop et al., 2008; Swyngedouw, 2004). The widely agreed and applied structuralist accounts of scale have been subject to critiques from within political economic traditions as well as from post-structural perspectives. From within, scholars have criticized the overemphasis on economic factors and the state's role in capitalist circulation, and called for *cultural* approaches (Smith, 1993; Sum & Jessop, 2013) and more explicit accounts of extra-economic factors in the construction of scale – such as, cultures, meanings, and institutional processes; as well as the relations of social reproduction at the scales of home and body (Marston, 2000).

The post-structuralist critiques have centred on ontological debates, arguing that although political economic views consider scales as fluid and contingent, they still conceptualize them as 'real' entities. Instead, they argue that, 'there is no necessary correspondence between material conditions and scale representations', even though 'scalar representations can... have material effects' (Moore, 2008, pp. 204–205). For post-structuralists, scale is: a 'representational trope' (Jones, 1998, p. 27), a narrative (Gonzalez, 2006), a performative discourse (Kaiser & Nikiforova, 2008) or an assemblage (Allen et al., 1998). Some have even called for a 'flat ontology' and the abandoning of the term scale altogether (Marston et al., 2005).

Rather than abandoning a term that is useful for the links it maintains with entrenched imaginaries of scales in practice, we suggest a new way of conceptualizing scale as a performative imaginary. This, we argue, helps to forge connections between materialist and idealist approaches which have long created unhelpful dividing lines between the structuralist and the post-structuralist understandings of scale, despite some commendable bridge-making attempts (MacKinnon, 2011). While the cultural turn has provided rich insights into the role of discourse in the making and fixing of scales, less attention has been paid to the role of imaginaries which are constitutive of, and in part constituted by, both material and discursive practices, as discussed below. What follows aims to fill this gap by providing a conceptual understanding of spatial imaginaries.

Spatial imaginaries

> The image, the imagined, the imaginary – these are all terms that direct us to something critical and new...: the imagination as a social practice. ... The imagination is now central to all forms of agency, is itself a social fact.
>
> (Appadurai, 1996, p. 31)

The concept of imaginary has a long intellectual history going back to the works of nineteenth century philosophers and sociologists such as Hegel's notion of 'spirit of a people' and Durkheim's notion of 'collective consciousness'. The use of the term itself can be traced to Mills (1959) and Castoriadis (1975). Combining Marxist and psychoanalytic theories, Castoriadis (1975 [1987], p. 101) considered 'the category of imaginary' as 'a unifying factor that provides a signified content and weaves it with the symbolic structure'. More recent adaptations of the concept by, for example, Marcus (1995), Ezrahi (2012) and Jasanoff and Sang-Hyun (2015) draw primarily on Anderson's (1991) and Taylor's (2004) works. Anderson (1991, p. 4) argues that what binds together a heterogeneous and spatially dispersed political community, such as a nation, is their shared social imaginaries which are represented in and performed by various mediums such as census data, maps, and territorics. His notion of 'imagined communities' resonates with Agnew's (1997) work on politics of scale that shows how Italy as a 'national space' was articulated differently by different political parties to create geographically differentiated political identities.

The introduction of the concept of imaginary into geographical and planning scholarship has been largely inspired by Said's *Orientalism* (1978). He revealed how the spatial imaginary of 'the Orient' was constructed and circulated through myriads of ideas and artefacts in order to pursue colonial ambitions and practices. Adopting a Foucauldian perspective, he highlights how spatial imaginaries legitimize certain political goals through a nexus of power, knowledge and geography; a nexus which, as we argue below, has driven the production and sedimentation of the ECC city-regional imaginary. Contrary to the mental mapping tradition of behavioural and environmental geographers, Said's imaginative geographies 'are profoundly ideological landscapes whose representations of space are entangled with relations of power' (Gregory, 1995, p. 474). However, his early insight into the performativity of spatial imaginaries has attracted limited scholarly attention. As Watkins's (2015, p. 508) review of the literature shows – with some exceptions (e.g., Bialasiewicz et al, 2007) – 'geographers have explained spatial imaginaries as representational discourses about places and spaces'. These portray imaginary as a 'static linguistic representation', rather than a performative act through which socio-spatial relations are reproduced and contested, and political projects are consolidated. Performativity foregrounds relations of power in which contestation and resistance are ever present. It highlights that the embedding of scalar imaginaries involves strategic struggles for coalition building and for mobilization and legitimization of ideological goals (Kaiser & Nikiforova, 2008; Jessop, 2010). It urges us to attend to questions such as: why, what and how certain scalar imaginaries are called into being, and what makes some stick and become institutionalized and others fade away or get side-lined. We understand performativity as 'the reiterative and citational practice' (Butler, 1993, p. 2) by which individual imaginations become deeply held and collective imaginaries.

Seen in terms of a performative imaginary, rescaling implies a process whereby ideal and material, discourse and interest, and real and illusive fold into each other to reinforce their effects and structure our understanding of what is or is becoming 'solidly material' (Butler, 1993, p. 188) and 'what qualifies as "being"' (Watkins, 2015, p. 517). Scalar imaginaries animate and are implicated in the dialectical tensions between relationality and territoriality (Paasi, 2010), and between scales' ontological fluidity and socio-political ambitions to rigidify them into bounded territories (Riding & Jones, 2017). Indeed, the remarkable staging power of imaginaries lies in their blurring of perceived facts and fictions and of precision and fuzziness in the political processes of scalar fixing. Through the fusion of material and discursive practices, scalar imaginaries are performed, given meanings and become taken for granted, collective understandings of what and where a particular scale is.

The politics of scalar fixing is, therefore, inescapably bound up with the political struggle over normalizing and institutionalizing certain scalar imaginaries. At the risk of over-simplification, we consider the political project as the *why* of fixing (what political goals are pursued), the scalar fix as the *what* (what scale is enacted as best serving the political goal), and the scalar imaginaries as the *how* (what are the key drivers through which the fixing is pursued, and by *whom*). In line with Eraser's (2010) work on scalecraft and Pemberton and Searle's (2016) work on the link between scalecraft and statecraft, we suggest that successful institutionalization of a particular scale is dependent upon, though not determined by, how closely these three aspects are aligned and reinforce each other. Having said that, the outcome of scalar fixing is complex, dynamic, historically contingent, and influenced by the sociocultural contexts, institutional and analytical traditions, and the interplay between alternative scalar imaginaries, as shown in the following example of city-regionalization attempts in England.

Scalar imaginaries and the fixing of scale: the english experience

In this part, we focus on the evolving rescaling of English subnational governance and argue that since the 1970s the answer to the *why* question has been determined by neoliberal political ideologies. The response to the *what* question has enacted the regional and city-regional scales. And a key driving force for the *how* question has been the production and circulation of two forms of knowledge by two groups of theorists and analysts: one rationalizing city-regional *scale,* the other demarcating city-regional *space.* Together, these have animated and legitimated a distinct imaginary of the city-region as an ECC space.

Regionalization and the neoliberal scalar strategy: the what and the why

In England, regionalization has been a recurring state scalar strategy of successive governments since the early 1970s, as opposed to a bottom-up or popular project (Jones & MacLeod, 2004). Knowing this history is important for understanding the emergence of city-regionalism, because the latter is a continuation of the former (Harrison, 2012), albeit with some differences which we highlight in our discussion of the *how* question.

Throughout the early 1970s, various forms of regional institutions were configured from the top down in pursuit of managerial and administrative efficiency, Keynesian welfare delivery, redistribution of Fordist national economic accumulation, and planning coordination (Brenner, 2003). Their administrative boundaries remained similar to that of the civil defence regions which were created between the two World Wars, and later became known as the 'standard regions' in England. It is argued that the 1970s' centrally imposed local and regional institutions served 'primarily as transmission belts for national economic and social polities' (Jessop, 2002, p. 71). By the 1990s, the shift to post-Fordism triggered a renewed enthusiasm for regionalization. This time, however, the enacting of the region as the scalar fix was because of a radically different political project: that of neoliberalism. Emphasis was put on the promotion of economic competitiveness, endogenous growth, entrepreneurial governance, and 'regions for themselves' (Brenner, 2003). The establishment of eight regional institutions in England as a part of the state's devolution agenda became a marker of the shift towards neoliberal ideology and is vividly reflected in their: name (regional development agencies), governing bodies (business-led boards appointed by central government), and remit ('trailblazers' of economic growth) (Danson & Lloyd, 2012; Jones, 2001). Couched in the depoliticizing, managerial language of 'modernisation', the remit set for the regions – in an official document – was to 'contribute to the prosperity of their own communities and the whole nation' (Department of the Environment, Transport and the Regions (DETR), 1997, p. 3). Interestingly, this document's narrative of 'bringing regions to the fore' (p. 8) speaks directly to the ways certain scalar imaginaries are called into being, both discursively and materially, as part of a political project.

However, the state's imposed regionalization in England was short lived. The rejection of an elected regional government in the North East Region in the 2004 referendum was followed by the dismantling of all regional institutions in 2010. This was justified by the state's expedient use of the critique that 'regions' are 'unnatural blocks' made up of 'arbitrary dividing lines across the country for bureaucratic convenience' (Pickles, 2010, p. 1). The search for a new scalar fix which began after the collapse of the Fordist-Keynesian institutional settlement ended with the death of regionalization, but it also led to the birth of city-regionalization in the 2000s (Harrison, 2012; Pike & Tomaney, 2004). The 'city-region' was invoked in the pursuit of a new neoliberal scalar fix. However, its invocation constituted a highly selective imaginary of city-region, which has been largely driven by the production of knowledge/power, as discussed below.

City-regional imaginary: the how and by whom

> The concept of the city-region, like all concepts, is a mental construct. It is not, as some planners and scholars seem to think, an area which can be presented on a platter to suit their general needs.
>
> (Dickinson, 1964, p. 227)

Although the resurgence of the city-region as a neoliberal scalar fix in England is recent, the city-regional imaginary has a much longer history, at least in spatial planning. An early example is the bird's eye view of Chicago that illustrates the cover of Daniel Burnham's *Plan of Chicago* (Burnham &

Bennet, 1909), showing the city and its surrounding landscape. Another 1915 example, which has remained the touchstone in the debate about the demarcation of city-regional boundaries, is Patrick Geddes' notion of conurbation. The term itself was coined in 1947 by Robert Dickinson whose above statement echoed earlier insights by sociologists suggesting that, 'the boundaries of the modern community ... are blurred, if not indeterminate' (Howley, 1950, p. 248).

These early imaginaries saw city-regions as spaces of multiple, fluid, socio-spatial and environmental interactions, especially those between urban and rural areas.[1] Central to these imaginative geographies was the interrelationship between *the city* and its wider *environs*. However, over the years while the 'cityness' of the imaginary has been intensified, the 'environs' component has been reduced to a narrow set of economic relations, creating a normalized imaginary of the city-region as an ECC space (Davoudi, 2008) that is neatly aligned with the neoliberal obsession with city-led economic growth imperatives. How such a reductive city-regional imaginary has evolved and how its performativity[2] has been associated with the 'historical constitution of knowledge' (Kaiser & Nikiforova, 2008, p. 544) are the questions to which we now turn.

We argue that there are two distinct, yet interrelated, ways through which knowledge production by key actors and institutions – such as academics, consultants, think tanks (e.g., Institute for Public Policy Research (IPPR), 2006) and international organizations (e.g., Organisation for Economic Co-operation and Development (OECD), 2007) – has helped create and legitimize the ECC city-regional imaginary: the rationalization of vertical scalar hierarchies (the vertical ordering of the state's power across scales), and the demarcation of the horizontal bounds of city-regional space (horizontal ordering of socio-spatial relations across space). To use the traditional geographical lexicons, we argue that academic theories, analytical reasoning and cartographical techniques have played a key role in producing, propagating and provisionally fixing both the 'level' (the relation with other scales) of the city-regional imaginary and its 'size' (its areal extent).

While there are counties s studies on the role of both economic theories in the rationalization of scale and statistical analyses and cartographical traditions in the demarcation of space, these two bodies of literature have remained largely separate, with little conceptual or empirical exploration of how the two processes *reinforce* each other to invoke not just the city-region per se as a scalar fix, but also a distinct imaginary of it as an ECC space. By bringing these together and focusing on the interactions between scalar (vertical) and spatial (horizontal) ordering, we aim to advance the debate and attend to Brenner's (2001, p. 616) call for *plural* understanding of the politics of scaling in which discursive and material production of *scale* (aided by political economic rationalization) and *space* (aided by demarcation methodologies) become intertwined.

Vertical ordering of city-regional scale

Charles Taylor's definition of imaginaries as *emergent* suggests that, 'although imaginaries are not theories or doctrines *per se,* they may start by discursive practices of theorists' (Davoudi, 2018, p. 102). As these discursive practices gain traction through deliberation, repetition and circulation, they 'generate more and more far reaching claims on political life' (Taylor, 2004, p. 5). While regional and economic theorists are not the sole progenitors of scalar imaginaries, their theorisations and rationalisations play a significant part in the emergence of them, as is also shown by Kaiser and Nikiforova (2008) in relation to the role of scalar discourses.

Since the 1990s, the search for scalar fixes in England and the invocation of scalar imaginaries (of region and city-region) have been supported and justified by a distinct epistemic rationality known as the 'new regionalism' (Keating, 1997; Levering, 1999). As Jones (2001, p. 1194) suggests, the regionalization project has been indicative of 'the new regionalist *orthodoxy in action',* referring to the proliferation of academic literature in the 1990s that proclaimed the 'hollowing out' of the nation state (Ohmae, 1995) and foregrounded 'the regions' as: the agents of wealth creation (e.g., *Regional Studies,* 2002, 2007), the 'crucible' of economic development in the post-Fordist era, and the 'prime focus' for post-Keynesian governance regulation and planning. Furthermore, economic geographers and scholars of regional development sparked a host of normatively charged claims' (Jones & MacLeod, 2004, p. 435) about what makes some regions prosper and others lag behind.

By theorizing and propagating imaginaries of idealized places, they not only invoked what a city-region is, but also provoked what it ought to be. Idealized imaginaries, as a meeting place between the ideal and the material, exacerbate spatial inequalities and create binary visions of: the world as 'Orient' and 'Occident'; Europe as 'core' and 'periphery'; and England as 'north' and 'south' (Davoudi, 2018). A particularly prescriptive imaginary is that of 'global city-regions' (such as Silicon Valley, Northern Italy and South East England) (Hudson, 2005). Proclaimed as 'basic motors' of global economic growth and 'the leading-edges of the contemporary post-Fordist economy' (Scott, 2001, p. 818), they project a sense of inevitability which goes beyond describing and prescribing to prophesies of how successful city-regions *will be* in the future (Golubchikov, 2010). Like globalization, which disseminates narratives of its own inevitability (Massey, 2007), the global city-regional imaginary has become a 'self-fulfilling prophecy' (Watkins, 2015, p. 513). The discourse used in the UK official documents (e.g., HM Treasury, 2006, p. 13) is indicative of the extent to which new regionalism has become a taken-for-granted, collective imaginary of the elites.

As mentioned above, the failure of regionalization led to the search for a new wave of rescaling which in turn led to re-imagining and privileging of city-region as the new neoliberal scalar fix. Once again, the process was driven and legitimated by political economic theories and often by the same 'new regionalist' scholars mentioned above. These invoked the city-region as the new 'engine' of local economic growth in the face of globalization (Scott, 2001) and the saviour of capitalist endemic crises. It was argued that the successful extraction of benefits from globalizing capital rests on city-regional agglomeration economies (Scott & Storper, 2003; Storper, 2013) and the benefits of concentrated urban economies would stretch beyond the city through 'ripple out' and 'trickle down' processes. Citations and reiterations followed in policy statements and some government's commissioned studies, claiming that, 'competitive cities create prosperous regions through a potential chain reaction' (Harding et al., 2006, p. 6).

Although in the search for a new scalar fix, city-regionalization emerged from the ashes of regionalization (Harrison, 2012), there is an important difference between the two processes that is premised on the weight given to the centrality of *the city* in the distinct ECC city-regional imaginary. The emphasis on the city is evident in both government's strategies and official documents as well as scientific rationalizations (Harrison & Heley, 2015; Pemberton & Shaw, 2012). The latter is reflected in the mushrooming of academic narratives which revolve around the 'triumph of the city' (Glaeser, 2011) and 'planetary urbanism' (Brenner & Schmid, 2015) whereby the 'metropolis' is imagined as 'a significant and revealing element of the world in emergence' (Scott, 2011, p. 858). It is argued that for the new 'knowledge economy', the city – dubbed as 'ideopolis' – is as important as factory floor space was for the industrial economy (Jones et al., 2006). As Luukkonen and Sirvio (2019, p. 17) suggest, '"urban" has become an *episteme* of our time'.

Together, the urban bias and the economic imperatives have invoked and entrenched, at least in policy processes and practices, a cityand economic-centric imaginary of city-regions which is aligned with and rationalizes the neoliberal obsession with *economy first* and *'city first',* as the basis of not just spatial demarcation (discussed below), but also of state politico-spatial selectivity. There are numerous official statements that show how deep this imaginary has penetrated into elites' policies and practices, such as the exhortation 'to ensure maximum impact by better aligning decision-making with real economic geographies such as city-regions' (Department of Communities and Local Government (DCLG), 2006, p. 73). The match between the *episteme* and the political project is further revealed by a government's commissioned study announcing that, 'an economic focus on City-Regions fits well with the current logic of Government policy' (Harding et al, 2006, p. 6). These broader theoretical rationalizations of the two components of the ECC city-regional imaginary (city and economy) have at once reinforced and been strengthened by the analytical and cartographical practices that have long dominated the demarcation of the horizontal bound of city-regional space; to which we now turn.

Horizontal ordering of city-regional space

Defining what constitutes a city-region conceptually or geographically has preoccupied planners, geographers and statistical analysts since city-regional imaginaries were first evoked. While proliferation of myriads of narrative definitions has turned the city-region into 'an object of mystery' (Harrison, 2012, p. 1246), its statistical definitions have followed a clearer path. But the path has turned into a cul-de-sac where one particular method has foreclosed the potential for alternatives, as the following brief historical account shows.

In Britain, although Geddes's (1915, p. 34) notion of conurbation referred to 'town aggregates', implying the importance of rural linkages, it was Fawcett's (1922) morphological definition of built-up areas that became institutionalized as the initial delineation of city-regions. By the 1970s economic definitions which had been used, since Gras (1922), to delineate America's metropolitan areas were adopted by British academics (notably Hall et al., 1973) to delimit the so-called standard metropolitan labour areas. What defined these imagined metropolises was the radial commuting pattern of the workforce from the periphery to the centre(s) where jobs were located. These widely circulated analytical methods and mapping practices invoked the imaginary of the city-region as a functional economic area (FEA). Coined in 1968 by Brian Berry (Berry et al., 1968), the FEA[3] approach has since essentialized city-regional space as a self-contained and integrated economic entity, bounded primarily by the lines of commuting patterns.

The emphasis on work-related economic flows reflects and reinforces the economic rationalization of the scalar position of city-regions that we discussed above. The ECC imaginary of city-region has been performed by successive geographers, spatial analysts, planners and cartographers who have advanced, fine-tuned, applied and circulated it as the 'natural' and self-evident representation of 'reality'. In the last two decades it has been further normalized by a series of pan-European studies supported by a key funding institution, ESPON.[4] These have been particularly prolific in producing maps and other visualizations of functional economic imaginaries of city-regions. We now turn to discuss in more detail how the *urban* and the *economic* biases are reflected in and reinforced by the methodological choices made and the assumptions smuggled into the FEA analyses and city-regional maps.

The most common method for delineating and mapping FEAs is top-down and deductive and follows a twostage process: the selection of 'core cities' and the delineation of their 'hinterlands' which are often designated as cities' sphere of *economic* influence. 'The inner core' and 'the outer surrounding area' have been given different labels, but the mapping process is often the same. The core city is imagined as a container bounded by morphological attributes such as contiguous built-up areas. Their selection is based on criteria such as population size and economic strength (measured by gross domestic product – GDP). The weight given to these criteria determine which cities are considered as the core, around which hinterlands are defined and mapped (Robson et al., 2006). This 'city first' (Coombes, 2014) methodological choice works at two levels: it excludes cities and towns that are not deemed part of 'the core', and it prescribes the total number of FEAs in a given national territory. The 'hinterlands' for the selected cities are delineated either by calculating the percentage of people who travel from surrounding areas to work in the core city, or by using a proxy, based on an assumed convenient commuting distance from the core. Both are somewhat arbitrary selections and prone to manipulation. Regarding the former, the *lower* the percentage, the *larger* the FEA and vice versa. The choice of threshold determines which towns and villages are included/excluded in the resulting city-region. When the threshold is set high, many places are left off the map even if they have strong environmental, cultural, historical or even administrative ties with them (Davoudi, 2008).

Economically driven geometries trump all others, such as geographies of waste flows (Davoudi, 2009), the catchment areas of rivers (Omernik, 2004), or the terrains of cultural landscapes (Davoudi & Brooks, 2019; Matless, 2017), and, hence change the relations of power. Places that are left off the map (not included in any city-region) and rendered invisible rarely attract policy attention or investment. Conversely, when the threshold is set low, many places are engulfed into the hinterlands of core cities, even if they have distinct historical, cultural or political place identity. This happened to the historic city of York in England, which was cast as the hinterland for the larger city of Leeds at the height of FEA mapping enthusiasms in the early 2000s, creating considerable contestation in strategic planning processes (Dabinett, 2009). Delineation and mapping processes not only make us see the city-region as an economic space. They also reduce the complexity of economic relations to mere travel-to-work flows, disregarding other economic interactions such as: travel to shops, schools, leisure destinations, or the interactions between businesses which take place through virtual space. Alternative, bottom-up methodologies have been promoted by, for example, Coombes (2014) 'region first' approach, or Harrison and Heley's (2015) relational 'hub and spoke' approach, but none has reached the leverage of the dominant top down FEA method and its ability to garner political action.

The key point is that what appears to be an arbitrary, technical exercise of selecting thresholds and cut-off points is a contested social process in which the infusions of ideas (methods and ways of knowing), discourses (naming and narrating), and materials (maps and images) into performative spatial imaginaries are constitutive of the politics of scalar fixing. Although city-region maps often have 'fuzzy' boundaries, despite or because of their fuzziness, they are highly performative and act as instruments of power. As Said (1994, p. 7) suggests in the context of colonialism, 'the struggle over geography is not only about soldiers and cannons, but also about ideas, forms, images and imaginings'. Drawing arrows, fixing lines, and colour-coding zones as cores, hinterlands or peripheries render certain areas and certain relations visible and remove others from sight. Cartographical practices and their hidden methodological assumptions perform a certain imaginary of city-region which is at once their product and their producer. Neatly aligning with and reinforcing the vertical ordering of scale, demarcation practices are integral parts of enacting, normalizing and solidifying not just the city-regional imaginary per se (the what) as the scalar fix of capitalist crises, but also the cityand economy-first version of that imaginary (the how), which fits so well with the neoliberal political project (the why) in which the imaginary is implicated and by which it is invoked. In his critique of structuralist approaches, Moore (2008) argues that their treatment of scale as a 'category of analysis' reifies scale as an ontological entity. Instead, he suggests that scale should be treated as 'a category of practice'. Our conceptualization of scale as an imaginary considers the relationship between the two categories not as binary but as co-constitutive. Inspired by the Foucauldian knowledge/power dyad, we argue that scalar fixing involves the synchronization of analyses and practices, as well as the political projects in which they are implicated. But, as the following discussion of city-regionalization will show, such an alignment is not a guarantee for successful institutionalization of the intended scalar fix.

Institutionalization of city-regional scale?

The above discussions demonstrate that the city-region has been an enduring spatial imaginary for at least a century. Even its more limited ECC version has been around since the 1970s and has been periodically recalibrated as part of a crisis-induced rescaling of the state. However, while as a *spatial imaginary* the ECC city-region has been kept alive, as a *scalar fix* it has failed to become institutionalized into a formal subnational scale of governance in England, as we sketch out below.

An early attempt to instil FEAs through a 1969 government commission was largely unsuccessful and throughout the 1980s and 1990s, the city-region remained a dormant imaginary. Any prospect of city-regionalization was quashed by the abolition of the metropolitan county councils, the closest institutional alignment to FEA at the time. Among various political motivations were the neoliberal disdain for 'big government' and the party-political tactics for reducing the power of these (mostly opposition-run) subnational governments. In the 2000s, the city-regional imaginary resurfaced in the debate about the 'Missing Middle' (New Local Government Network (NLGN), 2000) of English governance structure. By the middle of that decade, fuelled by the epistemic rationalization of city-centric economic growth, political enthusiasms for the city-regional scale gathered pace and led to the establishment of various institutional arrangements for collaboration across FEA boundaries. However, the city-regionalization project was as short lived as the regionalization which we discussed earlier

(Shaw & Greenhalgh, 2010); and by 2007, the transition of the ECC city-regional imaginary into formal governance structures was halted. Instead, a seemingly more inclusive, region-centric rescaling was initiated based on animating 'the more politically-palatable' imaginary of 'sub-regions' (Harrison & Heley, 2015, p. 1120). Thus, through clever political manoeuvring, the city-regional *spatial* imaginary was expanded to include areas that were left off the map, notably rural areas but, once again its *scalar* imaginary turned into a dormant neoliberal scalar fix.

The failure of fixing became clear as the opportunities for creating statutory governance structures were lost in 2010 (except in Manchester and Leeds) when a new government not only abolished all regional institutions, but also shifted the political emphasis towards localism and the instalment of Local Enterprise Partnerships. These were run by centrally appointed members from the public and private sectors and charged with local economic development. Their designated boundaries were legitimated on the basis that they 'reflected real FEAs' (HM Government, 2010, p. 13), yet in practice they followed neither the citycentric nor the economic-centric basis of FEAs (Harrison & Heley, 2015). Thus, despite the persistence of the ECC city-regional *spatial* imaginary, its alignment with boundaries of sub-national governance has failed to live up to its technically calculated 'ideal' FEA. Instead, it has been recast into politically crafted variable geometries (Pemberton & Searle, 2016). The mismatch is evident in the most recent experimentation with scalar fixing, notably the creation of 'Devolution Deals'. These are contractual agreements between local and central governments by which the former can be endowed with additional funding if they agree to work with adjoining local authorities on strategic policies. While the 'deals' are initiated by localities, central government calls the shots. This latest rescaling experiment has further complicated the patchwork quilt of coalitions of varying capacity and collaborative intents, and created a variable *spatial* geometry and *scalar* allocation of state power. They show a 'world of difference' with the idealized imaginary of the functional economic areas and the elites' desire for 'an orderly transition to a comprehensive and effective tier of subregions and city-regions' (Harding, 2010, p. 8).

Conclusions

In this paper, we have brought together two sets of literature – on scale and on imaginaries – to initiate a new conceptualization of scale as a performative imaginary in order to overcome the dualism between materialist and idealist theorizations of scale. We have deployed the concept of scalar imaginary to explore the politics of contemporary scalar fixing in England, focusing particularly on how a distinct form of city-regional imaginary as ECC has played an integral part in the political project of city-regionalization. We highlighted how theorists, analysts and cartographers have helped with legitimating this project by scientific rationalization of the city-regional *scale,* and by technical demarcation of city-regional *space.* We further demonstrated that despite the endurance of the ECC city-regional *spatial* imaginary, a corresponding city-regional governance and planning scale has ebbed and flowed. While the search for a contingently stable scalar fix is ongoing and the city-region remains a strong scalar candidate, it would be useful to sketch out some of the reasons for its, as yet, limited institutionalization.

At a wider level, a key reason is the spatio-temporal contingency of scalar fixing itself which can never offer a lasting solution to capitalist crises. This is compounded by the contested nature of scalar imaginaries even when they are normalized. City-regional space is subject to multiple alternative imaginaries which compete for a position of dominance. The ECC city-regional imaginary is no exception. It has been/continues to be subject to various forms of resistance which, although not operating independently, they often involve different coalitions of political interests. Short of a fuller analysis which would be beyond the scope of this paper, we highlight some of the key tensions.

First, there is resistance to the economy-centredness of ECC by alternatives which, as we mentioned in the introduction, focus on historical, cultural, political or ecological significance of city-regional imaginaries. Ecologists, in particular, call for an imaginary of city-regional space which is attentive to the unbounded metabolic 'hinterlands' of cities (Omernik, 2004). Although, as we have shown, these alternatives are either lost or suppressed by the hegemonic economic imaginary, they still exert influence and forge compromised outcomes. Another source of resistance comes from those who subscribe to the economy-centredness of the city-regional imaginary but object to its *city*-centrism, and call for a more inclusive imaginary of regional space which encompasses rural areas, in particular. Advocates of rural interests who feel they are being treated as 'carriages' pulled along by the 'locomotive' of economic growth (Shucksmith, 2008, p. 63) have been particularly vocal in lobbying against city-centric configurations.

A third form of resistance is to the rescaling project per se and its inevitable repercussions for 'power geometries' (Massey, 2005). This resistance operates primarily in the politico-administrative space and is concerned with the unsettling of actors' existing powers, responsibilities and resources. In city-regional rescaling, much depends on the repositioning of actors in the 'cores', 'hinterlands', or somewhere in between that is made invisible on the map. There is also (fourth) resistance to disruption of the status quo. Institutional path-dependencies make the wholesale transformation of deep-seated governance structures and distribution of political power and professional responsibilities difficult, if not impossible, to implement.

Fifth, there is a big gap between scientific or technocratic imaginaries (such as FEA) and the kinds of imaginaries held by wider communities (Harvey et al, 2011; Jones & MacLeod, 2004; Riding & Jones, 2017; Shields, 1991). To paraphrase Seton-Watson (1977, p. 5), a city-region can only become a socially embedded imaginary when a significant number of people imagine themselves as belonging to a city-regional community. Without such an 'imagined community' city-regionalization continues to be an elite enterprise to which people remain either indifferent or opposed. Finally, there is the 'messy world' of policy making (Davoudi, 2006) which is far from the idealized image of an evidence-based, rational process of perfectly synchronizing an elite-driven ECC city-regional imaginary with the spatial contours of governance structures. While ideological projects such as neoliberalism steer the direction of rescaling, its paths have to be negotiated along the way to take account of social, cultural, institutional and practical contexts. Such negotiations often result in scalar configurations that resemble not a perfect match with the ideal and the intended project, but a *collage* of compromises and a layering of past, present and future imaginaries.

The implications for planning regional futures are profound, not least because planning is about politics of place and its policies and practices are simultaneously the producers, the carriers, and the products of spatial and scalar imaginaries. Recognizing this is a first step towards unsettling taken-for-granted imaginaries, and asking questions (Davoudi, 2019) such as: how do such spatial and scalar imaginaries come about? Through what mediums do they get circulated and galvanized? What roles are played by planning thoughts and practices in invoking, reiterating, enacting or resisting certain imaginaries? Why do certain imaginaries stick while others fade away or get sidelined? And, more importantly, what is at stake, and who and what values stand to lose or to gain? Addressing these questions matters because how we imagine the spatiality of 'the region' or the 'city-region' has profound impacts on how we plan for regional/city-regional futures and to where future development investments are directed.

While making the invisible visible is a necessary step, it is not enough for disrupting taken-for-granted imaginaries and offering effective alternatives. For that, planners and other stakeholders need to recognize and mobilise the power of transformative imagination which, as Castoriadis (1987, p. 81) put it, is 'the capacity to see in a thing what it is not, to see it other than it is'. It is the capacity to see beyond the engrained spatial and scalar imaginaries and imagine how cities and regions might be otherwise.

Acknowledgements

Earlier versions of this paper were presented at the 2018 and 2019 Regional Studies Conferences in London, the 2019 BeMine Conference in Helsinki, and the 2019 AESOP Conference in Venice. The authors thank the conference participants, guest editors of the special issue and three anonymous referees for thoughtful and constructive comments on earlier versions of the paper.

Disclosure statement

No potential conflict of interest was reported by the authors.

Funding

This paper draws on research funded by the Academy of Finland [grant number 303553].

Notes

1 An emphasis which has resurfaced in OECD (2011).
2 As well as its implications in terms of, for example, directing infrastructure to certain places (Royal Institute of Town Planning (RTPI), 2019) or exacerbating spatial inequalities (Pike & Tomaney, 2009).
3 Berry et al. used the term function urban regions (FURs). It is also known as functional urban areas (FUAs).
4 See www.espon.eu/.

ORCID

Simin Davoudi ⓘ http://orcid.org/0000-0001-6299-3675
Elizabeth Brooks ⓘ http://orcid.org/0000-0001-7692-3221

References

Agnew, J. (1997). The dramaturgy of horizons: Geographical scale in the 'reconstruction of Italy' by the new Italian political parties, 1992–1995. *Political Geography, 16*(2), 99–121. https://doi.org/10.1016/80962-6298(96)00046-7

Allen, J., Massey, D., & Cochrane, A. (1998). *Re-thinking the region.* Routledge.

Anderson, B. (1991). *Imagined communities: Reflections on the origins and spread of nationalism.* Verso.

Appadurai, A. (1996). Disjuncture and difference in the global cultural economy. In *Modernity at large: Cultural dimensions of globalization* (pp. 27–47). University of Minnesota.

Berry, B. J. L., Goheen, P. G., & Goldstein, H. (1968). *Metropolitan area definition: A re-evaluation of concept and statistical practice* (Working Paper No. 28). US Bureau of the Census.

Bialasiewicz, L., Campbell, D., Elden, S., Graham, S., Jeffrey, A., & Williams, A. J. (2007). Performing security: The imaginative geographies of current US strategy. *Political Geography, 26*(4), 405–422. https://doi.org/10.1016/j.polgeo.2006.12.002

Brenner, N. (2001). The limits to scale? Methodological reflections on scalar structuration. *Progress in Human Geography, 25*(4), 591–614. https://doi.org/10.1191/030913201682688959

Brenner, N. (2003). Metropolitan institutional reform and the rescaling of state space in contemporary Western Europe. *European Urban and Regional Studies, 10*(4), 297–324. https://doi.org/10.1177/09697764030104002

Brenner, N., & Schmid, C. (2015). Towards a new epistemology of the urban? *City, 19*(2–3), 151–182. https://doi.org/10.1080/13604813.2015.1014712

Burnham, D. H., & Bennet, E. H. (1909). *Plan of Chicago.* Commercial Club of Chicago.

Butler, J. (1993). *Bodies that matter: On the discursive limits of 'sex'.* Routledge.

Castoriadis, C. (1987 [1975]). *The imaginary institution of society* (Trans. K. Blarney). MIT Press.

Coombes, M. (2014). From city-region concept to boundaries for governance: The English case. *Urban Studies, 51*(11), 2426–2443. https://doi.org/
10.1177/0042098013493482

Dabinett, G. (2009). New approaches to space and place in the Yorkshire and Hum-
ber regional spatial strategy. In S. Davoudi & I. Strange (Eds.), *Conceptions of
space and place in strategic spatial planning* (pp. 147–180). Routledge.

Danson, M., & Lloyd, G. (2012). Devolution, institutions, and organisations:
Changing models of regional development agencies. *Environment and Planning
C: Government and Policy, 30*(1), 78–94. https://doi.org/10.1068/cll45r

Davoudi, S. (2006). Evidence-based planning: Rhetoric and reality. *DisP: Planning
Review, 42*(2), 14–24. https://doi.org/10.1080/02513625.2006.10556951

Davoudi, S. (2008). Conceptions of the city-region: A critical review. *Proceedings
of the Institution of Civil Engineers – Urban Design and Planning, 161*(2), 51–60.
https://doi.org/10.1680/udap.2008.161.2.51

Davoudi, S. (2009). Scalar tensions in the governance of waste: The resilience of
state spatial Keynesianism. *Journal of Environmental Planning and Management,
52*(2), 137–156. https://doi.org/10.1080/09640560802666495

Davoudi, S. (2018). Imagination and spatial imaginaries: A conceptual framework.
Town Planning Review, 89(2), 97–107. https://doi.org/10.3828/tpr.2018.7

Davoudi, S. (2019). Imaginaries of a 'Europe of the regions'. *Transactions of the Association of European Schools of Planning, 3*(2), 85–92. https://doi.org/10.24306/
TrAESOP.2019.02.001

Davoudi, S., & Brooks, E. (2019). *Landscape quality: A rapidreview of the evidence.* DEFRA Science Advisory Council. Retrieved from https://www.gov.uk/
government/publications/landscape-quality-a-rapid-review-of-the-evidence

Department of Communities and Local Government (DCLG). (2006). *Strong and
prosperous communities: The local government white paper.* DCLG.

Department of the Environment, Transport and the Regions (DETR). (1997). *Building partnerships for prosperity: Sustainable growth, competitiveness and employment in the English regions* (Cm 3814). The Stationery Office (TSO).

Dickinson, R. E. (1964). *City and region: A geographical interpretation.* Routledge &
Kegan Paul.

Duncan, O. D. (1960). *Metropolis and region: Resources for the future.* Johns Hop-
kins Press.

Ezrahi, Y. (2012). *Imagined democracies, necessary political fictions.* Cambridge University Press.

Fawcett, C. (1922). British conurbations in 1921. *Sociological Review, 14*(2), 111–122.
https://doi.org/10.1111/j.1467-954X.1922.tb02860.x

Fraser, A. (2010). The craft of scalar practices. *Environment and Planning A: Economy and Space, 42*(2), 332–346. https://doi.org/10.1068/a4299

Geddes, P. (1915). *Cities in evolution.* Williams & Margate.

Glaeser, E. L. (2011). *Triumph of the city: How our greatest invention makes us richer,
smarter, greener, healthier, happier.* Penguin.

Golubchikov, O. (2010). World-city-entrepreneurialism: Globalist imaginaries, neoliberal geographies, and the production of new St Petersburg. *Environment and
Planning A: Economy and Space, 42*(3), 626–643. https://doi.org/10.1068/a39367

González, S. (2006). Scalar narratives in Bilbao: A cultural politics of scales approach to the study of urban policy. *International Journal of Urban and Regional
Research, 30*(4), 836–857. https://doi.org/10.1111/J.1468-2427.2006.00693.X

Gras, N. S. B. (1922). *An introduction to economic history.* Harper.

Gregory, D. (1995). Imaginative geographies. *Progress in Human Geography, 19*(4), 447–485. https://doi.org/10.1177/ 030913259501900402

Hall, P., Thomas, R., Gracey, H., & Drewett, R. (1973). *The containment of urban England: Urban and metropolitan growth processes or megalopolis denied.* Allen & Unwin.

Harding, A. (2010). *Economic development and regeneration: An early reading of coalition government runes, election unplugged II; northern reflections on the coalition's programme for government.* IPPR North.

Harding, A., Marvin, S., & Robson, B. (2006). *A framework for city-regions.* Office of the Deputy Prime Minister (ODPM).

Harrison, J. (2012). Life after regions? The evolution of city-regionalism in England. *Regional Studies, 46*(9), 1243–1259. https://doi.org/10.1080/00343404.2010.521148

Harrison, J., & Heley, J. (2015). Governing beyond the metropolis: Placing the rural in city-region development. *Urban Studies, 52*(6), 1113–1133. https://doi.org/10.1177/0042098014532853

Harvey, D. (2000). *Spaces of hope.* Edinburgh University Press.

Harvey, D., Hawkins, H., & Thomas, N. (2011). Regional imaginaries of governance Agencies: Practising the region of South West Britain. *Environment and Planning A: Economy and Space, 43*(2), 470–486. https://doi.org/10.1068/a43380

HM Government. (2010). *Local growth: Realising every place's potential.* The Stationery Office (TSO).

HM Treasury. (2006). *Devolving decision making 3 – Meeting the regional economic challenge: The importance of cities to regional growth.* The Stationery Office (TSO).

Howley, A. (1950). *Human ecology: A theory of community structure.* Ronald.

Hudson, R. (2005). Region and place: Devolved regional government and regional economic success? *Progress in Human Geography, 29*(5), 618–625. https://doi.org/10.1191/0309132505ph572pr

Institute for Public Policy Research (IPPR). (2006). *City leadership – Giving city-regions the power to grow.* Centre for Cities.

Jasanoff, S., & Sang-Hyun, K. (Eds.). (2015). *Dreamscapes of modernity, sociotechnical imaginaries and the fabrication of power.* University of Chicago Press.

Jessop, B. (2002). *The future of the capitalist state.* Polity.

Jessop, B. (2010). Cultural political economy and critical policy studies. *Critical Policy Studies, 3*(3–4), 336–356. https://doi.org/10.1080/19460171003619741

Jessop, B., Brenner, N., & Jones, M. (2008). Theorizing sociospatial relations. *Environment and Planning D: Society and Space, 26*(3), 389–401. https://doi.org/10.1068/d9107

Jones, A., Williams, L., Lee, N., Coats, D., & Cowling, M. (2006). *Ideopolis: Knowledge city-regions.* Work Foundation.

Jones, K. (1998). Scale as epistemology. *Political Geography, 17*(1), 25–28. https://doi.org/10.1016/S0962-6298(97)00049-8

Jones, M. (2001). The rise of the regional state in economic governance: 'Partnerships for prosperity' or new scales of state power? *Environment and Planning A: Economy and Space, 33*(7), 1185–1211. https://doi.org/10.1068/a32185

Jones, M., & MacLeod, G. (2004). Regional spaces, spaces of regionalism: Territory, insurgent politics and the English question. *Transactions of the Institute of British Geographers, New Series, 29*(4), 433–452. https://doi.org/10.1111/j.0020-2754.2004.00140.x

Kaiser, R., & Nikiforova, N. (2008). The performativity of scale: The social construction of scale effects in Narva, Estonia. *Environment and Planning D: Society and Space, 26*(3), 537– 562. https://doi.org/10.1068/d3307

Keating, M. (1997). The invention of regions: Political restructuring and territorial government in Western Europe. *Environment and Planning C: Government and Policy, 15*(4), 383–398. https://doi.org/10.1068/c150383

Lefebvre, H. (1991 [1976]). *The production of space.* Blackwell.

Lovering, J. (1999). Theory led by policy: The inadequacies of the 'new regionalism' (illustrated from the case of Wales). *International Journal of Urban and Regional Research, 23*(2), 379–395. https://doi.org/10.1111/1468-2427.00202

Luukkonen, J., & Sirvio, H. (2019). The politics of depoliticization and the constitution of city-regionalism as a dominant spatialpolitical imaginary in Finland. *Political Geography, 73,* 17–27. https://doi.org/10.1016/j.polgeo.2019.05.004

MacKinnon, D. (2011). Reconstructing scale: Towards a new scalar politics. *Progress in Human Geography, 35*(1), 21–36. https://doi.org/10.1177/0309132510367841

Marcus, G. E. (Ed.). (1995). *Technoscientific imaginaries, Conversations, profiles, memoirs.* University of Chicago Press.

Marston, S. (2000). The social construction of scale. *Progress in Human Geography, 24*(2), 219–242. https://doi.org/10.1191/030913200674086272

Marston, S., Jones, J. P., & Woodward, K. (2005). Human geography without scale. *Transactions of the Institute of British Geographers New Series, 30*(4), 416–432. https://doi.org/10.1111/j.14755661.2005.00180.x

Massey, D. (2005). *For space.* Sage.

Massey, D. (2007). *World city.* Polity.

Matless, D. (2017). Writing regional cultural landscape. In J. Riding, & M. Jones (Eds.), *Reanimating regions: Culture, politics and performance* (pp. 9–26). Routledge.

Mills, C. W. (1959). *The sociological imagination.* Grove.

Moore, A. (2008). Rethinking scale as a geographical category: From analysis to practice. *Progress in Human Geography, 32*(2), 203–225. https://doi.org/10.1177/0309132507087647

New Local Government Network (NLGN). (2000). *Is there a 'missing middle' in English governance?* NLGN.

Ohmae, K. (1995). *The end of the nation-state.* Free Press.

Omernik, J. (2004). Perspectives on the nature and definition of ecological regions. *Environmental Management, 34*(Suppl. 1), S27–S38. https://doi.org/10.1007/s00267-003-5197-2

Organisation for Economic Co-operation and Development (OECD). (2007). *Competitive cities in the global economy.* OECD Publ.

Organisation for Economic Co-operation and Development (OECD). (2011). *2011 OECD rural policy reviews: England, United Kingdom.* OECD Publ.

Paasi, A. (2004). Place and region: Looking through the prism of scale. *Progress in Human Geography, 28*(4), 536–546. https://doi.org/10.1191/0309132504ph502pr

Paasi, A. (2010). Commentary. *Environment and Planning A: Economy and Space, 42*(10), 2296–2301. https://doi.org/10.1068/a42232

Pemberton, S., & Searle, G. (2016). Statecraft, & alecraft and urban planning: A comparative study of Birmingham, UK, and Brisbane, Australia. *European Planning Studies, 24*(1), 76–95. https://doi.org/10.1080/09654313.2015.1078297

Pemberton, S., & Shaw, D. (2012). New forms of sub-regional governance and implications for rural areas: Evidence from England. *Planning Practice and Research, 27*(4), 441–458. https://doi.org/10.1080/02697459.2012.682476

Pickles, E. (2010, September 10). How we rebuild our local economy. Conservative Party. Retrieved from https://www.conservativehome.com/localgovernment/2010/09/eric-pickles-mp-how-we-rebuild-our-local-economy.html

Pike, A., & Tomaney, J. (2004). Subnational governance and economic and social development: Guest editorial. *Environment and Planning A: Economy and Space, 36*(12), 2091–2096. https://doi.org/10.1068/a37130

Pike, A., & Tomaney, J. (2009). The state and uneven development: The governance of economic development in England in the post-devolution UK. *Cambridge Journal of Regions, Economy and Society, 2*(1), 13–34. https://doi.org/10.1093/cjres/rsn025

Regional Studies. (2002). Special Issue: Devolution and the English Question. *Regional Studies, 36*(7), 715–797.

Regional Studies. (2007). Special Issue: Whiter Regional Studies? *Regional Studies, 41*(9), 1143–1270.

Riding, J., & Jones, M. (Eds.). (2017). *Reanimating regions: Culture,* politics and performance. Routledge.

Robson, B., Barr, R., Lymperoupolou, K., Rees, J., & Coombes, M. (2006). *Mapping city-regions.* Office of the Deputy Prime Minister (ODPM).

Royal Institute of Town Planning (RTPI). (2019). *A smarter approach to infrastructure planning: Overcoming complexity in city-regions and counties.* RPTI.

Said, E. W. (1978). *Orientalism.* Penguin.

Said, E. W. (1994). *Culture and imperialism.* Vintage.

Scott, A., & Storper, M. (2003). Regions, globalization, development. *Regional Studies, 37*(6–7), 579–593. https://doi.org/10.1080/0034340032000108697a

Scott, A. J. (2001). Globalism and the rise of city-regions. *European Planning Studies, 9*(7), 813–826. https://doi.org/10.1080/09654310120079788

Scott, A. J. (2011). A world in emergence: Notes toward a resynthesis of urban-economic geography for the 21st century. *Urban Geography, 32*(6), 845–870. https://doi.org/10.2747/0272-3638.32.6.845

Seton-Watson, H. (1977). *Nations and states: An enquiry into the origins of nations and the politics of nationalism.* Methuen.

Shaw, K., & Greenhalgh, P. (2010). Revisiting the 'missing middle' in English sub-national governance. *Local Economy: Journal of the Local Economy Policy Unit, 25*(5–6), 457–475. https://doi.org/10.1080/02690942.2010.525999

Shields, R. (1991). *Places on the margin: Alternative geographies of modernity.* Routledge.

Shucksmith, M. (2008). New labour's countryside in international perspective. In M. Woods (Ed.), *New labours countryside: Rural policy in Britain since 1997* (pp. 57–76). Policy Press.

Smith, N. (1993). Homeless/global: Scaling places. In J. Bird, B. Curtis, T. Putnam, G. Robertson, & L. Tickner (Eds.), *Mapping the futures: Local cultures, global change* (pp. 87–119). Routledge.

Storper, M. (2013). *Keys to the city: Howe economics, institutions, social interactions and politics shape development.* Princeton University Press.

Sum, N. I., & Jessop, B. (2013). *Towards a cultural political economy: Putting culture in its place in political economy.* Edward Elgar.

Swyngedouw, E. (2004). Globalisation or 'glocalisation? Networks, territories and rescaling. *Cambridge Review of International Affairs, 17* (1), 25–48. https://doi.org/10.1080/0955757042000203632

Taylor, C. (2004). *Modern social imaginaries.* Duke University Press.

Watkins, J. (2015). Spatial imaginaries research in geography: Synergies, tensions, and new directions. *Geography Compass, 9*(9), 508–522. https://doi.org/10.1111/gec3.12228

Two logics of regionalism: the development of a regional imaginary in the Toronto–Waterloo Innovation Corridor

David Wachsmuth● and Patrick Kilfoil

Introduction

Kitchener-Waterloo is a small metropolitan region located about 100 km west of Toronto in Ontario. It has long been recognized as the centre of Canada's tech sector, and in particular it is the home to BlackBerry – once the world's largest smartphone manufacturer. The erosion of BlackBerry's competitive position in the early 2010s under pressure from the iPhone and Android urgently raised the question of how the region's tech economy would adapt, and particularly whether the sector's centre of gravity would shift to the Toronto region. The latter has emerged as a global hub of finance and was rapidly adding high-tech jobs as BlackBerry was declining.

However, instead of the Waterloo region ceding its position to Toronto, or reasserting its dominance, actors in the two regions started to collaborate, marketing the entire 100-km stretch joining the two regions as the Toronto-Waterloo Innovation Corridor (TWIC). In a few years, an entirely new 'region' has sprung into existence, with an array of partnerships, initiatives and strategies mobilizing some version of this corridor which, a short while earlier, would not have been recognized as a region at all.

This paper uses the case of the TWIC to answer the question: Why and how do regional politics develop outside the context of a coherent regional economy? We introduce a distinction between two 'logics of regionalism': a familiar logic of territorial alliances or growth coalitions rooted in a city-regional structured coherence, and a less familiar logic of regional imaginaries actively constructing regional strategies in novel scalar and territorial configurations. We suggest that, in the presence of a strong policy common sense that regionalism is strategic, but in the absence of a city-regional focus for that strategy, regional politics can develop through the proliferation of varied and contradictory regional imaginaries. Through a detailed case study of the TWIC, we show how the organization of economic strategic action within this novel spatial configuration has been driven by a constitutive tension between the region understood as the 'real' space of economic activity, and the region as an ephemeral concept which can support numerous concrete projects. We highlight in particular three important forces: *the, productive ambiguity* of the region as a spatial and strategic concept; the centrality of *regionalism entrepreneurs* in actively constructing a regional political agenda; and the importance of *extrospective policy-making* in establishing a rationale for collaboration.

Fieldwork was conducted in 2018 and consisted of a review of key policy documents and plans, as well as 14 semi-directed interviews with policymakers, public servants, economic development officials and business leaders. Questions covered the history of the innovation corridor, including the circumstances that led to it developing into an economic development partnership, the goals and ambitions of stakeholders, the incentives for regional collective action, and the factors that contributed to the identification of the innovation corridor as a regional strategy worth pursuing.

Competitive regions, competitive regionalisms

How do the place-bound interests of local economic actors translate into politics? A long tradition of critical urban scholarship, often referred to as the 'new urban polities' (Cox, 1993; MacLeod & Jones, 2011), has approached this question by exploring the centrality of local economic development to urban politics, and the diffuse coalitions of actors who collectively steer urban development processes. This tradition encompasses the interrelated literatures on growth machine theory (Logan & Molotch, 2007), urban entrepreneurialism (Harvey, 1989), new regionalism (Storper, 1997) and city-regionalism (Harrison, 2007).

The new urban politics provides its most compelling account at the local and city-regional scales, where the economic conditions for growth and development map relatively cleanly onto the institutional levers for controlling those conditions. The central insight of the growth machine approach is the empirical observation that a set of place-bound elites, termed the 'growth coalition', has a shared interest in intensifying land use and systematically intervenes in – and indeed attempts to establish the very structures which constitute – local politics to act on this shared interest (Logan & Molotch, 2007). Since the institutions that control land use are frequently located at the local and city-regional scales, there is a strong correspondence between the growth machine's 'space of dependence' and its 'space of engagement' (Cox, 1998), which makes coordinated political action easier to achieve.

The self-organization of growth machines at these scales is not an onto-logical necessity, but rather an outcome of a long-term stability in specific scalar structures of the state (Brenner, 2009). And over the last 30 years local growth politics have partly been rescaled beyond the city-region (Wachsmuth, 2017a). Growth coalitions still seek land-use intensification, but their scope of action is increasingly extra-local and regional, which has contributed to the emergence of new regional growth coalitions made up of formerly and still competing actors at different scales of the state and civil society. In the context of the knowledge economy, moreover, growth coalitions are increasingly concerned with economic development broadly defined, which fosters the creation of opportunistic public-private partner-ships at various regional scales that overlap and often conflict in their objec-tives. New synthetic regions thus constitute an emerging institutional spatial fix for the knowledge economy, with innovation being positioned as the key factor in achieving economic competitiveness for the region.

The result is not a single model for regionalism and regional governance – a 'new new regionalism' – but instead an array of regional partnerships taking form in different regions. Several authors document the fascinat-ing bubbling of institutional experimentation currently taking place in North America (Addie & Keil, 2015; Cox, 2010; Jonas et al., 2014; Keil & Addie, 2015; Wachsmuth, 2017b). However, most of these studies analyse US cases. By contrast, Canadian regional governance in the 21st century remains a relatively unexplored terrain, save for a small number of studies of metropolitan governance, particularly in the Montreal metropolitan area (Boudreau et al., 2006; Lafortune & Collin, 2011; Tomas, 2012), regional transportation planning (Addie, 2013; Krawchenko, 2011) and suburbani-zation (Addie & Keil, 2015; Ekers et al., 2012; Keil & Addie, 2015). In par-ticular, large-scale regionalism has not yet been analysed in the Canadian context. Here we are particularly interested in what Wachsmuth (2017a) calls 'competitive multi-city regionalism' (CMCR) – regional economic govern-ance initiatives that connect the growth coalitions of multiple city-regions. CMCR builds on the concept of competitive city-regionalism, but argues that growth coalition action at the multicity scale is qualitatively different from the local and city-regional scales at which it is traditionally analysed. Without the shared labour and property markets of the city-region, multi-city growth coalitions must seek different foundations for collaboration and must stave off different challenges such as intra-regional competition and tax-base protectionism.

Two logics of regionalism: territorial alliances or regional imaginaries?

We argue that the complexity of regional alliance formation can be helpfully decoded by distinguishing between two logics of regional collective action, or more succinctly: *two logics of regionalism*. In making this distinction we are inspired by Offe and Wiesenthal's (1980) classic political economic analysis 'Two logics of collective action', which contrasts the constraints and opportunities facing workers' and capitalists' ability to undertake organized political action in a capitalist society. Applying this heuristic device – that the mode of social organization can give rise to divergent structures of collective action – to the very different question of regional alliance formation, we suggest that there are two common but contrasting logics of regional action corresponding to two common but contrasting modes of regional political and economic organization. We suggest that only one of these logics has been widely recognized in regional studies, and therefore provide a more systematic account of the other one.

To begin with, what is a 'logic of regional collective action'? 'Collective action' refers to the conditions under which groups of social actors collaborate, either durably or sporadically, to achieve common goals (Tilly, 1985). Implicit in this definition – and key to the way it applies to the question of regional politics – is that there is always the possibility of *not* undertaking collective action. In other words, alongside the important questions of 'to what goals is collective action aimed' and 'did it achieve its goals' is the question of 'why work collectively at all'? Offe and Wiesenthal's insight is that the position of social actors within the class structure of capitalist society produces systematically different incentives to collaborate on common goals, as well as systematically different constraints on what kinds of collective action will be effective. In the context of regional studies, the problem of regional collective action can thus be described as the dual questions of regional incentives and regional constraints: *why* social actors collaborate on a regional scale, and what factors influence the *success or failure* of such collaboration?

The new urban politics provides coherent answers to both of these questions, in an account of regional politics that emphasizes the manner in which common interests in local economic development drive the formation of growth coalitions to advance those interests in the arenas of subnational politics. This is what we term the 'first logic of regionalism', and it is the logic, in Harvey's (2001) terms, of 'structured coherence' and the 'territorial alliance':

> There are processes at work... that define regional spaces within which production and consumption, supply and demand (for commodities and labor power), production and realization, class struggle and accumulation, culture and lifestyle, hang together as some kind of structured coherence within a totality of productive forces and social relations.
>
> (p. 329)

Harvey observes that patterns of economic activity have a systematic tendency to arrange themselves along territorial lines and ascribes this tendency to the fact that investments in infrastructure and fixed capital are required to allow other capital to circulate more smoothly. This investment in the land gives an urban region a specific set of infrastructural and organizational forms that constrain production and consumption alike, and thereby creates powerful shared interests in defending the value of that investment. The first logic of regionalism thus answers the question of why social actors collaborate regionally with: *to defend thenshared place-bound interests in a regional economy*. And it answers the question of what factors influence the success or failure of regional collective action with: *the extent to which the structured coherence of the regional economy harmonizes interests across a sufficiently wide set of state, capitalist, and labour actors*.

Structured coherence in the midto late twentieth century was facilitated by the Fordist-Keynesian consensus in North America and Western Europe, where regional development was coordinated by territorial alliances made up of locally rooted interests operating according to a local mode of regulation for urban development. State institutions sometimes acted as participants within these alliances (as with the classic model of the urban growth coalition, wherein municipal governments play a coordinating role) and sometimes acted as external facilitators of the conditions of alliance formation (as with the 1960s and 1970s US federal posture toward regional governance in the United States or the 'spatial Keynesianism' of national governments in post-war Western Europe). These territorial alliances formed the basis for the system of inter-urban competition which developed in that era and subsequently consolidated under the twin guises of the new regionalism and neoliberalism (Brenner & Wachsmuth, 2012). As Feiertag et al. (2020) note:

> The geographical basis on which these institutions operated was predetermined and bore the legacy of spatial Keynesian state territoriality. There was, in many cases, no debate over the spatial logic of regions (and other subnational territorial units) being mobilised in the implementation of new region – alist-inspired institutions, policies, and planning styles.
>
> (p. 158)

And yet, the very stability of the Fordist-Keynesian system of local structured coherence misleadingly suggests that stable territorial alliances should be the norm. Under ongoing suburbanization and neoliberal restructuring the coherence of city-regional economies – and the growth coalitions acting to defend them – has progressively weakened (Jessop et al., 1999; Kirkpatrick & Smith, 2011; Phelps, 2012; Purcell, 2000; Wachsmuth, 2017a; Weber, 2010). Regional collective action is a straightforward problem only to the extent that the strategic pathways available to growth coalitions are similarly straightforward – in other words, under conditions of structured coherence. Where there is no strong structured coherence in the urban political-economic system, how do political actors generate spaces of engagement in response to their spaces of dependency (Cox, 1998)?

This is a particularly fraught question at supra-city scales, because, as an economic development concept, the region is simultaneously real and ephemeral. On the one hand, a range of growth coalition actors takes the region to be a 'real' space of economic activity. On the other hand, the region as a politico-strategic concept is constitutively ephemeral: it exists on few maps and corresponds to few institutional frameworks. While formal governments work within territorial boundaries, actually existing governance frequently transcends these boundaries (Hincks et al., 2017), and in the absence of strong institutionalization, the region is thus a 'soft space' (Allmendinger & Haughton, 2009). It embodies a generative tension between reality and ephemerality, and the outcome of this tension is a simultaneous call to action and ambivalence about the form that action should take.

The implication is that, while the region is often mobilized in academic literature and in policy discourse as a political-economic space formally similar to the city or the nation-state, this conceptualization only properly applies to the first logic of territorial alliances mobilizing to defend a regional structured coherence. Where regional collective action occurs in the absence of this coherence, the region might be more accurately described as an *imaginary:* a collective spatial rationality which justifies and gives meaning to a range of political-economic practices while being in turn sustained by the functional results of those practices. This is the second logic of regionalism: coalitions speculatively constructing regional imaginaries in the absence of structured coherence.

The core insight of literature on imaginaries in regional studies is that spatial practice always entails some form of spatial imagination, and that this imagination is often constitutive – not merely reflective – of the processes of governance, socioeconomic activity and everyday life with which it is intertwined (Healey, 2006). This emphasis on the necessary role of imagination in the formulation of spatial categories has particular resonance at the regional scale, which at least since Allen et al. (1998) has been understood as much as a particular way of seeing space as an objective scale. Described by Jessop (2012) as a 'simplified, necessarily selective "mental map" of a supercomplex reality' (p. 17), a regional imaginary constitutes a curated *representation* of a region, whether real or prospective, that provides a semblance of coherence to the process of assembling, stabilizing and providing recognition to regional formations.

Where strategic pathways are uncertain, contested or transient, interpretative work is required on behalf of actors to uncover (indeed construct) these pathways in conceptual terms. In short, contemporary regionalisms flow from a growth politics whose incentives for collective action are different from those of a previous era and emerge around regional geographies that are neither predefined nor selfevident. Unpacking this second logic of regional imaginaries and incoherent economic geographies thus requires a different set of explanatory tools. We focus on three interrelated ideas.

First, the *productive ambiguity* of the region facilitates the formation of many coalitions, strategies and geographies around an imprecisely defined spatiality. In the realm of local economic development, the conviction that regional action is necessary or desirable is widespread, although this conviction has historically been focused on achieving agglomeration economies and competitive advantage at local or city-regional scales. Under conditions of strong structured coherence, where economic activity and territorial state politics operate within similar spatial parameters, the classic 'territorial alliance' mode of regional strategic action is viable. But in the absence of a specific structured coherence to defend, local elites can – are even impelled to – mobilize around a larger range of fuzzy but overlapping visions for the region. While in principle these fuzzy regional visions could consolidate around any number of different geographies and different substantive political or economic objectives, a particularly important recent development is the emergence of new economic possibilities in logistics and related large-scale transportation and communication infrastructure at the multi-city corridor scale. Wachsmuth (2017b) has termed the growth coalitions assembling to advance regional strategies at this scale 'infrastructure alliances'.

Second, *regionalism entrepreneurs* – a core of visionaries to 'think the region' – are a necessary driving force of political strategies under the second logic of regionalism. Where there is no single hegemonic regional space, in either territorial or scalar terms, the system of regional strategic action features a larger number of 'degrees of freedom', and thus the importance of proactive, entrepreneurial approaches to regionalism is heightened. The success or failure of collective action in the soft spaces of multi-city regions or corridors may thus be contingent on the ability of these entrepreneurs to institutionalize these spaces in the absence of any single unambiguous pathway for doing so. In this regard, the second logic of regionalism implies a more significant role for the importance of leadership than the new urban politics has tended to recognize (cf. Stone, 1989, for a prominent exception).

Third, *extrospective policy-making,* particularly mimicry and competitive upscaling, provides the foundation of the regional imaginary's legitimacy. As urban governance has become increasingly oriented towards benchmarking and other exterior indicators of competitiveness, spatial imaginaries modelled on globally recognizable regional powerhouses such as Silicon Valley become correspondingly intuitive – to some extent regardless of specific local circumstances. Meanwhile, the same tendency toward extrospective urban governance has driven a trend toward 'competitive upscaling', the attempt by political actors to resolve local competitive pressures by repositioning their localities as the components of a larger competitive entity (Wachsmuth, 2020). Extrospective policy-making thus simultaneously supplies an incentive to large-scale regional action and a constraint on what forms of regionalism will be plausible to pursue.

To be clear, we do not understand the two logics of regionalism as mutually exclusive empirical possibilities; it is perfectly possible (and in fact occurs in our case study which we discuss below) for 'structured coherence' style regionalism to coexist with 'regional imaginary' style regionalism. Instead, our account of the 'second logic of regionalism' provides an account of *incentives* and *constraints* around regional action which contrasts sharply with the more common 'first logic' of city-regional growth coalitions, and thus describes the circumstances under which each might be expected to occur. Under the second logic, regional action is driven not by a motivation to defend or promote a commonly understood structured coherence, but to speculatively construct a new regional imaginary. This form of regionalism is thus constrained by the ability of its proponents to institutionalize across spaces which lack formal governance structures, and to establish a new regional imaginary as commonsensical in a world of competitive regions.

Regionalism and economic geography in southern ontario

Toronto is the financial capital of Canada and is surrounded by a sprawling urban fabric which is home to a variety of longstanding and emerging Toronto-centred regions and regionalisms (Figure 1). The most prominent is the Greater Toronto Area (GTA), which encompasses the commuter shed of the core city of Toronto. The GTA is home to 6.4 million people, 2.8 million of whom live in the City of Toronto itself. A more recent outgrowth of that region, the Greater Toronto and Hamilton Area (GTHA; also known as the 'Golden Horseshoe'), includes the Hamilton region to the south-west, which brings the total population to just over 7 million. It is at this scale that the Province of Ontario conducts its regional transit planning, through Metrolinx, a regional transit coordinator and operator established in 2006.

Just over 100 km west of Toronto is the region of Kitchener-Waterloo. This area, despite a modest population of 535,000, has a history of high-innovation firms and research institutions, with the best-known being Research In Motion (RIM), the company behind the BlackBerry. Beginning in the mid-2000s, two specific regionalism initiatives have attempted to connect Kitchener-Waterloo to Toronto. The first, more spatially circumscribed, vision focuses on improving transit accessibility in the corridor through the promotion of allday, two-way rail transit between Toronto and Waterloo. A second, expanded idea, which became known as the Toronto-Waterloo Innovation Corridor (TWIC), attempted to coordinate and market the region as a high-tech powerhouse, and formed the foundation of Toronto's 2017 Amazon HQ2 bid (*Toronto Global,* 2017). TWIC brings together a region of 8.2 million people and about *25%* of Canada's gross domestic product (GDP). A newer group leveraging a similar geography and imaginary is Canada's Innovation Corridor Business Council – an alliance of boards of trade trying to improve goods movement throughout the corridor. A final, even larger, regionalism initiative is the NGen Advanced

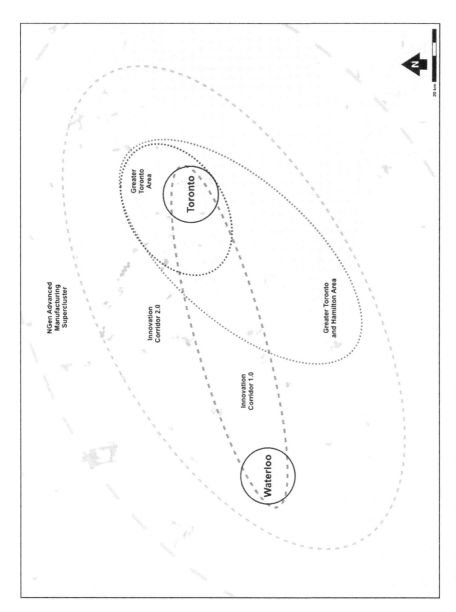

Figure 1 The multiplication of regionalisms around Toronto.
Source: Authors.

Manufacturing Supercluster, which encompasses most of southern Ontario. This project responded to a 2017 federal funding initiative which seeks to root emerging industrial sectors in specific regions across the country. The local leaders in Toronto and Waterloo who spearheaded the supercluster bid responded to the request for proposals by further extending the innovation corridor concept.

In Canada, land-use and development regulation is a provincial responsibility. However, provincial governments tend to limit their role to 'policy designer and custodian of the planning regime' (Pond, 2009, p. 242), delegating day to-day administration of land to local authorities while reserving the right to intervene to pursue provincial objectives (Leffers, 2018). Regional governance arrangements have accordingly ebbed and flowed as provincial governments changed. Under Fordism–Keynesianism, these structures typically aimed at addressing collective-action issues such as coordination between municipalities, planning at the metropolitan scale and local public service provision (Horak & Doyon, 2018). Municipal and regional boundaries reflected commuter sheds, thus allowing local growth coalitions to control local land development. However, ongoing urban growth, particularly along highway corridors, has expanded land markets beyond these boundaries, meaning that growth coalitions can no longer limit their action to their original political preserves (Wachsmuth, 2017a). Without a strong policy intent at the provincial level, the door is left open for other actors to develop new development visions at new planning scales.

Regionalism initiatives in the Toronto area through the 20th century generally followed the first, 'structured coherence' logic of regionalism. By the 1950s, the city had largely filled out its boundaries, at which time suburbanization became the dominant form of development. The Metropolitan Municipality of Toronto (Metro Toronto) was formed in 1954, encompassing Toronto and 12 surrounding municipalities. This arrangement remained in place until the 1990s, when Mike Harris's Progressive Conservatives swept to power on their Common-Sense Revolution, a neoliberal platform which involved the reorganization of municipal and regional governance across the province, most significantly in the GTA. Metro Toronto was reorganized as a single-tier municipality through the merger of all member municipalities in a single local authority. The province chose not to install regional governance mechanisms in the sprawling region, and the role of regional planning is now largely played directly by the provincial government (Frisken, 2001), with local institutions such as regional boards of trade filling in the gaps when needed (e.g., when regional issues become irritants for business). The governance void at the regional scale and the increasingly active role assumed by business interest groups has paved the way for new regionalisms and the instrumentalization of regional imaginaries for the purpose of economic development.

Spatial strategies since the 1990s have taken both topdown and bottom-up forms. The Places to Grow regional growth management framework was established in 2006, however its implementation proved difficult due to on-going antagonism between urban Toronto-centred elites and their suburban counterparts. A companion regional transportation plan, The Big Move, provided C\$50 billion over 25 years to maintain and grow transportation networks at the same time as it reshaped transportation governance through the creation of Metrolinx, a regional coordination body and transit opera-tor. Together, Places to Grow and The Big Move form the policy foundation of the provincial vision for regionalism in the Toronto region, a regionalism premised upon growth management and continued but 'smarter' suburban-ization (Keil & Addie, 2015). Horak (2013) has described this recent set of provincial initiatives as the result of a shift from 'jurisdictional' to 'task-specific rescaling' strategies, with a result being weak institutionalization and chronic instability.

The other side of the coin is a bottom-up regionalism led by local cham-bers of commerce and other local economic development interests: the TWIC. Unlike the provincial government's regional project, which builds on the assumption that the region is an outward extension from a densely populated and economically dominant central city into a suburban hinter-land undergoing significant transformations, the TWIC aims to create a new regional project in territories that are not traditionally thought of as belonging to a single coherent territorial unit. The TWIC exists neither as a recognized statistical region nor as an economic development agency or formal partnership, but it is increasingly important as a regional imaginary anchoring a range of spatial strategies.

The development of a regional imaginary in the Toronto-Waterloo Innovation Corridor (TWIC)

The TWIC spans about 100 km between downtown Toronto and the twin cities of Kitchener-Waterloo, encompassing a population of about 7 million living in the central city of Toronto, five regional municipalities (Durham, Halton, Peel, Waterloo and York) as well as the Guelph urban area. The en-terprise is led by the mayors of the three largest municipalities in the Water-loo Region (Kitchener, Waterloo and Cambridge) and the mayor of Toronto, as well as Communitech and MaRS, two local economic development-cum-innovation hubs based in Kitchener and Toronto, respectively. The Brampton and Mississauga boards of trade, two of Canada's fastest grow-ing municipalities located between Toronto and the Waterloo Region, have also taken on key facilitation roles. This set of actors typically take part in most activities and endeavours taking place under the TWIC umbrella, but each pursues its own set of objectives.

Economic development leaders in the Kitchener-Waterloo region were the first to push for the recognition of Toronto-Waterloo as a single regional unit in the early 2000s. While Ontario was undergoing the neoliberal Common-Sense Revolution, the Waterloo Region was reaping the rewards of another revolution with very local roots: RIM's exponential growth and dominance of the early, pre-iPhone smartphone market with its BlackBerry devices. The close relationship between RIM and the University of Waterloo constituted the foundation of the regional economy and innovation ecosystem for much of the period between the 1990s and early 2010s. After losing its dominant position in the smartphone market, RIM's labour force shrunk from over 19,000 (2011) to just 3200 (2018). BlackBerry's demise was a call to arms for the local business and political community, which increasingly recognized the dangers of relying on a single corporate entity to represent the urban area globally. Diversification thus became the paramount objective of efforts to secure the Waterloo brand. A new regional economic development partnership – Waterloo EDC – was established in 2016, but while Kitchener-Waterloo has become less dependent on a single actor, this growth strategy is facing significant challenges, notably talent attraction and retention, and access to venture capital.

At the same time, Toronto was growing a healthy tech sector rivalling Kitchener-Waterloo in size. Most interviewees, whether Toronto or Waterloo based, agreed that Toronto has selling points that cannot be matched by Waterloo: size, international clout, brand recognition, cultural capital and financial services. But Waterloo has advantages, too: more organized tech business development organizations, a larger share of tech entrepreneurs in relative terms, a culture of learning-by-doing, and an increasing reliance on related variety in the regional economy.

> I think Waterloo brings a globally significant pool of engineering, computer science, mathematics talent that strengthens ... the talent pool for Toronto in a very significant way. What Toronto gives us that we don't have is scale, density, customers, products, money, its critically important capital.
>
> (Waterloo interview 2)

While each could have decided to compete with one another for pre-eminence in the Canadian tech centre, actors at both ends of the corridor agreed to a different strategic objective: competing together to become a top urban tech economy in the world. The objective was given further credence in a 2016 McKinsey report on the economic potential of the TWIC. The goal was to replicate success found in places such as Silicon Valley, Cambridge-London and Tel Aviv-Haifa in order 'to achieve non-linear gains in both job creation and economic value accumulation' (McKinsey & Co., 2016, p. 3). However, while Toronto and Waterloo's labour supply is similar to their counterparts, McKinsey identifies access to venture capital as the region's (and indeed Canada's) weakness. Somewhat murkily, the report argues that the window of opportunity to emerge as a global tech cluster is closing rapidly, claiming, according to 'observers', that '80% of cluster gains will accrue to five global superclusters in the medium to long term' (p. 3).

Developing an effective economic strategy where the regional 'call to action' is strong but there is no pre-existing institutional infrastructure for collaboration has required elites to actively construct the region as a coherent and intuitive territory. Despite its enviable advantages, Waterloo economic leaders came to recognize by the mid-2000s that the city lacked two key elements of what they understood to be successful innovative regions: name recognition and size. Both lacunae could be addressed if Waterloo came to be seen as part of the same region as Toronto, its large and dynamic neighbour.

The original innovation corridor concept mimicked Silicon Valley, given that the distance between Toronto and Waterloo was that between San Francisco and San Jose.

> That's where this corridor notion came from. ... Trying to explain to them that the distance between Kitchener and Waterloo and Toronto is no different than the distance between San Francisco and Silicon Valley, right? That it's the same sort of area, that this is a relationship kind of in the same model, like they have Stanford, we have [University of Waterloo]. This is how it all fits together.
>
> (Toronto interview 2)

As much as the distances were comparable, though, Silicon Valley formed a single labour market for high tech workers due to all-day two-way rail transit (CalTrain), something that was missing between Toronto and Waterloo. Local governments in the Waterloo region produced the maps shown in Figure 2, which suggests that, despite comparable geography and high tech economies, efficient rail transit is the missing link to construct a regional imaginary around innovation (City of Kitchener 2014). Much of the early policy advocacy around the TWIC focused on convincing higher orders of government to fund and build reliable commuter rail infrastructure between the two poles. As Addie and Keil (2015) and Wachsmuth (2017b) highlight, transit infrastructure projects can act as important catalysts for new regional imaginaries.

Local economic leaders and policy-makers in the Waterloo Region were behind the initial push, but there was little interest from Toronto until John Tory's election as mayor in 2014. Mayor Tory's interest in the region was predicated on personal connections with the hightech business community and good relations with several of his counterparts in the Waterloo Region. The corridor is now being used by Waterloo and Toronto economic developers as a sales pitch for the Waterloo Region. Sowing the idea that Waterloo and Toronto constitute a single economic region renders capital and, to a lesser extent, talent attraction efforts easier simply because of name recognition.

As the TWIC project has matured, commuter rail has receded as the main common objective, partly due to Ontario's sluggish infrastructure and transit politics. While funding has been secured to improve rail connections between the two hubs – although not enough to bring it on a par with CalTrain – only a minority of interviewees identified transit as a key aspect of the project as it currently exists. More fundamentally, the provincial government has not proven to be a willing partner in reorienting regional institutions to the corridor, continuing to focus instead on the Toronto-centric concepts of the GTA and GTHA. As a result, local corridor proponents have generally narrowed their focus to strategic opportunities over which they have more direct control: place marketing, talent attraction and retention. The three-pronged marketing strategy is geared towards firm nurturing, retention and attraction, as seen in a TWIC mayoral tour of Silicon Valley in 2016. The goal is to connect two innovation ecosystems in conceptual – and therefore strategic – terms to make them appear as one, both internally and externally.

The second logic of regionalism in the Toronto-Waterloo corridor

The emergence of the TWIC imaginary can be explained through three factors following from the second logic of regionalism: the *productive ambiguity* of the 'the corridor' as a spatial development concept; the presence of a core group of *regionalism entrepreneurs* who champion the idea; and *extrospective policy-making* as a form of rhetorical legitimization. Collectively, these factors have facilitated the development of a set of spatially overlapping economic development strategies across a regional space that until recently was not understood as such.

Productive ambiguity

The TWIC does not exhibit the economic integration which has traditionally been at the heart of the concept of the metropolitan region. In particular, functional connections via daily commuting are very low across the corridor. Figure 3 shows the percentage of commuters from each census tract in southern Ontario who commute to the census metropolitan areas (CMAs) of Kitchener-Cambridge-Waterloo (Figure 3A) and Toronto (Figure 3B) and to the cities of Kitchener and Waterloo (Figure 3C) and Toronto (Figure 3D). Figure 3 indicates that the City of Toronto and the Cities of Kitchener and Waterloo attract most of the commutes from their wider regions. And while some workers commute from the Kitchener-Waterloo area to the western-most fringe of the GTA, effectively zero workers commute from Kitchener–Waterloo to Toronto itself. Toronto-to-Waterloo commuting flows are even sparser. In short, the two CMAs are strongly functionally integrated as labour-sheds, but the wider corridor shows very little evidence of such integration.

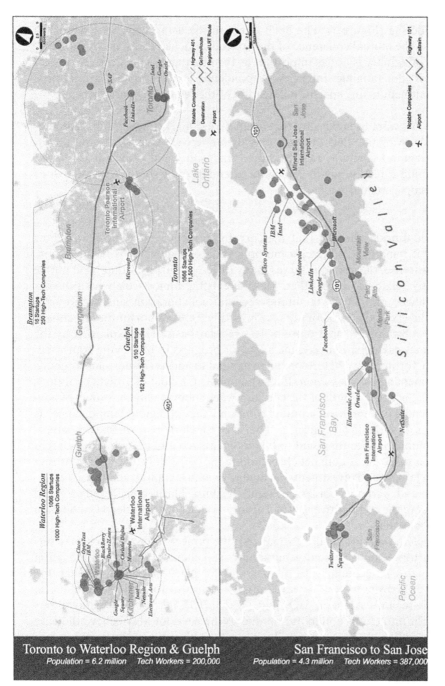

Figure 2 The Toronto-Waterloo Innovation Corridor (TWIC) as a replica of Silicon Valley.
Source: Communitech.

And yet, despite the relative lack of functional integration across the corridor, the sheer number of 'innovation corridor' initiatives taking shape is bewildering (Figure 1). The devil is not in the detail here; as a rhetorical device, the mutual coherence of the projects attached to the innovation corridor imaginary is not as important as the fact that they collectively render the corridor tangible. Interview respondents demonstrated relatively little commitment to any specific delineation of the regional geography:

> I just want to make sure that when we are marketing abroad, that people recognize that this is a very dynamic, very talentrich, and investmentand company-rich corridor. And you could extend it west, you could extend it north, you could extend it to the south. Any number of people could drive it.
>
> (Waterloo interview 2)

On the flipside, the fact that the corridor is recognizable, no matter how fuzzy it remains, facilitates a multiplication of regionalisms in the region. In this sense, the corridor serves many different purposes that need not be directly related to each other. Despite existing almost solely as a discursive device, the TWIC facilitates regional collaboration since it provides key players in the burgeoning region with various opportunities to collaborate substantively on a more or less regular basis. This explains why the informal partnership overcame a lack of progress in improving transit between Toronto and Waterloo, and to expand to address issues such as goods movement across the region. It also augments the clout of growth coalitions across the entire length of the corridor when lobbying higher orders of government. They can form a united front on issues of regional importance, as well as on more local concerns. This is particularly true of smaller, suburban municipalities that tend to be less organized and have fewer resources at their disposal. A core belief sustaining the corridor is that it helps attract and retain capital investment, particularly venture capital, and talent to Waterloo and, perhaps to a lesser extent, Toronto. This is considered essential to ensure the competitiveness of Toronto-Waterloo, and indeed Canada, on a global scale.

Since the corridor is not formalized, the projects attached to it take different forms and different geographies. Stakeholders from the innovation and high-tech economy use the corridor for place-marketing through the TWIC's website as well as trade missions. It also formed the foundation of the region's Amazon HQ2 bid (*Toronto Global,* 2017). Organizations brought into closer collaboration due to the corridor also believe they are better equipped to react to breaking events, such as the recent round of federal funding to create five 'superclusters' across Canada (Innovation, Science and Economic Development Canada, 2018) where firms, universities and economic development corporations in the corridor quickly agreed on an advanced manufacturing concept.

2016 daily commuting in Southern Ontario by city/region of destination

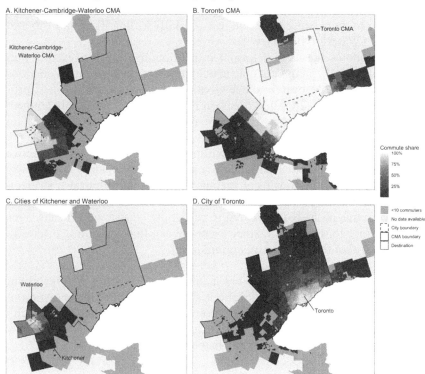

Figure 3 Functional integration in the Toronto-Waterloo Innovation Corridor (TWIC).

Source: Authors.

The case of the corridor demonstrates how non-permanent coalitions can be formed around loosely defined regional imaginaries and regional objectives. This is what Allmendinger and Haughton (2009, p. 631) call 'the functionality of fuzzy boundaries and soft spaces in providing room for strategic and tactical manoeuvre'. In contrast, it appears more difficult to build similar coalitions around issues such as transit, for which formal decision-making processes and structures already exist. A regional imaginary can more easily be used to respond to wicked problems in policy fields lacking ownership on the part of state actors. Ambiguity regarding what regionalism seeks to achieve provides the corridor with enough dynamism and flexibility so that, at worst, most concerned players find no reason to object to the idea. There remains a productive tension that no formal governance exists: efforts are constantly required to keep the group of regional entrepreneurs together, but it also creates a capacity to constantly reinvent the region and jump on opportunities as they arise. As a Waterloo-based economic development official argued: 'Maybe the beauty of this Corridor thing is, you don't ever want a formal kind of leadership team because then you're essentially killing its dynamism and flexibility' (Waterloo interview 1).

The flipside of the lack of formal institutionalization, however, is that relatively few of the many possible articulations of the innovation corridor have proven durable, even in the few years since the concept was first proposed. In particular, an initial focus on transit and infrastructure connectivity between the Toronto and Waterloo nodes has receded in the face of an uncooperative provincial government. By contrast, in the cases where the provincial government has been a willing participant, regional collective action has had a smoother path. This is perhaps most evident in Toronto's Amazon HQ2 bid. Figures from various spatial scales are drawn strategically to dress the region in its best clothes. The innovation corridor is mentioned by name in the bid book, but in very loose geographical terms. This was not cause for complaint, since everyone can find something it likes in one or several of the prospective regionalisms.

> If you look at the Amazon bid it talks about Toronto, it talks about Kitchener–Waterloo, it talks about all the universities in the region, it talks about Markham and Brampton and Mississauga and the capacity they have for advanced manufacturing. It allowed us to tell that story holistically, which I think really helped bring it together.
>
> (Toronto interview 2)

The goal of the corridor is not simply to define and defend a self-evident regional economy, but rather to use the ambiguity to everyone's advantage. A Toronto-based economic development official summarized the thoughts of many interview respondents in blunt terms:

> I don't know where the hell this came from. I arrived on the scene. Apparently the Toronto–Waterloo Corridor was a website. When I looked at it, I said, 'What is that?' Nobody could tell me what it was. So, I said, 'Well, until I know what it is, we're not doing anything on it', but I'm happy to speak about the Toronto–Waterloo region and what it is that we're doing and where the advantages are.
>
> (Toronto interview 1)

This is a common view among corridor economic actors: as long as the imaginary remains useful, its fuzziness does not prohibit them using it if it helps them achieve their goals. But coexisting alongside this relatively unambitious framing of the corridor has been the sense that concretely more positive strategic action has been possible thanks to the shared imaginary of a common region across what was formerly understood as disparate metropolitan regions. The coordination necessary to achieve a unified Amazon HQ2 bid is the clearest example of this outcome:

> [When] the Amazon bid came forward ... you had to apply as a metropolitan area. ... And it was like Toronto is going to [apply] and then Mississauga's going to and Markham's going to and Kitchener–Waterloo's going to do it and Hamilton, and it just seemed a bit ridiculous. So the Province got involved and said, 'Let's do this as a coordinated thing ....' Everybody will be a part of it, but we're not going to have seven different bids, and we're not going to call it the Toronto–Brampton–Mississauga–Guelph bid, we're going to call it the Toronto region bid.
>
> (Toronto interview 2)

The prior existence of a range of economic development collaborations across a sprawling, ill-defined corridor helped facilitate a higher level of collaboration than would have been possible in the absence of the regional imaginary.

Regionalism entrepreneurs

One of the implications of the 'incoherent' regional economies which facilitate the second logic of regional collective action is that regional governance strategies are underdetermined, in the sense that there are potentially multiple strategic equilibria. Regardless of any consensus among economic actors about the importance of regional action, regions in the absence of strong structured coherence do not 'exist' as policy objects to be targeted. Even where regionalism initiatives are densest, and even among the political actors most committed to regionalism, it is rare to find any consensus about the definition or identity of the region. This constitutive uncertainty provides an opportunity for *entrepreneurialism* in the domain of growth coalition formation and regional collective action. If there is no consensus about the form or purpose of the region, then it falls to regionalism entrepreneurs to construct and 'sell' a regional imaginary, in the hopes that locally situated elites will be receptive to their efforts to build coalitions around new governance objectives or configurations. Many different ideas of the region become plausible. Emerging regionalisms thus require dedicated champions who can both create a plausible imaginary as well as legitimize it to internal and external publics. The result is that, among regional actors, the development of regional initiatives is widely interpreted by participants in these initiatives as a leadership problem.

In the context of the TWIC, the key regionalism entrepreneurs have been based in Kitchener-Waterloo, which has most to gain through an economic development partnership with its larger neighbour Toronto. But several respondents also pointed to the specific inclination of Toronto Mayor John Tory to work collaboratively with other mayors despite Toronto's far greater ability to go it alone if necessary. The fact of Toronto's willingness to participate in the TWIC partnership is perhaps the single most important indicator of the importance of entrepreneurship in explaining why regionalism initiatives following the second logic of regionalism emerge. In 'objective' economic terms, Toronto has no need to partner with its much smaller neighbour, and a more strictly Toronto-centric 'structured coherence' style of regionalism is almost certainly more intuitive than a corridor partnership. Indeed, city-regional initiatives in Toronto have continued apace, led by a strong elite civil society amidst the relative lack of formal regional institutions (Boudreau et al., 2006). But aggressive attempts by political and economic leadership in Kitchener and Waterloo to enrol their counterparts in Toronto into a different, larger scale shared vision of a region have been successful. The larger scale regionalism vision is not irrational from the perspective of Toronto elites – it mobilizes an 'infrastructure alliance' style of possible economic agglomerations which is increasingly common (Wachsmuth, 2017b) – but it also is not *necessary*, and explanations for the emergence of the TWIC therefore need to account for this contingency. One Toronto-based respondent summarized the genesis of the corridor initiative almost entirely in the language of leadership and policy entrepreneurialism:

> I think it's just aggressive marketing by Waterloo. Ironically, the latest effort between Kitchener–Waterloo and Toronto is being led by the Kitchener mayor, not by the Waterloo mayor. And by Communitech, which covers both. And there are personal contacts. ... The success and failure of a lot of the stuff in the end comes down to: do the key people who lead the organizations see the merit and the sense of combining?
>
> (Toronto interview 4)

A striking aspect of the multiplication of regionalisms in the TWIC is the overlap in the membership of leadership groups. The same names and organizations came up as the faces and makers of the regional imaginary. Other than the mayors, state actors are typically afforded a secondary role at best. There is a belief among members of the business community that they understand what the region needs, and that higher levels of governments cannot meet those needs swiftly enough (Harrison, 2020). Business leaders see it as their responsibility to act because they view the region as emerging from the economic flows they help create. These actors include leading municipal governments, universities, innovation hubs, financial institutions, chambers of commerce, regional economic development agencies and logistics/transportation operators.

Until recently, these actors worked at the city-regional scale, understanding their respective regions as an urban core with suburban and rural hinterland around it. In the late 1990s and early 2000s, suburban chambers of commerce came to see themselves as part of a regional ecosystem, at the same time as Toronto-based economic development actors came to understand their mandate as more regional rather than just local in scope. A sign of this shift in perception was the renaming of the Toronto Board of Trade to the Toronto *Region* Board of Trade in 2012. At the same time, Waterloo-based economic development actors were confronting the structural limits related to the small size of Kitchener-Waterloo in the global economy. Rapprochement between Toronto and Waterloo had happened under the leadership of leading innovation hubs (MaRS in Toronto and Communitech in KitchenerWaterloo). Both were early adopters of the notion that the technology sector labour market in southern Ontario had to be understood as a single entity, even if actual functional integration of the labour market was relatively minimal (Figure 3) such an understanding of the spatiality of the innovation economy in southern Ontario sowed the seeds of a more meaningful regionalism. Interestingly, the region-building effort was largely led by Waterloo, at least initially, which is the smaller of the two nodes. This testifies to the innovation corridor operating under a different logic – a peripheral centre attaching itself to its neighbouring global city – from a more familiar city-regionalism – a region growing from a core city to absorb territories around it.

Extrospective regionalism

Two decades ago, Peck and Tickell (2002, p. 394) identified a tendency towards 'extrospective' urban policy under neoliberalism: a 'reflexive, and aggressive posture on the part of local elites and states, in contrast to the inward-oriented concerns with social welfare and infrastructure provision under the Keynesian era'. McCann (2013) elaborated this idea in the context of local policy boosterism, whereby local policy-making happens through externally facing efforts by cities to market themselves as policy leaders. Under the conditions that characterize the second logic of regional collective action, extrospective concerns are also central. Regional imaginaries rely on external points of comparison to establish their legitimacy, particularly where these points of comparison allow regionalism entrepreneurs to project an image of a large, powerful, globally competitive region.

The TWIC project is emblematic of these ideas. Various region-building exercises have focused less on achieving internal coherence and institutionalization and more on projecting the corridor to the world (and to local policymakers and residents) as a globally competitive economic entity. To do so, TWIC leaders have relied on images of roughly similar territorial configurations that have gained recognition as leading regions in the knowledge economy: Silicon Valley in particular has been pegged as the model to follow. The buzz is not limited to the business community; a recent article in Canada's leading public affairs magazine asked: 'What if the Toronto-Waterloo corridor really becomes the next Silicon Valley?' (Lee, 2018).

The equation is simple: there are highly competitive regions configured as corridors in other parts of the world, therefore southern Ontario needs one too. Mimicry as a legitimization tool has a dual objective: marketing the new region to the world to attract venture capital and tech talent, but also convincing local business communities, policy-makers and publics of the usefulness and necessity of the corridor. This is the appropriate context in which to understand a TWIC mayoral tour of Silicon Valley in 2016. Southern Ontario leaders visited California to generate interest in the TWIC as an investment opportunity for California tech firms, but arguably more importantly to build a collective regional consciousness *among the TWIC mayors* that the two corridors were comparable. The notion that the innovation corridor can – will? – match the success of Silicon Valley sustains continued work on the initiative.

Alongside mimicry sits 'competitive upscaling', the idea that bigger is better in the global economy (Wachsmuth, 2020). Marketing materials for the corridor are rife with claims of its capacity to rival other places because of its size. An oft-repeated assertion is that the innovation corridor is a top-20 start-up ecosystem in the world, whereas Toronto and Waterloo would not figure in the rankings individually. This fact does not increase the economic output of the region in concrete terms, but adding together the numbers for Toronto and Waterloo makes it appear to be a bigger fish in the global pond:

> [Our] goal on this is quite clear. We want to be one of the top five tech systems in the world. We don't have the scale to do that in Waterloo. For us to compete on a global level, with Silicon Valley, with Israel, with London, it has to be the Toronto–Waterloo corridor.
>
> (Waterloo interview 1)

The idea of competitive upscaling is not purely rhetorical; from a local economic-development perspective, it recognizes the importance of scale to attracting large firms with equally large staffing needs, which is a particularly important concern in Waterloo:

> It's one of the reasons why we joined the Amazon bid. We're too small a community. We don't have room for 50,000 people. We only have 10 million square feet. ... How can a community that can only accommodate 3,000 [new employees] in five years try to land [a firm like Amazon]? So I'd rather have a much smaller percentage of something than 100% of nothing. It's that philosophy. It's better to partner because, again, when Toronto's strong, Waterloo region is strong.
>
> (Waterloo interview 2)

Importantly, while competitive upscaling provides a kind of omnipresent pressure on local economic actors to consider larger partnerships, it is compatible with a variety of different specific territorial and scalar imaginaries. Toronto could get 'bigger' through ongoing monocentric development, or through a corridor partnership, or through both.

Conclusions: the pandora's box of regionalism

The purpose of this paper has been to answer the question: Why and how do regional politics develop in the absence of a coherent regional economy? We introduced a distinction between two 'logics of regionalism' with contrasting incentives and constraints: a familiar logic of territorial alliances rooted in a city-regional structured coherence, and a less familiar logic of regional imaginaries actively constructing regional strategies in novel scalar and territorial configurations. In the presence of a strong policy common sense that regionalism is strategic, but in the absence of a regional 'structured coherence', regional politics in the TWIC has developed through the proliferation of varied and contradictory regional imaginaries.

To conclude, we return to the simple observation of *how many* different versions of the innovation corridor have proliferated in a few short years (Figure 1). Above, we discussed the reality/ephemerality tension at work in supra-city-regional scales, where the 'region' is understood as a key economic space around which to build political strategies and yet has no clear-cut definition or boundaries. Because the reality/ephemerality tension simultaneously urges regional governance experiments while leaving ambiguous the precise form they should take, the result can be something of a Pandora's box. Once a specific regional imaginary takes hold, it becomes imaginatively available more broadly, increasing the likelihood that new permutations of regionalism will be attempted, albeit with no guarantees that they will avoid the longstanding weaknesses of previous modes of regional governance (Harrison, 2007). Regionalism, in this configuration, is not a question to be answered by implementing what Cox (2010) calls the 'good geography', but a restless, dynamic strategy space that abounds with a constant churn of initiatives, institutions and geographies that are not expected to remain stable over time. The TWIC is an illustration of this tendency: the new corridor geography has not replaced pre-existing city-regional geographies. Instead, geographies are steadily being made and remade to meet different objectives, respond to different shortterm imperatives and suit different actors. These geographies are generally weakly institutionalized and sometimes transient, but they collectively amount to an emerging new spatial imaginary.

The transition from the structured coherence of the Fordist-Keynesian era to a structured *incoherence* under suburbanized neoliberalism has allowed regions to become 'floating signifiers', where many potential projects and priorities can become attached to a given regional imaginary. In the case of the innovation corridor, what was initially a push to improve transit connectivity and efficiency between Toronto and Waterloo mutated into a broad but loose forum for regional cooperation on issues such as attracting investment, growing the innovation economy, addressing logistical bottlenecks and ensuring a smooth transition towards advanced manufacturing. All these issues are articulated through the lens of the innovation corridor, but projected at different geographical scales. The many projects and coalitions made possible through its conceptual ambiguity, the belief among key members of local business communities – regionalism entrepreneurs – that the region constitutes the appropriate space of economic activity, and its malleability to project size are all key elements of these new regional dynamics. As such, the endpoint of the regional imaginary cannot be found in a single regional strategy, but in a proliferation of strategies in the region.

Disclosure statement

No potential conflict of interest was reported by the authors.

Funding

This work was supported by a McGill University Internal Social Science and Humanities Development grant [number 243783]; and by the Social Science and Humanities Research Council of Canada [grant number 767-2015-2389].

ORCID

David Wachsmuth ⓘ http://orcid.org/0000-0001-5689-9527

References

Addie, J. P. (2013). Metropolitics in motion: The dynamics of transportation and state reterritorialization in the Chicago and Toronto city-regions. *Urban Geography, 34*(2), 188–217. https://doi.org/10.1080/02723638.2013.778651

Addie, J. P., & Keil, R. (2015). Real existing regionalism: The region between talk, territory and technology. *International Journal of Urban and Regional Research, 39*(2), 407–417. https://doi.org/10.1111/1468–2427.12179

Allen, J., Cochrane, A., & Massey, D. (1998). *Re-thinking the region.* Routledge.

Allmendinger, P., & Haughton, G. (2009). Soft spaces, fuzzy boundaries and metagovernance: The new spatial planning in the Thames Gateway. *Environment and Planning A: Economy and Space, 41*(3), 617–633. https://doi.org/10.1068/a40208

Boudreau, J.-A., Hamel, P., Jouve, B., & Keil, R. (2006). Comparing metropolitan governance: The cases of Montreal and Toronto. *Progress in Planning, 66*(1), 7–59. https://doi.org/10.1016/j.progress.2006.07.005

Brenner, N. (2009). Is there a politics of 'urban' development? In R. Dilworth (Ed.), *The city in American political development* (pp. 121–140). Routledge.

Brenner, N., & Wachsmuth, D. (2012). Territorial competitiveness: Lineages, practices, ideologies. In B. Sanyal, L. J. Vale & C. D. Rosan (Eds.), *Planning ideas that matter: Livability, territoriality, governance and reflective practice* (pp. 179–204). MIT Press.

City of Kitchener. (2014). *Innovative regional economies and strategic infrastructure: The business case for two-way urban commuter rail on the CN North Mainline.* Policy report. Available online at https://www.kitchener.ca/en/resourcesGeneral/Documents/ED_GO_Train_Business_Case.pdf

Cox, K. R. (1993). The local and the global in the new urban politics: A critical view. *Environment and Planning D: Society and Space, 11*(4), 433–448. https://doi.org/10.1068/dll0433

Cox, K. R. (1998). Spaces of dependence, spaces of engagement and the politics of scale, or: Looking for local politics. *Political Geography, 17*(1), 1–23. https://doi.org/10.1016/S0962-6298(97)00048-6

Cox, K. R. (2010). The problem of metropolitan governance and the politics of scale. *Regional Studies, 44*(2), 215–227. https://doi.org/10.1080/00343400903365128

Ekers, M., Hamel, P., & Keil, R. (2012). Governing suburbia: Modalities and mechanisms of suburban governance. *Regional Studies, 46*(3), 405–422. https://doi.org/10.1080/00343404.2012.658036

Feiertag, P., Harrison, J., & Fedeli, V. (2020). Constructing metropolitan imaginaries: Who does this and why? In K. Zimmermann, D. Galland, & J. Harrison (Eds.), *Metropolitan regions, planning and governance* (pp. 155–172). Springer.

Frisken, F. (2001). The Toronto story: Sober reflections on fifty years of experiments with regional governance. *Journal of Urban Affairs, 23*(5), 513–541. https://doi.org/10.1111/0735-2166.00104

Harrison, J. (2007). From competitive regions to competitive city-regions: A new orthodoxy, but some old mistakes. *Journal of Economic Geography, 7*(3), 311–332. https://doi.org/10.1093/jeg/lbm005

Harrison, J. (Forthcoming 2020). Seeing like a business: Rethinking the role of business in regional development, planning and governance. *Territory, Politics, Governance.* https://doi.org/10.1080/21622671.2020.1743201

Harvey, D. (1989). From managerialism to entrepreneurialism: The transformation in urban governance in late capitalism. *Geografiska Annaler: Series B, Human Geography, 71*(1), 3–17. https://doi.org/10.1080/04353684.1989.11879583

Harvey, D. (2001). The geopolitics of capitalism. In *Spaces of capital* (pp. 312–344). Routledge.

Healey, P. (2006). Relational complexity and the imaginative power of strategic spatial planning. *European Planning Studies, 14*(4), 525–546. https://doi.org/10.1080/09654310500421196

Hincks, S., Deas, L, & Haughton, G. (2017). Real geographies, real economies and soft spatial imaginaries: creating a 'more than Manchester' region. *International Journal of Urban and Regional Research, 41*(4), 642–657. https://doi.org/10.1111/1468-2427.12514

Horak, M. (2013). State rescaling in practice: Urban governance reform in Toronto. *Urban Research & Practice, 6*(3), 311–328. https://doi.org/10.1080/17535069.2013.846005

Horak, M., & Doyon, A (2018). Metropolitan governance in Canada: Lessons from Toronto and Vancouver. In R. Tomlinson & M. Spiller (Eds.), *Australia's metropolitan imperative* (pp. 109–122). CSIRO Publ.

Innovation, Science and Economic Development Canada. (2018). *Government of Canada's new innovation program expected to create tens of thousands of middle-class jobs.* Retrieved from https://www.canada.ca/en/innovation-science-economic-development/news/2018/02/government_of_canadasnewinnovationprogramexpectedtocreatetensoft.html

Jessop, B. (2012). Economic and ecological crises: Green new deals and no-growth economies. *Development, 55*(1), 17–24. https://doi.org/10.1057/dev.2011.104

Jessop, B., Peck, J., & Tickell, A. (1999). Retooling the machine: Economic crisis, state restructuring, and urban politics. In A. E. G. Jonas & D. Wilson (Eds.), *The urban growth machine: Critical perspectives, two decades later* (pp. 141–159). State University of New York Press.

Jonas, A. E. G., Goetz, A. R., & Bhattacharjee, S. (2014). City-regionalism as a politics of collective provision: Regional transport infrastructure in Denver, USA. *Urban Studies, 51*(11), 2444–2465. https://doi.org/10.1177/0042098013493480

Keil, R., & Addie, J. P. (2015). 'It's not going to be suburban, it's going to be all urban': Assembling post-suburbia in the Toronto and Chicago regions. *International Journal of Urban and Regional Research, 39*(5), 892–911. https://doi.org/10.1111/1468-2427.12303

Kirkpatrick, L. O., & Smith, M. P. (2011). The infrastructurallimits to growth: Rethinking the urban growth machine in times of fiscal crisis. *International Journal of Urban and Regional Research, 35*(3), 477–503. https://doi.org/10.1111/j.1468-2427.2011.01058.x

Krawchenko, T. (2011). Regional special purpose bodies for transportation and transit in Canada. *Canadian Journal of Regional Science, 34*(1), 1–8.

Lafortune, MÈ, & Collin, J. P. (2011). Building metropolitan governance capacity: The case of the Communauté métropolitaine de Montréal. *Canadian Public Administration, 54*(3), 399–420. https://doi.org/10.1111/j.1754-7121.2011.00182.x

Lee, A. (2018). What if the Toronto-Waterloo corridor really becomes the next Silicon Valley? *Maclean's,* https://www.macleans.ca/economy/what-if-the-toronto-waterloo-corridorreally-becomes-the-next-silicon-valley/

Leffers, D. (2018). Real estate developers' influence of land use legislation in the Toronto region: An institutionalist investigation of developers, land conflict and property law. *Urban Studies, 55*(14), 3059–3075. https://doi.org/10.1177/0042098017736426

Logan, J. R., & Molotch, H. L. (2007). *Urban fortunes: The political economy of place.* University of California Press.

MacLeod, G., & Jones, M. (2011). Renewing urban politics. *Urban Studies, 48*(12), 2443–2472. https://doi.org/10.1177/00420 98011415717

McCann, E. (2013). Policy boosterism, policy mobilities, and the extrospective city. *Urban Geography, 34*(1), 5–29. https://doi.org/10.1080/02723638.2013.778627

McKinsey & Co. (2016). *Primer on technology superclusters and a fact base on Canada's Toronto–Waterloo Innovation Corridor,* https://www.mckinsey.eom/~/media/McKinsey/Featured%20Insights/Americas/Tech%20North/Toronto-Waterloo%20Innovation% 20Corridor%20white%20paper%20-%20fact%20base-20161213.ashx

Offe, C., & Wiesenthal, H. (1980). Two logics of collective action: Theoretical notes on social class and organizational form. *Political Power and Social Theory, 1,* 67–115.

Peck, J., & Tickell, A. (2002). Neoliberalizing space. *Antipode, 34*(3), 380–404. https://doi.org/10.1111/1467-8330.00247

Phelps, N. A. (2012). The growth machine stops? Urban politics and the making and remaking of an edge city. *Urban Affairs Review, 48*(5), 670–700. https://doi.org/10.1177/1078087412440275

Pond, D. (2009). Institutions, political economy and land-use policy: Greenbelt politics in Ontario. *Environmental Politics, 18*(2), 238– 256. https://doi.org/10.1080/09644010802682619

Purcell, M. (2000). The decline of the political consensus for urban growth: Evidence from Los Angeles. *Journal of Urban Affairs, 22*(1), 85–100. https://doi.org/10.1111/0735-2166.00041

Stone, C. (1989). *Regime politics*. University Press of Kansas.

Storper, M. (1997). *The regional world*. Guilford.

Tilly, C. (1985). Models and realities of popular collective action. *Social Research, 52*(4), 717–747.

Tomàs, M. (2012). Exploring the metropolitan Trap: The case of Montreal. *International Journal of Urban and Regional Research, 36*(3), 554–567. https://doi.org/10.1111/j.1468-2427.2011.01066.x

Toronto Global. (2017). Toronto region response to amazon HQ2 RFP. *Toronto Global*. Retrieved from https://torontoglobal.ca/amazon

Wachsmuth, D. (2017a). Competitive multi-city regionalism: Growth politics beyond the growth machine. *Regional Studies, 51*(4), 643–653. https://doi.org/10.1080/00343404.2016.1223840

Wachsmuth, D. (2017b). Infrastructure alliances: Supply-chain expansion and multi-city growth coalitions. *Economic Geography, 93*(1), 44–65. https://doi.org/10.1080/00130095.2016.1199263

Wachsmuth, D. (2020). Competitive upscaling in the state: Extrospective city-regionalism. In S. Moisio, N. Koch, A. E. G.Jonas, C. Lizotte, & J. Luukkonen (Eds.), *The handbook on the changing geographies of the state* (pp. 355–367). Edward Elgar.

Weber, R. (2010). Selling city futures: The financialization of urban redevelopment policy. *Economic Geography, 86*(3), 251–274. https://doi.org/10.1111/j.1944-8287.2010.01077.x

Planning megaregional futures: spatial imaginaries and megaregion formation in China

John Harrison◉ and Hao Gu◉

Introduction: planning megaregional futures

> if regional planning is challenging, the megaregional level would be even harder.
>
> (Wheeler, 2015, p. 100)

> Although the importance of promoting urbanisation is fully recognised by political and academic circles, due to their late development – less than 35 years ago in China, which is around 80 years later than Western countries – the basic connotations, spatial delineation, degree of development, and construction foci of urban agglomerations in China are less certain and more contentious.
>
> (Fang, 2015, p. 1007)

The expansion of globalizing cities into larger city-regions and, most recently, megaregions is posing fundamental questions about how best to plan and govern 21st-century urban regions. Owing to the relentless pace of urban economic expansion, emergent transmetropolitan landscapes - so-called 'megaregions', but often referred to by other monikers including mega-city regions (Xu & Yeh, 2011), multi-city regions (Wachsmuth, 2017), megalopolis (Lang & Knox, 2009), polycentric metropolis (Hall & Pain, 2006) and mega-conurbations (Friedmann & Sorensen, 2019) – are identified as globalization's newest urban form. With this, the clamour call that megaregions represent the ideal scale for policy intervention continues to grow. For their part, advocates argue that ever larger urban-regional economies are superseding nations as the fundamental drivers of growth in the global economy (Florida, Gulden, & Mellander, 2008; Khanna, 2016). What they cannot agree on is the spatiality of megaregions. This is important because how megaregions are imagined defines the spatial scale over which institutions have jurisdiction and responsibility, policies are designed and implemented for, and planning enacted.

Today, boosterist accounts of megaregions being globally competitive territories par excellence are offset by a growing body of critical work examining the politics of megaregion formation (Harrison & Hoyler, 2015; Schafran, 2014; Wachsmuth, 2017). These accounts do not deny the strong geoeconomic logic explaining the rise of megaregions, nor do they necessarily undermine the concept of megaregion as a new spatial and planning imaginary; instead, they reveal how actors increasingly 'megaregionalize' space to exert influence by encouraging the privileging of certain locations, policies and programmes when decisions on major new strategic investments for capital expansion, infrastructure and social provision are being made (Jonas & Moisio, 2018). Acting as an important point of confluence between these geoeconomic and geopolitical perspectives is the recognition that megaregional spaces are supported by inadequate urban economic infrastructure, planning and governance arrangements (Harrison & Hoyler, 2014; Kantor, Lefèvre, Saito, Savitch, & Thornley, 2012; Xu & Yeh, 2011). What we have arrived at is a situation whereby the megaregion concept is providing both the fuel and the vehicle for demands to design and implement more apropos forms of planning and governance.

Nowhere is the challenge of planning megaregional futures more acute than China. Today, China has an urban population of 831 million, a figure currently increasing by approximately 20 million per annum. More than this, the 2017 urbanization rate was 1.2 percentage points higher than 2016, and 6 percentage points higher than 2012, while over the past decade the percentage urban population has increased from 45.9% to 59.6% (National Bureau of Statistics of China (NBS), 2019). Looking further ahead, the stated aim of the Communist Party of China (CPC) is for the urban population to reach 70% within the next decade. Not surprisingly, the concept of megaregion has become increasingly prominent in China's national and regional level plans for urbanization and spatial development (Fang, 2015; Wu, 2015) (see below).[1] Nonetheless, despite an expanding body of work mobilizing the concept of megaregion to understand China's urban development, for the most part this has been focused on their functionally networked characteristics (by measuring integration via intra-regional city connectivity and degrees of polycentricity; Li & Phelps, 2017; Taubenböck & Wiesner, 2015; Zhang, Derudder, Wang, & Shen, 2018), territorial-scalar characteristics (by assessing their emergence as 'new state spaces'; Li & Wu, 2018; Sun & Chan, 2017; Wu, 2016), or land-use characteristics (by quantifying the rate of urban expansion and assessing its economic, social and environmental impact; Tan, 2017). Allied to this, there is a tendency in most intellectual and practical debates about planning and governing megaregions in China to focus on (one of) the three main coastal megaregions – the Pearl River

Delta (PRD), Yangtze River Delta (YRD) and Beijing-Tianjin-Hebei (also known as Jing-Jin-Ji, or JJJ). What is missing is a clear understanding of the political project that is Chinese megaregionalism and its planning implications therefrom.

Starting from the position that we need to debunk some of the inherent assumptions surrounding megaregions in China, we aim to broaden our horizons beyond the narrow focus on what people have come to assume are China's megaregions to consider megaregionalism in China for what it actually is: an always evolving political-economic project orchestrated by the CPC through a combination of spatial development strategies and urbanization policies to manage the complex relationship between increased exposure to external global capitalist market forces while maintaining tight authoritarian control over internal domestic matters. We attach importance to this because understanding how the megaregion concept is being reimagined to manage urban and regional development is a 'crucial, yet somewhat under-researched, dimension of megaregional research' (Harrison & Hoyler, 2015, p. 22). China is no different, with the selection of megaregions increasingly 'subject to strong government leadership' and departing from the basic premise of their development (Fang, 2015, p. 1014). All of which raises a fundamental question, namely: can we actually plan megaregional futures?

The aim of the paper is to reveal the largely untold story of megaregion formation in China and consider its planning implications. To achieve this, the next section offers a brief history of the link between megaregions and planning, identifying the importance of recognizing the politics of megaregion formation, before setting the context for understanding how the politics of megaregionalism has risen to prominence alongside China's urban expansion. Analysing the evolving cartographic representation of China's attempts to megaregionalize national urban systems from 2005 onwards, the third section examines how and why the megaregion concept is being mobilized, adapted and moulded on behalf of the state and its interests. Finally, the fourth section distinguishes between *planning megaregions* (as discursive and imagined) and *megaregional planning* (as concrete and actual) to make a series of wider points about the purpose of planning and the scope to plan megaregional futures, drawing interviews with those directly involved in advising the framing of China's megaregions.

Planning megaregional pasts, presents and futures

Megaregions and planning: a brief history

For over a century there has been a close link between megaregions and planning.[2] This dates to the pioneering Scottish town planner Patrick Geddes, who, some 40 or so years before Jean Gottmann, mobilized 'megalopolis' as a concept for understanding cities of exaggerated size and as a place when identifying the 500-mile urban corridor along the US Atlantic coast as the exemplar (Geddes, 1915). Adopted and subsequently developed by the American Lewis Mumford, the link between megaregions and planning in the first half of the 20th century saw a firm belief not in planning *for* megaregional futures but planning *to avoid* megaregions. The thinking was that to achieve the status of being a megaregion was not something to aspire to; rather, it was a sure sign of imminent and cataclysmic disintegration (Mumford, 1938). In contrast, a new planning paradigm emerged for the second half of the 20th century centred on the contribution of Gottmann and his enthusiasm for megaregions epitomizing the very essence of progressive urbanism (Gottmann, 1957). Despite their undoubted differences, all three advocated comprehensive regional planning as opposed to piecemeal local planning confined to city limits.

The link between this era and the modern-day interest in megaregions is the British planner Peter Hall. In his study of 'Megalopolis England', Hall (1973) highlights how Gottmann never clearly defined what he meant by 'megalopolis', and reveals how in England at least, while the functional existence of a megalopolis could be claimed to exist, its physical existence had been denied by planning and the insistence on curbing urban sprawl. Three decades on, Hall returned to lead a major study documenting the characteristics of megaregions in Europe (Hall & Pain, 2006). This study demonstrated the profound consequences of megaregions for spatial planning and regional development in Europe, and, by implication, other parts of the world, because by this time megaregions were a 'truly global concept' (Harrison & Hoyler, 2015). Developments at this time in the United States, where the Regional Plan Association had identified 10 megaregions as key to their future competitive, Europe, for whom the London-Paris-Milan-Munich-Hamburg 'pentagon' was established through the European Spatial Development Perspective as its megaregional future, and Asia, where urban expansion and investment in infrastructure at the scale of urban megaregions (most notably high-speed rail links), ensured that assessing the 'usefulness of the megaregion and spatial planning' became an – and for some, *the* – urgent task for planners and policy-makers alike (Ross, 2009, p. 3). Fuelled by boosterist accounts trumpeting megaregions as globalization's newest urban-economic form, alongside international organizations advocating how megaregions were coming to represent the ideal scale for 21st-century spatial planning and policy intervention, this was also the time that China began actively to formulate a top-down national-level plan for urbanization and spatial development centred on megaregions.

Rethinking the geography of megaregions: the politics of megaregion formation

Today, there is a growing convergence of academic interest in exposing the need to 'rethink the geography of megaregions' for planning and governance purposes (Schafran, 2014, p. 90). This convergence is not especially new in regional studies per se, but it does highlight once more the remarkable fissure that exists between the economics and politics of regions. Looking retrospectively, in the 1990s it was a global mosaic of regions (Scott, 1998), then in the 2000s it was a network of city-regions (Scott, 2001), and now in the 2010s it is a brave new world of competitive megaregions (Florida et al., 2008) which are to be found front and centre of powerful and appealing 'new regionalist' claims that the nation-state, and the wider state system more generally, are being supplanted in globalization. Each time a discourse of competitiveness underpins these new growth-oriented orthodoxies (Harrison, 2007), itself derived from the 'new economic geography theory that growth in globalization results from self-perpetuating agglomeration (or spatial concentration) in economically advantageous locations, and which could increasingly be seen permeating policy-making and planning practices as actors desperately seek to promote and sustain urban and regional development within their jurisdiction.

The implication is that political actors – most notably national state governments – are increasingly passive in, and responsive to, the megaregionalization of geographical space. But this is not the case. For what has been demonstrated is just how active state (and other) actors are in promoting and sustaining these large-scale agglomerations (Harrison & Hoyler, 2015). Megaregions may be an urban-economic reality, but they are also a calculated political project. Accepting this, Jonas and Moisio (2018, p. 355) have taken to revealing how '[as the] concept becomes enrolled in the service of the state, it is in turn adapted and moulded to fit the state's wider policy agendas'. From this vantage point, megaregions suddenly appear very different. They appear as the outcome of economic and political processes,[3] something which requires a new narrative to be written if we are genuinely to understand the geography of megaregions and, accordingly, plan megaregional futures (cf. Scott, 2019).

It follows that if state territorial interests and geopolitical processes are essential elements in planning and governing megaregions, then we must build them into our theories. Ergo, there is no better starting point for considering megaregional futures than China. For nowhere is the emergence of transmetropolitan polycentric urban regions more self-evident, and yet planning coordination for megaregions 'remains one of the most neglected policy areas in China' (Xu & Yeh, 2011, p. 214).

China's megaregions: in search of a plan[4]

In the early 2000s, the Chinese central government embraced the global trend towards megaregions and began actively to megaregionalize the national space economy. This marked a significant change in approach because before this megaregional growth was actively discouraged a la Geddes and Mumford, rather than embraced a la Gottmann. To reveal the unfolding megaregion project in China, we align our framing with Wu's (2016) analysis of changing state spatial selectivity in China as centring on three distinct phases: state socialism (1949–78), early market reform (1979–2000) and post-World Trade Organisation (WTO) market society (2001-present).

1949–78: Centrally planned period of anti-urban ideology

In the pre-reform era, an emphasis on promoting balanced regional growth was linked to an anti-urban ideology that discouraged rural to urban migration in China. From the 1st Five-Year Plan (1953–57) a fundamental principle of strictly controlling the excessive growth of cities, especially the size of large cities, existed and remained all the way through to the 10th Five-Year Plan (2001–05). Urbanization proceeded very slowly, with the spatial focus prioritizing China's interior rural areas and a small number of interior industrial cities. Politically, the planning system was very hierarchical, controlling and served to enforce state control. By implication, horizontal linkages were not considered important. Regions were dependent on their centres and inward-looking, such that networked cities hardly existed.

1979–2000: Post-reform economic transition and the onset of early megaregionalism

China's post-reform macroeconomic strategy shifted from equity-oriented balanced spatial development ideology to an efficiency-oriented competitiveness ideology based on facilitating economic growth by embracing more entrepreneurial modes of economic governance and capitalizing on locational advantages. Part of this saw top-down interest in exploring horizontal linkages between cities and regions by recognizing economic regions and establishing informal government coalitions and institutional alliances. A notable example, highlighted by Wu (2016), was the Shanghai Economic Region, which was established by the State Council in 1982 to operate across 10 cities and five provinces in the YRD and charged with preparing its own regional development strategy. Albeit centrally mandated, these economic regions were freed from the political control of the hierarchical planning frameworks for enforcing state control and encouraged to be more experimental and entrepreneurial in the pursuit of growth. Locational advantages derived from their industrial and infrastructure base resulted in the spatial focus for economic activities and resources switching from interior cities and rural areas to coastal cities. This said, politically, central government policy remained unchanged on the fundamental principle that the size of large cities should be strictly controlled, with the emphasis placed on actively expanding the size of small and medium-sized cities (Zhang, 2019).

2001-Present: Comprehensive reform and megaregions unleashed

In the early 2000s it was clearly unsustainable to promote economic growth focused on coastal cities while at the same time politically restricting large city growth. Having started to recognize the locational advantages of the PRD, YRD and JJJ as megaregional spaces in the 1980s and 1990s, the central government gradually began to plan accordingly. By the time of the 10th Five-Year Plan (2001–05), the fundamental principle of strictly controlling the size of large cities was abandoned in favour of promoting the coordinated development of large, medium and small-sized cities. This was not to be at the expense of interior cities and provinces but sought to capitalize on China's coastal megaregions by replicating their success through state support for targeted industrial planning and fiscal policies towards interior provinces, alongside a coordinated national strategy to develop horizontal linkages and networked cities.

China's 11th Five-Year Plan (2006–10) went a stage further, advocating megaregions as 'the main entity for driving urbanisation' and thus the 'the main players' in how urban development should be planned. The critical distinction was that China's spatial planning framework was no longer centred on large individual cities and their urban expansion, but on functionality and the connecting of key cities, national-level megaregions and internationally competitive megaregions in a nationally networked urban system (Li & Jonas, 2019). This coincided with, and was to be enabled by, the central government's *2004 Railway Network Plan* (State Council, 2004), which called for four high-speed lines running north-south (verticals) and four lines running east-west (horizontals) to construct a high-speed rail network connecting China's largest cities by 2020.[5] Further evidence for this strategy came in the 12th Five-Year Plan (2011–15) which included two horizontal and three vertical axes of urbanization intersected by megaregions.

Prompting the change from discriminating to embracing megaregion development were a series of economic (*competitiveness*) and political (*control*) factors:

- The widening gap between coastal and interior areas.
- The requirement for new models of economic growth as China's economy matured that went beyond the exportoriented 'workshop of the world' growth model that marked early post-reform expansion.
- The need to address the problem of political fragmentation caused by decentralization in the 1980s and 1990s which had weakened the planning and governing capacities of China's largest urban regions.
- The belief that strategic planning at the megaregion scale was a key political strategy – for provincial and central governments – to regain and reassert control over local and regional development.
- The recognition that for all the endeavours to restrict large city growth, economic agglomeration continued to overcome state administrative controls.

- The competition between provinces for national recognition escalating once they saw the three coastal megaregions securing preferential central government support by virtue of having the kitemark of being identified in planning and policy circles as a megaregion.

This last point is most evident in the current 13th Five-Year Plan (2016–20). Megaregions remain the fundamental spatial unit for state planned urbanization, but there is a refocusing of attention on securing the international competitiveness of the three coastal megaregions over and above the development of national-level megaregions. More generally, megaregionality is now so rife in the Chinese psyche that it is 'making entry to urban agglomerations into political projects' as actors see inclusion being key for cities to thrive, while exclusion is feared to bring about dependency and stunted growth (Fang, 2015, p. 1014) (see also below). The argument here is that at this most discursive level, we can see that the Chinese state is constantly dealing with the task of managing seemingly conflicting priorities, that is, planning *with* megaregions: namely, orchestrating how the megaregion concept can be mobilized to project their international competitiveness externally while simultaneously managing internal domestic challenges.

Governing future urban systems: planning, imaginaries and the politics of megaregion formation in china

The aim in the remainder of the paper is to reveal how the megaregion concept is being mobilized in China. In this way we are directly responding to Jonas and Moisio's (2018, p. 353) contention that 'state territorial interests and geopolitical processes remain for the most part absent from mainstream policy and planning literatures' on city-regionalism and megaregionalism by examining how and why the megaregion concept is being adapted and moulded on behalf of the state and its interests. To achieve this, we analyse the evolving cartographic representation of China's attempts to megaregionalize the national urban systems plan from 2005 onwards through a series of representative maps. We do this because not only are cartographic representations powerful instruments in the planning process but also they provide a lens through which researchers can uncover the politics of state spatial planning – something Dühr (2007, p. 1) explains:

> Cartographic representations can help to focus dialogue and to shape discourses, but they may also be used to manipulate other participants in the process by distorting or highlighting certain facts. ... The decision on what should be 'put on the map', and how it is going to be presented, opens up great potential to shape discourse, to empower some parts of the public or the territory, and to disadvantage others.

In much the same way, Boria (2008) introduces the notion of 'geopolitical cartography' to remind us of the persuasive potential of maps. For Boria, what matters is the 'cartographic message', because simplified cartographic visualizations are only used when there is the intention to communicate with a large audience. To this end, simplified maps cannot be gauged by technical standards such as cartographic precision and scientific accuracy but by their communicative effectiveness, which is inherently open to subjectivity, persuasion and political bias.

From our perspective, cartographic representations are important in how they make visible the politics of 'planned' megaregionalism. They reveal how actors are actively megaregionalizing space. They attempt to translate a complex reality to its simplified configuration. Tensions, conflicts, overlaps and contradictions are worked through and made complementary alternatives, even though the empirical reality is very different. This is a deeply politicized process, one open to subjective and biased interpretations of spatial development trends, but which makes visible what are hitherto often concealed processes and interests.

Perhaps the most instructive part though is their potential to facilitate dialogue across different contexts. Recognizing that megaregionalism takes on national and regionally specific forms, a key challenge is to establish ways that promote greater engagement and comparison across contexts and territories. Comparative regionalism places a requirement on common tools, shared vocabulary and clear analytical frameworks to enable the cross-fertilization of ideas (Paasi, Harrison, & Jones, 2018). We would argue that spatial maps are an important tool in facilitating this due to the ease of translation across, and comparison between, different geographical contexts.

To this end, the following section examines four spatial maps produced in the period since 2005 when the state government first produced a strategic spatial map of megaregions. The four maps were selected on the basis that they reflected the three key stages in the framing of China's megaregions – National Urban Systems Plan (2005–06), National Main Functional Area Plan (2010–14) and National New-Type Urbanisation Plan (2014–) – with two maps selected in the first stage to highlight the politics at play as the initial 'outline' vision quickly morphed into a heavily reworked version of essentially the same spatial map by the time the plan came to be 'adopted' only one year later.

Stage 1: National urban system planning and the politics of upscaling

Planning in China is a tripartite system. Since the 1990 City Planning Act, the Ministry of Housing and Urban-Rural Development (MOHURD[6]) has been responsible for urban and regional planning, and the preparation of a national urban system plan to guide provincial urban system planning and urban master planning. In 1998, responsibility for land-use planning was with the Ministry of Land Resources, now part of the new Ministry of

Natural Resources established in 2018. Finally, there is the National Development Reform Commission (NDRC) which has been preparing five-year social and economic development plans since 1953.[7] Each has had an important role in shaping megaregionalism as a political project, beginning in 2005 when the MOHURD started to prepare the National Urban System Plan (2005–20).

The 2005–20 plan was significant in upscaling the spatial framing of urban systems planning and marked the first time the state government produced a strategic spatial map of megaregions (Figure 1). The 2005 outline map proposes a 3 + 4 + 4 + 13 model, emphasizing the strategic importance of the three main internationally competitive megaregions (PRD, YRD, JJJ – denoted by extra-large red circles), four national-level megaregions (Liaozhongnan, Wuhan, Xi'an, Chengdu-Chongqing – large red circles), four regional-level megaregions (Shandong, Haixia, Zhengzhou, Changsha-Zhuzhou-Xiangtan – medium orange circles), with a further 13 developing urban agglomerations (small blue circles). The three coastal megaregions are each shown to contain a network of cities comprising a combination of globally-nationally important (red dots) and regional-level cities (green dots), while 19 of the remaining 21 comprise a single regional-level city. Alongside this is an infrastructure framework based on 4 vertical + 4 horizontal axes, and nationally differentiated into three levels: a primary coastal megaregion

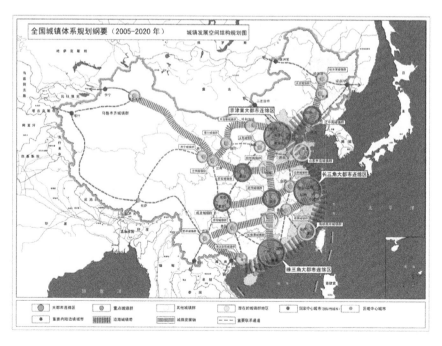

Figure 1 The 'outline' National Urban System Plan, 2005–20.
Source: China Academy of Urban Planning and Design (2005).

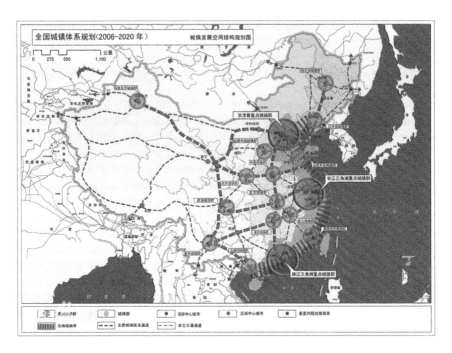

Figure 2 The 'adopted' National Urban System Plan, 2006–20.
Source: Ministry of Construction (2007, p. 45).

belt connecting the PRD-YRD-JJJ, secondary belts connecting all 24 urban agglomerations and tertiary links connecting with regional-level cities located outside of urban agglomerations and border cities.

By 2006 the discursive framing of China's megaregions already showed signs of shifting priorities. The National Urban Systems Plan (2006–20) adopted map changed from a 3 + 4 + 4 + 13 urban structure to a much simpler 3 + 14 model (Figure 2). The plan assigns far more strategic importance to the three coastal megaregions, PRD-YRD-JJJ, by effectively removing second-tier megaregions. In 2005, the national-level megaregions were identified by the same red circle as PRD-YRD-JJJ. The only differentiation was the size of the symbol. In 2006, the red circle symbol is reserved for PRD-YRD-JJJ and increases in size, while at the same time Liaozhongnan, Wuhan, Xi'an and Chengdu-Chongqing are now demarcated by the smaller green circle previously assigned to third-tier megaregions. Special status in the spatial framing is further enabled with the 'belt' symbol reserved solely for the coastal belt connecting PRD-YRD-JJJ, with all second-tier infrastructure seeing the secondary urban belt symbolism replaced and represented by primary links. A series of additional connecting lines are added in the west and north-east. A second notable development is the declassification of seven regional-level agglomerations: one is captured by the enlarged

YRD megaregion, while the other six – each located towards the western and northern edges of megaregionalized East China – appear only as regionally important cities.

The problem facing the MOHURD was that for its national urban systems planning to become more than a rhetorical and discursive framing device it would require the NDRC to support and develop it into a national economic development strategy. This is because although the MOHURD is an important institutional component in China's tripartite planning system, it lacked the power to implement policy directly and this plan was never enshrined in statutory planning practice.

Stage 2: National main functional area planning – a new 'scientific' approach to megaregional planning

In 2006, the State Council empowered the NDRC to prepare the National Main Functional Area Plan (*zhuti gongnengqu guihud*). Published in 2010, this plan gained traction because unlike the MOHURD, the NDRC has the authority over economic development and resource allocation to start putting theory into practice. Once more megaregions were the fundamental basis for the spatial structure, but in stark contrast to the hierarchy of megaregions created by the MOHURD, the NDRC vision is of a far more horizontal and spatially balanced urban system (Figure 3). The number of NDRC megaregional spaces (21) is midway between the 2005 (24) and 2006 (17) MOHURD plans, but no differentiation is made between any of the 21 megaregions, 37 cities, or axes connecting them. The NDRC also replaces the MOHURD base map of three macro-regions – West, Central, East, which were coloured light-mid-deep yellow to represent their degree of urban-industrial development – with China's underlying ecological footprint. The major lines on the base map are no longer political-administrative boundaries, which have been removed entirely, but rivers and topography. And instead of three levels of belts and axes, only one appears, with smaller functional links removed to leave only two horizontal and three vertical major axes connecting all but one megaregion – Lhasa in Tibet.

All of which reflects the NDRCs endeavour to depoliticize the new spatial imaginary of China's megaregions, aided and abetted by a new 'scientific' approach to delimiting megaregions (Fan, Sun, Zhou, & Chen, 2012). But this belies what remained a deeply politicized vision. First and most obviously, the spatial differentiation of China's megaregions became very confusing as JJJ (rebranded as the Bohai Economic Rim) was represented by far the largest megaregional configuration, the YRD becomes comparable with the neighbouring Middle Yangtze megaregion of Wuhan–Nanchang–Changsha, and the PRD appears as one of the smaller megaregions. This is despite the PRD-YRD-JJJ continuing to be singled out in the plan itself as being of superior strategic importance.

The primary intention of the NDRCs plan was to manage development spatially by identifying four main functional areas: *prioritized* for industrial and urban growth; *optimized* for industrial areas that require moving away from resource-intensive modes; *restricted* due to ecological concerns; and *prohibited* where development is not permitted. This zoning was applied to megaregions in two ways: the PRD–YRD–JJJ were identified as development-optimized megaregions, with the remaining 18 megaregions earmarked for development prioritized (Fan et al., 2012); and megaregions were the zones identified for growth and upgrading, but prohibited in ecological zones for containment and preservation. Within this reaffirmation of the PRD–YRD–JJJ as distinct megaregions, there was though a singling out of JJJ as 'the *main region* in which China participates in economic globalization' and reflected in the importance afforded to this megaregion in Figure 3 (State Council, 2010, emphasis added).

A deeper analysis of the NDRC map reveals many more politicized aspects. First, and although the axes of development have been flattened to remove any prioritization, some primary links from the MOHURD maps are removed altogether (Nanning-Kumming, Chengdu-Lanzhou, Guiyang-Changsha-Nanchang-Ningbo), while others have been upgraded (Chongqing-Xi'an) or added (Xi'an-Yinchuan). Second, Wuhan, Changsha and Nanchang, which were previously separate regions, are conjoined to form the Middle Yangtze megaregion; while further north, the much more proximate cities of Taiyuan and Shijiazhuang remain separate due, in part, to the latter being in Hebei and more aligned with JJJ. Perhaps most revealing is how despite the 'Belt and Road Initiative' providing the centrepiece of China's new foreign policy since 2013 – the basis of which is developing interconnectivity of infrastructure development that places China as the focal point strategically, economically and politically – all axes now stop short of the border, such that all development is internalized and stops at the final megaregion on each axis.

Stage 3: National new urbanization – combining 'imagined' and 'actual' geographies of megaregions

March 2014 saw the CPC Central Committee State Council approve the implementation of China's National New Urbanisation Plan (2014–2020), which included the latest spatial vision for planning development in and through megaregions. This remained identical to Figure 3 except for the axes which were all removed (NDRC, 2014). Significant change was to come though when the NDRC prepared a new map for the 13th Five-Year Plan (2016–20) (Figure 4). The basic spatial pattern of three vertical and two horizontal axes remains unchanged, as does the geography. The major change is the representation of megaregions to appear even less hierarchical, and project a much more balanced urban system. First, the large JJJ megaregion has been reconfigured from one very large (JJJ) and two small megaregions

(Shandong, Shijiazhuang) into three equally sized megaregions (JJJ, Liao, Shandong), which also sees Shijiazhuang formally part of JJJ. This is indicative of a broader trend to equalize the size of megaregions, with all smaller megaregions now appearing visibly larger.

A second key observation is the transition from stylized representations of megaregions (Figures 1–3) to a new representation that comprises both stylized elements (the political representation of megaregions – dashed orange lines – and development axes) and actual urban-economic and political geographies (Figure 4). This takes on three forms. First, we have an attempt to concretize the spatial form of urban agglomeration at the megaregion scale. By this we mean the introduction of new symbolism to map urban form as agglomeration, with differentiation between dense (red) and less-dense (pink), and often extending beyond the stylized denoting of the megaregion and its limits. Second, we see the return of administrative boundaries representing China's 23 provinces and five autonomous regions (*zìzhìqū*).[8] This reveals how all except two can claim to be included in China's megaregional future by virtue of having one megaregion (or part thereof) within their jurisdiction. The two exceptions are the territories of Tibet and Taiwan, which both contain key cities outside of megaregions (in Tibet, Lhasa has been downgraded from its previous megaregion status, while Taipei is recognized for the first time) alongside the special administrative regions (*tèbié xíngzhèng qū*) of Hong Kong and Macau. And related to this, third, cities that are not globallynationally-regionally important are now evident for the first

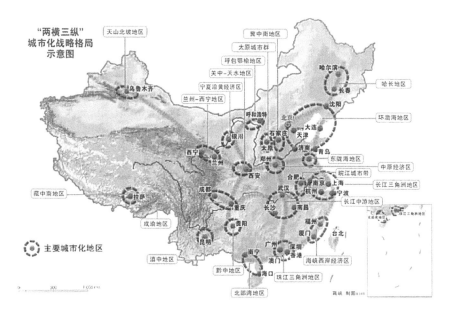

Figure 3 The National Main Functional Area Plan.
Source: NDRC (2010).

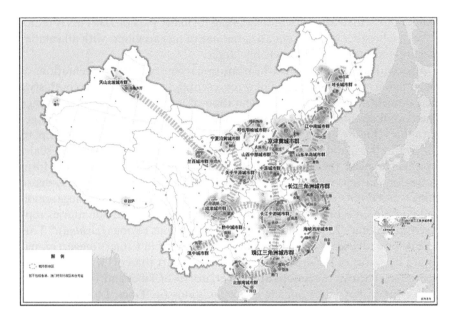

Figure 4 The national new-type urbanization plan.
Source: NDRC (2016, p. 64).

time. This includes significantly more cities located outside megaregions than it does within. Moreover, there is the added dimension which is that it is now far more difficult to identify those globally-nationally-regionally important cities (red dots, red circles) vis-à-vis medium (white) and smaller sized (dot) cities, and on the map overall.

What we have across these four spatial visions is a series of steps to flatten out the megaregionalization of the Chinese space economy into what now appears to be a more spatially balanced and inclusive urban system. This has involved transitioning from an imaginative and symbolic representation of megaregionalization to layering this evolving spatial imaginary onto actually existing geographies. In this way, Figure 4 also reveals attempts to make complementary China's two spatial organizing patterns: the *imagined* horizontal networked urban system centred on two vertical and three horizontal axes consisting of 19 megaregion agglomerations; and the *actual* hierarchical spatial pattern of large, medium and small-sized cities around which traditional planning is oriented (Fang & Yu, 2016). It also belies the hidden geographies of megaregions.

Megaregionalism beyond the map

Analysing the evolving cartographic representation of China's attempts to megaregionalize national urban systems reveals the politics of the megaregion formation in national spatial planning. What these maps cannot indicate, however, is what, if anything, makes these megaregional imaginaries meaningful in any significant way. In other words, can we actually 'do' planning at the megaregion scale? It is with this in mind that we find it useful to distinguish between *planning megaregions* (as discursive and imagined) and *megaregional planning* (as concrete and actual): the former relating to what we have discussed to this point, whereas the latter directs us to where the debate needs to move towards. Indeed, drawing on this distinction allows us to offer some cautionary remarks about the extent to which we can begin to think about planning megaregional futures.[9]

First, we must never assume that planning competencies lay behind these cartographic representations of megaregions. As one well-placed interviewee reflected:

> JJJ, YRD, PRD are the three megaregional growth poles. Everyone wanted to be number four. But they just want the name, the tide. It is actually meaningless. Even the three megaregion growth poles, there is no spatial policy for them.

While this interviewee might refer to the 'meaningless' pursuit of megaregional status when considering the planning strategy and competencies that accompany it, it is anything but meaningless to those stakeholders representing cities and regions located outside the three internationally recognized coastal megaregions. Indeed, for many, they are so fixated on the planning megaregions mantra that they neglect the purpose of planning altogether and consider megaregion status to be *the* achievement:

> Some local governments even treat whether their jurisdiction was elected to be part of an urban agglomeration [megaregion] as a performance assessment and political task. ... If a city was absorbed into an urban agglomeration [megaregion], it will be treated as a victory. If not, it will induce a lot of complaints.
>
> (Fang & Yu, 2016, p. 185)

As one interviewee went on to explain:

> The name means nothing. But for local governors, if others have it, they say 'we need it'. Hunan province didn't want one, but when they found out that other provinces had it, they wanted it too.

While it may be possible to point to examples of megaregional planning, what this reveals is the link between 'megaregions' and 'planning' does not always result in megaregional planning – or even planning at the megaregion scale. At worst they are the latest in a long line of growth-oriented, competitiveness-fuelled games that distract from the purpose of planning. At best we would have to consider some of these megaregions to be anticipatory planning and governance spaces, that is, imaginaries constructed in the hope that planning competencies and governance capacity might follow to institutionalize actual planning practice at this spatial scale. Either way, you would be hard pushed to say megaregions amount to a coherent planning space and tool.

Second, we must never assume the megaregion(s) under investigation: for as the third section reveals, there is no fixed geography to megaregionalism. Despite the underlying economic logic for megaregions remaining pretty constant across space and time, the politics of megaregionalism are always in a state of dynamic flux. Understanding how and why actors' endeavours to megaregionalize space result in the megaregional geographies they do might not be so important when it comes to planning megaregions, they can however provide meaningful windows to understanding the competing pressures on the state at any one time and how they plan to harness the megaregion concept as a 'geopolitical device not simply to manage domestic problems of territorial distribution but also to promote the international competitiveness and territorial integrity of the nation-state' (Li & Jonas, 2019, p. 71). In such a scenario, we must always consider the politics of spatial planning because as this interviewee reveals:

> In the western area, according to theoretical definition, it is not a real agglomeration [megaregion]. They are using it politically because we should have something in the national plan. They are always thinking about political balance.

Third, the focus on planning and megaregions is a prime example of how we have arguably forgotten that there is a purpose for regional planning beyond growth and infrastructure roll-out (Harrison, Galland, & Tewdwr-Jones, 2020). In the case of China, this interviewee reveals how:

> For the railway and the highway system and airport, we are starting to see local government talking about the need to see the city cluster [megaregion] and integrating things, but outside of this there are no discussions.

This aligns with developments globally whereby investing in infrastructure to enable supply chain expansion has quickly become the basic principle for planned urbaneconomic expansion and underpinned the rise of new megaregional spaces of planning and governance (Wachsmuth, 2017). But with it comes a recognition that although infrastructure can unite otherwise disparate actors in collective action at the megaregion scale it is only one activity and the chance of more holistic growth strategies are unlikely to be enabled by megaregionalism (Wheeler, 2015). The rise of megaregions and the notion of planning megaregional futures will likely therefore magnify the planninggrowth-infrastructure axis as opposed to adding weight to those arguing – rightly in our view – that there is a purpose for regional planning beyond simply growth and infrastructure roll-out.

Fourth, it would be seriously misleading to imply that because China has successful megaregions and a planned economy, they have megaregional planning in place and a coherent plan for so doing. Figures 1–4 reveal, at one level, the evolving and at times contradictory nature of the discursive framing of megaregions. At another level, our interviews reveal the practical challenges of embedding megaregions into China's extant institutional landscape:

> Since the llth Five Year Plan we said we should have major functional zones but in fact we just had some concept. The policy did not follow the zones. And the problem is these functional zones do not relate to urban agglomerations [megaregions].
>
> We talk about why we need this type of [megaregional] plan. We use a lot of ideas from Europe's Spatial Development Perspectives and the NUTs regions. But what is the base unit for China? Is it the provinces? Is it the city? Is it the county? In Europe it is just the NUTs regions. In China there are no clear units. This is why the policies and plans for urban agglomerations [megaregions] cannot be implemented properly because where is the unit?

Of course, the lack of clear units for Chinese megaregions is just one of the many factors that impedes the implementation of megaregion planning in China (others include, for instance, the lack of responsible government bodies, competition among different cities within the same region, which have previously been discussed at length by others; Li & Jonas, 2019; Sun & Chan, 2017; Wu, 2016) but we choose to focus on this one in particular because the final quote brings us to a fifth remark: who is learning from whom with regards to how to plan? In the 2000s when the Regional Plan Association launched their America 2050 megaregion programme, it was framed in terms of responding and learning from what they saw as their 'competitors' in Western Europe and South East Asia were already succeeding at regarding infrastructure investment in high-speed rail across extended urban areas. In the UK, new megaregional imaginaries such as the Northern Powerhouse are being constructed around what actors see as the 'incredible feat' of China's recent economic development, such that following China's megaregion development is what the then Chancellor of the Exchequer George Osborne lauded as being 'precisely what we're trying to achieve ... with our great industrial cities of the north of England' by connecting them up and framing them as a new megaregional space (Osborne, 2015). And yet while everywhere else is seemingly looking to China, the Chinese are looking the other way, as this interviewee explains:

> In China we do not have a real national spatial plan. We make policies based on some economic data and population data – density, growth

rates – and physical landscape. The Development Research Centre think that Germany has some very good national spatial plans and we are trying to convince our leaders of this.

All in all, then, while the perception of planning megaregional futures may exist, the practice suggests there is a long way to go before we can reasonably argue that megaregional planning exists in any meaningful way. What it amounts to is a narrow focus on infrastructure-enabled growth, and a discourse to exert influence, as this interviewee neatly surmises:

> Currently, it [megaregional status] is nothing other than a bargaining tool. It is very important when trying to get approvals from central government. That is why the local governor likes to put some beautiful name to it when making their case. If we have some tide this is very good reason why we can get approval. Beyond that? I am not sure.

In this way, megaregions *are* a planning tool but not for planning megaregions per se; rather, they are a way of enabling (some aspects of) what actors have otherwise planned for by providing the case for approval and investment.

Conclusions: looking ahead

This paper opens debates about the hitherto untold story of megaregion formation in China and its planning implications. Focusing on the Chinese state governments attempts to megaregionalize their national space economy, it contributes to wider debates recognizing the need to rethink the geography of megaregions for planning and governance purposes (Schafran, 2014). Our approach of using cartographic representations of China's evolving megaregional geography has provided a lens through which to reveal the politics of spatial planning at the scale of megaregions, and a basis from which to interrogate the capacity for planning megaregional futures. From this our analysis highlights three important considerations when examining future links between 'planning' and 'megaregions'.

First, and for all the economic boosterism surrounding megaregions, the mobilization of megaregions as a planning tool owes as much to (national) territorial politics as it does economic logic. Indeed, as our analysis of the cartographic representations of China's evolving megaregional geography reveals, with the passing of time the geographical basis and form that planning with megaregions takes arguably becomes an entirely political game. The inherent problem is the distraction this causes from the actual practice of planning.

This brings us to our second point, which is that understanding the geographical basis of megaregions in Chinese urban and regional planning tells us more about Chinese spatial politics than it does about megaregional planning per se. As a spatial planning concept, megaregions are mobilized and moulded by the CPC as part of an evolving political-economic project to manage the complex relationship between increased exposure to external global capitalist market forces while at the same time trying to maintain control over internal domestic matters. There is no doubt that this amounts to a version of planning, but in this guise it is far from reflecting the essence and hallmarks of planning, nor does it seem to engender the purpose and values we would hope for planning moving forward (Harrison et al., 2020).

This brings us to our final point, which is the question of whether we can even begin to consider planning at the megaregion scale? At one level, planning at the regional level has had a mixed history of success so the idea that we can plan at the megaregional level presents a daunting challenge (Wheeler, 2015). And yet, at another level, this should not be presented as a question but arguably it must be framed as an assertion. This is because large extended urban landscapes – megaregions – are an empirical reality. They exist and forecasts for urbanization indicate they will become more, not less, important as we move through this century. Therefore, the question is not if we should, but how can we, plan in, with and for megaregions. Gottmann recognized this and so must we:

> Megalopolis is a spectacular and fascinating phenomenon. Facts so huge and so stubborn can only be caused by the convergence of many powerful and sustained forces. ... [However, its] problems will not be solved by the easy wish of decentralization. The whole evolution of modern society may be at stake. *Society will have to learn to manage large urban regions.*
>
> (Gottmann, 1976, pp. 110–111; added emphasis)

In this regard, we still have a long way to go.

Disclosure statement

No potential conflict of interest was reported by the authors.

Funding

Hao Gu thanks Hunan University for financially supporting him in writing this paper through its 'Research Talent Project' [ID No. 531118010145].

Notes

1 In China, *chengshiqun* is used to identify these large urban regions, which has been variously translated into English as 'urban clusters' and 'urban agglomerations' rather than megaregions. To avoid obvious confusion, this paper will refer to these urban-regional configurations as megaregions throughout.
2 Even before this, the very origin of the concept 'megalopolis' owes itself to *Megalopolis,* the name given to a new city-state which a group of ancient Greeks

planned for on the basis that it would develop on a grandiose scale (Baigent, 2004).

3 We do not make any assertation here as to the balance of superiority between these two processes. This is a matter that must be resolved ex post and empirically rather than a priori and theoretically. We must also recognize that megaregions, as with all sociospatial configurations, are social constructs and therefore historically contingent.

4 A full history of the transformation of Chinese cities and city-regions into megaregions is beyond the scope of this paper, but see Fang (2015) or Zhang (2019).

5 In 2016, the NDRC announced this would be extended yet further to create an 'eight vertical, eight horizontal' network.

6 Previously the Ministry of Construction, of which the China Academy of Urban Planning and Design (CAUPD) is a subsidiary.

7 The NDRC was formally established in 2003. Previously it fulfilled this function as the State Planning Commission (1952–1998) and State Development Planning Commission (1998–2003).

8 Functional areas are removed at this point because they never related to megaregions; rather, they overlapped meaning policy and planning could never follow both.

9 This section draws on interviews conducted with actors selected because of their direct involvement in advising the framing of China's megaregions. This is a small population and, given the nature of doing qualitative research in China with public officials, to preserve anonymity we are required not to provide any identifying information in the attribution of interviews. All are engaged nationally and close to the process. Interviews were conducted in 2018 and lasted up to two hours. Audio recording was not permitted, meaning the conversations were recorded in note form. Interviews were conducted in English, enabling almost complete notes to be transcribed for the full conversation. Some quotations appearing in the paper have been corrected for grammar, albeit there are no changes to any of the substantive content or emphasis.

ORCID

John Harrison ⓘ http://orcid.org/0000-0002-6434-5142
Hao Gu ⓘ http://orcid.org/0000-0001-7456-0033

References

Baigent, E. (2004). Patrick Geddes, Lewis Mumford and Jean Gottmann: Divisions over 'megalopolis'. *Progress in Human Geography, 28,* 687–700. doi:10.1191/0309132504ph514oa

Boria, E. (2008). Geopolitical maps: A sketch history of a neglected trend in cartography. *Geopolitics, 13,* 278–308. doi:10.1080/14650040801991522

China Academy of Urban Planning and Design. (2005). *Outline of urban system planning 2005–2020.* Beijing: Ministry of Construction.

Diihr, S. (2007). *The visual language of spatial planning: Exploring cartographic representations for spatial planning in Europe.* London: Routledge.

Fan, J., Sun, W., Zhou, K., & Chen, D. (2012). Major function oriented zone: New method of spatial regulation for reshaping regional development pattern in China. *Chinese Geographical Science, 22,* 196–209. doi:10.1007/s11769-012-0528-y

Fang, C. (2015). Important progress and future direction of studies on China's urban agglomerations. *Journal of Geographical Sciences, 25,* 1003–1024. doi:10.1007/s11442-015-1216-5

Fang, C., & Yu, D. (2016). *China's new urbanization: Developmental paths, blueprints and patterns.* Berlin: Springer.

Florida, R., Gulden, T., & Mellander, C. (2008). The rise of the mega-region. *Cambridge Journal of Regions, Economy and Society, 1,* 459–476. doi:10.1093/cjres/rsn018

Friedmann, J., & Sorensen, A. (2019). City unbound: Emerging mega-conurbations in Asia. *International Planning Studies, 24,* 1–12. doi:10.1080/13563475.2019.1555314

Geddes, P. (1915). *Cities in evolution: An introduction to the town planning movement and to the study of civics.* London: Williams & Norgate.

Gottmann, J. (1957). Megalopolis or the urbanization of the northeastern seaboard. *Economic Geography, 33,* 189–200. doi:10.2307/142307

Gottmann, J. (1976). Megapolitan systems around the world. *Geografski Glasnik, 38,* 103–111.

Hall, P. (1973). *The containment of urban England.* London: Allen & Unwin.

Hall, P., & Pain, K. (Eds.). (2006). *The polycentric metropolis: Learning from megacity regions in Europe.* Abingdon: Earthscan.

Harrison, J. (2007). From competitive regions to competitive city-regions: A new orthodoxy, but some old mistakes. *Journal of Economic Geography, 7,* 311–332. doi:10.1093/jeg/lbm005

Harrison, J., Galland, D., & Tewdwr-Jones, M. (Forthcoming 2020). Whither regional planning? *Regional Studies.*

Harrison, J., & Hoyler, M. (2014). Governing the new metropolis. *Urban Studies, 51,* 2249–2266. doi:10.1177/0042098013500699

Harrison, J., & Hoyler, M. (Eds.). (2015). *Megaregions: Globalizations new urban form?* Northampton: Edward Elgar.

Jonas, A. E. G., & Moisio, S. (2018). City regionalism as geopolitical processes: A new framework for analysis. *Progress in Human Geography, 42,* 350–370. doi:10.1177/0309132516679897

Kantor, P., Lefevre, C., Saito, A., Savitch, H., & Thornley, A (2012). *Struggling giants: City-region governance in London, New York, Paris,* and Tokyo. Minneapolis: University of Minnesota Press.

Khanna, P. (2016). *Connectography: Mapping the future of global civilization.* New York: Random House.

Lang, R., & Knox, P. (2009). The new metropolis: Rethinking megalopolis. *Regional Studies, 43,* 789–802. doi:10.1080/00343400701654251

Li, Y., & Jonas, A. E. G. (2019). City-regionalism as countervailing geopolitical processes: The evolution and dynamics of Yangtze River Delta region, China. *Political Geography, 73,* 70–81. doi:10.1016/j.polgeo.2019.05.014

Li, Y., & Phelps, N. (2017). Knowledge polycentricity and the evolving Yangtze River Delta megalopolis. *Regional Studies, 51,* 1035–1047. doi:10.1080/00343404.2016.1240868

Li, Y., & Wu, F. (2018). Understanding city-regionalism in China: Regional cooperation in the Yangtze River Delta. *Regional Studies, 52,* 313–324. doi:10.1080/00343404.2017.1307953

Ministry of Construction. (2007). *National urban system planning 2006–2020.* Beijing: Ministry of Construction.

Mumford, L. (1938). *The culture of cities.* New York: Harcourt.

National Bureau of Statistics of China (NBS). (2019). *China statistical yearbook 2019.* Beijing: NBS.

National Development Reform Commission (NDRC). (2010). *National main functional zone plan.* Beijing: NDRC.

National Development Reform Commission (NDRC). (2014). *National New Urbanisation Plan.* Beijing: NDRC.

National Development Reform Commission (NDRC). (2016). *The 13th Five-Year Plan for national economic and social development.* Edition 8, Chapter 33, Section 1. Beijing: NDRC.

Osborne, G. (2015). *Chancellor speech in Chengdu, China, on building a Northern Powerhouse.* Retrieved from https://www.gov.uk/government/speeches/chancellor-speech-in-chengdu-china-on-building-a-northern-powerhouse

Paasi, A., Harrison, J., & Jones, M. (2018). New consolidated regional geographies. In Paasi, A., Harrison, J., & Jones, M. (Eds.), *Handbook on the geographies of regions and territories* (pp. 1–20). Cheltenham: Edward Elgar.

Ross, C. (Ed.). (2009). *Megaregions: Planning for global competitiveness.* Washington, DC: Island.

Schafran, A. (2014). Rethinking mega-regions: Sub-regional politics in a fragmented metropolis. *Regional Studies, 48,* 587–602. doi:10.1080/00343404.2013.834043

Scott, A. J. (1998). *Regions and the world economy: The coming shape of global production, competition, and political order.* Oxford: Oxford University Press.

Scott, A. J. (2001). Globalization and the rise of city-regions. European *Planning Studies, 9,* 813–826. doi:10.1080/09654310120079788

Scott, A. J. (2019). City-regions reconsidered. *Environment and Planning A: Economy and Space, 51,* 554–580. doi:10.1177/0308518X19831591

State Council. (2004). *National medium and long-term railway network plan.* Beijing: State Council.

State Council. (2010). *National main functional area planning – Building an efficient, coordinated and sustainable land and space development pattern.* Retrieved from www.gov.cn/zwgk/201106/08/content_1879180.htm

Sun, Y., &Chan, R. (2017). Planning discourses, local state commitment, and the making of a new state space (NSS) for China: Evidence from regional strategic development plans in the Pearl River Delta. *Urban Studies, 54,* 3281–3298. doi:10.1177/0042098016665954

Tan, M. (2017). Uneven growth of urban clusters in megaregions and its policy implications for new urbanization in China. *Land Use Policy, 66,* 72–79. doi:10.1016/j.landusepol.2017.04.032

Taubenböck, H., & Wiesner, M. (2015). The spatial network of megaregions – Types of connectivity between cities based on settlement patterns derived from EO-data. *Computers, Environment and Urban Systems, 54,* 165–180. doi:10.1016/j.compenvurbsys.2015.07.001

Wachsmuth, D. (2017). Competitive multi-city regionalism: Growth politics beyond the growth machine. *Regional Studies, 51,* 643–653. doi:10.1080/00343404.2016.1223840

Wheeler, S. (2015). Five reasons why megaregional planning works against sustainability. In J. Harrison & M. Hoyler (Eds.), *Megaregions: Globalization's new urban form?* (pp. 97 118). Northampton: Edward Elgar.

Wu, F. (2015). *Planning for growth: Urban and regional planning in China.* London: Routledge.

Wu, F. (2016). China's emergent city-region governance: A new form of state spatial selectivity through state-orchestrated rescaling. *International Journal of Urban and Regional Research, 40,* 1134–1151. doi:10.1111/1468-2427.12437

Xu, J., & Yeh, A. G. O. (Eds.). (2011). *Governance and planning of mega-city regions: An international comparative perspective.* London: Routledge.

Zhang, W., Derudder, B., Wang, J., & Shen, W. (2018). Regionalization in the Yangtze River Delta, China, from the perspective of inter-city daily mobility. *Regional Studies, 52,* 528–541. doi:10.1080/00343404.2017.1334878

Zhang, X. (2019). Transformation of Chinese cities and city-regions in the era of globalization. In R. Yep, J. Wang, & T. Johnson (Eds.), *Handbook on urban development in China* (pp. 137–154). Northampton: Edward Elgar.

Understanding heterogeneous spatial production externalities as a missing link between land-use planning and urban economic futures

Haozhi Pan⊕, TianrenYang⊕, Ying Jin,
Sandy Dall'Erba and Geoffrey Hewings⊕

Introduction

Land-use planning serves as an efficient policy tool to promote regional economic performance and prosperity. Kim (2011) claims that policy interventions in land use lead to the economic growth/decline through spatial (re) arrangement where housing supply, labour market and the spatial configuration of socioeconomic activities interact. For instance, the growing density in urban centres often accounts for higher productivity (Glaeser, 2008; Lucas & Rossi-Hansberg, 2002) as a result of the zoning regulation and market response. The nature and strength of spatial production externalities, as a function of land-use planning, vary at different spatial scales (Chung & Hewings, 2019; Kim & Hewings, 2013). However, the findings from urban/regional economies' literature tend to focus on large spatial scales such as cities and counties, while land-use planning often addresses block-level concerns. Without a sound theoretical framework applied to a *spatial* scale that planners can address, the issues of how and to what extent land-use regulations and policies influence production has long been overlooked.

To explore the missing link between land-use planning and urban economic development, this paper uses highperformance computing techniques within a spatial econometric framework on block-level land-use data inventory publicly available for Chicago, Illinois. Two research questions are addressed:

- How do spatial production externalities affect urban economic growth?
- What are the land-use planning and urban design implications regarding the heterogeneity in production externalities?

A spatial economic model is constructed based on the theory of sector-specific equilibrium wages and sectorspecific factors of production and externalities (Bishop & Gripaios, 2010; Glaeser, Kallal, Scheinkman, & Shleifer, 1992; Hanlon & Miscio, 2017). With regards to landuse planning and regulation, we further compare the outcomes from the economic growth model with the official land-use planning vision for Chicago from the Chicago Metropolitan Planning Agency (CMAP) to examine how official land-use planning matches with the market-driven trend for the optimization of spatial production externalities.

This paper has three major contributions: (1) to enhance the literature on how land-use configuration affects urban economic growth with high-granular spatial land-use data; (2) to add to the literature on competitive and complementary relations between regional economic sectors through an examination of matrices of spatial proximity between land use and establishments that belong to different industrial sectors; and (3) to compare the market-oriented growth with planned growth in a scenario simulation to gain practical insights for planners and decision-makers. The outcomes and methodologies of this study can be used to support and evaluate sectorbased economic impacts by land-use planning and regulations.

The paper is structured as follows. It begins with a literature review of the theoretical and empirical studies, examining heterogeneous agglomeration economies. The third section presents the theoretical model and outlines the data sources. The fourth section discusses the impacts of various types of production externalities on urban economic growth, and further compares market-driven growth and local planning outcomes in a scenario simulation. Section five concludes with planning implications.

Literature review

Land-use planning and urban economic growth

Urban spatial structure, as largely affected by land-use planning, has proved to be closely related with the operation of the land market since the work of Alonso (1964). The bidrent locational choices of various land uses determine the spatial distribution of economic activities. Fujita, Krugman, and Venables (2001) further link location theories with the trade network between firms, examining the positive effects of spatial proximity. 'Efficiently managed growth', as argued by Cervero (2001), contributes positively to urban economic performance, while negative externalities such as congestion yielded by weak land-use planning inhibit economic growth and public welfare improvements (Glaeser, 2011). Specifically, higher employment density and better access to large labour markets with an efficient transport network result in higher labour productivity. This can be achieved through a series of planning tools such as urban growth boundary designation, infrastructure provision and zoning (Kim, 2011).

Despite the efforts of planning interventions that improve density and accessibility, the generated positive externalities differ between industries and development periods. For example, traditional manufacturing industries tend to be highly localized with related industries and those with long-term upstream-downstream ties (Ellison & Glaeser Edward, 1997; Ottaviano & Thisse, 2004). Modern service industries, on the other hand, are more information oriented and tend to be clustered in central business districts (CBDs) (Nam & Kim, 2017). These phenomena have been long documented in both planning and urban/regional economies' literature, while the latter provides a more consistent theoretical foundation by illustrating the existence of spatial production externalities through the analysis of empirical, longitudinal data.

Heterogeneous spatial production externalities

Location-based externalities generated through spatial (re)arrangement have been a key in the urban land-use structure literature (Bishop & Gripaios, 2010), but this relationship is further complicated when production externalities of sector difference are explored (Chung & Hewings, 2015). The major sources of production externalities can be distinguished into three types: specification externalities that operate within the same industrial sector (Marshall, 1961), diversity externalities produced from a variety of sectors (Jacobs, 2016), and urbanization externalities derived from urban size and density (Rosenthal & Strange, 2004).

The impacts of different externalities vary between the types of the local district and the nature of industry. As argued by Glaeser et al. (1992), diversity externalities are more likely to operate within metropolitan areas where industries are not heavily overrepresented. Compared with low-tech industry sectors in small local districts, specification and diversity externalities appear more influential in high-tech sectors located in business districts of larger cities (Paci & Usai, 1999). For traditional and cuttingedge manufacturing sectors, the specialization effect is more powerful in the former one, whereas both specialization and diversity economies are important in the latter case (Henderson, Kuncoro, & Turner, 1995).

Following Glaeser et al.'s (1992) empirical work on explaining city growth in temporal dimensions, the dynamics of externalities are further realized by Henderson (1997) who suggested that a three to four years' lag exists before the full effects of externality benefits take place. Such dynamics have also been empirically investigated by Yang, Pan, Hewings, and Jin (2019b) when exploring the location of the newly developed commercial establishments (2001–11) in comparison with the existing ones (pre-2001); the subcentres with sector-specific positive externalities seem to be generating stronger attractions for new commercial land use.

Despite their consideration of urban growth patterns, these studies are mostly limited to the measurement of economic performance or discovering temporal differences rather than unravelling the competitive and complementary relationships between particular sectoral groups. This neglects the heterogeneity in spatial externalities from diverse and/or related economic sectors when understanding urban growth. Among a few related studies, Bishop and Gripaios (2010) examine the externalities of different types and their impact on local employment growth, where specialization and diversity play opposite roles in employment creation. Similar empirical findings have been reached by Hanlon and Miscio (2017) using long-run city-industry panel data.

In addition, most of the literature examining diversity, specialization and relatedness in spatial externalities has been explored at a relatively large spatial scale, such as cities, counties or census tracts (Boschma, Eriksson, & Lindgren, 2014; Boschma, Minondo, & Navarro, 2012; Frenken, van Oort, & Verburg, 2007; Porter, 2003; Wixe & Andersson, 2017). However, production externalities are more likely to be detected with greater geographical disaggregation (Beaudry & Schiffauerova, 2009). The argument is in line with a growing but still rather limited literature that moves beyond broad spatial representations by exploring micro-level data. Aggregating firm-level panel data into $1 \times 1 \text{ km}^2$ grid, Andersson, Larsson, and Wernberg (2019) find positive, within-grid externalities from both specialization (stronger) and diversity (smaller) economies, while the influences from the neighbouring grids are not discernible. An extremely rapid distance decay of scale externalities, where agglomeration benefits approach zero beyond 750 m, are witnessed from the advertising agency industry in Manhattan (Arzaghi & Henderson, 2008). Many other industries also have highly localized agglomeration forces, with a possible exception of manufacturing (van Soest, Gerking, & van Oort, 2006).

This paper is situated at the confluence of planning and urban/regional economies' literature examining heterogeneous spatial production externalities, and is motivated by the need to explore the nature and strength of spillovers at different spatial scales as a function of land-use planning. First, it introduces finer scale landuse data at the block level (100 x 100 m) building upon the increasing understanding of the rapid attenuation of externalities. The model development and application, when performed at smaller spatial scales, improves in robustness and becomes more informative taking account of urban hierarchical regimes (Andersson, Klaesson, & Larsson, 2016; van Oort, 2007). In response to the first research question (see the introduction above), we expect to find that sector-specific spatial spillover at local scales affect local employment change on top of influences from regional economy, technology change and urbanization effects.

Second, this research has a particular focus on the reciprocal relationships across specific business sectors within a city, through the lens of economic growth and land-use planning. A comparison between market-driven trend and planned vision bridges the interdisciplinary gap (Hu, Yang, Yang, Tu, & Zhu, 2019; Yang, Jin, Yan, & Pel, 2019a), and provides empirical evidence for plan-making that stimulates future employment attraction. This is in response to the second research question (see the introduction above) where we aim to find out how official planning vision can be optimized with new knowledge discovered.

Methods and data

Theoretical models

The Glaeser et al. (1992) model is adopted as the theoretical framework with the incorporation of the later modifications from Bishop and Gripaios (2010) and Hanlon and Miscio (2017). Assume that a firm has a production function with a single labour input:

$$A_t f'(l_t) \tag{1}$$

where A_t and I_t is technology and labour input, respectively, at time t. Profit maximization yields the standard condition:

$$A_t f'(l_t) = w_t \tag{2}$$

where w_t is the wage rate. After taking the logs and including the spatial (i) and sectoral (r) dimensions, the growth rates can be written as:

$$\log\left(\frac{A_{i,r,t+1}}{A_{i,r,t}}\right) = \log\left(\frac{w_{i,r,t+1}}{w_{i,r_t}}\right) - \log\left(\frac{f'(l_{i,t+1})}{f'(l_{i,r,t})}\right) \tag{3}$$

According to the literature, the growth in technologies is related to within-industry spillovers (speciality), acrossindustry spillovers (diversity), national technology growth and urbanization economy. Thus:

$$\log\left(\frac{A_{i,r,t+1}}{A_{i,r,t}}\right) = $$
$$g\left(\begin{array}{cc} \text{within industry spillover} & \text{cross industry spillover} \\ \text{regional industry technology growth} & \text{urbanisation economies} \end{array}\right) \tag{4}$$

Setting:

$$f(l_t) = l^{1-\alpha} (0 < \alpha < 1) \tag{5}$$

yields:

$$\alpha \log\left(\frac{l_{i,t+1}}{l_{i,r,t}}\right) = -\log\left(\frac{w_{i,r,t+1}}{w_{i,t}}\right) + g(\blacksquare) \tag{6}$$

Assuming that wage growth and the growth of technology do not vary across regions, equation (6) implies that employment growth can be explained by the measures of externalities in $g(\blacksquare)$. The externalities include spillover effects within the same industries, spillover effects across related industries and the urbanization effects due to the location of the commercial establishments within the cities.

Measuring crossand within-industry spillovers

The Chicago land-use inventory provided by the CMAP (2016) is used and manually cleaned to best match the two-digit North American Industry Classification System (NAICS) and of the Chicago Regional Econometric Input-Output Model (CREIM) database (Figure 1).

The rasterized land-use data are then transformed into a matrix with each grid denoting the sector code of a land-use cell. Non-industrial and non-commercial land-use grids are denoted as zero. For all cells belonging to each sector i, a 'proximity' index n_{ij} is calculated to all other sectors j by:

$$n_{i,j} = \sum_{i,j \, in \, S} 1[k_{j,r} \, in \, D(i)] \tag{7}$$

where n_{ij} is the 'proximity' index for between sectors i and j; S is the set of all sectors; $1[\blacksquare]$ is the operator that results in 1 if the conditions in $[\blacksquare]$ are satisfied, and otherwise 0; $k_{j,r}$ is cell k from sector j in location r; and $D(i)$ represents the immediate neighbourhood of cells in sector i. The 'immediate neighbouring' rule means that by 'proximity' we mean two commercial establishments are within one block (100 m) away. To test if this is an overly strong assumption, we loosen the threshold to 200, 300, 400 and 500 m; the results are discussed in the third section.

To avoid over-parameterisation of the model, spatial spillover effects measured from equation (7) are simplified into a dummy representation of a 'most related' economic sector for each sector i:

$$r_i - j \text{ s.t. } \max_j(n_{i,j}) \text{ and } j \neq i \tag{8}$$

Thus, there is a 'most related' sector for each sector i (excluding sector i itself) and a dummy variable is created for each spatial block of whether a

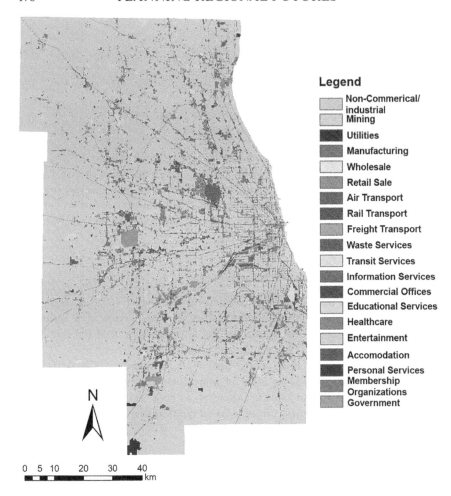

Legend

- Non-Commerical/industrial
- Mining
- Utilities
- Manufacturing
- Wholesale
- Retail Sale
- Air Transport
- Rail Transport
- Freight Transport
- Waste Services
- Transit Services
- Information Services
- Commercial Offices
- Educational Services
- Healthcare
- Entertainment
- Accomodation
- Personal Services
- Membership Organizations
- Government

N

0 5 10   20   30   40
km

Figure 1 Land-use inventory of Chicago with subsector detonations.
Note: Some sectors have extremely sparse land use that is not visible on the map.

most-related sector establishment (excluding the same sector) is within the distance threshold as an instrument for cross-industry spillover. This approach highlights the effects of relatedness in the discussion of how diversity influences economic growth (e.g., Bishop & Gripaios, 2010). Similarly, a dummy variable is also created for each spatial block of whether a same sector establishment is within the distance threshold as an instrument for 'within-industry' spillovers.

Data and empirical model

The sector classification involved in this study provides a cross-match between the CREIM database and the landuse inventory including 19 sectors.

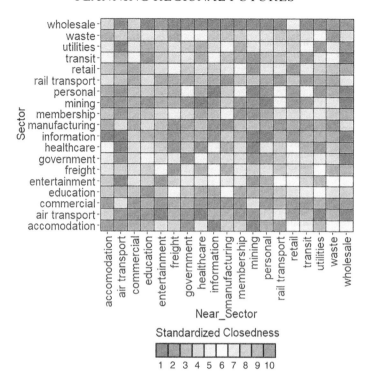

Figure 2 Standardized 'proximity' index between sectors.
Note: The colour scale is constructed by 10 quantiles of the 'proximity' index.

We estimate by ordinary least squares (OLS) how sectoral growth is influenced by the various sources of externalities including withinand crossindustrial spillover as well as urbanization economies (these are included in the $g(\blacksquare)$ function). The specification problems and tests are discussed in the third section. The present section focuses on the data used for the OLS estimation in addition to the withinand cross-industrial spillover variables that were already explained above.

The base year (t) of the model is 2010. A large amount of census information and land-use inventory data are available through public databases for Chicago that year. The end year ($t + 1$) is set to be 2016. The log of sectoral employment growth over the period 2010–16 is used as the dependent variable derived from the CREIM database. An obvious limitation to the study is the relative short period (six years) of observing employment growth. The main reason for choosing this time period is because it was one in which the region enjoyed positive economic growth, and stable levels of diversity and, consequently, the impact of withinand cross-industry spillover can be examined in the absence of major changes in the economic structure. Aggregated using the county-level employment of US Bureau of Labour Statistics, the study region (the seven-county Chicago Metropolitan region) has

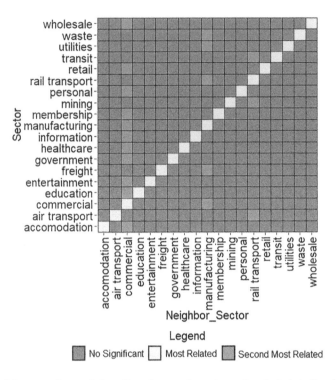

Figure 3 Most proximate (related) and second most proximate (related) neighbours of each economic sector.

employment growth from about 3.7 million to 4.0 million (6.7% growth) in this period.

Regional factors, including wage growth and employment growth by sector, are derived from the CREIM database. Employment density and local income data are derived from the Economic Census. The data are sampled on 55 'economic places' defined by the Economic Census within the Chicago Metropolitan region that have employment headcount within each place. They are then interpolated by spatial smoothing to all cells to avoid employment numbers changing dramatically at the boundary between economic places. In this study, the section on urbanization economy (one component in $g(\blacksquare)$ function as proposed by Glaeser et al., 1992) is based on Yang et al. (2019b) and Pan, Deal, Chen, and Hewings (2018). The latter authors find that employment growth at patch level in Chicago is influenced by their connectivity to major population centres, urban amenities and transportation hubs. The present paper includes the relevant measures of connectivity (acquired through the data repository provided by the original studies and then resampled to the spatial resolution of this paper) as control variables in the OLS model. Table 1 describes the data included in the OLS model. Key variables including the employment growth and urbanization economy

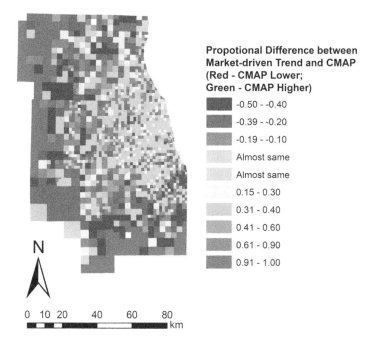

Propotional Difference between
Market-driven Trend and CMAP
(Red - CMAP Lower;
Green - CMAP Higher)

-0.50 - -0.40
-0.39 - -0.20
-0.19 - -0.10
Almost same
Almost same
0.15 - 0.30
0.31 - 0.40
0.41 - 0.60
0.61 - 0.90
0.91 - 1.00

N

0 10 20   40   60   80
km

Figure 4 Comparison of 2040 employment growth between Chicago Metropolitan Planning Agency (CMAP) vision and market-driven trend (model simulation).

measured by connectivity are mapped in Appendix A in the supplemental data online.

Robustness check

The first potential issue of the model is the selection of the spatial unit of analysis and the definition of distance threshold for proximity. The original model uses 'direct neighbouring' (within 100 m) as a rule for the existence of cross and within-industry spillover effects. To examine whether the model results are robust to different selections of distance threshold, alternative analyses are applied for different distance thresholds including 200–500 m with 100-m intervals.

Another robustness check requires one to verify whether the sources of externalities measured in the $g(\blacksquare)$ function are truly exogenous. The risk of endogeneity they present is based on the fact that the location of some industries and employment centres is subject to urban planning policies such as the designation of a new industrial zone accompanied by location subsidies such as tax rebates and infrastructure support. If that is the case, the current model would fail to account for the correlation between the planned industrial zones and the existing industrial agglomerations.

Table 1 Definitions and descriptive statistics of the variables.

Variable	Definition	Mean	Standard deviation	Minimum	Maximum
Independent variables					
LOG(SWG)	Logarithm of sector wage growth from 2010 to 2016	−0.049	0.086	−0.190	0.192
LOG(REG)	Logarithm of regional sector employment growth from 2010 to 2016	0.014	0.100	0.353	−0.148
EMPDENS	Employment density spatially interpolated on the cell level	2.265	0.353	1.789	3.335
POP-C	Connectivity to population centres as measured by Pan et al. (2018)	0.006	0.003	0.004	0.017
TRANS-C	Connectivity to transportation hubs as measured by Pan et al. (2018)	0.002	0.003	0	0.043
POI-C	Connectivity to a point of interest (POI) (such as restaurants and parks) as measured by Pan et al. (2018)	0.004	0.015	0	0.385
LOC-INCOME	Local income spatially interpolated on cell level	0.069	0.029	0	0.250
WITHIN-SPILL	Dummy variable on whether industrial establishments of the same sector appear within the distance threshold	0.076	0.266	0	1
CROSS-SPILL	Dummy variable on whether most-related industrial establishments of the same sector appear within the distance threshold	0.010	0.100	0	1
Dependent variable					
LOG(SEG)	Logarithm of sector employment growth from 2010 to 2016	−0.026	0.081	−0.157	0.172

In order to avoid this issue, we apply a two-stage least squares (2SLS) estimation process developed by Duranton and Turner (2012) and adopt as an instrumental variable (IV) the economic sector coding from CMAP (treated as fixed effects) of each land-use cell. It is reasonable to assume that the economic sector coding of any specific place does not reflect the growth of an economic sector as a whole, while economic land-use regulation is highly related to the sources of externalities within or neighbouring the locality. As usual in the literature, exogeneity will be tested by the Hausman-Wu test and overidentification will be tested by the Wald F-test.

Additional robustness tests of incorporating within – and cross-industry spillovers at all distance thresholds and of adding county-level fixed effects to address timeinvariant heterogeneity effects are conducted; these are available in Appendix B in the supplemental data online. We find that the

IV-2SLS models for 100–400 m distance threshold (run separately) to be the most appropriate model specifications, while adding county-level fixed effects do not change the results and conclusions.

Market-driven growth versus plan comparison

As noted above, this paper compares a market-driven industrial land-use configuration with the official CMAP 2040 vision of subsectional employment growth (CMAP, 2016). According to CMAP's documented methodology (CMAP, 2015), several factors are considered for modelling job growth allocations to subsections, including proximity to density and green infrastructure, land-use planning and regulation, as well as local (neighbourhood or community levels) consensus-building and debates through local technical assistance (LTA) programmes. It is noticeable that local spatial production externalities that are found to be significant for employment growth in this study are not included by CMAP in their vision of the job growth expected by 2040.

This counterfactual check provides a practical factcheck of whether land-use regulation and planning would result in an optimization of land-use externalities to maximize sources of positive spatial production externalities. More specifically, the economic growth model provides an end forecast year that corresponds with that for CMAP (2040) to determine the land use of each available undeveloped land by:

$$k_i = \max_i\left[-\log\left(\frac{w_{i,r,t+1}}{w_{i,r,t}}\right) + g(\blacksquare)\right] \tag{9}$$

which is a simulation function showing the optimal land use (k_i) of each 100×100 m block for the maximum employment growth with the economic sector i as the only variable that can be altered. It is noteworthy that because withinand cross-sector spillover dummy constructs are different for each sector (i), this simulation model needs to be run 19 times for each i and an optimal land use is then selected from all simulations to maximize the perspective employment growth on each land-use cell. Total employment growth until 2040 from the CREIM database is then allocated to each land-use cell based on its sector designation. This result is aggregated to the subsections of the CMAP 2040 vision plan and a comparison is made between optimal employment growth allocation based on spatial production externalities ('market-driven scenario') and the CMAPvision employment growth by 2040.

Results

Cross-and within-industry spillover results

Figure 2 shows the row and column standardized 'proximity' index between sectors for a 100-m threshold. The horizontal axis reports the number of sector establishments that appear within 100 m of at least one establishment

Table 2 Ordinary least squares (OLS) growth model results.

Threshold distance	Dependent variable: LOG(SEG)				
	100m	200m	300m	400m	500m
LOG(SWG)	−0.172***	−0.187***	−0.128***	−0.241***	−0.311***
	(0.002)	(0.005)	(0.008)	(0.011)	(0.014)
LOG(REG)	0.587***	0.599***	0.635***	0.654***	0.713***
	(0.002)	(0.004)	(0.007)	(0.010)	(0.012)
EMPDENS	0.950**	−1.096	0.938	−4.726**	−8.504***
	(0.950)	(0.888)	(1.412)	(2.083)	(2.640)
POP-C	−0.486***	0.097***	0.602**	0.901*	2.015***
	(0.065)	(0.065)	(0.240)	(0.460)	(0.605)
TRANS-C	0.728***	0.806***	0.993***	0.744**	1.774***
	(0.050)	(0.120)	(0.223)	(0.342)	(0.474)
POI-C	0.099***	0.145***	0.111**	0.158**	0.202***
	(0.011)	(0.027)	(0.045)	(0.070)	(0.071)
LOC-INCOME	3e-4	2e-4**	1e-4	2e-4	2e-4**
	(2e-4)	(1e-4)	(1e-4)	(1e-4)	(1e-4)
CROSS-SPILL	0.011***	0.007***	0.020***	0.022***	−0.025***
	(0.001)	(0.001)	(0.003)	(0.003)	(0.007)
WITHIN-SPILL	−0.035***	−0.016***	−0.009***	−0.002	−0.003
	(0.001)	(0.001)	(0.001)	(0.003)	(0.002)
Constant	−0.011***	−0.037***	−0.054***	−0.061***	−0.068****
	(0.001)	(0.001)	(0.002)	(0.003)	(0.004)
Observations	136,248	30,333	11,404	5573	3282
R^2	0.428	0.439	0.489	0.514	0.567
Residual standard error	0.061	0.061	0.059	0.059	0.057
F-statistic	11,333***	2634***	1212***	673***	475***

Note: *p < 0.1; **p < 0.05; ***p < 0.01.

in the sector displayed in the vertical axis. The first obvious pattern is that establishments within the same sector co-locate within the same vicinity. This is intuitive because establishments in the same sector usually have similar locational decisions that generate agglomeration economies. Whether 'proximate to self agglomeration pattern promotes sector growth is subject to examination by the growth model.

Figure 3 reports the most proximate (most related) and second most proximate (second most related) neighbouring sectors to each sector. This information is then coded into a dummy variable used as input into the OLS model (explained in detail in the fourth section). It is not surprising that every sector is most related to itself. Thus, for the variable 'within-sector spillover', 1 is assigned to a land-use cell that has any establishment in the same sector within the distance threshold, and 0 otherwise. The second most related sector varies across all sectors and is defined as the most related source of 'cross-industry spillover' in this study. Note that the related matrices are row standardized, thus the percentage rather than the total number of proximate sectors determine the 'most related' and 'second related' sectors.

The results for the 'second related' source of externalities in Figure 3 generally fit the intuition. All the second related sectors are establishments that belong to commercial offices, manufacturing and rail transportation. Note that because the absolute number of offices within distance thresholds is column-standardized to remove the impacts of the total number of existing establishments of all sectors, these results show that a higher percentage of these three industrial sectors appear to be very close (within 100 m) to other industrial sectors. The reasoning is that these three sectors create spatial production externalities. Commercial offices provide consulting and other business services that require more face-to-face meetings than other services. Manufacturing establishments that are part of a supply chain may find that spatial proximity to customers or sources of inputs can save costs. Proximity to rail transportation can save costs for many other economic sectors and, as a result, many sectors have rail transportation establishments in their proximity. Similar to 'within-industry spillover' dummy, the growth model treats the land-use cells with 'second most related' establishments in their proximity to have a 'cross-industry spillover' dummy value of 1, and otherwise 0.

Growth model results

Table 2 presents the OLS results. The robustness check shows that models using 100–400 m distance thresholds for withinor cross-industry spillovers produce very similar results. The results indicate that employment growth is negatively affected by wage growth, which is consistent with the theoretical expectations (equation 6). These findings suggest that the model results are consistent and robust with the theoretical predictions at least with a threshold range between 100 and 400 m. We also find across all specifications that the 'within-industry spillover' effect has a significant and negative impact on sector job growth while the 'cross-industry spillovers' affect job growth positively.

Among all the urbanization factors, connectivity to transportation hubs and urban amenities (points of interest – POIs) show consistently significant and positive impacts on sectoral employment growth. This result is consistent with previous findings of Pan et al. (2018) and Yang et al. (2019b). Some other spatial variables, including employment density in 2010, connectivity to population centres, as well as the local wage level (sector wage growth – SWG) in 2010 are either not significant or do not demonstrate consistent results with a different distance threshold. The results on connectivity to population centres are understandable because the improvement of transportation technology makes commuting less important as a factor in determining local economic growth. The results on employment density further

Table 3 Two-stage least squares (2SLS) instrumental variables (IV) model results.

Dependent variable: LOG(SEG)

Threshold Distance	100m	200m	300m	400 m	500m
LOG(SWG)	−0.117***	−0.220***	−0.252***	−0.228***	−0.436***
	(0.005)	(0.009)	(0.010)	(0.013)	(0.032)
LOG(REG)	0.596***	0.670***	0.717***	0.687***	0.873***
	(0.005)	(0.008)	(0.010)	(0.011)	(0.031)
EMPDENS	7.257***	−2.929*	3.195*	−1.201	−4.394
	(0.963)	(1.636)	(1.842)	(2.371)	(5.338)
POP-C	−5.264***	−2.100***	0.001	−0.531	4.186***
	(0.171)	(0.370)	(0.314)	(0.531)	(1.256)
TRANS-C	−2.404***	−1.678***	−0.978***	0.923**	0.868
	(0.121)	(0.235)	(0.315)	(0.438)	(1.040)
POI-C	−0.506***	−0.243***	0.018	0.156**	0.182
	(0.027)	(0.051)	(0.059)	(0.079)	(0.145)
LOC-INCOME	4e-4	0e-4	1e-4	2e-4**	1e-4**
	(5e-4)	(2e-4)	(1e-4)	(1e-4)	(2e-4)
CROSS-SPILL	0.169***	0.110***	0.091***	0.152***	−0.751***
	(0.005)	(0.010)	(0.008)	(0.010)	(0.080)
WITHIN-SPILL	−0.437***	−0.256***	−0.128***	0.003	−0.060***
	(0.005)	(0.007)	(0.007)	(0.008)	(0.015)
Constant	0.376***	0.175***	0.043***	−0.067***	−0.036****
	(0.005)	(0.006)	(0.006)	(0.007)	(0.013)

Note: *$p<0.1$; **$p < 0.05$; ***$P<0.01$.

confirm the findings of Pan et al. (2018) and Yang et al. (2019b) of a shift out of the CBD of new commercial growth post-2011.

The model results with a distance threshold of 500 m display substantial differences with the results of the other models. This indicates that the mechanisms for spatial production externalities may not hold at larger spatial resolutions.

Using the 100-m threshold, the Hausman-Wu test statistics (32,114 with d.f. = 2; 136, 236) rejects the null hypothesis of exogeneity at the 95% confidence level, while the null hypothesis of an instrument is rejected for both cross-and within-industrial spillover dummies by the Wald *F*-test statistics (351 with d.f. = 16; 136, 24 and 585 with 351 with d.f. = 16; 136, 24, respectively). These results imply that the choice of the instrument that was used is warranted and a 2SLS approach is required. Similar diagnostic results are obtained for models using 200–400 m threshold values. Endogeneity is found and thus an IV approach can help identify the causality. The IV results for distance thresholds from 100 to 400 m show that the significance and direction of cross-and within-industry spillovers do not change in comparison to the OLS, although the coefficients have grown larger and indicate a downward bias from OLS models (Table 3).

On the other hand, 'urbanization economy' factors, such as connectivity to transportation and urban amenities (POIs), either lose significance or direction of impacts in the IV models. The IVs used in the 2SLS models intend to correct the simultaneous effect that planned developments have on employment growth and spatial production externalities. Here, the model results indicate that urbanization economy factors do not promote employment growth and urbanization economies at the same time. This means that the economic development plan in Chicago during this time period prioritizes development in places with better connectivity to transportation hubs and urban amenities for higher job growth. However, the growth model results indicate that when we remove the planned zoning effects, better connectivity to transportation hubs and urban amenities do not generate a causal relationship with employment growth. Instead, the major drivers of job growth are places that feature better cross-industry spillovers and places that have diverse and related activities based on the consistent within-and cross-spillover coefficients.

Market-driven growth versus plan comparison

This section explores the difference between the planned employment growth from the CMAP official 2040 vision at the subsectional spatial resolution and the model simulation of the spatial configuration that maximizes spatial production externalities.

The results displayed in Figure 4 indicate that the downtown area has mostly similar job growth predictions (< 15% difference) between the CMAP vision and the market-driven trend (model forecast). The major difference occurs in the north-western and southern parts of Chicago where the market-driven trend predicts much higher employment growth. If Figure 1 is used as a reference base, it can be observed that these two parts of Chicago (south of Cook County) have a diverse economic base. In Figure 4, they are identified as the 'red' areas where the market-trend simulation almost doubles the employment growth provided in the CMAP vision. Northwest Chicago features a diverse economy growth and a strong emerging trend of new commercial offices. The areas south of Cook County have a similarly diverse growth with more weight on manufacturing growth. Thus, the model simulation forecasts that under a market-driven trend, emerging establishments will highly value the spatial production externalities of commercial and manufacturing establishments and create strong employment growth in these two parts of Chicago. The CMAP vision expects employment growth in the south-west corner of Chicago, which is most likely because there is an important intersection between Interstate 1–55 and Highway 50. It is understandable for economic planning to highlight major intersections for future employment growth. However, the lack of existing commercial establishments in that region makes it much less attractive for new establishments under a market-driven scenario.

Discussion and policy implications

This analysis has highlighted the importance of understanding the heterogeneity in agglomeration effects at a spatial scale familiar to planners. Echoing Ellison and Glaeser Edward (1997), the results indicate that, for an establishment, proximity to another establishment in a sector relevant to its supply chain is beneficial for employment growth. On the other hand, proximity to an establishment in the same sector (specialization) leads to negative job growth externalities at local (block) level.

The important practical takeaway from this study is the comparison of each sector's employment growth as expected under CMAP vision versus the market-driven one. The findings of 2SLS models suggest that urbanization economies are endogenous to planned development while spatial production externalities with the most related industrial sectors have shown consistent and non-endogenous impacts. This is further supported by the varying results of employment density impacts over distance on employment growth since the new commercial establishments tend to locate outside the traditional CBD for other higher sector-specific agglomeration economies (Yang et al., 2019b).

When compared with CMAP 2040 visions, the projections of the employment growth generated by our econometric model confirm the prior point. While places such as highway interchanges traditionally generate strong attractions for economic development (Pan et al., 2019), our econometric results show the opposite. Therefore, critical discrepancies are present between the CMAP visions that favour transportation hubs while the market-driven trend extrapolation suggests spatial production externalities are more important. It is noteworthy that the findings of this paper focus on the location of job growth. The factors that affect households or population growth can be different and are not in the scope of this paper. For example, the demographic drivers of development may have important feedback effects on the location of economic activity.

These new trends and evidence call for a reconsideration of the current economic and land-use planning methods in locating future urban growth. First, the fundamental roles of heterogeneous spatial production externalities in stimulating urban economic growth, though often noted at the city-regional level, prove to be more critical to urban design and land-use planning at the block level. More finetuned local policy measures should be advocated to provide a complementary perspective that maximizes the benefits from localization economies under the regional economic development goals. Second, policy-makers should be cautious about the sources of agglomeration that emerge in places beyond the traditional city centre and transport hubs. As employment density may no longer play a dominant positive role in employment attraction for job growth, the suburbanization of employment should be more often in the spotlight as a potential source of new subcentres with sector-specific spatial production externalities. Similarly, the bottom-up approaches that encourage the specialized clustering of business establishments may prove to be more preferable to city-level land-use planning for local economic growth based on improved regional connectivity. The outcomes of this paper add further evidence to the previous findings by Kim (2011) on how policy interventions in land use lead to the economic growth/ decline through spatial (re)arrangement, and, especially, the arguments of Glaeser (2008) and Lucas and Rossi-Hansberg (2002) on the way that the growing density in urban centres often accounts for higher productivity as a result of the zoning regulation and market response. We demonstrate that the zoning policies that aim at 'densification' for higher productivity need to incorporate the sectorspecific related spatial production externalities to realize the policy goal.

Conclusions

This paper explores the relationship between spatial configuration of land use and spatial externalities for production across various economic sectors. For the first research question concerning the effects of local sectorspecific spillover on employment growth, it identifies the main determinants, especially the heterogeneous spatial production externalities, that contribute to local employment growth. For the second research question on how official planning vision can be further optimized by the new discovery on spatial production externalities, a comparison between market-trend-based simulation and CMAP vision of development reveals the limitations of the assumptions traditionally used in planning (e.g., Kim, 2011) in that economic development does not only occur in highly accessible and highly dense areas, but is more likely to take place in local hotspots with stronger production potential in cross-industrial spillovers. In addition, the results at a finer spatial resolution resonate with the rapid distance-decay effects of production externalities (e.g., Andersson et al., 2019; van Soest et al., 2006) in the Chicago case. This informs local planners and urban designers on the importance of tapping into the potential of localized economies at the block level.

Based on these findings, this paper calls for an interdisciplinary research agenda that should be explored at the intersection of land-use planning and urban economic development. The missing components of economic concerns in local plan-making should be supplemented through the revealed reciprocal relationships across specific business sectors in the local context. In addition, the increasingly available disaggregated data from land-use plans have their untapped potential in providing micro-and intra-city level insights (e.g., the importance of block-level diversity and related spatial production externalities for job growth) to the economics literature.

Further research could look into the site-scale development patterns in specific areas to support the local policies better. It is noteworthy that although this study provides consistent evidence with previous work, it cannot yet be concluded that production externalities across scales are materialized through the same mechanism. For example, the spatial production externalities found at the local level (100–400 m) take place through face-to-face knowledge exchange. In comparison, the mechanisms at the city-regional scale may rely more on shared infrastructure or knowledge spillover through labour mobility.

Acknowledgements

This paper benefited greatly from the comments and suggestions received at the Regional Studies Association (RSA) Winter Conference in 2018. The authors thank the guest editors, John Harrison, Daniel Galland and Mark Tewdwr-Jones, as well as three anonymous referees for constructive feedback and comments.

Disclosure statement

No potential conflict of interest was reported by the authors.

Funding

This work was supported by Cambridge Commonwealth and the European and International Trust.

ORCID

Haozhi Pan http://orcid.org/0000-0002-0709-632X
Tianren Yang http://orcid.org/0000-0002-3547-5853
Geoffrey Hewings http://orcid.org/0000-0003-2560-3273

References

Alonso, W. (1964). *Location and land use: Toward a general theory of land rent*. Cambridge, MA: Harvard University Press.
Andersson, M., Klaesson, J., & Larsson, J. P. (2016). How local are spatial density externalities? Neighbourhood effects in agglomeration economies. *Regional Studies, 50*, 1082–1095. doi:10.1080/00343404.2014.968119
Andersson, M., Larsson, J. P., & Wernberg, J. (2019). The economic microgeography of diversity and specialization externalities – Firm-level evidence from Swedish cities. *Research Policy, 48*, 1385–1398. doi:10.1016/j.respol.2019.02.003
Arzaghi, M., & Henderson, J. V. (2008). Networking off Madison Avenue. *Review of Economic Studies, 75*, 1011–1038. doi:10.1111/J.1467–937X.2008.00499.x

Beaudry, C., & Schiffauerova, A. (2009). Who's right, Marshall or Jacobs? The localization versus urbanization debate. *Research Policy, 38,* 318–337. doi:10.1016/j.respol.2008.11.010

Bishop, P., & Gripaios, P. (2010). Spatial externalities, relatedness and sector employment growth in Great Britain. *Regional Studies, 44,* 443–454. doi:10.1080/00343400802508810

Boschma, R., Eriksson, R. H., & Lindgren, U. (2014). Labour market externalities and regional growth in Sweden: The importance of labour mobility between skill-related industries. *Regional Studies, 48,* 1669–1690. doi:10.1080/00343404.2013.867429

Boschma, R., Minondo, A., & Navarro, M. (2012). Related variety and regional growth in Spain. *Papers in Regional Science, 91,* 241–256.

Cervero, R. (2001). Efficient urbanisation: Economic performance and the shape of the metropolis. *Urban Studies, 38,* 1651–1671.

Chicago Metropolitan Planning Agency (CMAP). (2015). 2040 *Forecast of population households and employment.* Retrieved from https://datahub.cmap.illinois.gov/dataset/2040-forecast-of-population-households-and-employment

Chicago Metropolitan Planning Agency (CMAP). (2016). *Land use inventory for Northeast Illinois,* 2010. Retrieved from https:// datahub.cmap.illinois.gov/dataset/land-use

Chung, S., & Hewings, G. (2019). A short exercise to assess the effects of temporal and spatial aggregation on the amounts of spatial spillovers. In R. Franklin (Ed.), *Population, place, and spatial interaction, new frontiers in regional science: Asian perspectives* (pp. 35–56). Heidelberg: Springer.

Chung, S., & Hewings, G. J. D. (2015). Competitive and complementary relationship between regional economies: A study of the great lake states. *Spatial Economic Analysis, 10,* 205–229. doi:10.1080/17421772.2015.1027252

Duranton, G., & Turner, M. A. (2012). Urban growth and transportation. *Review of Economic Studies, 79,* 1407–1440. doi:10.1093/restud/rds010

Ellison, G., & Glaeser Edward, L. (1997). Geographic concentration in U.S. manufacturing industries: A dartboard approach. *Journal of Political Economy, 105,* 889–927.

Frenken, K., van Oort, F., & Verburg, T. (2007). Related variety, unrelated variety and regional economic growth. *Regional Studies, 41,* 685–697. doi:10.1080/00343400601120296

Fujita, M., Krugman, P. R., & Venables, A. J. (2001). *The spatial economy: Cities, regions, and international trade.* Cambridge, MA: MIT Press.

Glaeser, E. (2011). Cities, productivity, and quality of life. *Science, 333,* 592–594. doi:10.1126/science.1209264

Glaeser, E. L. (2008). *Cities, agglomeration, and spatial equilibrium.* Oxford: Oxford University Press.

Glaeser, E. L., Kallal, H. D., & heinkman, J. A., & Shleifer, A. (1992). Growth in cities. *Journal of Political Economy, 100,* 1126–1152. doi:10.1086/261856

Hanlon, W. W., & Miscio, A. (2017). Agglomeration: A long-run panel data approach. *Journal of Urban Economics, 99,* 1–14. doi:10.1016/j.jue.2017.01.001

Henderson, V. (1997). Externalities and industrial development. *Journal of Urban Economics, 42,* 449–470. doi:10.1006/juec.1997.2036

Henderson, V., Kuncoro, A., & Turner, M. (1995). Industrial development in cities. *Journal of Political Economy, 103,* 1067–1090. doi:10.1086/262013

Hu, L., Yang, J., Yang, T., Tu, Y, & Zhu, J. (2019). Urban spatial structure and travel in China. *Journal of Planning Literature.* doi:10.1177/0885412219853259

Jacobs, J. (2016). *The economy of cities.* Visalia: Vintage.

Kim, J. H. (2011). Linking land use planning and regulation to economic development: A literature review. *Journal of Planning Literature, 26,* 35–47. doi:10.1177/0885412210382985

Kim, J. H., & Hewings, G. J. D. (2013). Land use regulation and intraregional population—employment interaction. *Annals of Regional Science, 51,* 671–693. doi:10.1007/s00168-013-0557-l

Lucas, R. E., & Rossi-Hansberg, E. (2002). On the internal structure of cities. *Econometrica, 70,* 1445–1476. doi:10.1111/1468-0262.00338

Marshall, A. (1961). *Principles of economics: An introductory volume.* London: Macmillan.

Nam, K., & Kim, B. H. S. (2017). The effect of spatial structure and dynamic externalities on local growth in Seoul metropolitan area. *Urban Policy and Research, 35,* 165–179. doi:10.1080/08111146.2016.1159554

Ottaviano, G., & Thisse, J.-F. (2004). Agglomeration and economic geography. *Cities and Geography, 4,* 2563–2608. doi:10.1016/S1574-0080(04)80015-4

Paci, R., & Usai, S. (1999). Externalities, knowledge spillovers and the spatial distribution of innovation. *Geojournal, 49,* 381–390. doi:10.1023/A:1007192313098

Pan, H., Deal, B., Chen, Y, & Hewings, G. (2018). A reassessment of urban structure and land-use patterns: Distance to CBD or network-based? — Evidence from Chicago. *Regional Science and Urban Economics, 70,* 215–228. doi:10.1016/j.regsciurbeco.2018.04.009

Pan, H., Page, J., Zhang, L., Chen, S., Cong, C., Destouni, G., ... Deal, B. (2019). Using comparative socio-ecological modeling to support climate action planning (CAP). *Journal of Cleaner Production, 232,* 30–42. doi:10.1016/j.jclepro.2019.05.274

Porter, M. E. (2003). The economic performance of regions. *Regional Studies, 37,* 549–578. doi:10.1080/0034340032000108688

Rosenthal, S. S., & Strange, W. C. (2004). Evidence on the nature and sources of agglomeration economies. In J. V. Henderson & J.-F. Thisse (Eds.), *Handbook of regional and urban economics* (pp. 2119–2171). Cambridge, MA: Elsevier.

Van Oort, F. G. (2007). Spatial and sectoral composition effects of agglomeration economies in the Netherlands. *Papers in Regional Science, 86,* 5–30. doi:10.1111/j.l435-5957.2006.00088.x

Van Soest, D. P., Gerking, S., & van Oort, F. G. (2006). Spatial impacts of agglomeration externalities. *Journal of Regional Science, 46,* 881–899. doi:10.1111/j.l467-9787.2006.00488.x

Wixe, S., & Andersson, M. (2017). Which types of relatedness matter in regional growth? Industry, occupation and education. *Regional Studies, 51,* 523–536. doi:10.1080/00343404.2015.1112369

Yang, T.Jin, Y, Yan, L., & Pei, P., (2019a). Aspirations and realities of polycentric development: Insights from multi-source data into the emerging urban form of Shanghai. *Environment and Planning B: Urban Analytics and City Science, 46,* 1264–1280. doi:10.1177/2399808319864972

Yang, T., Pan, H., Hewings, G., &Jin, Y. (2019b). Understanding urban sub-centers with heterogeneity in agglomeration economies — Where do emerging commercial establishments locate? *Cities, 86,* 25–36. doi:10.1016/j.cities.2018.12.015

Spatial planning, nationalism and territorial politics in Europe

Claire Colomb and John Tomaney

Introduction

Over the past decade, nationalist parties have gained power at the regional level (alone or in coalitions) and augmented their claims for more autonomy or independence in several European countries. This resurgence of substate nationalism concerns the recasting of the 'politics of territorial solidarity' (Béland & Lecours, 2008). Although cultural claims and identity narratives remain important in regionalist and substate nationalist politics, challenges to existing constitutional and fiscal arrangements increasingly mobilize an economic discourse – a language of efficiency, competitiveness and good governance – as the basis of demands for more autonomy or independence (Rodriguez-Pose & Sandall, 2008). Simultaneously, new discourses about social policy and infrastructure requirements are promoted by nationalist parties to demand decentralization of power and resources (Beland & Lecours, 2008; Colomb et al., 2014).

Despite these trends, little academic attention has been paid to the link between substate nationalist claims and spatial planning, infrastructure and territorial management policies, even if the management of land use and territory is based on cultural and political choices about the built and natural environment, in which particular 'models of society' are materialized (Faludi, 2007). We should expect spatial planning to be an arena through which nationalist political actors (parties and civic movements)[1] invoke a distinctive 'collective territorial imagination' (Peel & Lloyd, 2007), and seek to distinguish the present, and future, character of their territory. In this paper we explore how spatial planning is mobilized by nationalist actors, through which they may seek to *envision* and shape their territory in substate contexts characterized by demands for more autonomy or independence. Specifically, we examine the territorial politics of spatial planning in Scotland (UK), Catalonia (Spain) and Flanders (Belgium). All three territories have achieved significant degrees of self-government, notably in spatial planning and cognate fields.

In contrast to traditional 'land-use planning', which is limited to the regulation of land and property uses, the location of activities and the control of development at the local scale, 'spatial planning' as a state activity engages with complex, multifaceted problems in an integrated way and aims to envision shared territorial futures. It seeks to balance demands for economic development, environmental protection, and social and territorial equity through the distribution of key infrastructure and collective amenities, to protect areas of natural, environmental or historic value, and to coordinate the spatial impacts of sectoral policies such as transport, housing and economic development (e.g., Albrechts et al., 2003). The reality of planning policies and practices often differs, however, from this ideal definition of 'spatial planning'. Planning is an intrinsically political activity, shaped by shifting ideologies, governmental agendas and interest presentation, and attendant conflicts on the relationship between state, market and civil society (Nadin & Stead, 2008). Any form of (public) planning is an attempt to influence social, economic and environmental processes through various forms of regulation, policy instruments and modes of state action. Redistributive conflicts are at the heart of planning, which deals with fundamentally 'wicked problems' (Rittel & Webber, 1973) requiring trade-offs that benefit some interests and social groups at the expense of others (Campbell, 1996).

The paper is structured as follows. It first reviews the literature from a range of disciplines on the relationship between spatial planning (and territorial management activities), nation-building, state formation, regional decentralization and (substate) nationalist claims. We note the virtual silence in classical studies of nationalism on how public policies shape the organization of territory, a gap which this paper addresses. Second, the paper considers each case in turn, analysing the extent to which nationalist parties have mobilized spatial planning and territorial management issues in their discourses, and whether they have developed distinctive planning and territorial management policy agendas as part of their claims. Finally, the paper identifies similarities and differences between the three cases, outlines possible explanatory factors and ponders further research.

Envisioning the nation: spatial planning and territorial politics in contested states

Planning and the making of national state territories in Europe

If the nation is an 'imagined community' (Anderson, 1983), it is materialized in canals and ports, roads and railways, electricity grids and reservoirs. Long before the field of 'planning' was codified into extensive legislation, modern state formation involved the creation of postal services, statistical offices, cadastral and mapping exercises (Gellner, 1983; Scott, 1998). The planning and construction of strategic transport and communications infrastructure, together with the provision of public services, was a vital component of state-building in Europe (Williams & Smith, 1983). In France after 1870, as Weber (1976, p. 218) memorably states, roads and railways 'welded several parts into one' and turned 'peasants into Frenchmen'. Such infrastructure planning connected, bounded, subdued and unified the territory 'to assimilate or incorporate culturally distinctive territories' via a process of 'state building nationalism' (Breuilly, 1993). Similar practices were witnessed in Spain (Bel, 2010, 2011), the UK (Hewitt, 2011) and Belgium (De Vries, 2015), albeit reflecting variable national configurations of political and social forces.

In the 20th century, forms of territorial planning were instrumental in the formation and consolidation of 'Keynesian welfare states', alongside national demand management and social programmes which in Europe took a range of forms (Brenner, 2004). The provision of collective goods such as public housing, education and transport was intended to achieve social and territorial cohesion and required planning on a large scale. 'Spatial Keynesianism' typically involved the centralization of regulatory capacities, the creation of uniform systems of local government and efforts to equalize public investment and infrastructure across the territory. However, the way states have intervened to shape economy, society and the territory varies from country to country (Esping-Andersen, 1990). In planning studies, this is reflected in attempts to compare, classify and typologize national planning systems, practices and cultures in Europe (e.g., Commission of the European Communities (CEC), 1997; Nadin & Stead, 2008; Newman & Thornley, 1996; Knieling & Othengrafen, 2009).

The unifying ambitions of the central state were always frustrated, however, in part because 'high modernist schemes in liberal democratic settings must accommodate themselves sufficiently to local opinion in order to avoid being undone at the polls' (Scott, 1998, p. 102). 'Spatial Keynesianism' became destabilized by processes of economic restructuring unfolding from the 1970s onwards, which reinforced some pre-existing 'centre–periphery' cleavages which historic processes of national state formation had not erased (Rokkan & Urwin, 1983). Demands for decentralization emerged or intensified in many West European countries and led to reforms of uneven pace and scope. Decentralization to the 'meso-level' of regions has been driven by various factors (Keating, 2013), not least by regionalist electoral insurgencies reflecting a contested 'territorial politics' (Keating, 2008). However, decentralization reforms did not quench demands for more autonomy: over the recent decades, in several European countries, regionalist/nationalist parties have won power at the regional level and strengthened their claims for increased autonomy or even outright independence, as shown below.

(Substate) nationalism and the making of the territory

Nationalism is 'an ideological movement for attaining and maintaining autonomy, unity and identity for a population which some of its members deem to constitute an actual or potential "nation"' (Smith, 2001, p. 9). A nation, meanwhile, is 'a named human community occupying a home- land, and having common myths and a shared history, a common public culture, a single economy and common rights and duties for all members' (p. 13). Nation and state are not necessarily congruent – there are many 'stateless nations' and some multinational states. In classical discussions of nationalism, it is notable that the role of 'territory' is frequently omit- ted, or merely treated as a container for a (latent or existing) nation, whose borders may be contested. Smith (2001), however, emphasizes the threefold importance of 'homeland' in the emergence of nationalist claims. First, homeland acts:

> as a tide-deed, a political claim to a specified area of land and its re- sources, often in the teeth of opposition from rival claimants. From this perspective, the homeland is indispensable for economic well-being and physical security, and the exploitation of its agricultural and mineral resources becomes a prime nationalist consideration.
>
> (pp. 31–32)

Second, 'the homeland constitutes an historic territory, the ancestral land' of the people and the setting for 'foundational' historical events (and their sites of memory). Third, Smith highlights the profound effect of 'land- scapes' (and their representations) on the self-understanding of members of the nation.

According to Etherington (2003, 2010), the neglect of territory in foun- dational studies of nationalism is attributable to the tendency to naturalize the relationship between the two, and to focus on the temporal, rather than the spatial/geographical, dimension of nation-building (Etherington, 2010, p. 323). 'National territorial belonging' is a distinctly modern phenomenon (Billig, 1995), shaped by the practices of states in 'territory making' and in the 'naturalisation of links between territories and people' (Paasi, 1997, p. 41). This is achieved, first, through the incorporation of physical features of the territory into representations of national identity and, second, at a symbolic level through nationalist (re)interpretations of the territory fusing the homeland with elements of identity such as culture, language, common myths and history, religious buildings, fields or even trees (Etherington, 2010). Among the instruments that have been used to legitimate nationalist territorial claims and promote territorial belonging are geography teaching, cartography (Agnew, 1987; Nogué, 1998), practices such as hiking, or the celebration and reproduction of landscapes in painting, poems and songs (Hooson, 1994; Nogué & Vicente, 2004; Schama, 1995).

Williams and Smith (1983) additionally emphasize how the *remaking of the environment* is a key part of nationalist projects:

> The manner in which nationalists 'activate' and mould their territories to fit their visions – the construction of ports and waterways, the regulation of law and rights, the use of development plans for industrialization, the strengthening of borders, the construction of tariffs, the use of settlements, communication networks and trade flows to alter the physical and occupational balance within a territory testify to the shaping of 'national' space economies'.
>
> (p. 514)

Additionally, the relationships between urban and rural areas, between city and country, have often been recurring themes in (substate) nationalist debates (Nel·lo, 2013a). The conservative Catalanist cultural-political movement of the early 20th century, for example, was rooted in a mystified image of rural life and shaped by a fear of the potential social and political upheaval brought about by 'revolutionary', working-class Barcelona, the distrusted modern industrial city (Nel·lo, 2013a, 2015). This later filtered into an insistence on decentralizing population and activities from the city and 'balancing' the territory.[2]

Few studies of (substate) nationalism, however, examine how public policies shape the territory and the organization of the 'homeland' – either the policies of the larger state whose authority and legitimacy is contested, or the policies proposed or developed by insurgent (substate) nationalist parties. This is important because 'if state processes are a reflection of distinctiveness and national identity, planning as a state process should be a reflection of and motivation for identity and distinctiveness' (Allmendinger, 2001, p. 44). If nationalist ideologies and movements have 'well-defined goals of collective self-rule, territorial unification and cultural identity' (Smith, 2001, p. 21), spatial planning and territorial management policies should be crucial in achieving those ends, as well as operationalizing 'national' socioeconomic projects materialized in space.

Béland and Lecours (2008) have shown that debates on social policy have become central to processes of substate identity formation and territorial mobilization, because this policy field represents a tangible manifestation of the existence of a political community. In contentious regions such as Québec, Scotland or Flanders, nationalist leaders suggest that autonomy or independence is needed because their population has distinctive social and economic preferences and constitutes a separate 'world of welfare' (Esping-Andersen, 1990). Here, we consider the extent to which nationalist actors also argue that their population have different preferences in terms of spatial and territorial organization, development and policies. The following sections analyse the extent to which nationalist parties have mobilized spatial planning and territorial management issues in their political discourses, and whether they have developed (distinctive) planning and territorial management policy agendas as part of their claims. Beforehand, however, we provide an overview of the current state of decentralization, spatial planning and territorial political conflicts in the three regions analysed in this paper.

Decentralization, regionalism/ nationalism and spatial planning in scotland, catalonia and flanders

Over the past decades, Scotland, Catalonia and Flanders have asserted historical claims for autonomy within their respective states and experienced decentralization (Table 1). Each territory now has its parliament and government and a broadly similar range of administrative powers: in addition to key competences such as language, culture and education, these include fields which shape the organization of the territory, for example, rural development, regional transport, local government, housing, environment, tourism, economic development, land-use and spatial planning. In each case, with some variation, the central state retains competences in constitutional matters, foreign affairs, defence, social security, immigration and nationality, energy regulation, key national infrastructure networks, and taxation.

Comparative studies of the effect of regional decentralization in Europe have tested whether new 'territorial policy communities' and divergent policy trajectories have emerged as a result (Keating, 2005, 2013; Keating et al., 2009). Political scientists have focused on fields such as social policy, culture, language and education, but much less so on spatial planning and territorial management policies. In parallel, in the field of planning studies, comparative approaches to planning systems in Europe have primarily focused on the national scale, neglecting how distinctive planning agendas and practices may emerge at other spatial scales. Yet, decentralization is generally seen to facilitate the operation of strategic spatial planning, providing frameworks of political accountability and enabling the promotion of regional social, cultural and environmental assets in ways which central governments have failed to achieve (Albrechts et al., 2003). In Scotland, Catalonia and Flanders, the decentralization of planning competences was reflected in the enactment of new legislation (Table 1) and led to signs of divergence in approaches to territorial management, at least at the level of policy discourses. A shift to more strategic spatial planning was witnessed in all three cases.

In the UK, devolution has allowed greater experimentation in planning strategies and delivery styles, generating a diversity of 'spatial plannings' *between* and *within* the four home nations (Allmendinger & Haughton, 2010; Colomb & Tomaney, 2015; Tewdwr-Jones & Allmendinger, 2006; Tomaney & Colomb, 2018). Scotland always remained a distinct jurisdiction with its own body of planning law. Planning reforms introduced by the first two Scottish governments after 1999 (Labour-Liberal Democrat coalitions) – notably the

Table 1 Scotland, Catalonia and Flanders: basic institutional setting and planning system.

	Scotland (UK)	Catalonia (Spain)	Flanders (Belgium)
Size	78,387 km^2 UK: 243,610 km^2	32,114 km^2 Spain: 505,992 km^2	13,522 km^2 Belgium: 30,528 km^2
Population	5.42 million UK 66.04 million (mid-2017 estimate)	7.54 million Spain 46.73 million (January 2018 estimate)	6.55 million Belgium 11.38 million (January 2018 estimate)
Density	69 inhabitants/km^2	235 inhabitants/km^2	484 inhabitants/km^2
Languages	English (Scottish Gaelic, Scots)	Catalan, Spanish	Flemish (Dutch)
Official structure of the nation-state	United Kingdom of Great Britain and Northern Ireland: unitary parliamentary constitutional monarchy with devolved governments	Kingdom of Spain: unitary parliamentary constitutional monarchy with 'autonomous communities'	Kingdom of Belgium: federal parliamentary constitutional monarchy
Key legislation for regional autonomy	Scotland Act 1998	Spanish Constitution of 1978: right to self-government of the 'nationalities and regions of Spain' = 17 autonomous communities plus two autonomous cities. For Catalonia: 1979 and 2006 Statutes of Autonomy	1980, later expanded. Three regions (Flanders, Wallonia, Brussels Capital) plus three linguistic communities (Dutch, French, German). Flemish community and Flemish region are merged
Institutions of regional government	Since 1999: Scottish Parliament; Scottish Government headed by a First Minister	Since 1979: Parlament de Catalunya; Generalitat de Catalunya headed by a President	Since 1980: Vlaams Parlement; Vlaamse Regering headed by a Minister-President
Sub-administrative units	32 unitary authorities/local councils (regional councils 1975–96, abolished)	4 provinces (Diputacions) 41 comarcas (aggregations of municipalities); 947 municipalities	5 provinces; 22 arrondissements; 308 municipalities
Spatial planning competence acquired	1999	1979	1980/88

(Continued)

	Scotland (UK)	Catalonia (Spain)	Flanders (Belgium)
Main spatial planning legislation	Town and Country Planning (Scotland) Act 1997 Chapter 8 as amended by the Planning etc. (Scotland) Act 2006	Llei de Política Territorial 1983 Llei d'Urbanisme revised version of 2010 plus various laws 2003–10	Decrees on spatial planning of 1996 and 1999 (and revisions)
Strategic spatial planning at the regional level	National Planning Framework (NPF); first in 2004, second in 2008, third in 2014	Pla Territorial General de Catalunya 1995; Plans Territorials Sectorials	Spatial Structure Plan for Flanders 1997; New Spatial Policy Plan for Flanders in preparation since 2011
Sub-regional plans	4 city-regional Strategic Development Plans	7 Plans Territorials Parcials	5 Provincial Structure/Implementation Plans
Local plans	Development Plans for 32 council areas and two national parks	Plans Directors Urbanístics (supramunicipal); Plans d'Ordenació Urbanística Municipal	Municipal Structure Plans/ Implementation Plans

Source: Authors.

Planning, etc (Scotland) Act 2006 – were generally similar to those enacted in England and Wales by the then New Labour government (Lloyd & Peel, 2009). The electoral victory of the Scottish National Party (SNP) in Scotland in 2007, and of a Conservativeled coalition in the UK in 2010, contributed to a divergence in planning agendas between England and Scotland, with a pro-market turn in the former and evidence of a more interventionist, pluralistic and corporatist policy-making approach in the latter (Tomaney & Colomb, 2013, 2018). The extent of this distinctiveness has, however, been debated (Allmendinger, 2006; Keating, 2005; Morphet & Clifford, 2014; Tomaney et al., 2019).

Catalonia and Flanders have been described as pioneers in their country with regards to the emergence of more strategic approaches to planning. In Catalonia, between 2003 and 2010, while the Spanish government was promoting a deregulatory agenda, the regional government – led by a coalition of three left-wing parties – enacted several laws to create a wide-ranging system of spatial plans covering the whole territory, to protect coastal areas, tackle urban sprawl and support integrated urban regeneration in deprived neighbourhoods (Nel·lo, 2012). In Belgium, the decentralization of planning competences led to divergent trajectories of spatial planning policies between the three regions. In Flanders, a shift from traditional land-use planning to new forms of strategic spatial planning was started by the CVP-SP-VU government (1991–95) and then continued by the Christian Democrat-Socialist coalition (1995–99) (Van den Broeck et al., 2014), in contrast to Wallonia where strategic spatial planning remained less developed. This was expressed by the 1997 Spatial Structure Plan for Flanders (Albrechts, 1999, 2001), which promoted polycentric development around the 'Flemish Diamond' (Brussels, Antwerp and Ghent), designated infrastructure corridors, and required urban growth boundaries to be drawn in order to halt sprawl (De Decker, 2011). The local planning permission system was tightened to restrict greenfield development (Van den Broeck & Verachtert, 2016).

The link between decentralization and the rise of new forms of – and agendas for – spatial planning is not straightforward, however. In Catalonia, the Generalitat had possessed spatial planning competences since 1979, but only exercised them in significant ways in the 2000s. In all three cases, the shift to a spatial planning approach was enacted when left-of-centre political parties or coalitions came to power, and was influenced by a new generation of academic and professional planners, as well as environmental and social movements (Albrechts, 1999; Nel·lo, 2003; Nogué & Wilbrand, 2010; Van den Broeck & Verachtert, 2016). This shift, as expressed in the case of Flanders by a senior planning scholar involved in the process of preparing the Spatial Structure Plan, encouraged different government departments to 'reflect on what kind of [region] they wished'.

Despite the high degree of decentralization achieved in the three territories, none has reached a stable consensus about the distribution of powers between different tiers of government. In all three cases, nationalist parties attained power, in coalition governments or alone: in 1999 (and more markedly in 2004) in Flanders, in 2007 in Scotland and in 2010 in Catalonia. Moreover, the post-2008 economic crisis fuelled renewed claims about the 'politics of territorial solidarity'. Central government austerity reinforced Catalan demands for greater fiscal autonomy on the grounds that the region (which accounts for one-fifth of Spanish economic output) returns more to the centre than it receives (Bel, 2015). In Belgium, Flemish nationalists argued that Flanders should not be subsidizing poorer Wallonia. Under the Barnett formula, Scotland benefits from the system of financial allocation to the devolved administrations of the UK. However, grievances about the exploitation of oil resources on Scottish territory was an important theme in the independence referendum debates in 2014, in the context of austerity imposed by the UK Conservative government since 2010 (which affects Scotland in fields such as social security).

Spatial Planning In Substate Nationalist Agendas

We now analyse to what extent nationalist parties have mobilized spatial planning and territorial management issues in their discourses, and whether they have developed (distinct) planning and territorial management policy agendas as part of their claims. Our analysis is based on exploratory research conducted in the three territories between 2013 and 2018 using two main methods:

- Qualitative content analysis of primary documentary sources including the electoral manifestos of the main nationalist parties at regional elections since 1999 (Scotland), 2004 (Flanders) and 2010 (Catalonia); key official publications on the Scottish referendum and on the right to self-determination in Catalonia; strategic planning policy documents; and statements by relevant organized interests (e.g., civil society organizations or professional associations in fields related to planning).
- Thirty semi-structured interviews with key stakeholders involved in spatial planning and territorial management policies: officials from the (regional) ministries of planning; academic experts; elected members of the regional parliaments (in particular from nationalist parties); and representatives from professional planning associations and related interest groups.

Scotland

Following the 2011 elections, the SNP was able to form a majority government on the promise of a referendum on Scottish independence. In October 2012, the UK's Prime Minister and Scotland's First Minister signed an agreement on the terms of the referendum, which took place in September 2014. The prospect of establishing a progressive social policy in Scotland was at the core of the SNP's argument for independence (Béland & Lecours, 2008). The SNP is generally described as a moderate, left-of-centre party. Its supporters often associate Scottish national identity with notions of egalitarianism, social justice and progressive social policy preferences (Béland & Lecours, 2008), including greater support for state intervention, although the supposed prevalence of such values in Scottish society is debated (McCrone, 2017).

Spatial planning in Scotland acquired a relatively high profile on the agenda of the SNP governments, although it figured only intermittently in the party's electoral manifestos during this period. From 2010 onwards, the UK government – a coalition of Conservatives and Liberal Democrats – set out to reform the English planning system through the 2011 Localism Act, which dismantled strategic spatial planning initiatives in England. A divergence between the planning policy agendas of the Scottish and UK governments thus became more apparent (Tomaney & Colomb, 2013), although some similarities remained in the discourses of the two governments (e.g., an emphasis on 'sustainable economic growth' and efficiency in the planning permission process). Yet, unlike the anti-planning rhetoric of the Conservatives, the SNP government was keen to state the value of planning as a positive means of steering spatial development. Respondents from the public and private sectors and from various political parties remarked that that there seems to be a 'national consensus' about planning in Scotland, and that Scottish Conservatives have not sought to dismantle or vilify planning as has, at times, been the case in England.

The strategic and visionary element of planning supports the SNP's vision of an independent Scotland. The 3rd National Planning Framework (NPF) for Scotland (Scottish Government, 2014), published just before the independence referendum, contains a 30-year vision for the territory in support of sustainable economic growth and the transition to a low-carbon economy. It was presented as the spatial expression of the SNP government's Economic Strategy (Scottish Government, 2010), and emphasized the need to balance economic growth with environmental protection, the stewardship of natural resources and the development of renewable energy. Additionally, themes of social, regional and intergenerational equity figured prominently in the NPF and the Economic Strategy in ways that were absent in the UK government's National Planning Policy Framework for England (Department for Communities and Local Government (DCLG), 2012; Tomaney & Colomb, 2013). Interviewees stated that there were time pressures to finish NPF3 before the referendum of September 2014, and that it had to be 'aspirational, offer something for all of Scotland, and avoid controversial and divisive developments' (senior planner, Scottish government). The preparation of NPF3 generated, according to an official involved in the process, healthy discussions about the geography of Scotland and how certain parts of Scotland are represented. The identification of strategic national development projects as part of the document was, additionally, characterized by relative consensus. For instance, major infrastructure proposals for the Highlands and Islands were all accepted, in order to counterbalance the weight of the Central Belt.

The NPF (and associated policy guidance) is supposed to shape planning decisions in a range of sectors, such as economic development, regeneration, energy, environment, transport and digital infrastructure. Whether it effectively influences the investment decisions of public authorities and private investors remains unproven. The Scottish government's room for manoeuvre is limited by its inability to borrow directly on capital markets to fund infrastructure projects, and the UK parliament's remaining competences in key policy areas such as taxation, energy and airports. Energy policy is a source of contention because the SNP rejects nuclear power and fracking for shale gas. The devolution of spatial planning allowed the Scottish government to foster a de facto renewable energy policy (which already makes up 40% of Scotland's electricity generation), by promoting the development of wind farms, banning fracking and refusing the building of new nuclear power stations. However, the Scottish government's ambitions come up against the constraints of the national electricity grid, which remains a UK government regulatory responsibility.

Before the 2014 Referendum, the Scottish government published its prospectus for independence in a document entitled *Scotland's Future* (Scottish Government, 2013). It set out its ambitions 'for the type of economy and society that captures Scotland's distinct values and build distinct economic, industrial and social policies which reflect these aims' (p. 94). It asserted that independence would allow 'an alternative economic policy' to that 'which disproportionately benefits London and the South East of England' (p. xii), leading to stronger connections between urban and rural, island and mainland, national and international. Independence would also enable the alignment of transport policy with energy policy to achieve declared carbon reduction targets.

Much of the case for independence rested on the benefits arising from full control of Scotland's rich natural resources, such as the seabed and oil and gas reserves, claimed to be 'central to our identity as a country and as a people' (p. 288). It was proposed that independence would 'enable a regulatory approach that is tailored to specific Scottish conditions that influence the costs of keeping homes warm, such as our climate, our mix of urban, rural and remote communities and our distinctive housing stock' (p. 169). It was asserted that 'the harsher Scottish climate and the challenges of heating remote homes call for an ambitious approach to energy efficiency and carbon emissions reduction' (p. 167). It is worth nothing that this narrative is, in the UK context, not unique to Scotland: Jones and Ross (2016) have analysed how nationalists in Wales have claimed that 'sustainable development that is allegedly more attuned to Welsh national values and identities', and 'is being used to imagine new and possibly more inclusive kinds of futures for the Welsh nation' (p. 54).

The Scottish independence referendum took place on 18 September 2014. Independence was rejected by 55% to 45%. After the referendum, there were further changes to the devolution settlement as the full provisions of the 2012 Scotland Act were rolled out. A commission was set up to prepare proposals for further devolution (Smith Commission, 2014), whose recommendations were included in the revised Scotland Act 2016. It gave extra power to the Scottish Parliament, for example, the management of the Crown Estate in Scotland, the setting of rates and thresholds of income tax, air passenger duty, the licensing of onshore oil and gas extraction, and rail franchising.

After 2014, some planning-related activities of the Scottish government strengthened the contrast with the planning agenda in England, in particular through the Community Empowerment Act 2015 and the Land Reform Act 2016, which grants some power to the Scottish government to force the sale of private land to community bodies so that land 'can be best managed in the public interest to ensure it is of benefit to all of the people of Scotland' (SNP, 2015, p. 32), a contentious issue in a country where large landlords historically own a sizable part of the territory (for a discussion, see Wightman, 2019). These reforms illustrate an approach to 'localism' and community empowerment by the SNP, which is markedly different than the 'new localism' agenda of the UK government in England. A further reform of Scottish planning legislation was announced by the Scottish government, with a new Planning (Scotland) Bill presented to parliament in 2017. The legislation had a fractious passage through the Scottish parliament, with the government claiming it streamlined the planning process, while opponents asserting it centralized power at the expense of local councils and communities (Tomaney et al., 2019).

Catalonia

In 2006, a new Statute of Autonomy for Catalonia was approved in the Spanish parliament, but judicially challenged by the right-wing Partido Popular (PP). In 2010, the Spanish Constitutional Court culled significant parts of the Statute, which led to massive protests in Catalonia and an increase in support for independentist parties (Table 2). Following the regional election of 2010 (and others in 2012, 2015 and 2017), Catalonia has been governed by pro-independence parties spanning from the far left to the right of the political spectrum (Table 2), while the Spanish government was governed by the PP from 2011 until 2018. The Catalan separatist movement is additionally fuelled by powerful civil society associations and movements (such as the Catalan National Assembly), able to mobilize large crowds for the Catalan National Day on 11 September (Crameri, 2015). These organizations helped the Catalan government organize a referendum on self-determination on 1 October 2017, albeit declared illegal by the Spanish government. The vote was violently repressed by the Spanish police and followed by the temporary suspension of Catalan regional autonomy and enforcement of direct rule

Table 2 Regional parties and governments in Scotland, Catalonia and Flanders, 1999–2019.

		Scotland	Catalonia	Flanders
Regional political parties advocating independence or maximum autonomy	Left		Candidatura d'Unitat Popular (Popular Unity Candidacy) (CUP)	
	Centre left	Scottish National Party (SNP)	Esquerra Republicana de Catalunya (Republican Left of Catalonia) (ERC)	
	Right		Partit Demòcrata Europeu Català (European Catalan Democratic Party) (PDeCAT), known as Convergència Democràtica de Catalunya (Democratic Convergence of Catalonia) (CDC) before 2016. Note: CDC plus UDC coalesced into Convergencia i Unió (Convergence and Union) (CiU) 1978–2015	Nieuw-Vlaamse Alliantie (New Flemish Alliance) (N-VA) (previously VU)
	Far right			Vlaams Belang (Flemish Interest) (VB)
Other main regional political parties	Left	Scottish Greens	Iniciativa per Catalunya Verds & Esquerra Unida i Alternativa (Initiative for a Green Catalonia and United and Alternative Left) (ICV & EUiA) Catalunya en Comú (CatComú)–Podem (Catalonia in Common-We Can)	Groen (Green)
	Centre left	Scottish Labour Party Scottish Liberal Democrats	Partit dels Socialistes de Catalunya (Socialist Party of Catalonia) (PSC)	Socialistische Partij Anders (Socialist Party-Differently) (sp.a) (previously SP)
	Right	Scottish Conservative Party	Unió Democràtica de Catalunya (Democratic Union of Catalonia) (UDC), dissolved 2017. Note: CDC plus UDC coalesced into Convergencia i Unió (Convergence and Union) (CiU) 1978–2015 Ciutadans (Citizens) (Cs) Partit Popular de Catalunya (Popular Party of Catalonia) (PPC)	Open Vlaamse Liberalen en Democraten (Open Flemish Liberals and Democrats) (Open Vld) (previously VLD) Christen-Democratisch en Vlaams (Christian Democratic and Flemish) (CD&V) (previously CVP)
	Far right			

Year of regional elections and subsequent governments			
1999	Scottish Labour Party	CiU (CDC plus UDC)	Coalition: VLD, SP, Agalev (Greens) and VU
2000			
2001			
2002			
2003	Scottish Labour Party	Coalition: PSC, ERC, ICV	(until 2003)
2004			Coalition: CD&V, N-VA, sp.a and Open VLD
2005			
2006			
2007	Coalition: SNP–Scottish Liberal Democrats	Coalition: PSC, ERC, ICV	
2008			
2009			Coalition: CD&V, N-VA and sp.a
2010		CiU	
2011	SNP		
2012		CiU	
2013			
2014			Coalition: N-VA, CD&V and Open Vld
2015		Coalition: Junts pel Sí (CDC plus ERC), with ad hoc support from CUP	
2016	SNP		
2017		Coalition: Junts per Catalunya (PDeCAT plus independent), ERC	
2018			
2019			Coalition: N-VA, CD&V and Open Vld

Source: Authors.

until new regional elections in December 2017, at which pro-independence parties, reflecting the deep divisions in Catalan society, retained only a small majority.

Three phases can be identified in the planning and territorial management policy agenda of Catalan governments since 2010. The years 2010–12 were marked by a liberalizing approach. The economic crisis was used as a legitimizing argument to support large-scale urban development projects that were highly controversial in socioeconomic and environmental terms. New laws were passed partly to deregulate development control procedures. Austerity led to the freezing of the urban regeneration programme set up by the previous government. The revision of the General Territorial Plan of Catalonia – started in 2009 – was halted and some planning-related public agencies were dissolved. Nevertheless, several laws passed by the previous government were retained, in particular on landscape protection.

Between 2012 and 2017, the liberalizing drive of the Catalan government was somewhat weakened, partly to secure the support of other pro-independence parties (the Esquerra Republicana de Catalunya (ERC) and Candidatura d'Unitat Popular (CUP), respectively, on the centreleft and far left of the political spectrum) in the governing coalition. The manifestos of the main Catalan parties for the 2012 and 2015 regional elections reveal a degree of discursive convergence around objectives such as sustainable mobility; a compact urban model; tackling climate change; better management of natural resources; landscape protection; supporting renewable energy; and increasing affordable housing (with the exception of the PP, which does not mention these issues). In practice, however, as revealed in interviews with members of the Catalan parliament, there have been tensions within the governing coalition regarding particular policy issues (e.g., ring roads and motorway extensions).

The regional election campaign of 2015 focused on the right to self-determination and brought to power a coalition named Junts pel Si ('Together for Yes'), which focused its activities on enforcing that right and setting a 'roadmap' to independence. This generated fierce opposition from non-independentist parties, and meant that debates on key substantive policy issues, largely, have taken the back seat in the Catalan parliament. Draft proposals for a new regional 'Law of Territory' and 'Law on the Planning of Coastal Areas' were launched in 2014–15, but progress stopped in 2017 after the 'unauthorized' referendum. The Catalan government's White Paper on the so-called 'national transition' (GenCat, 2014) focuses on the steps to be taken to exercise the right to self-determination and achieve independence. It refers to the creation of 'state structures' (e.g., tax collection and social security institutions) as well as measures to ensure the continuity of energy, transport and water supply. However, it does not contain references to any substantive policy objectives for its nation-building project, which contrasts starkly with the detailed policy debates that preceded the Scottish referendum.

The pro-independence forces in Catalonia mainly mobilize claims about national identity and sense of community (i.e., language and education policy); economic viability (fiscal relations with the central state); and future opportunities in a global world (issues of infrastructure, especially transport) (Bel, 2015). Spatial planning in a strict sense does not figure prominently in those arguments. None of the electoral manifestos of pro-independence parties included an overall vision of the territory in the sense of a 'territorial model for Catalonia', which would offer a framework for all public policies (Societat Catalana d'Ordenació del Territori (SCOT), 2015, p. 6), with the possible exception of the left-wing anti-capitalist party CUP, which offers a radical vision of decentralized endogenous development and degrowth for Catalonia, with radical policies in relation to energy, water and food sovereignty. The strong territorial imbalances within Catalonia remain surprisingly unaddressed (e.g., rural depopulation or the lack of attention to the southern part of Catalonia, often forgotten in nationalist imaginary). As a senior Catalan planning scholar argued in a 2016 interview, 'spatial planning is not used for a national project'.

The lack of attention of the pro-independence political forces towards spatial planning contrasts strongly with the central importance of urban planning and related fields in the agenda of the parties that have governed Barcelona for most of the post-Franco period: the Socialist Party until 2011 and, after 2015, the new political force Barcelona en Comú. The latter has placed the right to housing, improvements to public transport, tackling air pollution, public energy and water management, and the return to a more 'socially focused' urban planning at the heart of its agenda, arguing that distributional questions should come first in the city's politics – not the 'national' question. Additionally, an emerging metropolitan-scale planning vision (Pla Estratègic Metropolita de Barcelona) has been developed by a not-for-profit association promoted by Barcelona City Council and the Metropolitan Area of Barcelona as an instrument for identifying the potential of the city-region's territory in the medium term, thus pointing towards a specifically metropolitan 'planning imaginary'.

These differences between the urban/metropolitan and regional political agendas reflect a longstanding historical cleavage in the electoral-political geography of Catalonia, between the Barcelona metropolitan region and the rest of the territory. In the former, left-wing, non-independentist parties gain the most votes, whereas in the latter, regionalist or pro-independence parties (both rightand left-wing) are most supported. The share of the votes for pro-independence parties has, however, increased in Barcelona from the early 2010s onwards. These parties have had to change their traditionally hostile vision of the city, and of metropolitan and urban issues, as a result. As expressed by a member of the Catalan parliament from the ERC party interviewed in 2016, there is 'no new nation without a strong capital city'.

Territorial management issues are nonetheless present in the narrative of pro-independence parties in relation to three themes. First, there are strong grievances about the 'unfair' fiscal transfers and distribution of public investment by the Spanish state between Autonomous Communities. Catalan governments have continually criticized the centralizing transport investment policies of successive Spanish governments, historically favouring the convergence of networks towards Madrid in what Bel (2010, 2011) terms a consolidation of the 'radial State' since the 17th century. Nationalists declaim the lack of financial support by the Spanish state for the Mediterranean rail corridor (linking the south of Andalusia through Catalonia to the Rhone Valley) and for the secondary railway network in Catalonia, while demanding control over airport and port management.

Second, the Spanish state and Catalan actors have clashed over the management of natural resources, notably water, such as the proposal by the PP government in 2000 to redirect water from the River Ebre which generated strong protests in Catalonia (although the then Convergencia i Unió (Ci-U)-led Catalan government initially supported the proposal).

Third, left-wing, pro-independence Catalan political parties and social groups associate control over natural resources with broader claims for a more egalitarian and ecologically sensitive national project, reflecting historical linkages between the Catalan environmental movement and the left-wing part of the independentist movement (Nogué, 1998).

Flanders

Flemish nationalism has its origins in the demand for equal status for the Dutch language in Belgium in relation to French, which was the language of the 19th-century ruling elite. After the Second World War, the rise of Flemish nationalism prompted the transformation of the Belgian state through a series of six constitutional reforms between 1970 and 2011, which have failed to quench Flemish demands for more autonomy. At present, around 58% of the population of Belgium is Dutch speaking and 31% French speaking. In the early 2000s, two Flemish nationalist parties became increasingly popular: the Nieuw-Vlaamse Alliantie (N-VA), a right-wing party founded in 2001 out of the previous Volksunie (1954–2001), and the Vlaams Belang (VB), a far-right party (earlier called Vlaams Blok, which gained strength in the late 1980s), which began to lose popularity after 2009 but regained 12% of the vote in the 2019 Belgian federal elections.

In 2004, the Flemish regional elections brought to power a coalition of Christian-Democrats, Social-Democrats and the N-VA. Since then, the N-VA has continued to attract a strong vote at local, regional and national elections, and been part of all Flemish governing coalitions (Table 2). The N-VA does not openly advocate independence, but a confederal model for Belgium which would move 'the centre of gravity of the socio-economic policy ... to the federated entities so that they can implement a policy at the level of their own inhabitants and economy' (N-VA, 2019, n.p.). Its manifestos express grievance about the level of fiscal redistribution between Flanders and

Wallonia. The N-VA favours low tax and limited state intervention, in particular in land-use management and private property rights. Under the leadership of Bart De Wever, the party moved to the right, with tougher stances on immigration and security. In its 2009 regional election programme, the N-VA also described itself as a 'green' party, advocating support for public transport and renewable energy – an emphasis which was lost thereafter.

Since 2004, Flanders has been governed by coalitions between the Christian Democratic and Flemish (CD&V), N-VA, and other parties (Table 2). The Flemish political consensus is often defined as 'right-wing', whereas the largest political party in Brussels and Wallonia is the Parti Socialiste. The notion of 'right-wing Flanders' and 'left-wing Wallonia' is a powerful trope in Belgian politics, although, arguably, this has less to do 'with "objective" socio-economic differences, but rather with a curiously persistent identity construction' (De Wever, 2011, p. 4). In the coalition system, individual ministers have extensive autonomy over their policy domains. The Ministry of Spatial Planning has moved between the Open Vlaamse Liberalen en Democraten (VLD) (1999–2009), N-VA (2009–14) and CD&V (2014–19).

In this political context, since the 2000s land-use planning has been blamed for hindering development, which has led to reforms facilitating greenfield development (Van den Broeck & Verachtert, 2016). The strategic spatial planning approach developed in the 1990s was weakened and spatial planning was reoriented towards the protection of private property, hampering 'the capacity of government to implement a coherent spatial policy and collective spatial projects' (Van den Broeck & Verachtert, 2016, p. 388). This reflected historic Flemish social and cultural preferences for private home ownership and unconstrained individual housebuilding, expressed in a popular distrust of government interference in planning (De Vries, 2015). This has been reflected in the enactment of widespread exceptions to zoning restrictions, a lax enforcement of planning regulations, local clientelist practices and illegal constructions (Van den Broeck & Verachtert, 2016).

In 2011, a process was launched to replace the Spatial Structure Plan for Flanders by a new Policy Plan for Town and Country Planning (Departement Ruimte Vlaanderen (DRV), 2016), still underway at the time of writing. A Green Paper (DRV, 2012) set out key principles for the future plan, including the rejection of urban sprawl and preference for the protection of green spaces. A 2016 White Paper further acknowledged the spatially dispersed, sprawling and car-dependent urbanization pattern of Flanders, defining the key objective of the future plan as 'doing more with less space' (DRV, 2016) by stopping all new construction on unused open space by 2040. In July 2018, the Flemish government approved the 'Strategic Vision' of the future Flanders Spatial Policy Plan (DRV, 2018), which confirmed the commitment to reduce greenfield development, although this has been undermined in practice by recent planning decisions (Tomaney & Colomb, 2014) and the pro-growth political agenda of Flemish governments since 1999.

The Strategic Vision does not include any map or visualizations of future development patterns for the whole Flemish territory. Moreover, it contains a strong localist rhetoric, calling for 'provinces, cities and municipalities [to be] given more responsibilities' to 'determine for themselves which town and country planning projects they will focus on'. It abandons 'the notion of a strict planning concept, imposed by the Government of Flanders' (p. 30), and limits the role of the Flemish government to determining large-scale transformation projects. Intermunicipal cooperation is proposed to deal with issues such as water management, housing development and mobility management, but with little indication of how it should be incentivized.[3]

More notably, there has been little interregional cooperation at the political level between the three regions of Belgium on key, transregional planning issues. Before the decentralization of planning to the regions, the Belgian national planning system initially permitted a national plan, but none was ever produced. The lack of coordinated strategic planning to guide the growth of the Brussels metropolitan area is a particularly pressing issue, as its functional urban economy extends far beyond the administrative boundaries of the capital city-region. The Flemish government has been standing with its back to Brussels', as expressed by a senior planning scholar. Land-use planning in the Flemish municipalities around Brussels is highly politicized and has been used as a mean of pursuing 'language wars' (Boussauw et al, 2013). As French has become the majority language in Brussels, in the Dutch-speaking 'Flemish Fringe' that encircles the city, there is resistance to the growth of new Francophone communities. The growth of the Brussels functional urban area and extended commuter flows is seen as posing a threat to the national (linguistic) identity of Flanders, and Flemish municipalities have used restrictive planning policies to contain the 'francisation' of their territory, for example, by attaching conditions to the sale of public land or social housing allocation (stipulating that prospective buyers or tenants should have a link to the municipality), or by setting height limits to new housing development (as done in the district of Brussels-Halle-Vilvoorde). In December 2011, the Flemish government adopted a specific development perspective for the 'Flemish Strategic Area around Brussels' (VSGB), which delineates an urban growth boundary aimed at containing the growth of Brussels. The (Socialist) Minister-President of the Brussels-Capital Region subsequently filed a complaint with the federal Council of State against this plan in the summer of 2012.

Conclusions: spatial planning, substate nationalism and the politics of territory in Europe

The three cases explored here reveal that spatial planning and territorial development issues *can* be mobilized politically to support the autonomist or separatist political agendas of substate nationalist parties. However, the present research shows that such issues are rarely central compared to social or linguistic policy issues, although as the Flanders case shows, planning laws can be used as a means to prosecute language wars. Taking Beland and Lecours' (2008) analysis one step further, we showed that spatial planning and territorial management issues gained prominence in such agendas, sometimes indirectly, because they contain redistributive demands linked with interterritorial fiscal transfers and, centrally, because they reflect the relationship between state, market and civic society in the management of land, wherein 'models of society' (Faludi, 2007) and 'worlds of welfare' (Esping-Andersen, 1990) are expressed. However, in none of the three cases does one witness the formulation of a cohesive and comprehensive spatial vision for the whole territory, although the NPF (in the Scottish case) comes closest to that. The absence of a strong spatial planning strategy 'does not necessarily imply the absence of a collective spatial project' (De Vries, 2015, p. 2160) – though it may be an implicit one. The development of a coherent and overarching strategic spatial strategy and policy – if it exists – remains overshadowed by decisions taken in other policy areas and at other scales of government – for example, large-scale road and rail infrastructure development, retail siting, and property taxation. In Flanders, for example, the 1997 RSV provided a long-term vision for the region, but it played a marginal role in the allocation of public resources (Tomaney & Colomb, 2014; Van Den Broeck, 2008) – reflecting the 'missing link' between strategic plans, public budgets and projects witnessed in many other contexts (see Moore-Cherry & Tomaney, 2019, for the Irish case).

When comparing the findings from the three cases, it is clear that nationalist parties mobilize spatial planning and territorial management to varying extents and in diverse ways. In Scotland, the SNP's planning discourse has been more strategic, interventionist and positive compared with that of the N-VA in Flanders. The claim that Scottish political culture is more consensual, egalitarian and favourable to state intervention (than its English counterpart) figured prominently in the case for Scotland's independence. There is evidence of the performativity of such proclaimed values in the Scottish strategic planning discourse, in part as a reaction to the 'anti-planning' rhetoric of the Conservatives in England. In Flanders, the N-VA – in coalition with other right-wing political parties and influenced by landowners and the building sector (Van den Broeck & Verachtert, 2016) – has favoured the liberalization of planning controls and shown scepticism about previous strategic planning approaches. The case of Catalonia is more ambiguous: because the three main parties advocating the right to self-determination are located from the radical left (CUP), via the moderate left (ERC) to the right of the political spectrum (Convergencia Democratica de Catalunya (CDC), which turned into the Partit Democrata Europeu Catala (PDeCat) in 2016), there are differences in policy agendas in relation to planning and territorial management policies, but also a degree of 'centrist' consensus because of the coalition dynamics between these different parties.

Thus, the analysis shows that the observed *differences* between the three cases seem to depend on the political ideology of each nationalist party vis-a-vis the role of the state and the legitimacy of public policy interventions in market processes. Differences are rooted in the relative value that parties attach to particular objectives such as sustainability, the protection of private property, economic growth, etc. The positioning of each party on the traditional *left-right* political spectrum, rather than their broader 'nationalist' disposition, seems to be more decisive in influencing the extent to which spatial planning is mobilized in their political discourse and policy agenda. In that regard, it is significant that the shift to strategic spatial planning that happened in the 1990s-2000s in the three regions was *not* pressed by regionalist or nationalist parties, but by coalitions of centrist, left-wing and/ or green parties that broadly shared a progressive social-democratic and environmental agenda in relation to questions of territorial management, at a moment when existing models of urban growth and resource consumption were becoming increasingly criticized (in particular in Flanders and Catalonia).

This paper addresses the relative absence of a concern with the production of the territory in classic studies of nationalism, by focusing on the production of the national space through public policies related to the planning and organization of the territory. The literature on nationalism notes the importance of the 'homeland' to the nationalist project (Smith, 2001) and pays particular attention to the discursive aspects of nation building, but it is noted how the spatial planning and geographical dimensions are comparatively neglected. In this paper we have sought to redress this lacuna using the lens of spatial planning to contribute to analyses of contemporary forms of substate nationalisms in Europe. Nations are imagined communities. We have shown how the 'shaping of territory' is an important aspect of nationalist politics in the three cases (albeit to a variable degree). Spatial planning has been an instrument to that end, although strategic ambitions often are defeated by day-to-day *realpolitik*. This paper thus draws attention to the role of spatial planning in envisioning and forming the national territory, while noting the considerable variation in how spatial visions are developed and subsequently materialized, reflecting the way national priorities are contested often along conventional left-right axes. We suggest this is a fruitful area for future comparative studies.

In future research, more attention needs to be paid to the social actors and economic interest groups that form the constituencies of regionalist and nationalist parties: first, their geographical distribution (which can offer insights into intraregional divides, e.g., between metropolitan areas and other parts of the territory); and second, how their characteristics influence their attitude to land, property, ecological issues or their pro- or anti-urban bias. As emphasized by De Vries (2015) in his insightful comparison of Dutch and Flemish planning cultures, the 'combination of urban morphology, actor constellations and societal values can shape the planning project in particular countries or regions', in particular 'the size and orientation of key actors in the land and property development process' (p. 2161). There is a need to unpack the fraught spatial metaphors that are commonly used in political and media discourses through the 'recurring substitution of *social* actors with *territorial* abstractions': "'rich regions', "poor regions", "Catalonia", "Spain", "Madrid" ... are metaphors continuously used to mask the fact that what is in competition are not territories, but social groups, economic interests and political projects' (Nel·lo, 2013b, pp. 49–50; authors' translation). Finally, while we focused here on policy discourses and agendas, further enquiry is needed into the implementation and impacts of policies enacted by governments led (or co-led) by nationalist parties, and into the extent of policy distinctiveness in spatial planning and territorial management – as there is often a large gap between promises and the reality of public policy implementation.

Acknowledgements

The authors thank all the interviewees in Catalonia, Flanders and Scotland who generously gave their time and insights. They are grateful to colleagues who offered constructive comments on earlier versions of this paper, which were presented at seminars at the London School of Economics, Birmingham University, Institut d'Aménagement et d'Urbanisme de Lille, University of Santiago de Compostela, Open University of Catalonia and KU Leuven. Thanks to the three anonymous referees and guest editors for their positive, detailed and extremely helpful comments.

Disclosure statement

No potential conflict of interest was reported by the authors.

Funding

The authors thank the UCL BartLett School of Planning, as well as the former Institut d'Estudis Autonòmies (now Institut d'Estudis de l'Autogovern) of the Generalitat de Catalunya, for small travel and research grants which supported several field visits.

Notes

1 We use the term 'nationalist' in a neutral, non-pejorative sense to refer to political and social forces that advocate more autonomy, or secession, for their region/ nation from the larger state of which it is a part.
2 The authors are grateful to an anonymous referee for raising this point.
3 The regional government has set up some funding to support such intermunicipal cooperation projects (e.g., Strategic Projects REKOVER in Kortrijk, Regionet in Leuven, the City Region of Turnhout and the City Region of Antwerp).

References

Agnew, J. (1987). *Place and politics: The geographical mediation of state and society.* Allen & Unwin.

Albrechts, L. (1999). Planners as catalysts and initiators of change: The new structure plan for Flanders. *European Planning Studies, 7*(5), 587–603. https://doi.org/10.1080/09654319908720540

Albrechts, L. (2001). Devolution, regional governance and planning systems in Belgium. *International Planning Studies, 6*(2), 167–182. https://doi.org/10.1080/13563470123288

Albrechts, L., Healey, P., & Kunzmann, K. (2003). Strategic spatial planning and regional governance in Europe. *Journal of the American Planning Association, 69*(2), 113–129. https://doi.org/10.1080/01944360308976301

Allmendinger, P. (2001). The head and the heart. National identity and urban planning in a devolved Scotland. *International Planning Studies, 6*(1), 33–54. https://doi.org/10.1080/13563470120026523

Allmendinger, P. (2006). Escaping policy gravity: The scope for distinctiveness in Scottish spatial planning. In M. Tewdwr-Jones, & P. Allmendinger (Eds.), *Territory, identity and spatial planning: Spatial governance in a fragmented nation* (pp. 153–166). Routledge.

Allmendinger, P., & Haughton, G. (2010). Spatial planning, devolution, and new planning spaces. *Environment and Planning C, 28*(5), 803–818. https://doi.org/10.1068/c09163

Anderson, B. (1983). *Imagined communities.* Verso.

Bel, G. (2010). *Espana, Capital Paris.* Destino.

Bel, G. (2011). Infrastructure and nation building: The regulation and financing of network transportation infrastructures in Spain (1720–2010). *Business History, 53*(5), 688–705. https://doi.org/10.1080/00076791.2011.599591

Bel, G. (2015). *Disdain, distrust, and dissolution. The surge of support for independence in Catalonia.* Sussex Academic Press.

Béland, D., & Lecours, A. (2008). *Nationalism and social policy: The politics of territorial solidarity.* Oxford University Press.

Billig, M. (1995). *Banal nationalism.* Sage.

Boussauw, L., Allaert, G., & Witlox, F. (2013). Colouring inside what lines? Interference of the urban growth boundary and the political–administrative border of Brussels. *European Planning Studies, 21*(10), 1509–1527. https://doi.org/10.1080/09654313.2012.722952

Brenner, N. (2004). *New state spaces.* Oxford University Press.

Breuilly, J. (1993). *Nationalism and the state* (2nd ed.). Manchester University Press.

Campbell, S. (1996). Green cities, growing cities, just cities? Urban planning and the contradictions of sustainable development. *Journal of the American Planning Association, 62*(3), 296–312. https://doi.org/10.1080/01944369608975696

Commission of the European Communities (CEC). (1997). *The EU compendium of spatial planning systems and policies.* Office for Official Publications of the European Communities.

Colomb, C., Bakke, K., & Tomaney, J. (2014). *Shaping the territory in Scotland, Catalonia and Flanders* (Working Paper No. 5). UCL European Institute. Retrieved from https://www.ucl.ac.uk/european-institute/news/2012/aug/shaping-territory-scotland-catalonia-and-flanders

Colomb, C., & Tomaney, J. (2015). Territorial politics, devolution and spatial planning in the UK. *Planning Practice and Research, 31*(1), 1–22. https://doi.org/10.1080/02697459.2015.1081337

Crameri, K. (2015). Political power and civil counterpower: The complex dynamics of the Catalan independence movement. *Nationalism and Ethnic Politics, 21*(1), 104–120. https://doi.org/10.1080/13537113.2015.1003491

De Decker, P. (2011). Understanding housing sprawl: The case of Flanders, Belgium. *Environment and Planning A, 43*(7), 1634–1654. https://doi.org/10.1068/a43242

Departement Ruimte Vlaanderen (DRV). (2012). *Green Paper: Flanders in 2050: Human scale in a metropolis? Spatial Policy Plan.* Retrieved from https://www2.ruimte. vlaanderen.be/ruimtelijk/docs/groenboek%20ruimtelijke%20ordening%20 EN %20DEF.pdf

Departement Ruimte Vlaanderen (DRV). (2016). *Working together on the space of tomorrow. Brochure to the White Paper on the Spatial Policy Plan for Flanders.* Retrieved from https://www.ruimtevlaanderen.be/Portals/108/WhitePaperSpatial PolicyPlanFlanders_brochure2017_1.pdf

Departement Ruimte Vlaanderen (DRV). (2018). *Strategische Visie. Beleidsplan Ruimte Vlaanderen.* Retrieved from https://www.ruimtevlaanderen.be/ Portals/108/Strategische_Visie_rgb_1.pdf

Department for Communities and Local Government (DCLG). (2012). *National planning policy framework.* DCLG.

De Vries, J. (2015). Planning and culture unfolded: The cases of Flanders and the Netherlands. *European Planning Studies,* 2.3(11), 2148–2164. https://doi.org/10.1080/ 09654313.2015.1018406

De Wever, B. (2011). *Right-wing Flanders, left-wing Wallonia? Is this so? If so, why? And is it a problem?* Re-Bel. https://www.rethinkingbelgium.eu/rebel-initiative-files/ebooks/ebook-12/ReBel-e-book-12.pdf

Esping-Andersen, G. (1990). *The three worlds of welfare capitalism.* Polity.

Etherington, J. (2003). *Nationalism, national identity and territory. The case of Catalonia* [Unpublished doctoral dissertation]. Department of Political Sciences. Universitat Autonoma de Barcelona.

Etherington, J. (2010). Nationalism, territoriality and national territorial belonging. *Papers: Revista de Sociologia, 95*(2), 321–339. https://doi.org/10.5565/rev/papers/ v95n2.23

Faludi, A. (2007). The European model of society. In A. Faludi (Ed.), *Territorial cohesion and the European model of society* (pp. 1–22). Lincoln Institute of Land Policy.

Gellner, E. (1983). *Nations and nationalism.* Cornell University Press.

Generalitat de Catalunya. (2014). *Llibre Blanc de la Transició Nacional de Catalunya.* Sintesi.

Hewitt, R. (2011). *Map of the nation. A biography of the ordnance survey.* Granta.

Hooson, D. (ed.). (1994). *Geography and national identity.* Blackwell.

Jones, R., &Ross, A. (2016). National sustainabilities. *Political Geography, 51,* 53–62. https://doi.org/10.1016/j.polgeo.2015.12.002

Keating, M. (2005). Policy divergence and convergence in Scotland under devolution. *Regional Studies, 39*(4), 453–463. https://doi.org/10.1080/00343400500128481

Keating, M. (2008). Thirty years of territorial politics. *West European Politics, 31*(1–2), 60–81. https://doi.org/10.1080/014023807018 33723

Keating, M. (2013). *Reseating the European state. The making of territory and the rise of the meso.* Oxford University Press.

Keating, M., Cairney, P., & Hepburn, E. (2009). Territorial policy communities and devolution in the United Kingdom. *Cambridge Journal of Regions, Economy and Society, 2*(1), 51–66. https://doi.org/10.1093/cjres/rsn024

Knieling, J., & Othengrafen, F. (eds.). (2009). *Planning cultures in Europe. Decoding cultural phenomena in urban and regional planning.* Ashgate.

Lloyd, G., & Peel, D. (2009). New Labour and the planning system in Scotland: An overview of a decade. *Planning Practice and Research, 24*(1), 103–118. https://doi.org/10.1080/02697450902742197

McCrone, D. (2017). *The new sociology of Scotland.* Sage.

Moore-Cherry, N., & Tomaney, J. (2019). Spatial planning, metropolitan governance and territorial politics in Europe: Dublin as a case of metro-phobia? *European Urban and Regional Studies, 26* (4), 365–381. https://doi.org/10.1177/0969776418783832

Morphet, J., & Clifford, B. (2014). Policy convergence, divergence and communities: The case of spatial planning in post-devolution Britain and Ireland. *Planning Practice and Research, 29*(5), 508– 524. https://doi.org/10.1080/02697459.2014.976998

Nadin, V., & Stead, D. (2008). European spatial planning systems, social models and learning. *disP – Planning Review, 44*(172), 35–47. https://doi.org/10.1080/02513625.2008.10557001

Nel·lo, O. (ed.). (2003). *Aquí no! Els conflictes territorials a Catalunya.* Empuries.

Nel·lo, O. (2012). *Ordenar el territorio. La experiencia de Barcelona y Cataluña.* Tirant lo Blanch.

Nel·lo, O. (2013a). Barcelona y Cataluña: las raíces del debate sobre el policentrismo del sistema urbano Catalan. *Ciudad y Territorio. Estudios Territoriales, 176,* 317–332.

Nel·lo, O. (2013b). La crisis catalana: orígenes y alternativas. In J. Gómez Mendoza, R. Lois Gonzáles, & O. Nel·lo Colom (Eds.), *Repensar el Estado. Crisis economica, conflictos territoriales e identidades políticas en España* (pp. 41–52). Universidad de Santiago de Compostela.

Nel·lo, O. (2015, 10 August). Barcelona i Catalunya, de nou. *Blog Post.* http://oriolnello.blogspot.com/2015/08/barcelona-i-catalunya-de-nou.html

Newman, P., & Thornley, A. (1996). *Urban planning in Europe: International competition, national systems and planning projects.* Routledge.

Nogué, J. (1998). *Nacionalismo y Territorio.* Milenio.

Nogué, J., & Vicente, J. (2004). Landscape and national identity in Catalonia. *Political Geography, 23*(2), 113–132. https://doi.org/10.1016/j.polgeo.2003.09.005

Nogué, J., & Wilbrand, S. (2010). Landscape, territory, and civil society in Catalonia. *Environment and Planning D, 28*(4), 638– 652. https://doi.org/10.1068/d6209

N-VA. (2019). *Frequently asked questions.* Retrieved from https://english.n-va.be/frequendy-asked-questions

Paasi, A. (1997). Geographical perspectives on Finnish national identity. *Geojournal, 43*(1), 41–50. https://doi.org/10.1023/A:1006885503314

Peel, D., & Lloyd, G. (2007). Civic formation and a new vocabulary for national planning. *International Planning Studies, 12*(4), 391–411. https://doi.org/10.1080/13563470701745538

Rittel, H. W. J., & Webber, M. (1973). Dilemmas in a general theory of planning. *Polity Sciences, 4*(2), 155–169. https://doi.org/10.1007/BF01405730

Rodríguez-Pose, A., & Sandall, R. (2008). From identity to the economy: Analysing the evolution of the decentralisation discourse. *Environment and Planning C, 26*(1), 54–72. https://doi.org/10.1068/cav2

Rokkan, D., & Urwin, W. (1983). *Economy, territory, identity: Politics of West European peripheries.* Sage.

Schama, S. (1995). *Landscape and memory.* Vintage.

Scott, J. C. (1998). *Seeing like a state.* Yale University Press.

Scottish Government. (2010). *A low carbon economic strategy for Scotland.* Retrieved from https://www.webarchive.org.uk/wayback/archive/20170701133421/http://www.gov.scot/Publications/2010/11/15085756/0

Scottish Government. (2013). *Scotland's future.* Retrieved from https://www2.gov.scot/resource/0043/00439021.pdf

Scottish Government. (2014). *Ambition, opportunity, place: Scotland's third national planning framework.* Retrieved from https://www.gov.scot/publications/national-planning-framework-3/

Scottish National Party (SNP). (2015). *Stronger for Scotland. Manifesto 2015.* Retrieved from http://ucrel.lancs.ac.uk/wmatrix/ukmanifestos2015/localpdf/SNP.pdf

Smith, A. (2001). *Nationalism: Theory, ideology, history.* Polity.

Smith Commission. (2014). *Report of the Smith Commission for further devolution of powers to the Scottish Parliament.* Retrieved from https://webarchive.nationalarchives.gov.uk/20151202171017/ http:/www.smith-commission.scot/

Societal Catalana d'Ordenació del Territori (SCOT). (2015). *Forum 2012 Catalunya 21: 'Territori i Urbanisme. Estat i Alternatives'. Document d'alternatives.* SCOT.

Tewdwr-Jones, M., & Allmendinger, P. (eds.). (2006). *Territory, identity and spatial planning: Spatial governance in a fragmented nation.* Routledge.

Tomaney, J., & Colomb, C. (2013). Planning for independence? The evolution of spatial planning in Scotland and growing policy differences with England. *Town and Country Planning, 82*(9), 371–373.

Tomaney, J., & Colomb, C. (2014). Planning in a disunited Kingdom. *Town and Country Planning, 83*(2), 80–83.

Tomaney, J., & Colomb, C. (2018). Devolution and planning. In J. Ferm, & J. Tomaney (Eds.), *Planning practice: Critical perspectives from the UK* (*pp.* 20–35). Routledge.

Tomaney, J., Natarajan, L., Ilies, E., & Hamiddudin, I. (2019). Towards a second generation of spatial planning in the UK? *Town and Country Planning, 88*(11), 457–461.

Van Den Broeck, P. (2008). The changing position of strategic spatial planning in Flanders. A socio-political and instrument-based perspective. *International Planning Studies, 13*(3), 261–283. https://doi.org/10.1080/13563470802521457

Van den Broeck, P., Moulaert, F., Kuhk, A., Lievois, E., & Schreurs, J. (2014). Spatial planning in Flanders. Serving a by-passed capitalism? In H. Blotevogel, P. Getimis, & M. Reimer (Eds.), *Spatial planning systems and practices in Europe: Towards multiple trajectories of change* (pp. 190–209). Routledge.

Van den Broeck, P., & Verachtert, K. (2016). Whose permits? The tenacity of permissive development control in Flanders. *European Planning Studies, 24*(2), 387–406. https://doi.org/10.1080/09654313.2015.1045838

Weber, E. (1976). *Peasants into Frenchmen: The modernization of rural France 1870–1914.* Stanford University Press.

Wightman, A. (2019). Land matters. *Blog.* http://www.andywightman.com/

Williams, C. H., & Smith, A. D. (1983). The national construction of social space. *Progress in Human Geography, 7*(4), 502–518. https://doi.org/10.1177/030913258300700402

Towards a sustainable, negotiated mode of strategic regional planning: a political economy perspective

Ian Gordon● and Tony Champion●

Introduction: a rationale for decentring strategic regional planning

Planning is a contested terrain: not only in ideological terms (market liberalism versus social redistribution), materially (in the allocation of windfall gains) and culturally (as it cuts across diverse communities); but also *crucially* in relation to the authority of 'planners' vis-à-vis other specialist/professional groups. Coming late to the professional 'ball' – within the last century, after engineers, architects and public health practitioners – and without ongoing service delivery functions to sustain them, except in low-level development control activities, planners have generally experienced a structural weakness in securing their potential position as the integrators of societal activity at a city/regional scale. This insecurity has been reflected both in rotation between a set of legitimating heuristics (e.g., the planner as technician, bureaucrat, community advocate or normatively validated professional[1]) and fluctuating levels of political acceptance.

There have ensued (in the 'global "north"' at least) recurring phases of active debate about both 'planning theory' and appropriate forms of professional education (e.g., Fainstein & De Fillipis, 2015; Friedmann, 2012). Though such debates continue, with shifting emphases, the strongest pair of cards in marking planners' particular professional strength has long involved claims to: possession of a particularly *comprehensive* vision; plus particular attention to *spatial* relations and integration. Strategic spatial plans at regional scale (or beyond) assume an iconic status then, in embodying the highest forms of the planner's craft. As well as (hopefully), offering a more secure context (in social, economic and environmental terms) within which operational/regulatory planning can be undertaken across the gamut of public and private activity.

For practitioners, strategic planning's broader context seems to offer a welcome freedom from the inherited constraints and rivalries that beset everyday, localized planning and development control. It looks less of a contested terrain. The reality is, however, that any effective strategic planning (even in the most authoritarian settings) depends on somehow securing credible commitments from other agents with real power, on key lines of action they will take (or refrain from), given the vision they are being offered. Despite vigorous debates about the form and logic of strategic planning, this crucial general point tends to get lost – though Friedmann's (1993) argument for a new 'non-Euclidian planning model' notably emphasized the need for a more entrepreneurial perspective, with planners acting primarily as 'resource mobilisers who seek to concert public and private energies around innovative solutions to stubborn problems in the public domain' (p. 485).

Strategic planning can be characterized normatively as embodying a *longer run, spatially broader and more fundamentally grounded* perspective on choice issues. But it is also a matter of 'situated practice' (Albrechts et al., 2017), involving work as well as ideas, and needing to be pursued differently as the circumstances of a time and place affect how those functional requirements might best be met. And when it 'fails', the manner in which it does so will also reflect such situational influences – though there are likely to be some common, underlying factors.

Making use of experience to understand what is generally applicable, offering some kind of useful lesson of wider relevance, and distinguishing that from what is specific to particular types of situation, cannot, however, be simply a matter of induction from reported cases. It also depends on thinking more intensively about what has happened in a few situations (maybe one at a time), and the sorts of potentially generic factors underlying these – at least as hypotheses for wider testing. That is closer to the approach of this paper, which starts from a casual generalization about the problematic record of strategic regional planning, for which it seeks to offer some analytic explanation and suggest some possible general lessons for the future, using a single, familiar regional case for illustration (rather than corroboration).

Both the argument and the method reflect a critical approach – to the standard model of strategic spatial planning, its basis in planning theory and the disciplinary limits of planning research – which is rather close to that of Salet (2017). From a sociological perspective (and in the context of a collection of situated studies of strategic planning initiatives) he argued that work in this field has suffered from a planner-centric *subjectivism,* which evolved in the era of welfare state construction (and/or, we might say, industrial Fordism), but is completely out of place in the more uncertain times of recent decades. Maybe it was ever thus, but has just become more evidently so, as (and where) the political climate has become less supportive of strategic planning – and experience exposed its limitations. As Salet frames it, this subjectivism is largely an intellectual problem – of 'thought and action perspectives [which] tend to consider the planning subject (i.e., the planner) as the centre of all action'. But it is one that is compounded by a *voluntaristic* tendency for planners to frame projects in a manner driven by their own normative perspective, rather than seriously considering alternatives reflective of wider social forces (pp. 375–378). Both of these negative tendencies might be seen as reflecting claims to professional legitimacy based on planners' particular capacity to maintain a comprehensive viewpoint.

The other side of this planner-centrism, in research as well as in strategic planning practice has been a particular reluctance to engage with the power and reactive capacity of political or economic actors and institutions. At the level of planning theory, Friedmann (2012) suggested that:

> 'the biggest problem we face ... is our ambivalence about power': 'the rational planning paradigm studiously avoided talking about any form of power other than the power of the mind'; the knowledge/action paradigm was blocked from saying how new visions might be implemented 'because implementation requires an acknowledgement of power as a central issue'; and the communicative action paradigm had a 'Panglossian view of the power of dialogue to bridge the gap between those who command substantial power and those who do not'.
>
> (p. 137)

At the level of strategic planning practice, powerful economic and political processes tend to be treated either in some anodyne form as contextual elements or as purely exogenous factors to be handled through forecasts of their effects.

What is sadly missing is recognition of either kind of process as: a dynamic element responding opportunistically to plan proposals and forecasts; or involving agents whose potentially active support or resistance could be crucial, at both plan-making and implementation stages. For example, in the situated practice cases of Albrechts et al.'s (2017) handbook, direct references to market or political behaviour (as distinct from economic trends and policy decisions) rarely appear, with only a Chinese case (Xu & Yeh, 2017) addressing spatial politics as a significant factor. And Albrecht's own (2013) refraining of strategic planning in terms of a potential co-production model, while involving a loosening up of planners' direct control, does so on a basis even more driven by *their* idealistic norms, with no specific attention to how planning activity *actually* interacts with markets or politics, beyond generally baleful effects attributed to 'neo-liberalism'.

We agree with Albrecht (and other planning theorists) that a refraining of the conventional strategic planning model is required. And also with more practice-oriented colleagues about the urgent need, in England at least, for a revived and strengthened strategic element in development planning

(Bowie, 2018; Common Futures Network (CFN), 2017). Our view, however, is that a much more radical rethinking is required – in relation to theory, practice and research – of how that strategic element can be effectively (and positively) pursued, on a basis which is decentred, spatially, professionally and intellectually, from the classic focus on production of strategic regional plans.

We start from three basic propositions, that:

- the form, scale and complexity of currently pressing issues and uncertainties facing communities around the world requires a stronger strategic – longer term, spatially broader and more fundamental – dimension to city/regional planning;
- past efforts to pursue plan-based strategic approaches have commonly been bedevilled by a lack of durable support for them, falsified assumptions about the direction and scale of key changes, unconsidered barriers to desired policy impacts and important unintended consequences; and
- a common cause of such failure is inattention to strong economic and political forces outwith the direct control (and professional orientation) of strategic planners – remedying which is key to a more genuinely strategic planning process.

The following sections pursue this line of argument in three steps, moving from general processes via illustrative examples from the UK – focused particularly on the strategic challenges to governance presented by strong and contentious currents of population mobility across a much extended capital city-region (the Wider South East – WSE) – to implications for a more realistic and durable model of strategic planning, there and elsewhere. Two running themes are the need to think of the strategic planning process as itself a long-term, continuing activity; and to recognize practical attention to institution-building on a sustained basis as an integral part of that process. Our approach is identified as a political economy one, not because it follows one of the classic (macro-oriented) schools, but because it asserts the need to attend closely to interacting political and economic processes, if strategic regional planning is to be credibly worthwhile.

The argument: strategic regional plans versus effective strategic planning

In this section we develop the case for a decentred approach to strategic regional planning as a process-based and sustained enterprise, rather than one embodied in the development, implementation and occasional revision of an authoritative strategic plan. We start by outlining the set of ideas on which it draws from inside and outside the planning canon, before setting out a set of first principles, then summarizing ways in which significant

British strategic planning initiatives of the past 75 years have fallen short of reasonable expectation for them, and finally suggesting some generic lessons that might be drawn.

Sources in the literature

The conceptual underpinning of this paper draws on a mix of ideas from several distinct sources: classical and postmodern writing about planning theory; empirical research on metropolitan governance; and a political economy perspective on territorial competition. The sources (and provocations) are doubtless very many, drawn from past engagement with several mainstream literatures. But the originality of our argument generally comes from what we emphasize and combine rather than from specific sources, so the referencing is limited and indicative in character.

As a point of entry, we take two foundational distinctions from *classic planning theory* (as represented by Faludi, 1973). One distinction is that between a *comprehensive rational* approach to planning, with complex systems being managed through hierarchies of plans (from strategic to operational), and *disjointed incrementalism,* a piecemeal politically driven alternative, dealing reactively to 'signals' from interacting interest representatives (Lindblom's, 1965, 'partisan mutual adjustment') about what requires attention. The other distinction is between a static view

of planning as engaged periodically in the production of *blueprints* for future development and a more dynamic one involving a set *of processes* jointly shaping the path of change on a continuing basis. Our view leans toward the disjointed and process sides of these dualisms, but with an understanding that increments don't have to be modest when a pressing issue is seen to require more, and that key processes for management of change often lie outwith the 'planning system'.

From (a rich variety of) *post-modern re-theorizations of planning* we take another pair of ideas. One is that of *communicative rationality,* involving processes of critical and creative interaction between diverse parties with a realistic aim of securing enhanced understanding and progress toward better outcomes, rather than an agreed vision (Healey, 1992). The other is that of imagined communities or *spatial imaginaries* (Davoudi, 2018), involving shared understandings of identity and difference that are significantly political both in their effects in structuring arguments about change and in the experiences that shape them. Our particular take on both of these ideas is more strategic than most of their exponents advocate, involving a greater emphasis on coalition building processes than on normative democracy, and focusing on the significance of imagining not only friendly neighbours to band together with but also spatial enemies as constraints to be overcome.

From recent work on metropolitan governance we take one further set of related ideas involving: the importance of *voluntary collaboration* between local municipalities; the difficulties of achieving this in practice; and the key role of a notion *of civic capital,* involving shared understandings and thick networks. More specifically, it emphasizes the importance of leaders – people or organizations with capacities both as bridge-builders and catalysts for collective action through engagement in projects (Gordon, 2006; Nelles, 2012).

Finally, we draw another pair of ideas from writings about *territorial competition* (in relation to the advancement of place-based sets of economic interests). One is that representations of collective interests (of the kind deployed in strategic plans) emerge from a political interplay between actors with different types and degrees of *stake in place-specific outcomes* and with different levels of resources to deploy. The other is that the active engagement of actors in pursuit of their collective interests cannot be taken for granted, but depends on a judgement about *its likely efficacy* for them, where existence of a few players with very strong stakes and the ability to mobilize collectively may often be crucial for what happens (Cheshire & Gordon, 1996).

Rather little in the elements which we have picked out here explicitly addresses the possibility of worthwhile strategic planning. But together – and with an understanding of the centrality of self-oriented decision-making by very large numbers of independent agents for how city-regions evolve – they suggest to us where the scope for effective strategic action can be found, as well as why the classic model is unlikely to have it.

Some first principles

Our characterization of strategic planning suggests that it should be a more thoughtful activity than everyday planning, where robust standard operating procedures (SOPs) and assumptions are generally adequate. But as each of these literatures suggest, it cannot be a purely intellectual activity, if it is to command any attention, to make a (positive) practical difference *and* be sustained, in a real world where SOPs, short-term politics and/or privately directed strategies are the norm.

To focus attention on what else is required, we propose half a dozen key principles – starting from the functions expected of a strategic approach, the circumstances in which these particularly matter, relations with other types of strategically significant process, through to the crucial issue of securing relevant action:

• The distinctive function of the strategic dimension in planning is to secure a purposive and positive sort of coherence in the operation of a complex system with inherent sources of uncertainty. In a spatial context such complexity and uncertainty is particularly associated with larger urban regions, characterized by high levels of diversity in activities, peoples and place-types, with multiplex networks of interaction over extended territories.

- The challenges of securing coherence in such situations are beyond the strategic capacities of even the smartest single organization, profession (or indeed state), acting on their own. This applies even, or particularly, to establishing the directions in which it would be good for it to be steered – what might count as 'good steering' in a statement of planning objectives.
- The actual steering (i.e., governance) of cities/regions needs to be recognized as an amalgam of three interacting elements, including markets and informal institutions as well as planning. As well as authoritative policy-making and enforcement from official nodes (planning); these involve structured interaction between very large numbers of, more or less, self-serving agents (markets); and sets of beliefs/understandings, shared identities, and habits of cooperation/ antagonism (informal institutions). As a first approximation, these may be seen as independent and of comparable importance, but patterns of accommodation between them matter and may be shifted (Gordon, 2006, 2016).
- It is crucial for planners to recognize the real power of the other two elements of governance, particularly in terms of how their dynamic reactions to 'plans' can alter forecast outcomes. The temptation not to do so seems especially great for strategic planners who aspire to transcend more mundane, local and transient features. But planning that is blind to the importance of two-thirds of the governance system, how they respond to planned initiatives, and how these might be trained in more positive directions, cannot itself be expected to have positive strategic impacts.
- More specifically, it needs to be better understood that ignored market responses can lead to quite perverse effects from key policies. This is especially likely when investment markets actually embody a longer term view than planners effectively deploy – and/or when exaggerated notions of planners' influence have been cultivated.[2] Real influence depends on understanding how markets will respond – and similarly how institutional processes can engender either (unnecessary) resistance or lines of support, depending on how they are attended to (Gordon, 2016).
- Realistic planning for how implementation can be secured is a vital element of strategic planning, not an add-on. This is a matter of developing practice (and reflecting continuously on that, as Schon (1983) emphasized), as much as of sophisticated ideas. Working strategically to build cooperative relations, shared understandings, and credibility as a mobilizer of resources is intrinsic to pursuing a long-run approach, particularly where continuity of external patronage cannot be counted on.

Learning from past experience

The UK (particularly England) has a rather long history of engagements with strategic spatial planning, effectively starting with the internationally recognized example of Abercrombie's 1944 Greater London Plan, dating from war years with an unusual degree of economic planning and motivational drive toward designing a better future. This plan was archetypal in its neat logic, assuming effective economic restraint of aggregate growth across the region, designing a Green Belt to physically 'contain' the urban core, and providing for a system of planned population movement out to New Towns to relieve the overcrowding of housing in inner areas (Hall, 1988). In practice, restraint of a new service economy was ineffective, the achieved scale of New Towns was too small, and population decentralization was achieved very largely through private initiatives,[3] commonly by leapfrogging a Green Belt, the width of which got greatly extended in response to local community demands (Hall et al., 1973). That element was the only one to be fully implemented, because it simply involved saying 'no' and did not depend on infrastructural support. Growth was not really constrained, though population was decentralized on a very large scale, essentially through market forces which the plan had not considered (Buck et al., 1986).

During the following 75 years, strategic planning activity has been intermittent, whether because it was seen as laying down blueprints which only occasionally required servicing, or new governments opposed it in principle (as during the Margaret Thatcher years, and again since 2010). Or sometimes, because it seemed an answer to a problem briefly topping the national political agenda – consistent with Wannop's (1995) view of British regional planning as a 'mercurial, often ephemeral' form of crisis management (p. xv).

An example of the last of these was the appearance in the late 1960s, during a (Labour) government favourable to planning of all kinds, of a quite sudden upturn in national population growth projections. This stimulated a unique Long Term Population Distribution planning exercise, making a case for development of a set of substantial new cities (Department of the Environment, 1971). This was on grounds very largely independent of that population growth materializing – and a matter of conflict between rival physical and economic planning departments (O'Hara, 2007). But it was a deflation of the projections, and election of a new (Conservative) government, that led to abandonment of further strategic work.

At the sub-national scale within England, strategy/strategic plan-producing regional planning bodies also came and went, in two separate waves (appointed planning councils and then indirectly elected assemblies, both set up by Labour governments) with ad hoc policy impacts only (e.g., Baker & Wong, 2013; Breheny & Hall, 1984; Roberts & Lloyd, 1999). The one really sophisticated (and serious) experiment involved a Strategic Plan for the South East, with strong technical engagement from three levels of government (South East Joint Planning team (SEJPT), 1971). But even in this case a review after six years found there to have been no substantial impacts on infrastructure planning and resourcing (Development of the Strategic Plan for the South East Team (DSPSE), 1976, reported in Gordon, 2018).

At a city/sub-regional level, when elected London government was restored in 2000, after a 15-year hiatus, it was in the form of a directly elected mayor leading an explicitly strategic (Greater London) authority, with preparation of a spatial strategy as a keystone in its responsibilities. This is a formal strategic plan, binding on boroughs, though itself required to be in conformity with a national planning policy framework. It is scarcely a *regional* plan, however, since (as the next section will make clear) it only covers the core of a much more extensive functional region. And the issue of how the London Plan should engage with communities and authorities in this region (now identified as the WSE) in meeting expected shortfalls in housing delivery, has been a key stimulus for new debate about means of renewing strategic regional planning (Bowie, 2018; CFN, 2017).

Responses from (Conservative) ministers have so far displayed an inconsistency that reflects shifting political pressures. Ministers' reactions to proposals (from the inspector at one London Plan public examination) for some real engagement between London and authorities in neighbouring regions, have shifted from outright negativity in 2015 (Brandon Lewis writing to the Mayor of London) to evident impatience in 2019 that strategic cooperation was not advancing fast enough (Ministry of Housing Communities and Local Government (MHCLG) evidence to the next such examination[4]) – alongside growing national concern about housing supply shortfalls. And having swept away regional strategies in 2010 as part of a programme to 'end the hoarding of power within central government and top-down control of communities', the government's 2019 version of the National Planning Policy Framework involves vigorous enforcement of top-down local housing targets, directly from the centre.

Even from a very broad-brush review, this 75-year record of intermittent strategic regional planning practice in a country pioneering this activity, presents a very depressing picture. Some things are fundamentally wrong with the context, aspirations or the model from which we have been working. We have cases of:

- a classic (and classically statist) plan, with a clear vision but a shaky and rather blinkered analytic base, showing remarkable durability in the bluntest of its instruments, decades after their perverse effects were shown;
- a more sophisticated, better researched strategic plan which evidently failed in getting key public infrastructural resources redirected to implement it; and
- many more initiatives, institutions and bits of strategic policy that came and went with the minor eddies and shifting currents of an unstable national politics.

Doubtless each of these three types of failure owes something to particular features of the UK/English setting – and maybe economic regimes of the times, though chiefly in the dependence of the Abercrombie Plan on a wartime version of Fordism. What all three seem to illustrate in different ways, however, is the unlikelihood (in any context) of effective strategic planning being achieved on the basis of a 'strategic plan' produced in (professional) isolation from intellectual and practical engagement with the more powerful economic and political forces in play.

Four foundations for realistically sustainable strategic practice

Putting together the *principles* set out earlier with these reflections on the frustrating *limits on effective practice* in one illustrative national context, we identify four basic foundations for a decentred model of strategic planning better suited to realizing its defining functions. These involve:

- an emphasis on *building* collective understandings and *habits of co-operation* across agencies/areas (in a pluralistic way, not just across 'a region');
- reducing *incentives* to non-cooperation and boosting those for cooperation;
- *acquiring some enabling leadership* from sources with a capacity to *commit resources* on a relevant scale and a durable basis; and
- establishing the grounds for *negotiating acceptable deals* among parties, notably by building trust in sources of evidence on likely impacts and uncertainties.

These foundations imply supportive action from central government and continuing commitment to enhance the quality of regional governance in a broader national interest. But their goal is to reduce reliance on specific initiatives, enthusiasms and agencies established by central government and avoid the associated risks of disruption each time there is a shift in political control or professional personnel. For instance, government might valuably provide leadership, such as in the form of a territorial minister for a collection of regions who is able to provide authoritative and coherent responses to resource bids and retune incentive schemes – but not act as top-down patron for strategic planning activity. Similarly, in respect of professional engagement, it should go without saying that this kind of decentred planning model would need to be backed up by a lot of tactical and operational planning, that would include formal statutory plans – but without having an iconic Strategic Regional Plan as its focus.

An illustrative case: steering population dynamics in a mega-city region

Why migration flows are crucial for strategic planning of (super) metro regions

To illustrate in more concrete terms the problems and potential of different forms of strategic planning, we take the case of the extended functional region centred on London. This typifies the situation of a mature metropolitan region, with a single dominant core and a momentum of spatial extension that is mediated by the interaction of dozens of overlapping spatial sub-markets for labour and housing, generating patterns of residential segregation at scales broad enough to strongly differentiate the politics of local government units across the region.

In particular we focus on issues involving population movement, which though obviously important in relation to infrastructure and service provision, and as influences on perceived quality of life in different communities, are not readily or clearly understood in this complex kind of setting.

One of the sources of obscurity about these facts is the sheer size of this extended region, though the spatial extent of the relevant territory is itself both unclear and contested. What is clear is that it has grown greatly in scale in the decades since the Abercrombie Plan, through the interplay between three broad currents of migration. Two of these have involved net flows into this part of the country – from overseas and from the less economically dynamic British 'north'. The third has been a strong deconcentrating trend with net migration out of the denser and more central parts of this territory, driven by a combination of increasing demands for more residential space and inelastic supply within these areas.

The strength of each of these currents has varied over time, with distinct periods of high/low net migration from the two external origins, and with fluctuations in the deconcentrating stream reflecting both macroeconomic factors and the scale of displacement effects from the two longer distance inflows. Chains of displacement also occur within the deconcentrating current itself, because housing supply is inelastic in many of its destination areas (especially in the metropolitan ring immediately around London) as well as in the regional core. These chains convert the short distance moves which households make for housing or environmental reasons into currents shifting population over distances of 100 kms. plus, well beyond the metropolitan ring (Gordon et al., 2017).

These broad patterns and their dynamics are not only matters of strategic importance, but also have implications for how far issues arising from them can be effectively addressed, including of key importance: finding the right territorial focus for strategic analysis and governance; and appropriately relating forecasts, targets and scenarios in long-term planning.

Finding the right territorial focus for strategic planning

From a classic strategic plan-making perspective, a fundamental issue is how to define the region to be covered. Rationally this could be seen in terms of trying to maximize the proportion of relevant causal interactions contained within the planning region. But inclusion in these terms has to be traded off against something else lest all strategic plans become national in scope. Once such basis might be the degree of shared economic interest within the territory, though compromises over boundaries would still have to be made where two urbanized regions ran into each other – as in Warwickshire where the London and Birmingham migration regions join up. However, setting the problem up in this way runs into direct conflict with the notion that 'imagined territories' are of critical importance for a planning that depends on some degree of local popular consent for legitimacy and the build-up of support for desirable collective action. For long-run planning, there is also the issue that future development is liable to extend the effective bounds of the region in ways that cannot be wholly controlled.

In London's case, the likelihood of such change is highlighted by the truly enormous (some 40-fold) increase in the extent of its functional area over the past century (from that of the current Inner London to the London Metropolitan Region). This is due in part to its economic dynamism and a much extended public transport network. But it is also the result of motorization, the 'sprawl' which this induced, *and* the unintended consequences of strategic planning, via a Green Belt intended to check that process. Its failure to effectively achieve that led perversely to a much wider diffusion of population beyond the Green Belt (Champion, 2002; Hall et al., 1973) and the extended chains of outward population movement mentioned above.

The direct effect of movement out into the commuter belt around London was to create a metropolitan region (with an Outer Metropolitan Area – OMA), which was the focus of Hall's (1963) first work on London futures and remains close to researchers' definitions of its functional urban region (FUR), based essentially on commuter flows. With growing population displacement beyond the OMA, and the emergence of secondary employment concentrations both in the OMA and further out, a much more complex economic region has developed in the past 40 years or so, involving multiple interlinked FURs. As the Greater South East (GSE), this became the focus of Hall's (1989) second work on London futures and formed the prototype of a new concept of polycentric metropoles or mega-city regions (Hall & Pain, 2006). This is the scale at which informal moves toward some collaboration in planning have been discussed in the past five years, and more formal ones proposed (Bowie, 2018).

But recent research indicates that even this WSE combination of three former administrative regions does not represent the full scope of the migrational system of this agglomeration. The current reality is that the deconcentration current originating in London flows right through the OMA (much of it Green Belt) – with very little net effect on its population size, contrary to general belief into both the outer ring of the WSE *and a* substantial Fringe area beyond this on the western and northern sides (Gordon et al, 2017). Including this Fringe in the territory appropriately covered by strategic planning of the quadrant implies a Still Wider South East (or SWSE) with a population of over 30 million (Figure 1).

In contrast to this, the territory of 'London' government has been extended only once during this era, with the creation of Greater London in

1965 incorporating most of the city's pre-1939 extension. Though sometimes included in a South East administrative region, that never had effective planning responsibilities – despite the one-off Strategic Plan for the South East referred to above. And since the early 1990s London has been formally separated from even its immediate hinterland. This has both reflected and reinforced territorially distinct 'imagined communities' and left governance of their interrelations in the joint hands of national government and the market. The border between them is actually crossed by 200,000 or so migrants each year, but neither the dynamics of this interconnection nor how planning policies affect it are understood (or examined). And, unsurprisingly, weak efforts by central government in the early 2000s to mobilize a wider regional consciousness, in the national economic interest, made little impact (Cochrane, 2012), particularly at a time when national planning 'guidance' was reinforcing the defence of greenfield sites across the region. Since the re-establishment in 2000 of a London authority, in the form of an elected mayoral, with strategic responsibilities but dependence on the goodwill of central government for infrastructure funding, the consistent theme of London Plans developed by successive mayors (Ken Livingstone, Boris Johnson and Sadiq Khan, whose New London Plan (Mayor of London, 2019) is currently awaiting government approval) has been acceptance of responsibility for accommodating all the population growth associated with the city's continuing economic growth. As was noted at the outset (Hall & Gordon, 2002), this entailed an 'almost impossible' acceleration of housebuilding – dependent on a response from private developers that has proved consistently well below Plan targets. Actual population growth has been achieved largely through denser occupation of the existing stock by new migrants from poorer countries (Gordon, 2014). Despite arguments for alternative options (Outer London Commission (OLC), 2016b) the political imperative remains for London to 'consume its own smoke' in housing terms.

The imagined geographies (whether of politicians or citizens) are clearly at odds with the functional integration of the WSE. But if strategic planning is to involve more than very occasional one-off exercises and if this requires active sub-national participation in relation to imaginable spaces, it is clear that simply translating it to an SWSE level is no sort of an answer. Hardly anyone actually imagines themselves as bound up with this space. And rising populist feeling (signalled here as elsewhere by the Brexit referendum) will not encourage that. Nor is there any chance that national government is going to devolve strategic responsibilities for an area containing a majority of England's population. Other ways have to be found to broaden both understanding and action beyond localities and 'fortress London' – and beyond superficial shorttermism.

One useful positive step which has been proposed is reinstatement of technical support arrangements at a panWSE level, building on the model of the former SERPLAN 'standing conference' (Swain, 2018). But it needs a remit extended much further into the development and dissemination of

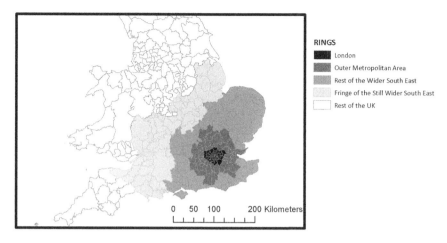

Figure 1 Zonal ring structure of the Still Wider South East (SWSE).

a common understanding of processes (not least those affecting population dynamics, as the report drawn on in this section was intended to do) across the various parts of the WSE and its external borders (OLC, 2016a; Swain, 2018). Application of this kind of intelligence at a strategic level and on the continuing basis that is required would have to rest on development of the kind of collaborative negotiated bases for advancing shareable interests discussed in the previous section, and emphasized in the OLC (2016a) agenda for the WSE.

Beyond this, however, it is important to understand the political dimension of selective outward migration within the region, which encourages defensive solidarities between political communities with shared suspicions about the interests of others. Thus, when (from 1998 to 2010) a South East region – comprised of those parts of the WSE, to the south-east, south-west, west and north-west of London – had an elected regional chamber, the one shared basis of communal identity involved resistance to incursions by more migrants from London. This tended to obscure *both* the very different positions within the regional migration system of places within the OMA versus those further out *and the* fact that an integrated housing market across the whole SWSE gave residents *of all areas* a similar stake in resolving housing supply constraints. From this perspective, if political integration of the extended region is unfeasible, collaborative arrangements cutting across the rings, are a much more promising route toward the development of positive-sum spatial strategies (Mace & Gordon, 2016).

One spatial framework for these is set of radial growth/ coordination corridors identified in the Key Diagram of successive London Plans, though with very limited practical development. A partial exception is the London-Stansted-Cambridge Corridor Consortium, a bottom-up initiative building on an idea from the Tony Blair government's 2003 Sustainable Communities

Plan. These corridors have been seen primarily as means of securing economic and social gains by promoting linkages between related activities with different locational requirements (London-Stansted-Cambridge Corridor Growth Commission, 2016). But because of their roles as migration and commuting corridors, cutting across the rings (with their different situations and populations) they could also offer the prospect of developing imagined geographies more conducive to collective strategic action, and credible deals made by partners with trustworthy records (Mace, 2019).

Thinking strategically about population dynamics: projections, forecasts and scenarios

With its focus on the longer term patterns of development, over broader territories and the scope for qualitatively different approaches the kind of information or guidance that strategic planning requires about likely and possible future developments is rather different from that required for statutorily-based operational planning – even in basic and familiar fields such as that of population change.

In the UK at least, practice with respect to demographic forecasting in the more routine contexts is heavily shaped by some combination of nationally mandated projections and accepted statistical methodologies. These are substantially trend based, except where there is some very strong policy guidance as to what should happen (e.g., to international migration). This is not only to make best use of available data but to secure some evident objectivity and independence from either speculative ideas or the vested interests of particular groups in different interpretations of trends or possible changes in these. One important example in the case of those areas which are 'open' in housing/labour market terms involves use of projections of future population or household numbers in deriving the scale of housing needs which authorities should plan for – notably in those regions where there is resistance to additional development.

When trend-based population projections are used as a key input into defining future need and setting building targets, there is an obvious element of circularity in the procedure, since areas which have built more houses in the past will find themselves with higher population projections and larger targets for future construction, while others which have failed in (or resisted) development in recent years are likely to face less challenging targets in future. That is not, in itself a legitimate technical ground for challenging *projections,* whereas the choice of base period to extrapolate migration trends or household formation rates can be an important one (Champion, 2019).

What is lost in this essentially technical process of sharing out responsibility for future growth (and/or entitlement to additional infrastructure/ services) is any concern with causality in terms of such key considerations as the reasons why a trend may be expected to 'bend', the policy/implementation options (locally or elsewhere) that would be expected to make a real difference, and the identifiable sources of major uncertainties that deserve particular monitoring, contingency plans or choice of more resilient strategies. Examples of all of these concerns may be found from analysis of the major migration currents into and within the WSE (Gordon et al., 2017).

An obvious example, though one that is consistently underplayed, is the growth in the importance of international migration to the region and especially to its core areas within the last 30 years, such that it has become a key push factor in the deconcentration current supplanting the previous main driver which had been the upward trend in real earnings (according to time series regression analyses by Gordon, 2016; Gordon & Champion, 2020).

For a genuinely strategic planning in the region, preparing for alternative futures and not merely setting targets based on projected levels of need or capacity growth, an understanding of the main sources of uncertainty about population trends, particularly the strength of this deconcentration current, should be really important. This applies both to underlying uncertainties about the future course of known influences (in this case those of real personal income growth and of international migration), and to those which are more conjectural – including possible differences in mid-life movement patterns of the millennial generation of urban migrants as compared with their baby-boom predecessors; and whether longer residence will push up the space expectations of recent immigrants (Gordon et al., 2017).

There also needs to be a much wider understanding of the (more certain) relation between 'compact city' type policies of restricting development in rings close to London and the continuing spatial extension of the region into its very much less 'compact' fringes. But both of these also require a longer-term vision of the governance function which is decentred from shorter-term, operational concerns about trend projections and the making of an authoritative strategic plan.

Learning from this case

Population mobility and its ramifications are clearly just one dimension of strategic regional planning in the WSE, and one which arguably receives too much attention and generates too many worries with top-down allocative forms of regional plan. But it offers a relatively simple porthole into grasping the complexities with which any worthwhile strategic planning has to deal – and with the blindness there can be to key facets of these within actual existent forms of planning and regional politics. Megacity regions present these in especially striking ways, and this particular region – with its distinctive functional and planning history – does so in its own way. But we would contend that it offers generic lessons (also relevant to places that are smaller, newer, more industrial and/or poorer) about the need to approach the challenges of strategic regional planning in a less classically monocentric fashion.

At one level, the lessons are ones of inadequate and unduly crude understandings – among practitioners, the policy community and to some extent among researchers too – of how the migration system and spatial housing markets actually function in this kind of region. In particular this involves:

- the pervasive role of (largely voluntary) displacement processes in the face of inelastic local housing supplies (in which planning plays a role) in channelling currents of (mostly short-distance) population movement over very long distances;
- the strong interlinkage of sub-regional housing markets; and
- the autonomy of housing developers in relation to the phasing of new build.

But the fact that debate over population planning has excessively focused on the immediate overspill from London into areas in the OMA; targets for additions to the London housing stock are set quite unrealistically in relation to observable patterns of delivery; plans are assumed to shape where people move to, and residents in many areas assume they can cater simply for local needs; *all* also reflect political, administrative and professional considerations that are open to understanding and reshaping. Just not by adding another 'strategic' level to the status quo.

Conclusions: building a more a durable form of strategic regional planning

The ambition to plan strategically – with long/wide horizons and attention to fundamental processes – is an old one, but with much greater salience in a world of increasingly complex, extended urban regions. Delivering on this ambition presents a series of challenges, of which probably the most fundamental is to accept that it is not simply a matter of enlarging the scope of established spatial planning processes and procedures. At the level of principle it needs to involve some of the kinds of decentring that we have discussed, away from the model of a single organization producing an overarching *Plan* as the guiding framework for action and investment. Attitudinally, however, it also needs recognition of the various kinds and sources of *failure* in past strategic planning initiatives, and of the need to learn from these about how to achieve more, better and durable impacts in the short, medium and long run – with minimal waste of effort and frustration of expectations.

The difference a strategic perspective should make

The potential of strategic regional planning depends very largely on it being clearly distinguished from mainstream day-to-day professional planning. The latter has to offer substantial degrees of certainty – about property rights, budgeting, demand for services, timetabling of infrastructure projects and so on – within the limits *of force majeure,* external shocks and internal failures that may cause some of these certainties to shift. Consistency, standard procedures to maximize coherence, and attention to formal regulations/policy frameworks all have value in this situation, as well as attention to relevant local influences and situations.

Adding a strategic perspective should involve questioning all of these, in relation to a broader, longer term view underpinned by a knowledge base about key processes, influences and interactions. In the classic rational planning tradition, however, there is no real disjunction between these levels, with strategic planning being just a more elevated (ideal-typical) version of the same activity, with a cleaner fact/value distinction, more opportunity to undertake rigorous analyses and a playing down of local/temporary situational factors. As such, it is clearly a top-down exercise focused on producing *a plan*, which even if light on physical design will have a blueprint aspect to it – not least because it involves the kind of data handling and marketing effort that cannot be repeated frequently, still less adapted as situations and knowledge evolve.

The alternative 'political economy perspective' pursued here simply amounts to insisting on recognition that planning and the systems which it seeks to control (or more realistically help steer) involve very strong political/economic forces that interact with each other. In our judgement, this is an essential precondition if strategic planning is to have more positive and durable impacts than we have recognized in our review of British experience. At one level, this means building an understanding of these processes – along with an appreciation of their likely reactions to policies, and of practicable responses to those – into the intellectual framework of strategic initiatives. But at another level it means accepting that these forces make the classic equation of strategic planning with producing a strategic plan both unworkable and actually undesirable, particularly in relation to the 'regional' context where they have seemed particularly appropriate.

One reason, we would argue, is that at this level – and particularly in relation to a (currently) functional rather than (historic) administrative territory – there will be much less established legitimacy for it as representing an imaginable community, with a commonality of interests and values, than is the case either more locally *or* at a national level. One important reason for this is the way in which residential mobility within functionally integrated regions naturally engenders socially and culturally distinct local political communities often with high degrees of self-consciousness. Without work to build collaboration, this can be problematic for executing change that makes strategic sense, but more grievously so for attempts to endow a pan-regional authority with the power to produce and impose a meaningful strategic plan.

If that cannot be effectively achieved on an independent basis, the default option is that of a central government initiative, which may be little more than symbolic, except in those few regions where a critical issue of national significance is identified. The main problem that we see (in the UK at least) is a lack of durable national-level commitment to meaningful action of the kind that strategic planning supposes. This is even more likely to be a fatal problem for proposals (such as CFN, 2017) to effectively integrate intraregional strategic planning into an interregional framework of activity redistribution.

Hence, the argument here is for pursuing this strategic dimension on a radically less 'centred' basis: actively encouraging bottom-up ad hoc collaborative groupings across ad hoc spaces (Cochrane, 2019); supporting development of strong bases of shared understanding and mutual trust, plus some identifiable 'leaders';[5] and thus enabling negotiation of compatible ways for furthering varied interests on a basis of durable resource commitments.

Recognizing and learning from past failures

One of the themes of this paper – exemplified from UK experience though surely not limited to this setting – is of a pattern of failure in past strategic spatial planning initiatives to deliver positively effective strategic outcomes, for reasons that may seem extrinsic to the activity itself, but which really need to be understood if strategic planning is to become a functional reality, in times when this increasingly matters. Three of the arguably 'extrinsic' factors that are recognized involve: failures of political will/consistency; inadequate channels of implementation; and deficiencies in the knowledge base from which planners worked. Our argument is that these are actually generic issues that need to be addressed, not only at the level of planning *practice,* but also at that of *theory,* since they involve intrinsic problems with the classically iconic plan/planner-focused model that require a radical re-thinking and opening up of the process.

Any scan of the literature of the last 20 years (only slightly reflected in our citations) will show numerous contributions with ideas for, and/or examples of, 'radical' reimaginings of strategic planning. Typically their radicalism is a normative one, focused on redressing recognized deficiencies in how strategic planning has addressed agendas of responsive governance, social cohesion, environmental sustainability and (even) economic competitiveness. In these respects they are progressive, but distinctively planner-centric in Salet's (2018) terms, and reflective of the problematic 'new conventional wisdom' (NCW) of the late 1990s (Gordon & Buck, 2005). More basically, they lack attention to how a collective capacity to effectively address strategic possibilities and challenges is to be developed in a real, material world where both political power and market forces have to be engaged with.

This may be seen even in the thoughtful and respected benchmark review by Albrechts et al. (2003) of lessons from three recent exemplars of a revived interest in strategic planning within European societies, under the strong influence of that NCW. Their cases involve three quite different settings:

one with a strongly institutionalized regional planning culture (Hannover); one in which land use planning had been relatively weak, regulatory and localized in focus (Flanders); and one in which such characteristics were subsidiary to concerns with peace-making in an historically divided society (Northern Ireland). The authors' conclusions embrace *both* an optimism that a broader revival of strategic planning is underway *and* identification of some key processes and governance structures that need to be worked on. But while the latter is grounded in the case histories, the optimism seems entirely exogenous – and somewhat qualified by Kunzmann's own cited argument that the NCW-inspired exercises are 'little more than a cosmetic covering that hides the growing disparities evolving in Europe' (Albrechts et al., 2003, p. 115).

The first two cases are presented in a very positive light, and related to (differently) advantageous circumstances: a strong tradition of city-regional collaboration and leadership commitment that enabled extended bargaining processes to be effectively and productively concluded, in the Hannover case; and consensus across multiple elites of the need for a more action-oriented form of regional planning to respond to pressures arising from its international neighbours (and draw in academic expertise to facilitate innovative approaches), in the Flanders case. In the third, Northern Irish, case, where underpinnings were weaker, and the spatial development strategy of less concern than confidence building and housing allocation, achievements seem both weaker and of less general relevance. The general lessons drawn from the first two cases in particular are entirely credible, with particularly perceptive observations about the importance of building institutional alliances and identifying approaches that are flexible, future-oriented, *and* politically acceptable. What such reviews crucially lack, however, is attention to cases where effective strategic action has not been forthcoming, whether analyses of contemporary ones where non-decisional barriers could be identified as operating, or reflection on historic cases of thwarted, ineffective or misdirected strategic activity. Understanding these might be expected to enable a more radical rethinking of how territorial governance can be made more (positively) strategic than is likely from observation of apparently effective examples.

What we offer here reflects a first approximation to what might be learned from giving greater attention to the collective experience of failed or non-strategic initiatives. The tide invokes two familiar, indeed hackneyed, concepts – but with a significant twist to each. By 'sustainable' we mean *not* 'simply' generating plans that could plausibly secure a long-term balance or rebalancing in/between key economic, social and environmental forces, but rather developing a set of processes and institutions to secure the basis for such planning and associated action itself to be pursued strategically over the long run. To borrow and re-anglicize the French label for sustainable, we are particularly concerned with how (positive) strategic planning can itself be made *durable* in ways that it has generally not been.

And by *'negotiated'* we do not mean the rationalized/ consistent representation within a planning document of a set of compromises arrived at by interactions with more/less diverse interests, which may or (often) not survive through subsequent 'implementation' processes. Rather, we are suggesting that for an effectively strategic dimension to planning, processes of negotiation and committing (or to put it more bluntly 'deal-making') should be seen as at the centre of a continuing and developing practice. This practice would engage with and be expressed in a variety of operational, shorter term, localized or more specialist plans, rather than according centrality to any singular 'strategic' plan of the conventional professional kind.

Acknowledgments

The paper has benefitted from discussions in the Regional Planning Futures sessions at the Regional Studies Association 2018 Winter Conference in London; with the London and Wider South East Strategic Planning Network convened by Duncan Bowie and Corinne Swain; and with colleagues at LSE London and CURDS at Newcastle University. More specifically, we appreciate the critical comments on earlier drafts from an anonymous referee and the editors, which led to a substantial strengthening of the paper's argument.

Disclosure statement

No potential conflict of interest was reported by the authors.

Notes

1 This is an adapted version of Rein's (1969) original taxonomy of available sources of legitimation for planning practice. In our version the role of a socially licensed professional represents a tamer, more institutionalized but politically defensible, counterpart to his 'guerrilla' role which has planners striving to enhance governmental competence and responsiveness by any means available. If not specifically one for 'planners', his guerrilla role does, however, have something in common with the view of strategic planning (as practice) for which we are arguing.

2 Either on their own behalf to build credibility in the competition for influence or by antagonists seeking a fallguy for unwanted outcomes of other forces.

3 Views about whether population and employment dispersal were a good thing vary. But its scale during the period when planners actively favoured it was (and is) commonly supposed to be a result of planning. In fact, however, even in a peak period planned movement accounted only 15% of net moves out of London (Department of the Environment, 1971), and a similarly modest proportion of London job losses (Buck et al, 1986, p. 59).

4 MCHLG written representation on Matter 16 of the London Plan's Examination in Public (see https://www.london.gov.uk/sites/default/files/ml6_mhclg_2631.pdf).

5 With a credible power to commit to a line of action.

ORCID

Ian Gordon ⓘ http://orcid.org/0000-0002-2170-8193
Tony Champion ⓘ http://orcid.org/0000-0001-5478-9682

References

Albrechts, L. (2013). Refraining strategic spatial planning by using a co-production perspective. *Planning Theory, 12*(1), 46–63. https://doi.org/10.1177/1473095212452722

Albrechts, L., Balducci, A., & Hillier, J. (Eds.). (2017). *Situated practices of strategic planning*. Taylor & Francis.

Albrechts, L., Healey, P., & Kunzmann, K. R. (2003). Strategic planning and regional governance in Europe. *Journal of the American Planning Association, 69*(2), 113–129. https://doi.org/10.1080/01944360308976301

Baker, M., & Wong, C. (2013). The delusion of strategic spatial planning: What's left after the Labour government's English regional experiment? *Planning Practice and Research, 28*(1), 83–103. https://doi.org/10.1080/02697459.2012.694314

Bowie, D. (ed.). (2018). Strategic planning for London and the Wider South East. *Town and Country Planning, 87*(10), 395–419.

Breheny, M., & Hall, P. (1984). The strange death of strategic planning and the victory of the know-nothing school. *Built Environment, 10,* 95–99.

Buck, N., Gordon, I. R., & Young, K. (1986). Decentralisation in the metropolitan region. In *The London employment problem* (ch. 3). Oxford University Press.

Champion, A. G. (2002). *The containment of urban Britain: Retrospect and prospect.* Franco Angeli.

Champion, A. G. (2019). How many extra people should London be planning for? *Geography, 104,* 160–165.

Cheshire, P., & Gordon, I. R. (1996). Territorial competition and the predictability of collective (in)action. *International Journal of Urban and Regional Research, 20*(3), 383–399. https://doi.org/10.1111/j.1468-2427.1996.tb00324.x

Cochrane, A. (2012). Making up a region: The rise and fall of the 'South East of England' as a political territory. *Environment and Planning C: Government and Policy, 30*(1), 95–108. https://doi.org/10.1068/cll49r

Cochrane, A. (2019). In and beyond local governance: Making up new spaces of governance. *Local Government Studies,* https://doi.org/10.1080/03003930.2019.1644321

Common Futures Network (CFN). (2017). *Towards a common future: A new agenda for England and the UK.* Retrieved from http://commonfuturesnetwork.org/mdocuments-library?mdocs-cat=mdocs-cat-28&att=null.

Davoudi, S. (2018). Imagination and spatial imaginaries. *Town Planning Review, 89*(2), 97–124. https://doi.org/10.3828/tpr.2018.7

Department of the Environment. (1971). *Long term population distribution in Great Britain: Report of an interdepartmental study group.* HMSO.

Development of the Strategic Plan for the South East team (DSPSE). (1976). Implementation. In *Review of the strategy for the South East*: Report of the resources group. Department of the Environment.

Fainstein, S., & De Fillipis, J. (2015). The structure and debates of planning theory. In S. Fainstein, & J. De Fillipis (Eds.), *Readings in planning theory* (4th ed., pp. 1–18) Wiley Blackwell.

Faludi, A. (1973). *Planning theory.* Pergamon.

Friedmann, J. (1993). Toward a non-Euclidean mode of planning. *Journal of the American Planning Association, 59*(4), 482–485. https://doi.org/10.1080/01944369308975902

Friedmann, J. (2012). Planning theory revisited. In *Insurgencies: Essays in planning theory* (ch.7). Routledge.

Gordon, I. R. (2006). Finding institutional leadership for regional networks: The case of London and the Greater South East. In W. Salet (Ed.), *Synergy in urban networks* (pp. 136–160). Sdu.

Gordon, I. R. (2014). Fitting a quart in a pint pot?: Development, displacement and/or densification in the London region. In B. Kochan (Ed.), *Migration and London's growth* (pp. 41–55). London School of Economics and Political Science (LSE).

Gordon, I. R. (2016). Functional integration, political conflict and muddled metro-politanism in the London region: 1850–2016. In A. Cole, & R. Payre (Eds.), *Cities as political objects* (pp. 31–55). Edward Elgar.

Gordon, I. R. (2018). Getting (more) real in planning for London and the Wider South East. *Town and Country Planning, 87* (10), 415–419.

Gordon, I. R., & Buck, N. H. (2005). Introduction: Cities in the new conventional wisdom. In N. H. Buck, I. R. Gordon, A Harding & I. Turok (Eds.), *Changing cities: Rethinking urban competitiveness, cohesion and governance* (ch. 1). Palgrave Macmillan.

Gordon, I. R., & Champion, A. G. (Forthcoming 2020). *The dynamics of migration flows and population shifts in England's metropolitan super-region.*

Gordon, I. R., Champion, A. G., McGregor, N., & Whitehead, C. M. E. (2017). *Migration influences and implications for population dynamics in the Wider South* (Report to the East of England Local Government Association). London School of Economics (LSE). http://lselondonhousing.org/wp-content/uploads/2018/01/EELGA-MIgration-Project_Main-Report_plusExec.pdf.

Hall, P. G. (1963). *London 2000.* Faber.

Hall, P. G. (1988). The city in the region: The birth of regional planning: Edinburgh, New York and London 1900–40. In *Cities of tomorrow: An intellectual history of planning and design in the twentieth century* (ch. 5). Blackwell.

Hall, P. G. (1989). *London 2001.* Unwin Hyman.

Hall, P. G., & Gordon, I. R. (2002). Postscript: The Mayor's London Plan. In N. Buck, I. R. Gordon, P. G. Hall, M. Harloe, & M. Kleinman (Eds.), *Working capital: Life and labour in contemporary London* (pp. 388–392). Routledge.

Hall, P. G., Gracey, H., Drewett, R., & Thomas, R. (1973). *The containment of urban England.* Allen & Unwin.

Hall, P. G., & Pain, K. (2006). *The polycentric metropolis: Learning from mega-city regions in Europe.* Earthscan.

Healey, P. (1992). Planning through debate: The communicative turn in planning theory. *Town Planning Review, 63,* 143–162.

Lindblom, C. E. (Ed.). (1965). *The intelligence of democracy: Decisionmaking through mutual adjustment.* Free Press.

London–Stansted–Cambridge Corridor Growth Commission. (2016). *Findings and recommendations: The next global knowledge region: Setting the ambitions and delivering the vision.* Retrieved from http://www.lsccgrowthcommission.org.uk/?p= 812.

Mace, A. (2019). How real is networked planning? When a corridor region meets green belt. Paper presented at the 'Planning Regional Futures' session of the Regional Studies Association (RSA) London conference on New Horizons for Cities and Regions in a Changing World.

Mace, A., & Gordon, I. R. (2016). *A 21st century metropolitan Green Belt.* London School of Economics (LSE). http://eprints.lse.ac.uk/68012/.

Mayor of London. (2019, December). *London plan: Spatial development strategy for London, intend to publish version.* Greater London Authority (GLA). Retrieved from https://www.london.gov.uk/sites/default/files/intend_to_publish_-_clean.pdf.

Nelles, J. (2012). *Comparative metropolitan policy: Governing beyond regional boundaries in the imagined metropolis.* Routledge.

O'Hara, G. (2007). *From dreams to disillusionment: Economic and social planning in 1960s Britain.* Palgrave Macmillan.

Outer London Commission. (2016a). *Coordinating strategic policy and infrastructure investment across the Wider South East* (5th Report to the Mayor of London). Greater London Authority (GLA).

Outer London Commission (OLC). (2016b). *Accommodating London's growth* (7th Report to the Mayor of London). Greater London Authority (GLA).

Rein, M. (1969). Social planning: The search for legitimacy. *Journal of the American Institute of Planners, 35*(4), 233–244. https://doi.org/10.1080/01944366908977227

Roberts, P., & Lloyd, G. (1999). Institutional aspects of regional planning, management, and development: Models and lessons from the English experience. *Environment and Planning B: Planning and Design, 26*(4), 517–531. https://doi.org/10.1068/b260517

Salet, W. (2017). Revisiting strategic spatial planning: a critical act of reconstruction. In Albrechts, L., Balducci, A., & Hillier, J. (Eds.). (2017). *Situated practices of strategic planning* (ch. 23). Taylor & Francis.

Schon, D. A. (1983). *The reflective practitioner: How professionals think in action.* Ashgate.

South East Joint Planning Team (SEJPT). (1971). *Strategic plan for the South East.* HMSO.

Swain, C. (2018). Towards a London city-regional intelligence base – The art of the possible. *Town and Country Planning, 87,* 398–401.

Wannop, U. (1995). *The regional imperative.* Jessica Kingsley.

Xu, J., & Yeh, A. G. O. (2017). Regional strategic planning for China's Pearl River Delta. In Albrechts, L., Balducci, A., & Hillier, J. (Eds.). (2017). *Situated practices of strategic planning* (pp. 25–44). Taylor & Francis.

Regional planning as cultural criticism: reclaiming the radical wholes of interwar regional thinkers

Garrett Dash Nelson ⓘ

Introduction

To think rigorously and creatively about the future of regional planning, it is necessary not only to engage with the present day and the startling speed of its transformations but also to locate these transformations within the historical accumulation of ideas and practices which have led up to the present. Although the specifically named discipline of regional planning is a relatively recent phenomenon, dating only to the beginning of the 20th century, the historical horizon of much work in regional studies is even more dramatically foreshortened. This article offers a juxtaposition between the dominant framing of regional problems in contemporary literature and the more radical cultural criticism that characterized the first phase of regionalism within the planning disciplines a century ago. The goal is to show that much of the ideological content of the early regional planning movement, though it achieved a brief moment of rhetorical dominance, now seems out of place in regional studies – a historical phenomenon that tracks the gradual shedding of cultural criticism from the work of regional planning and development. Although certain thinkers of this earlier moment are still recognized, at least in name, as progenitors of regional studies, few contemporary scholars engage with the substantive content of these early regionalists' ideas, pointing again at the contemporary eclipse of the themes which most interested these thinkers.

As a historical keyframe, the paper pivots around the first appearance of the term 'regional planning' in the 14th edition of the *Encyclopedia Britannica* (1929). Written by two members of the Regional Planning Association of America (RPAA), Benton MacKaye and Lewis Mumford, the encyclopaedia entry foreshadowed certain elements of regional planning's conceptual framework and practical concerns that would remain at the heart of the discipline nearly a century later. More striking, however, are the many elements in this 1929 definition that have retreated to the margins of regional planning or even been eliminated altogether from the catalogue of issues considered under the larger banner of regional studies. Rediscovering the commitments of regional planning through the framing of the term's early encyclopaedia definition is an exercise in reclaiming the lively and heterodox set of ideological currents that came together in the first moment where 'regional' was affixed as a geographical adjective onto the technical and administrative work of 'planning'. Crucially, it is a reminder that the introduction of the 'region' into the intellectual history of planning was not merely – or even primarily – a move that sought to redraw the geographical containers of planning jurisdictions. Rather, regionalism for these regional planners was the material container and the geographical nexus for a wide-ranging critique of the spatial conditions of modern life.

The keyframe of the 1929 appearance of regional planning in *Britannica* is an invitation to question why the literature on regional planning now bears so few measurable imprints of the field's early definers. To take just one startling indicator of this state of affairs, the term 'Lewis Mumford' appears in only seven regular articles in the entire *Regional Studies* archive, an absence that can hardly be explained simply by the journal's traditional bent towards UK topics and authors. The ambition of this article not to re-sanctify a canon of specific foundational thinkers such as Mumford, but rather more generally to insist on the importance of drawing on the full sweep of regional planning's intellectual history in order to grapple more effectively with the interlocking set of problems that face regional planning headed into the 21st century. Above all, this article seeks to reclaim material from a 'usable past' – to invoke a term used by Mumford and his interlocutor, Van Wyck Brooks (Brooks, 1918; Mumford, 1926; see also Susman, 1964) – that can be brought to bear on the question of what thinking and working with regions might look like in the present day.

Indeed, problems that may seem at first to belong exclusively to a period beginning somewhere in the last third of the 20th century – for instance, the emergence of functionally integrated megaregions, the neoliberal retreat from industrial policy, the weakening legitimacy of traditional expert-led planning schemes, or the challenges of global climate change – turn out upon closer reflection to have not only echoes but also direct lines of continuity with the problems that planners, theorists and scholars were grappling with nearly a century earlier. To take just one illustrative example, Mumford's complaint in a 1928 article that 'our big cities are burdened with a vast amount of obsolete equipment which continues to be used just because it is so costly to be replaced' could, almost without modification, appear in a modern critique of today's politics around urban infrastructure (Mumford, 1928, p. 132).

What complicates the issue of why regional planning's early radicalism has been so left out of much of today's discourse is the fact that these thinkers and their ideas can hardly be described as 'forgotten'. Quite to the contrary, even cursory histories of regionalism will typically mention figures such as MacKaye, Mumford and their RPAA colleagues, and, more crucially, certain benchmark works in regional studies have in fact spent time exploring this history of ideas, notably Peter Hall's comprehensive *Cities of Tomorrow* (1988) and the first part of John Friedmann and Clyde Weaver's *Territory and Function: The Evolution of Regional Planning* (1979). How, then, can we explain the fact that, on the one hand, the ideas of the early regionalists are recognized today (even if only through superficial gestures) as occupying a place of historical importance, while, on the other, these ideas have only the faintest purchase on present-day framings of the regional question?

Perhaps one answer is disciplinary: more sustained attention to the intersection of regional thinking with the broader history of ideas, politics and culture has been undertaken by historians and social theorists whose work is rarely invoked in contemporary debate over regional issues, such as Riesman (1947), Sussman (1976), Thomas (1988), Birch (1989), Blake (1990), Guha (1991), Parsons (1994), Rodgers (1998), Sutter (1999), Dalbey (2002) and Mittiefehldt (2013). Again, a search for this representative sample of works in the citations *of Regional Studies* shows just how infrequently these historical perspectives are brought to bear on the issue of regional planning in the present day. To be fair, regional studies scholars whose primary communicative circles are in the worlds of policy-making and presentist social science cannot always spend time buried in a deep history of ideas. Yet, it is precisely this shift – in which regional planning has become more focused on the region as a type of instrumental economic and administrative problem, and less on the region as an integrative territory of cultural, environment and environmental co-construction – that has left regional planning so unable to make productive use of its own rich theoretical endowment.

Another reason for why the echo of the early regionalists has grown fainter is the fact that little new work that specifically seeks to weave together regional studies with the history of regional thought has been undertaken since the 1970s, leaving the history of regional planning mostly unrevised by recent developments in the intellectual and institutional historiography of 20th-century Europe and the United States. Precisely because of the degree to which early regional planning was connected to lines of thought ranging from art history to forestry and community sociology, this history of regional planning is best treated not as the narrow origin story of a professional discipline, but rather as a moment where regional thinking reflected a broader discontent with the conditions of the status quo.

Friedmann and Weaver argue in a footnote following a brief excerpt of Mumford and MacKaye's (1929) definition that the 'distinguished list of intellectual contributors to the thinking of the RPAA deserves a separate study to itself, but that would take us far beyond the scope of the present work' (p. 29, n. 6; also p. 41, n.). That invitation to go 'beyond the scope' of the more pragmatic questions in regional studies is in some ways the starting-off point of this article, and in fact Friedmann himself had acknowledged in a 1956 paper that his own understanding of regional planning was descended from the definition laid out in the MacKaye–Mumford encyclopaedia article (Friedmann, 1956, p. 2, n. 3). After exploring conceptual threads that are woven both explicitly and implicitly into *Britannica* article's, a formative attempt to define the field of regional planning, the present paper draws on both published and archival sources from Mumford and MacKaye, as well as from sources that illustrate the intellectual milieu in which they operated at the time the encyclopaedia entry was drafted, to open up a question about what particular conceptualizations of the 'region' brought together this eclectic group of thinkers in the 1920s and 1930s to argue for its centrality in the planning movement.

Scrutinizing the interwar moment in regional planning theory illustrates the degree to which regional planners of this period were undertaking a cultural critique of modern industrial life that not only incorporated questions about politics, ethics and aesthetics but also made these elements central to a radically reformist view of planning's role in structuring communities. Seen from this perspective, the 'region', as invoked by the first regional planners, played a double role. On the one hand, it served as a functional *description* for an emergent pattern of geographical integration, an empirical observation about the new scale of economic organization and administrative rationality. On the other, the region portrayed a *desired* state of affairs for a reconstructed and renewed social order. In this latter sense, the essential work undertaken by regional planning was its proposed ability to suture back together divisions that had supposedly been ripped apart by the instrumental logic of the 19th century, and in particular the spatial ruptures of modernity. As such, the 'regional whole', as Mumford and MacKaye termed it, was at its conceptual core a view of the world that abolished distinctions between producers and consumers, humans and nature, work and leisure, and community and administration.

After considering the central role of this vital organicism in the particular intellectual setting in which the 1929 definition was worked out, the article provides a brief sketch of the afterlife of these ideas within regional planning, exploring how the idealism of interwar thinking about regional planning was gradually absorbed into the institutional structure of the administrative state. Through this process of formalization, regional planning gained power but also lost much of its oppositional attitude, shedding its origins in cultural critique in order to take up a formalized professional role within the post-war bureaucracy. Finally, the article concludes with a call to rethink what the interwar regional planners' emphasis on holism might look like in light of the future prospects of regional planning and regionalism. Some of the ideological content of interwar regional planning is undoubtedly impossible to extract from the particular anxieties of the historical moment in which it emerged. However, many of the problems posed in the 1929 definition of regional planning remain unsolved – and, more to the point, oftentimes entirely unconsidered – in the present day. It is argued that there exists a usable past in this material that can be productively brought to bear on what the conveners of this special issue describe as the 'intellectual and practical challenge of planning urban and regional futures'.

The organic ideology of interwar regional planning

In a 1928 letter to Patrick Geddes, Mumford wrote that 'you have doubtless heard from [Victor] Branford about the various contributions our Regional Planning Association is going to make to the new *Britannica'*. Mumford complained about the 'very sloppy' organization of the encyclopaedists, but admitted that the 'hit or miss ways' in which the 14th edition was being put together 'are partly responsible for the Regional Planning Association's share in the work' (Novak, 1995, pp. 276–277). The RPAA, after all, was a relatively obscure group of dissident planners, landscape architects, housing reformers and writers centred on New York City who had originally convened under the banner of 'garden cities' and only later came to a focus on 'regional planning', a term with barely any professional currency in the early 1920s (Parsons, 1994). Franklin Hooper, the encyclopaedia's American editor, retained John Dewey on his advisory board for philosophy and Isaiah Bowman for geography, and it is possible that one of these two may have provided the connection with the RPAA (Kogan, 1958).

Indeed, the conceptual location of 'regional planning', as the RPAA saw it, really did fall somewhere between and across philosophy and geography. Mumford and MacKaye's (1929) entry for *Encyclopedia Britannica* began with the following paragraph:

> **Regional planning,** a term used by community planners, engineers and geographers to describe a comprehensive ordering of the natural resources of a community, its material equipment and its population for the purpose of laying a sound physical basis for the 'good life.' In America the term has also been used to describe plans for city extension over wide metropolitan areas; this type of planning should properly be called metropolitan planning. Regional planning involves the development of cities and countrysides, of industries and natural resources, as part of a regional whole.

Four key points in this paragraph alone mark out the major features of regional planning that were central to the idealistic project of regional planning during the interwar period – some of which are still recognizable as defining characteristics of regional planning, and others of which barely register in today's thinking. First is the coupling of the professional triad of 'community planners, engineers and geographers' to the practical work of 'comprehensive ordering'. It was precisely the comprehensive nature of the three named fields – their ability to work across professional domains in order to emphasize the *relationship* of elements within an encompassing territorial matrix – that linked them to the emergent work of regional planning. The two authors' RPAA colleague Henry Wright had helped to define the term 'community planning' for the American Institute of Architects, arguing that the traditional practices of architecture urban design had given no consideration to the relationship of buildings to one another in larger community groups (Wright, 1921; see also Lubove, 1963). The inclusion of engineers signalled both authors' admiration for the economist Thorstein Veblen's suggestion that engineers would form a 'soviet' of rational revolutionary administration based on disinterested principles of social betterment (Veblen, 1921; see also Layton, 1962). Finally, geographers represented the academic discipline most responsible for advancing the concept of a 'region' as a distinct territorial object consisting of mutually structuring phenomenon ranging from biophysical conditions to economic practices. The entry named Vidal de la Blache, Frank Herbertson, Nevin Fenneman, J. Russell Smith and C. B. Fawcett amongst those whose research had portrayed the region 'as a definite unit, with its special individuality of geologic formation, climate, vegetation, landscape and human culture'.

The second remarkable point in this initial paragraph is the straightforward insistence on the 'good life' as the motivating purpose of regional planning. Quite in contrast to later forms of regional planning that hinged on the role of the state in shaping the geographical balance of economic sectors or overseeing the provisioning of a specific natural-resource complex such as hydropower, the definition of regional planning here directly implicates a question about what is not merely efficient, rational or productive – but the much more expansive question of what is *good*. As MacKaye had written in his description of the Appalachian Trail project, regional planning represented 'a new approach to the problem of living' (MacKaye, 1921, p. 325; MacKaye & Nelson, 2019). Through the deliberate use of these humanistic terms, MacKaye and Mumford were not only connecting regional planning to a normative debate about the ethical principles of modern life. They were also deliberately contrasting regional planning to the dominant attitudes in both economic theory and public administration that focused on optimizing existing ways of life rather than opening up a critique of the fundamental values of individual and group action. As Mumford put it in the magazine *Survey Graphic*'s 1925 special issue on regional planning, the one principle that bound together the 'hundred approaches to regional planning' was the commitment to 'promote a fuller kind of life, at every point in the region' (Mumford, 1925b, p. 151).

Third, the authors were at pains to distinguish proper *regional* planning from a mere extension of traditional city planning power over wider areas, a practice which they preferred to label as *metropolitan* planning. The radical regionalists shared a belief with many reform-minded planners that the geographical units of planning administration were poorly matched to the functional geographical conditions of industrial urban expansion. Metropolitan jurisdictions ranging from the creation of the London County Council in 1889 (Saint, 1989) to the creation of a metropolitan park district in Boston in 1893 (O'Connell, 2009) pointed the way towards a retooling of city-region boundaries that was well underway at the dawn of the 20th century. For MacKaye and Mumford, however, what was particular to regional planning was not merely the jump up in scale from traditional urban boundaries. Instead, it was about superimposing a regional vision in order to counter the hegemony of industrialized urban centres over the entire landscape. Regional planning, in this view, had much to do with countermanding the almost colonial form of centre-periphery power dynamics that had come to characterize metropolitan planning schemes – a principle that led the group into a pitched public battle against the Regional Plan of New York and Environs, which the RPAA regionalists felt reinscribed the dominance of the central city over its hinterland (Dalbey, 2002).

Fourth, and most tellingly for the purposes of this investigation, is the conclusion of this paragraph with the term 'regional whole'. In the effort to dissolve traditional distinctions such as cities and countrysides or industries and resources into the unifying totality of the region, MacKaye and Mumford showed the raw content of their ideological hand. For them, the region was hardly just an alternative type of territorial object existing somewhere on the scalar rank above the city but below the nation. Instead, it offered the conceptual basis on which to construct a radical critique of industrial modernity, with its exploitative system of hierarchies and divisions. The wholeness of the region rested not only on its inclusion of different land-use types and underlying resource patterns. Above and beyond this, it rested on the reassembly of the parts of human life which the radical regionalists believed had been severed by the instrumentalism of modernity.

These four themes, so strikingly idealistic in comparison with later formalizations of regional planning, set the frame for the rest of MacKaye and Mumford's encyclopaedia definition. In a turn of phrase drawn directly from MacKaye's (1928) book *The New Exploration: A Philosophy of Regional Planning* (repr. 1962) (see also MacKaye, 1940), the authors argued that regional structure was defined by 'force or "flow"' more than an inert territorial boundary. Such flows, they argued, made the region a dynamic entity, and the goal of regional planning would be to 'direct and modify these changes to the advantage of a whole community'. Here again, the almost mystical definition of wholeness – coupled now with 'community' rather than 'region' – reiterated the desire for an organic sense of social cohesion, akin in many ways to Tönnies's theory of the *Gemeimchaft* (Tönnies, [1887] 1963).

Because of the way that the region bound together concepts usually treated as separate, it allowed MacKaye and Mumford to point towards a heterogenous cast of intellectual referents for their definition of regional planning. 'Regional planning, following Ruskin,' they wrote, referring to the eclectic art theorist and critic of modernity, 'recognizes as the ultimate

product of human industry not money or commodities but human life.'
They pointed towards Progressive Era administrators such as Gifford Pinchot and Liberty Hyde Bailey as well as the work of the garden cities movement, anchored by Ebenezer Howard's treatise *To-Morrow: A Peaceful Path
to Real Reform* (1898), as examples of how to marry the desired state of regional holism to the practical work of planning and development.

The ideology of organicism, therefore, was absolutely crucial to the introduction of the 'region' into planning theory, for ultimately the purpose
of expanding the territorial boundary of planning's professional obliga-
tions was the ability of this expanded geography to put human life back
together. This belief is referred to here as an 'ideology' in the broad sense
of a set of interlocking worldviews that underly both cultural and political
beliefs – similar to what Mumford himself described as the 'idolum': 'all
the philosophies, fantasies, rationalizations, projections, images, and opinions in terms of which people pattern their behavior' (Mumford, 1922b,
p. 13). As Leo Marx correctly diagnoses it, 'the opposition between the organic and the mechanical ... dominates Mumford's thinking' (Marx, 1990,
p. 168). To understand the full weight of this intellectual tension-point, it
is necessary to strip off the semantic detritus that has attached itself to the
term 'organic' over the past century. Marx, connecting Mumford to both
19th-century Romanticism and the vitalist philosophy of Alfred North
Whitehead, argues that 'the most important and attractive aspect of organicism' is 'the primacy it imports to relatedness, order, or integration in human affairs'. Mumford's 'highest intellectual aim' can, therefore, in Marx's
view, be captured in terms of 'a coherent and comprehensive conception of
the whole of life, one that might yield the principles needed to order relations among the parts' (Marx, 1990, p. 178; on Mumford and vitalism, see
also Ekman, 2015).

Words such as cooperation, commonwealth and community, with their
emphasis on mutual bound-togetherness, are therefore absolutely crucial
in interpreting what, exactly, the region as a term of art for this early moment in regional planning. It conjoined the sociocultural concept of a whole
community – with its derivations from socialist reform, Utopian experiments and a sentimental notion of premodern organicism – with the ecological and geographical concept of the region as a kind of territory that skirted
around the instrumental social order of capitalist modernity. 'Briefly,' as
MacKaye and Mumford put it in their definition, 'regional planning deals
with the ecology of the human community.'

The region in description and desire

In a handwritten note from the early 1920s, Mumford posed a question for
himself that foreshadowed his turn to the region as a key explanatory category. 'The crux of the difficulty is the unit of investigation,' he jotted down.
What is a society or a community?'[1] This question about units was a key

puzzle for Mumford's during the years in which he set the course of his intellectual development. A set of neatly typed notecards from 1917 record some of the sources of his early attempts to answer this question. He had discovered the work of the French regional geographers, writing in one note that 'Vidal de la Blache, in his *Regions Françaises,* distinguishes three kinds of regions, each characteristic of a certain state of the arts.' Mumford followed Vidal in describing history as structured by a series of successive human–environment relationships, each with its own technical system operating within the frame of a different type of geographical unit. Beginning with the 'primitive or natural' region, 'in which geologic structure and climate and vegetation form a complex which definitely sets it apart', Mumford's notes on Vidal then moved to the 'cultivated region', where 'the soil-rooted peasant' met 'the wandering trafficker' and tied together new areas by market-centre focused economic exchange. Finally, as market trade gave way to industrial capitalism, society moved towards the 'energized region ... markt [*sic*] by a coalescence of cities ... and by the creation of an intensive urban life within the conglomerations'.[2] Another note suggests Mumford also read H. J. Fleure's 1917 article 'Regions Humaines', which he incorrectly attributed to Schader.[3]

Units of geographical organization, in this reading, both typified the social and economic possibilities of a given era, and also controlled the territories within which human groups modified the Earth's surface for their own needs. Mumford continued in his notes:

> Summing up we may say that the protagonist of the natural region is the peasant, and its civic expression the village; the protagonist of the cultivated region is the merchant, and its expression the city, while finally the chief figure in the energized region is the industrialist and the civic expression of great industry is the conurbation.[4]

But he was cautious to add that these eras did not transition perfectly from one to the other: 'one state does not finally leave the other behind it... the evolution of regions creates incompatibilities and anomalies in habits and institutions which make the transition from period to period one of difficult adjustment'.[5] Social patterns and institutions might outlive the conditions that had led to their creation, and this lag, Mumford believed, was one of the chief sources of friction which led to moments of conflict.

By reference to the historical lag between different units of geographical organization, Mumford believed he could diagnose two problems of maladjustment that marred the early 20th century. First:

> Administration in conurbations is hindered by the fact that the so called municipalities are 'independent' and their common activities are uncoordinated, as in the days when each city had a hinterland of its own to support it and none lived on that common hinterland which is the world.[6]

Second, he believed that a 'parasitic' relationship had developed between city and country, in which the city transformed the country into its recreational colony in a desperate attempt to reconnect with the authenticity found in nature and the outdoors. Meanwhile, the country 'goes in for an equally sterile life by living off the city'. The result was a 'social exhaustion of land', a 'vital depletion' and 'loss of the amenities and sanities and decencies', replaced by 'a sterilized, cranky, ugly, starved population'. All these changes had been driven by technological and material transformation: as cities grew larger to hold ever vaster concentrations of population and capital, and formerly distinct cities merged together through the mortarwork of capital, commerce and communication, it became impossible to plan properly for common needs – a problem which, at its root, lay in the lack of any units, either for the purpose of administration or for the purposes of defining a common cultural affinity, which might synchronize these new patterns of functional interaction.

The geography of raw agglomeration was a process that Mumford tied historically to the rise of nationalism, which, he explained, was 'developed in order to make the political States which were founded in Europe, from the fourteenth century onward, unified territories from which tribute might be extracted without difficulty' (Mumford, 1922a, p. 131). Owing to its acquisitive ambitions, 'the unity which is promoted by "nationalism" is a highly artificial condition' (p. 132). Regionalism, by contrast, 'emphasizes the corporate unity and the independence of the local community, focussed in its local capitals' (p. 133). In other words, an arbitrary unit such as the 'political States' served only the ruling class in their uptake of powers; a *true* unit was a democratic polity in which residents felt themselves to belong organically to a single geographical body.

A hand-drawn lecture note from the early 1920s gave a visual clue as to what Mumford meant. A sketch map of the 'arbitrary division' of North America into gridded states was accompanied by references to 'state-building 14–17 century', 'power politics extending blank unitary power states' and 'exploitation ... extending base of supplies for city-agglomerations'. It was a 'preoccupation with power, numbers, magnitude & money instead of with pattern of activity and quality of experience' that had produced these political units which were not actually unitary.[7] The borders of such areas were based on the logic of the military survey or the speculator's plat book: a geography which ignored the patterns of land and life in order to speed the processes of accumulation and agglomeration. On the same note, Mumford sketched out 'La ville tentaculaire', the destabilizing city that reached its feeding tubes into the countryside; the same type of urban form which the British planner Clough Williams Ellis would decry in his influential book *England and the Octopus* (1928) (see also Matless, 2012).

In the same set of notes, Mumford drafted out the principles of alternative path of a regionalized geography that founded its organizing logic on the 'underlying realities' of physiography, vegetation, climate, human occupance and city-region interdependence that had the potential to move beyond 'indefinite agglomeration & massing' and achieve an 'organic' principle in which 'access to nature' and 'access to culture' were guaranteed within the limits of stable, well-balanced geographical entities. 'Region' should be understood, according to Mumford in these notes, not simply as a territory of an intermediate scalar size, but 'as a value'.[8]

Mumford had begun working out the principles of regional unity on his own since the 1910s, but it was his reading of the works of the Scottish biologist, geographer and planner Patrick Geddes that fully convinced him of the necessity for regional reorganization of civilization in order to put community, economy and state back into their proper territorial relations. Geddes was, like Mumford, an intellectual gadabout: his interests sprawled across the many scientific disciplines which were just beginning to mark out their distinct responsibilities in the early 20th century. As Mumford put it, 'his work and his philosophy have spring out of the fulness of his life' (Mumford, 1925a, p. 523). It was precisely this integrative approach, in which Geddes surveyed all manner of human and natural forces and attempted to organize them within the overarching logic of a historical geography of places, that attracted Mumford.

Geddes, therefore, approached the problem of planning with the assumption that the planner needed to be at once a naturalist, a sociologist, a technician, a politician and an educator. Borrowing from the French sociologist Frédéric Le Play and the French geographer Elisée Reclus, he structured his thinking in terms of an interaction between natural possibilities, folk traditions and lifeways, and the evolution of cultures and states (Geddes, 1915; Mercer, 1997). In *The Coming Polity* (1917), co-written with the sociologist Victor Branford, Geddes synthesized regionalism, humanism, planning, socialism and anti-imperialism into an argument about readjusting social organization in terms of the lessons gleaned from an investigation undertaken 'from the standpoint of Place' (Branford & Geddes, 1917, p. 191). Surveying regions from an airplane, Geddes and Branford offered an intoxicating, and theoretically impressionistic, version of a 'coming polity', which, through a cultural readjustment made possible by a new way of thinking about society and space, would resynchronize modernity with the elemental forces of human life.

These writings from the late 1910s and early 1920s show that the problem of a unit area suitable for modernity was *the* foundational concept for Mumford: the wellspring from which he drew the source of both his regionalism, as a specific critique about planning and architecture, and his organicism, as a broader critique about culture and social life. A typescript report on The Background of Regional Planning' (*c.*1926) marks the zenith of the period during which Mumford centred *planning* as the discipline that would be forced to confront this question before all others.[9] The inheritance of that idea could be found in Mumford's draft RPAA report. In the second chapter of the report, 'The Region as a Geographic Unit', Mumford laid out the empirical case that it was now regions, not cities, that formed cohesive wholes under the conditions of 20th-century technological and economic systems. These regions ultimately rested their status on the configuration of the natural world. 'Underlying all our political conventions, our frontiers, our state boundaries, our various administrative districts,' he wrote, 'is the basic factor of the earth itself.' In long-settled areas – Mumford singled out New England as the sole American example – 'there is often a definite correspondence between the ancient political area and the geographical area itself.' However, with the dawning of the industrial era, and a misguided faith in 'the manmade or political' remaking of nature, people had come to divide up territory according to arbitrary schemes. The gridiron layout of the American West, he argued, 'implied a definite indifference to geographic facts'. It was only with the reawakening of the regional spirit, Mumford argued, that 'we have arrived at the notion of fitting the political fact to the geographic reality'.

This, in one sentence, encapsulated the dream of the unitary region: the dream of discovering a 'geographic reality', both naturally and humanistically defined, and then 'fitting the political fact' to match it. From this basic claim about the geographical reality of regions, Mumford could elaborate his cultural critique about regions as carriers of praiseworthy traditions. 'Each region has its own specific historic and geographical pattern, which cannot be ignored by anyone who would understand its life or its destiny,' he argued. Instead of 'a system of development which sacrificed the welfare of cities and regions to the pecuniary advantage of the great metropolises', one might envision instead a form of regional development which could 'integrate every function that grows out of the fact that men live and learn best... in communities'. Regionalism, in 'the ideal and the practical, the cultural and technical aspects', thereby formed the basis for 'a new attitude towards our political and industrial institutions, towards the human drama itself, towards the earth upon which it is staged'.

What is perhaps most striking about Mumford's theory of regions as the modern inheritors of communitarian, political, ecological and economic totalities was the way in which it took an unabashedly modernist and teleological view of history and bent it in the direction of an organic, anti-mechanistic vision based on romantic naturalism. Science, empirical observation and technical innovation set the conditions within which the region would be recognized and developed. However, a newly communitarian system of economic activity and political control, described in contradistinction to the mass systems of the bureaucratic industrial city, would be the result. As Robert L. Dorman argues, Mumford's 'regional civilization', in contrast to the mass coercion of Nazism and Stalinism, 'would be the exceptionalistic outgrowth of a process of "rational politics": citizens acting cooperatively from scientific disinterestedness and communal consciousness, values to be instilled within every individual through an intensive education in regional history, environment, myth, and aesthetics' (Dorman, 1998, p. 13).

Like Mumford, MacKaye's interests were wide-ranging, and did not fit easily into a course of study or a professional career. In 1898, he latched on to William Morris Davis's description of the breadth of human-environment studies in Harvard's 'Geography A' course. 'The subject of our study,' as he recalled Davis's introduction to geography 52 years later, was 'the earth as a habitable globe' (MacKaye, 1950, p. 439). Captivated by the theme of 'habitation', MacKaye went on to earn Harvard's first degree in forestry in 1905, and then began work in Gifford Pinchot's Forest Service. When the reformist Pinchot was dismissed by William Howard Taft and the agency began to lose its crusading zeal, MacKaye began travelling in more radical circles. His brother James, who worked for a time as secretary to the Harvard geographer Nathaniel Southgate Shaler (with whom MacKaye also studied), had moved to Washington, DC, and begun earning himself a reputation as a fresh-voiced theorist of a socialism which grew from the original ideas of the American experiment.

Increasingly, the younger MacKaye sought to devise a version of economic radicalism which acknowledged the foundational role of human-land interactions and community structure in determining the structure of social relations: a kind of political ecology that long predated today's use of that term. As such, his interest turned towards the question of how to overlay the mutuality of a community and the power of a polity onto total geographies that were shaped by the ways which people made a living from the land. In a 1918 article for the Bureau of Labor Statistics, he laid out an argument for the resettling or 'colonization' of soldiers returning from the First World War in forest communities that would allow labourers to self-organize: a principle which MacKaye felt would not only ease the way to socialist economics but also prevent the kind of exploitative logging practices that had denuded thousands of square miles of forestland. Under the argument that 'disintegration is gradually being replaced by integration of the Nation's sources of life', MacKaye began to outline the first principles of his own organic system (MacKaye, 1918a, p. 49; see also National Colonization Bill, 1916). Getting the geography correct was the fundamental first step, he argued: 'the natural unit of development here, from a physical standpoint, is the mountain basin' (MacKaye, 1918a, p. 52). No doubt imagining the apparent solidity of his New England hometown, MacKaye hoped such reforms would lead to 'permanent forest communities based upon continuous forest employment' – thereby setting up an opposition between settledness and nomadism which became key to the regionalists' social ideology (p. 54).

MacKaye's method for linking together these two problems – human and non-human – was similar to the one that Geddes had conceived: by beginning with place as an a priori container holding a total set of interactions. MacKaye concluded that lumbering communities needed to have a definite layout and composition, as against the pulverized and selfish organization of itinerant logger and absentee capitalist: 'The working circle within the National Forest – if it is to work – must be a unit and not, like the wandering minstrel, 'a thing of shreds and patches'. In short, the interests involved must be integrated' (MacKaye, 1918b, p. 212).

Independently of Mumford, MacKaye had come to believe that figuring out the unit was a 'a primal question'. He realized, moreover, that it was not only forestry that could be mapped – and subsequently reformed – by reference to the geographical units in which economic and community action took place. By 1921, MacKaye had begun to articulate the potential consequences for this line of thinking in terms of a wholesale reorganization of the geography of capitalism, and he sketched the way forward in a 'Memorandum on Regional Planning' drafted on Department of Labor stationery (MacKaye, 1921). He defined the task as such:

> Let us call it 'regional planning' – the conscious deliberate working out of a systematic method for developing, as far as still possible, the natural resources of a region (or locality) so as to convert those resources into human needs + welfare. This is a problem not alone of industrial and working conditions but of housing + living conditions. It is social engineering from the geographic standpoint.[10]

The absorption of regional planning into the developmental state

Although the article has focused specifically on the 1929 definition of regional planning and the intellectual milieu of its authors, it would be wrong to interpret this radical moment of interwar regional thought as belonging exclusively to MacKaye, Mumford and their immediate interlocutors. In fact, a diverse set of loosely related thinkers articulated parallel versions of regional planning as a cultural critique in a variety of institutional and national contexts. In the US South, Howard W. Odum developed a theory of regional planning that attempted to combine folk life, ecological thinking and economic development while also wrestling with the troubled racial history of Southern regional identity (Odum, 1934, 1939; Odum & Moore, 1938). Following very much in the pattern of MacKaye and Mumford, Odum argued in a 1951 symposium that the regional project was one which combined description and development, the goal being:

> to recognize and give foil credit to the folk personality of millions of people; to group geographic and culture areas into regional clusters of practical administrative proportions; to give them representation; and, finally, to integrate them in the total order.
>
> (cited in Jensen, 1951, p. 404)

In Britain, a generation of geographers who followed in Geddes's path produced shelves' worth of regional surveys, maps and descriptions that pointed towards a similar organic fusion of categories (Matiess, 1992). Here, again, the goal was not only rational order but also 'a full spiritual expression of mankind', as the geographer Robert Dickinson put it (Dickinson, 1934, p. 7; see also Dickinson, 1979). Even Karl Polanyi, observing the conflict between capitalism and communism in Eastern Europe at mid-century, could argue that it was regional planning which offered the best possibility of cutting through both chauvinistic nationalism as well as totalitarian communism (Polanyi, 1945). And when Paul and Percival Goodman proposed in 1947 their own form of communitarian Utopia heavily inspired by Mumford, they proposed a 'Patrick Geddes Regional Museum' on the town square (Goodman & Goodman, [1947] 1960).

Regional planning, then, from the 1920s to at least the 1940s, provided a rich site of attraction for a wide variety of thinkers concerned with the work of what Mumford called 'a counter-movement to the dehumanised specialisation and standardisation which was fostered by the older forms of industrialism' (Mumford, 1928, p. 140). Yet, within the course of just a few decades, regional planning became itself the subject of an extensive programme of 'specialisation and standardisation' as it shed its thoroughgoing cultural critique and came to occupy a position within the bureaucratic formality of the administrative state. What happened?

Friedmann and Weaver's (1979) text stands in many ways as the historical inflection point where regional planning lost its direct line of communication to the cultural criticism of the early regionalists. Concluding their first major chapter with the observation that the RPAA school 'advocated a counter position' to the growing dominance of economic development planning, they identified the absorption of RPAA's ideas into the river basin planning of the Franklin D. Roosevelt administration as the point where the cultural criticism of this strain of regionalism 'lost much of its theoretical purity' while simultaneously becoming the 'prevailing model of development planning'. As if to exemplify this very transition, Friedmann and Weaver *themselves* turn from the RPAA story of regional planning's intellectual origins into 'a spatial framework for capitalist planning'.

In an even more strikingly instructive historical juxtaposition, the term 'regional planning' no longer enjoys its own entry in *Britannica,* having been relegated to a synonym of 'regional development program'. The entry bears almost no relationship to Mumford and MacKaye's definition of 1929, describing it now as 'government program designed to encourage the industrial and economic development of regions that are stagnant or in which a large portion of the population is experiencing prolonged unemployment'. Where regional planning had once stood for the possibility of a new type of geographical scaffolding for the 'good life' in opposition to the dominant forms of state-led and capital-driven economic development, this oppositional sense has been almost entirely stripped away in the course of nearly a century of institutional and ideological shifts. Indeed, the post-war thinkers who did centre the organicist principles of the interwar regionalists were noteworthy specifically because of their marginal status within an increasingly functionalist profession of regional planning – concepts such as Artur Glikson's 'habitational unit' (Glikson, 1967), or Kevin Lynch's treatise on 'managing the sense of the region' (Lynch, 1976) were widely appreciated but rarely integrated into the formal undertakings of regional management.

Crucially, 'region' evolved from a term that fundamentally incorporated the interactions between 'climate, vegetation, minerals, power resources, landscape, economic and social institutions necessary to a flourishing human community', as in the 1929 definition, to a mere scalar container for the programmes of the developmental state, something mediating between local organization and the machinations of national policy. This move, in which the region lost its symbolic and Utopian elements and became little more than an administrative territory, was the necessary casualty that tracked regional planning's move into the centre of bureaucratic power.

Consider, for example, what MacKaye wrote in a 1940 article on human ecology in planning. Citing the *Britannica* definition, and noting that 'being the co-author ... of this definition... I feel at liberty to interpret it', MacKaye offered the following synonym: 'Regional planning is ecology. ... The region is the unit of environment' (MacKaye, 1940, pp. 350–351).

The equivalence between regional planning and ecology here demonstrates the central location of the organic principle for the early regionalists, in which the conceptual vocabulary of ecology promoted a version of regional development which was fundamentally opposed to the centrally led developmental programmes of the capitalist state. Simply put, it was impossible to carry over this ecological principle to a form of regional planning that sited the region as a post hoc construction of industrial and commercial geography and chained it to the bureaucratic and political logic of the developmental nation-state, since in the MacKaye–Mumford definition the region was precisely the form of geographical, economic and social order that ran against the spatial development patterns of nationalized capitalism.

In part, this move from an organicist regionalism, infused with cultural criticism and oriented in an adversarial position to the developmental state, to a bureaucratic regionalism, in which the region became a scalar intermediary between city and nation in state-led economic planning, was part of a much larger trend in the capitalist states during the post-war. Wary of the extreme revolutions on both the right and left that had characterized the interwar period, a managerial liberalism increasingly sought to implement welfare and planning regimes which were insulated from mass cultural movements. However, the chief obstacle for radical regionalism was simply the hardening of territorial units in the post-war period. While the century leading up to the 1920s had seen an astonishing reshuffling of empires, the consolidation of new nations in places such as Italy and Germany, and the invention of new kinds of metropolitan governments, the century following the 1920s saw a remarkable stasis in political geography, at least in the capitalist West. The nationstate retained its supremacy, and while countiess new kinds of special-purpose authorities ranging from neighbourhood redevelopment zones to natural resource management districts were established, hardly any new geographies of fully constituted *polity* emerged during this time. With its chief objective stymied – that is, the wholesale reorganization of group life into a new geographical pattern – what was left for a rump movement of regional planning was a technical absorption of into the administrative state.

Conclusions: reclaiming the radical wholes of regional planning

Because today's world is so obviously marked by the worldspanning forces of globalization, in which both the conceptual individuality and practical autonomy of smaller units such as regions have been hollowed out, it may seem that the early regional planners' insistence on the region as a radical whole is no longer a tenable proposition. Indeed, considerable work on the regional question in recent years has been undertaken in response to this very problem: does it even make sense to speak about and work with geographical units such as regions when the material, institutional and imaginative structure of the 21st century's spatial order is so relentlessly deterritorialized? As Harrison (2013) puts it in a survey of contemporary theoretical debates over the territorial status of regions, most regional theory has moved beyond a concept of the region as a distinctly bound geographical area in order to emphasize the multiple and non-overlapping forms of regional identification through contested political, social and economic practices.

Yet, the radical wholeness of this regional vision was *not* reliant on some absolute geography of bordered territorial enclosure. In fact, MacKaye and Mumford were at pains to make exactly this point: 'No region is a self-contained unit,' they argued in the 1929 *Britannica* definition, and 'economically and culturally no region has existed without contact with other regions.' Instead, they returned to the *conceptual* form of wholeness as the basis for regional planning: it was to be understood as a task which 'involves every aspect of a region's life'. Or, as Mumford wrote in the draft manuscript: 'In the reintegration of regional activities lies, perhaps, the main social foundation for a reintegrated life.'[11] Rather than treating the region as an object of functional spatial isolation and economic autarky – as both some regional planners as well as their critics have done – it is more appropriate to interpret the holism of the early regionalists as a geographical structure that sought to destabilize the conceptual divisions between such areas of human activity as economics, culture, environment and politics. As Friedmann and Weaver put it, the early regionalists 'attempted to champion the territorial principle of social integration, which was quickly disappearing before a growing flood of market relationships' (Friedmann & Weaver, 1979, p. 40).

It is a sign of changing times that the urgency of 'social integration' is once again ascending, after nearly a century's worth of a 'growing flood of market relationships'. What role does regional planning have to play in the renewed political task of finding some kind of rapprochement between ecological balance, social justice, cultural flourishing and the necessities of public administration? Because of the way that regional planning has shed most of the theoretical apparatus that once sited it at the centre of such discussions, few contemporary scholars, politicians or reformers see regional planning as occupying any place of importance in these questions. However, there are signs of change: for instance, the legal scholar Jedediah Purdy, in his 'search for a new commonwealth', written in sympathy with movements such as the putative Green New Deal that seek to fuse together environmental and social concerns, turns to Benton MacKaye as an example of a thinker who sought to make 'the whole human environment, from the workplace to the untouched woods, welcoming and stimulating, a good place to be alive' (Purdy, 2019, p. 126). This affixing of 'whole' to 'human environment' is a semantic move that both echoes the almost-forgotten past of regional planning's original comprehensive ambitions and also stands as a challenge to those who would plan regional futures today.

Disclosure statement

No potential conflict of interest was reported by the author.

Notes

1 LMP 188:8168. LMP citations refer to the box and folder at the Lewis Mumford Papers at the Kislak Center for Special Collections, University of Pennsylvania.
2 LMP 180:8028.
3 LMP 191:8228.
4 LMP 180:8028.
5 LMP 180:8028.
6 LMP 180:8028.
7 LMP 191:8228.
8 LMP 191:8228.
9 LMP 148:7095. The manuscript includes a note of 1963 by Mumford explaining its original purpose: 'Background of Regionalism done originally for pub. As pamphlet by Regional Planning Association of America. When pub. in Sociological Review Branford's introduction of errors & gratuitous interpolations made it impossible to use in that form. Some of it went into T&C [*Technics and Civilization*] & CofC [*Culture of Cities*].' The *Sociological Review* publications to which Mumford refers, in which much of this manuscript appears with Branford's edits, are Mumford (1927, 1928). The quotations are as they appear in the original manuscript version.
10 Rauner Library, Dartmouth College, Benton MacKaye papers, 177:2.
11 LMP 148:7095.

ORCID

Garrett Dash ⓘ *Nelson* http://orcid.org/0000-0003-2515-6514

References

Birch, E. L. (1989). An urban view: Catherine Bauer's five questions. *Journal of Planning Literature, 4*(3), 239–258. https://doi.org/10.1177/088541228900400301.

Blake, C. N. (1990). *Beloved community: The cultural criticism of Randolph Bourne, Van Wyck Brooks, Waldo Frank & Lewis Mumford.* University of North Carolina Press.

Branford, V., & Geddes, P. 1917. *The coming polity; a study in reconstruction. The making of the future.* Williams & Norgate. http://hdl.handle.net/2027/mdp. 39015028392283.

Brooks, V. W. (1918). On creating a usable past. *The Dial,* April, 337–341.

Dalbey, M. (2002). *Regional visionaries and metropolitan boosters: Decentralization, regional planning, and parkways during the inter*war years. Kluwer.

Dickinson, R. E. (1934). *The Le Play method in regional survey.* Le Play Society.

Dickinson, R. E. (1976). *Regional concept: The Anglo-American leaders.* Routledge.

Dorman, R. L. (1998). The regionalist movement in America, 19201945. In C. R. Wilson (Ed.), *The new regionalism* (pp. 1–18). University Press of Mississippi.

Ekman, P. (2015). Diagnosing suburban ruin: A prehistory of Mumford's postwar jeremiad. *Journal of Planning History, 15*(2), 108–128. https://doi.org/10.1177/1538513215598041.

Encyclopaedia Britannica Co. (1929). *The Encyclopedia Britannica: Fourteenth edition: A new survey of universal knowledge.*

Fleure, H. J. (1917). Regions humaines. *Annales de Geographic, 26*(141), 161–174. https://doi.org/10.3406/geo.1917.8623

Friedmann, J. (1956). The concept of a planning region. *Land Economics, 32*(1), 1–13. https://doi.org/10.2307/3159570

Friedmann, J., & Weaver, C. (1979). *Territory and function: The evolution of regional planning.* University of California Press.

Geddes, P. (1915). *Cities in evolution: An introduction to the town planning movement and to the study of civics.* Williams & Norgate.

Glikson, A. (1967). The concept of a habitational unit. *Ekistics; Reviews, on the Problems and Science of Human Settlements, 24* (141), 135–138.

Goodman, P., & Goodman, P. (1960). *Communitas: Means of livelihood and ways of life.* Vintage.

Guha, R. (1991). Lewis Mumford: The forgotten American environmentalist: An essay in rehabilitation. *Capitalism Nature Socialism, 2*(3), 67–91. http://www.tandfonline.com/doi/abs/10.1080/10455759109358458.

Hall, P. (1988). *Cities of tomorrow: An intellectual history of urban planning and design in the twentieth century.* Blackwell.

Harrison, J. (2013). Configuring the new 'regional world': On being caught between territory and networks. *Regional Studies, 47*(1), 55–74. https://doi.org/10.1080/00343404.2011.644239.

Howard, E. (1898). *To-morrow: A peaceful path to real reform.* Swan Sonnenschein.

Jensen, M. (Ed.). (1951). *Regionalism in America.* University of Wisconsin Press.

Kogan, H. (1958). *The great EB: The story of the Encyclopaedia Britannica.* University of Chicago Press.

Layton, E. (1962). Veblen and the engineers. *American Quarterly, 14* (1), 64. https://doi.org/10.2307/2710227.

Lubove, R. (1963). *Community planning in the 1920s: The contribution* of the Regional Planning Association of America. University of Pittsburgh Press.

Lynch, K. (1976). *Managing the sense of a region.* MIT Press.

MacKaye, B. (1918a). Labor and the war: The soldier, the worker, and the land's resources. *Monthly Review of the U.S. Bureau of Labor Statistics, 6*(1), 48–56. http://www.jstor.org/stable/41829258.

MacKaye, B. (1918b). Some social aspects of forest management. *Journal of Forestry, 16*(2), 210–214. https://doi.org/10.1093/jof/16.2.210.

MacKaye, B. (1921). An Appalachian trail: A project in regional planning. *Journal of the American Institute of Architects, 9*(10), 325–330.

MacKaye, B. (1928; repr. 1962). *The new exploration: A philosophy of regional planning.*

MacKaye, B. (1940). Regional planning and ecology. *Ecological Monographs, 10*(3), 349–353. https://doi.org/10.2307/1948509.

MacKaye, B. (1950). Geography to geotechnics: I. Growth of a new science. *The Survey,* October, 439–442.

MacKaye, B. (1962). *The new exploration: A philosophy of regional planning.* University of Illinois Press.

MacKaye, B., & Nelson, G. D. (2019). An Appalachian trail: A project in regional planning. *Places Journal.* https://placesjournal.org/article/an-appalachian-trail-a-project-in-regional-planning/

Marx, L. (1990). Lewis Mumford: Prophet of organicism. In T. P. Hughes & A. C. Hughes (Eds.), *Lewis Mumford: Public intellectual* (pp. 164–180). Oxford University Press.

Matless, D. (1992). Regional surveys and local knowledges: The geographical imagination in Britain, 1918–39. *Transactions of the Institute of British Geographers, 17*(4), 464–480. http://www.jstor.org/stable/622711. https://doi.org/10.2307/622711

Matless, D. (2012). Communities of landscape: Nation, locality, and modernity in interwar England. In R. Heynickx & T. Avermaete (Eds.), *Making a new world: Architecture & communities in interwar Europe* (pp. 42–55). Leuven University Press.

Mercer, C. (1997). Geographies for the present: Patrick Geddes, urban planning and the human sciences. *Economy and Society, 26*(2), 211–232. https://doi.org/10.1080/03085149700000012.

Mittlefehldt, S. (2013). *Tangled roots: The Appalachian Trail and American environmental politics.* University of Washington Press.

Mumford, L. (1922a). Nationalism or culturism? A search for the true community. *The Menorah Journal, 8*(3), 129–138.

Mumford, L. (1922b). *The story of Utopias.* Boni & Liveright.

Mumford, L. (1925a). Who is Patrick Geddes? *Survey, 53*(February), 523–524.

Mumford, L. (1925b). Regions – To live in. *Survey Graphic, 54*(May), 151–152.

Mumford, L. (1926). *The golden day: A study in American experience and culture.* Boni & Liveright.

Mumford, L. (1927). Regionalism and irregionalism. *The Sociological Review, a19*(4), 277–288. https://doi.org/10.1111/j.1467-954X.1927.tb01644.x

Mumford, L. (1928). The theory and practice of regionalism. *The Sociological Review, a20*(2), 131–141. https://doi.org/10.1111/j.1467-954X.1928.tb02897.x

Mumford, L., & MacKaye, B. (1929). Regional planning. In *The Encyclopedia Brittanica: Fourteenth edition: A new survey of universal knowledge,* vol. 19 (pp. 71–72). Encyclopaedia Brittanica Co.

National Colonization Bill: Hearings before the Committee on Labor, House of Representatives. 1916. Washington, DC: Government Printing Office.

Novak, F. G. (Ed.). (1995). *Lewis Mumford and Patrick Geddes: The correspondence.* Routledge.

O'Connell, J. C. (2009). How metropolitan parks shaped Greater Boston, 1893–1945. In A. N. Penna & C. E. Wright (Eds.), *Remaking Boston: An environmental history of the city and its surroundings* (pp. 168–197). University of Pittsburgh Press.

Odum, H. W. (1934). The case for regional–national social planning. *Social Forces, 13*(1), 6–23. https://doi.org/10.2307/2570212.

Odum, H. W. (1939). Regional development and governmental policy. *The Annals of the American Academy of Political and Social Science, 206* (1), 133–141. https://doi.org/10.1177/000271623920600122

Odum, H. W., & Moore, H. E. (1938). *American regionalism: A cultural–historical approach to national integration.* H. Holt & Co.

Parsons, K. C. (1994). Collaborative genius: The Regional Planning Association of America. *Journal of the American Planning Association, 60*(4), 462–482. https://doi.org/10.1080/01944369408975605.

Polanyi, K. (1945). Universal capitalism or regional planning? *The London Quarterly of World Affairs,* January, 86–91.

Purdy, J. (2019). *This land is our land: The struggle for a new commonwealth.* Princeton University Press.

Riesman, D. (1947). Some observations on community plans and Utopia. *The Yale Law Journal, 57,* 173–200. https://doi.org/10.2307/793022

Rodgers, D. T. (1998). *Atlantic crossings: Social politics in a progressive age.* Belknap/Harvard University Press.

Saint, A. (Ed.). (1989). *Politics and the people of London: The London County Council, 1889–1965.* Hambledon.

Susman, W. I. (1964). History and the American intellectual: Uses of a usable past. *American Quarterly, 16*(2), 243. https://doi.org/10.2307/2711041.

Sussman, C. (1976). *Planning the fourth migration: The neglected vision of the regional planning Association of America.* MIT Press.

Sutler, P. S. (1999). 'A retreat from profit': Colonization, the Appalachian Trail, and the social roots of Benton MacKaye's wilderness advocacy. *Environmental History, 4*(4), 553–577. https://doi.org/10.2307/3985401

Thomas, J. L. (1988). Lewis Mumford: Regionalist historian. *Reviews in American History, 16*(1), 158–172. https://doi.org/10.2307/2702081

Tönnies, F. (1963). *Community and society.* Harper & Row.

Veblen, T. (1921). *The engineers and the price system.* B. W. Huebsch.

Williams Ellis, C. (1928). *England and the octopus.* Geoffrey Bles.

Wright, H. (1921). Shall we community plan? *Journal of the American Institute of Architects, 9*(10), 320–324.

Future-proof cities through governance experiments? Insights from the Resilient Melbourne Strategy (RMS)

Sebastian Fastenrath ⓘ and Lars Coenen ⓘ

Introduction

In the face of increasingly tangible impacts of climate change, growing socioeconomic inequalities and environmental degradation, the debates around future-proofing cities are gaining rapid momentum. Current city practices are often ill-equipped to deal with the complexities and the urgency of today's urban challenges (Elmqvist et al., 2019). To make cities more resilient and sustainable, the United Nations' (UN) Sustainable Development Goal (SDG) 11 underlines the need for better urban planning and governance (UN, 2015). However, how can cities 'better' plan and build capacity for what is generally considered to require transformative change towards a more sustainable future?

Urban resilience strategies and actions constitute a relatively novel approach that challenges and potentially transforms urban policy and planning (Davidson & Gleeson, 2018). During the last few years, building resilience has become a key objective for many cities in the face of acute and often interrelated environmental, social and economic challenges. One example is the Resilient Melbourne Strategy (RMS) initiated through the Rockefeller Foundation's '100 Resilient Cities' (100RC) initiative, one of the most prominent city networks that advocates urban resilience activities. This strategy identifies placebased resilience challenges in metropolitan Melbourne, and implements actions to deliver, organize and coordinate urban services and infrastructures across a variety of contexts such as mobility, energy, housing, health, climate change, and social cohesion in new and more robust ways (Fastenrath et al., 2019). Scholars have described resilience as a new 'policy metaphor for embedding "foresight," robustness and adaptability into a variety of place-making and localist planning activities' (Coaffee, 2013, p. 325).

While resilience thinking and practice have been criticized for conceptual slippage, model transposition from natural to social sciences and being potentially defensive of authoritarian and/or neo-liberalvalues (e.g., Beilin &

Wilkinson, 2015; Cote & Nightingale, 2012; Kythreotis & Bristow, 2017; Leitner et al., 2018; MacKinnon & Derickson, 2013; Porter & Davoudi, 2012), others have acknowledged its status as a boundary object, called for a less dismissive view and highlighted the possibility of resilience for triggering newways of urban governance (Duit et al., 2010; Rogers, 2015; Schwanen, 2016). The latter perspective resonates with the debates around resilience as a catalyst for transformational change through new cross-sectoral formations of actors and institutional structures (Brand & Jax, 2007; Davoudi et al., 2012; Shaw, 2012). Resilience thinking and practice, when enacted through inclusive processes that involve institutional learning, might discourage 'planners from putting the emphasis on rigid and fixed plans and the attempt to command and control space and time' (Davoudi et al., 2013, p. 320).

Whether urban resilience strategies can deliver transformative change requires a more granular evidence base of the implementation processes and the outcomes of urban resilience actions (Coaffee et al., 2018; Fastenrath et al., 2019). More in-depth theoretical and empirical research is needed to understand further the ways in which resilience actions are implemented and shaping the capabilities of cities to innovate and transform their urban systems of provision in and across multiple urban domains.

In this paper we investigate the implementation of urban resilience actions and its transformative potential through the lens of 'governance experimentation' (Bos & Brown, 2012; Bulkeley et al., 2018; Caprotti & Cowley, 2017; Evans et al., 2016; Fuenfschilling et al., 2019; Raven et al., 2019; Sengers et al., 2016; Smeds & Acuto, 2018; Turnheim et al., 2018). This concept, often associated with urban sustainability transitions and/ or transformations, is defined as 'purposive interventions designed to respond to the imperative for climate change responses in the city, and with a more or less explicit attempt to innovate, learn or gain experience' (Bulkeley & Castán Broto, 2013, p. 362). Such governance experiments serve to reconfigure capacities, resources and agency of actors in urban contexts (Bulkeley & Castán Broto, 2013; Bulkeley et al., 2014; McGuirk et al., 2015). By providing a space in which to negotiate problem definitions and understandings, claims to resources, authority or dominant ideologies, experiments restructure the local institutions and through that have the potential to contribute to deep-structural change, that is, sustainability transitions (Hodson et al., 2017).

Increasingly the concept of governance experimentation is put to practice by mainstream policy and practice to test new cross-sectoral partnerships and forms of coordination to reshape and renew urban policy processes (Bulkeley et al., 2011; Frantzeskaki et al., 2017; Moore et al., 2018). The Intergovernmental Panel on Climate Change's (IPCC) 'summary for urban policy makers' concludes that what is required are transitions in social and ecological systems driven by policies that enable collaborative multilevel-stakeholder partnerships between public and private sectors, civil society and academia (IPCC, 2018).

There is wide agreement that cities need new governance approaches that are more inclusive, collaborative, reflexive and long-term (e.g., Elmqvist et al., 2019; Webb et al., 2018). Governments need to restructure activities that can break down bureaucratic silos and innovate beyond conventional 'predict-then-act' planning approaches (e.g., Davoudi et al., 2013). So far, the discussion around governance experimentation in city contexts has predominantly been linked to so-called living laboratories, urban laboratories or transition laboratories (e.g., Bulkeley et al., 2018; Fuenfschilling et al., 2019; Nevens et al., 2013). Albeit sympathetic concepts that emphasize inclusivity, participation and processes of open and democratic innovation, they at the same time run the risk of black boxing governance experimentation and keeping its organizational principles and institutional processes opaque.

To understand better how urban governance experiments are implemented and seek to drive transformational change, the paper introduces a framework that draws on Ferraro et al.'s (2015) theorization of tackling grand challenges through robust action. This framework is shaped to analyse single governance experiments focusing on three dimensions: coordination and structure; goals and understandings; and processes. Applying this framework by analysing actions of the RMS, the paper demonstrates how this approach is helpful for city practitioners and researchers to assess and compare actions at different stages.

The paper is structured as follows. The next section highlights the debates around urban resilience and outlines the current understandings and challenges. The paper then introduces the analytical framework and discusses urban experimentation. The following section discusses the empirical insights into RMS actions as case studies, before the conclusions are presented.

Urban resilience: from crisis management to the reduction of 'chronic stresses'

The conceptual foundations of resilience go back to the 1970s when engineers used the term to describe the capacity of materials to return to pre-existing conditions after being exposed to physical stresses. This idea was adopted by ecologists and used to describe how ecosystems return to stable states (equilibrium) after disturbances (Holling, 1973). Linking social and ecological systems and introducing ideas for a socio-ecological resilience to analyse human-environment dynamics opened the discussion for social sciences (Berkes, 2007; Berkes & Folke, 1998; Folke, 2006). While rationales of systemic 'bouncing-back', 'absorbing', and 'adapting' to shocks and hazards dominated the early debates, a wider understanding of resilience exists today. It is increasingly linked to ideas of 'proactive', solution-oriented actions that respond to systemic 'stresses' – challenges that disturb urban systems over a longer period of time.

During the last decade, resilience has become a key goal for cities in the face of acute and often interrelated environmental, social and economic challenges. Numerous cities have initiated resilience strategies and implemented actions to 'future-proof their cities. However, resilience thinking and practice are contested, particularly in the context of urban governance and public service provision (e.g., Beilin & Wilkinson, 2015; Cote & Nightingale, 2012; Kythreotis & Bristow, 2017; Porter & Davoudi, 2012). Critical scholars have found resilience initiatives often to be 'externally' and 'top-down' steered, lacking citizen participation and not open to alternative ways of collaboration and delivery of actions (e.g., Leitner et al., 2018; MacKinnon & Derickson, 2013). More specifically, they have critiqued resilience initiatives as an instrument of neoliberalism, characterized by prioritizing (vested) economic interests, undermining citizen engagement and reducing tasks of public authorities (e.g., Fainstein, 2018; Hay & Muller, 2014).

The increasing heterogeneity of opinions on urban resilience is the result of the continual diversification of understandings and practices (Meerow et al., 2016). During the last few years, resilience shifted from a dominant 'reactive' disaster management toward a more 'proactive' and selfreflective policy-making tool to drive urban transformational change (Coaffee et al., 2018; Fastenrath et al., 2019; Shaw & Maythorne, 2013). Moreover, the understanding of resilience as a static condition rather than an ongoing process has been challenged (e.g., Boschma, 2015; Davoudi et al., 2013; Martin & Sunley, 2015; Simmie & Martin, 2010). Therefore, the critical literature on urban resilience often seems one-sided, neglecting the increasing multiplicity of resilience (Schwanen, 2016) and lacking scrutiny of concrete actions and practice. Urban resilience-building actions have diversified from 'reactive' disaster management toward more proactive and selfreflective policy-making tools to drive transformational change (Coaffee et al., 2018).

The understanding of urban resilience as the capacity to tackle systemic 'shocks' and 'stresses' can be seen as a significant modification. Resilience is no longer solely understood as a 'back to normal' or back to pre-disaster status. In other words, there is a shift from resilience as a systemic 'bouncing back' toward also 'bouncing forward'. This changed resilience thinking is also linked to an understanding from systemic equilibrium towards a more open, experimental and non-linear ecosystem-thinking. These 'evolutionary' perspectives of resilience, as a critical response to the static understanding, are some of the most recent and important turning points in conceptualizing and understanding resilience. Following the definition of Davoudi et al. (2013), the approach of 'evolutionary resilience' can be understood as a process of transformative capacity-building through experimentation, social and institutional 'learning by doing', and 'cultivating flexibility, resource-fulness and cooperative networks' (p. 319). We argue that this theoretical thinking further opens the discussion for resilience as an 'agenda of change' (Rogers, 2015) and helps to analyse resilience actions and their embedded-ness in urban systems over time. It also (re)opens the debates of resilience as an innovative governance model to deal with processes of complex change (Duit, 2016; Duit et al., 2010).

Cities as key arenas for resilience-building actions and transformational change

The debates about urban resilience resonate with discussions around cities as key arenas for experimentation to drive transformational change. It be-comes clear that the grand challenges we are facing today call for innovation in collective action and urban governance (e.g., Bulkeley & Castán Broto, 2013; Burch et al., 2014; Elmqvist et al., 2019). To identify and implement solutions, knowledge and expertise need to be bundled from a variety of stakeholders linked to the public, private, academic and civic sector.

At present, urban resilience actions and strategies are mostly monitored by quantitative indicators and tools (e.g., Amp's City Resilience Index; Arup, 2019). These assess resilience building actions relative to achieving (static) conditions of urban resilience but pay less attention to dynamic and transformative socio-political processes (Chelleri et al., 2015; Matyas & Felling, 2015; Felling & Manuel-Navarrete, 2011; Rogers, 2015). Therefore, analytical frameworks are needed that help to investigate how strategies are actually translated into actions to complement quantitative analysis of actions' outcomes. In doing so, a closer look at goals and interests of spe-cific resilience actions is needed to explore how, and particularly by and for whom, urban resilience practices are initiated (Cretney, 2014; Meerow & Newell, 2016; Shaw & Maythorne, 2013).

Analysing urban resilience as urban governance experimentation

Empirical research on the implementation processes of resilience actions need more attention to understand the underlying experimental forms of capacity-building and agency; and based on this, to inform policy-makers and practice decisions (e.g., Coaffee et al., 2018; Rogers, 2015). Therefore, we argue that urban resilience actions need a reconceptualization as 'gov-ernance experiments'. The increasing number of contributions on 'urban experimentation' or 'experimental cities' have paid attention to several case studies and potential transformational areas (e.g., Bulkeley et al., 2018; Caprotti & Cowley, 2017; Evans et al., 2016; Fuenfschilling et al., 2019; Sen-gers et al., 2016). However, a conceptualization of urban resilience actions as governance experiments is lacking. The meaning and functions of urban experimentation differ fundamentally from 'classical' experiments in natural or engineering science (Turnheim et al., 2018). Rather, they should be understood as trial and testing processes of novel institutional arrangements to govern urban systems. However, how do cities and local governments organize urban experimentation? What are its organizational design principles? To unpack governance experiments we draw on Ferraro et al.'s (2015) theorization of tackling grand challenges through 'robust action'. They draw on the sociological concept of robust action (e.g., Padgett & Ansell, 1993; Padgett & Powell, 2012), which is understood as an openended practice in which actors have the ability to adapt over time to new and developing situations. In a context of grand challenges, such as poverty alleviation and climate change consequences, Ferraro et al. (2015) have analysed strategies focused on how public sector actors and organizations coordinate and restructure processes of transformative change. They identified three key components to such strategies:

- Participatory architecture: a structure and rules of engagement that allow diverse and heterogeneous actors to interact constructively over prolonged timespans.
- Multivocal inscription: interpretative flexibility around boundary objects to promote coordination without requiring explicit consensus.
- Distributed experimentation: iterative action that generates small wins, promotes evolutionary learning and increased engagement, while allowing unsuccessful efforts to be abandoned.

We argue that these three underlying complimentary dimensions can be used and applied as an analytical framework to analyse governance experimentation. Focusing on these three analytical entities allows one to compare single urban governance experiments such as actions related to resilience-building, sustainability transitions or other initiatives that are based on new governance models.

Participatory architecture (coordination and structure)

Governance experiments cannot be understood without the actors who initiate and drive learning processes and interact with other actors within this initiative. The 'architecture' of actions is seen as key to providing new structures and longer term involvement of a range of actors. As Ferraro et al. (2015) explain, 'Institutional change is not the result of individual entrepreneurial action, but rather, the efforts of multiple individuals and organizations that purposefully spearhead change and mobilize cooperation' (p. 368). Therefore, to create knowledge about how governance experiments are constructed, we need to understand how they are organized and coordinated. In other words, we need to identify the actors and their interactions to understand the underlying structures and processes. There is broad agreement that pathways of change rely on processes of agency (Garud & Karnoe, 2001; Garud et al., 2010). Coenen et al. (2010) demonstrate how agency shapes interactions and learning processes in 'local niche experimentation' driven by intermediary actors. However, we need to understand better how the drivers of experiments are interacting with higher policy levels (state, national and international) (Kythreotis, 2018; Smeds & Acuto, 2018). To overcome the challenges in creating cross-sectoral and cross-scale collaboration, Cash et al. (2006) suggest 'boundary or bridging organizations' than can fulfil an intermediary function by collecting and sharing information with participating stakeholders.

Multivocal inscription (goals and understandings)

This second type identified by Ferraro et al. (2015) is understood as the interpretive flexibility of common activities. This dimension draws on stakeholders' different expectations and understandings of problems and the tools to solve these. It helps to identify the discursive and material kit to drive longer term actions. As Cash et al. (2006) pointed out, the challenge in creating change through new cross-scale cooperation is the plurality of interests. Different actors seek to reach different goals based on new cooperation. To overcome this challenge, common goals and actions need to be identified through boundary or bridging organizations. Authors have pointed out that one of the attractions of resilience as a boundary object and bridging concept is that it allows multiple knowledge domains to interface (Brand & Jax, 2007; Meerow & Newell, 2016; Welsh, 2014).

Distributed experimentation (processes)

The third dimension, distributed experimentation, refers to the different processes of coordination of interventions. Ferraro et al. (2015) give examples of how purpose-driven experimentation may lead to novel institutional arrangements and socio-technical configurations. They argue that if experiments are understood and applied as ongoing and reflexive interventions, and include diverse actors with different understandings, there is increasing potential for innovation. We argue that urban governance experimentation is about flexibility, self-reflectivity, learning and knowledge transfer. Lessons learned can increase the transformative capacity of actors embedded in their socio-technical systems. However, as Ferraro et al. highlight:

> not every experiment will prove successful, at least not in realtime. This could be because the experiment has gone 'wrong' in the sense that it failed to deliver the hoped for results. Or the experiment itself can lead to the emergence of new and previously unidentified concerns.
>
> (p. 377)

Resilient Melbourne Strategy (RMS) actions

Analysing the implementation processes of the RMS provides the opportunity to assess more keenly urban resilience actions. In 2013, the City of Melbourne became a member of the 100RC network, under the condition that all 32 local governments of metropolitan Melbourne participated in the initiative. More than 1000 individuals and organizations from public, private and academic sectors across Melbourne helped to identify context-specific challenges, which were subsequently incorporated into the RMS, (Resilient Melbourne, 2016). These challenges are linked to a range of natural and human-induced related hazards as well as socioeconomic and sociotechnical challenges.

The results of the assessment of Melbourne's 'acute shocks' (sudden events that threaten a city) covered the following aspects: bushfires, floods, heatwaves, epidemics, infrastructure-related emergencies and extremist acts. Identified 'chronic stresses' (challenges that weaken the fabric of a city on a day-to-day or cyclical basis) were: rapid population growth, social inequality, pressures on natural assets, unemployment, climate change, alcoholism and family violence (Resilient Melbourne, 2016). The rapid population growth the city is facing is undoubtedly the dominant problem. It has implications for the population, but also for authorities that provide infrastructure and other public services and facilities (e.g., energy, transport, water, sewerage, green space, schools, health services).

The process resulted in 33 potential strategy actions to tackle Melbourne's identified challenges (Resilient Melbourne, 2016). Since 2017, several these actions have been prepared and partly implemented (Figure 1) under the lead of the Resilient Melbourne Delivery Office (RMDO). The RMDO seeks collaborations across state and local government, private and not-for-profit actors and academia, and monitors and reports on progress of actions.

Research design and data

The empirical insights are based on an ongoing research project conducted in cooperation with the RMDO. Using Resilient Melbourne Strategy Actions (RMSAs) as case studies, the goal of the project is to gain knowledge about how governance experimentation might help to lead transformative change by analysing structures, understandings and key processes. For this study, we selected two 'Flagship Actions': The Metropolitan Urban Forest Strategy (renamed as Living Melbourne – The Metropolitan Urban Forest Strategy) and the Metropolitan Cycling Network. In comparison with 'Supporting Actions' (Figure 1), Flagship Actions are 'key initiatives with the potential for metropolitan-wide involvement and transformational outcomes' (Resilient Melbourne, 2016, p. 3). These actions have been selected as comparative case studies because of their similarities in objective and remit, that is, to drive transformational change on a metropolitan scale, yet

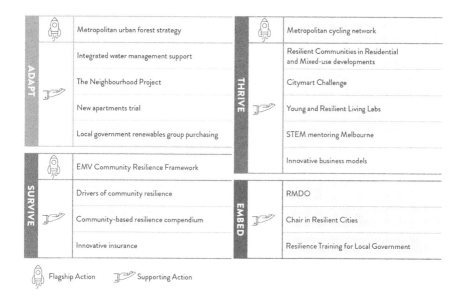

Figure 1 Overview of the Resilient Melbourne Strategy (RMS) actions.
Source: Resilient Melbourne (2019b).

be deployed in different urban systems. Also, they started at a similar time and involved stakeholders from the public, private and academic sectors.

We explored these two actions based on a qualitative research design that includes interviewing and document analysis. Referring to Flick (2004), the triangulation of methods is helpful when collecting and interpreting primary data. Combining different sources helps to ensure the legitimacy of a case study-based qualitative research design (Yin, 2014). The data were collected through semi-structured interviews and document analysis between July and December 2018 (Figure 2). Participants were selected through advice by the RMDO and via snowball sampling. The interviewees were directly involved in the actions or were experts of the actions' fields. Case studyrelated materials such as policy documents and project reports and drafts were provided by the RMDO or collected through desktop research. Aligned with the analytical framework, the interview guide was structured into five key topics that were discussed for each action: stakeholders; roles and motives in the action; goals and understandings; processes of learning; and knowledge transfer.

Metropolitan urban forest strategy

The flagship action of Resilient Melbourne is The Metropolitan Urban Forest Strategy, given the large number of actors involved, and the international

Metropolitan Urban Forest Strategy			Metropolitan Cycling Network		
9 semi-structured interviews			**10 semi-structured interviews**		
Date	*Sector*	*Code*	*Date*	*Sector*	*Code*
15/08/18	NGO	FOR-1	18/07/18	Local Government (Other)	CYC-1
24/08/18	Local Government (Urban planning)	FOR-2	05/10/18	Local Government (Urban planning)	CYC-2
27/08/18	Local Government (Urban planning)	FOR-3	17/10/18	Local Government (Urban planning)	CYC-3
04/09/18	Local Government (Urban planning)	FOR-4	25/10/18	Academia	CYC-4
07/09/18	Academia	FOR-5	26/10/18	Academia	CYC-5
09/11/18	Private Sector	FOR-6	07/11/18	Local Government (Urban planning)	CYC-6
22/11/18	Local Government (Urban planning)	FOR-7	09/11/18	Local Government (Urban planning)	CYC-7
29/11/18	Local Government (Urban planning)	FOR-8	09/11/18	Local Government (Urban planning)	CYC-8
12/12/18	Local Government (Other)	FOR-9	12/11/18	Local Government (Urban planning)	CYC-9
			12/12/18	Local Government (Other)	CYC-10

Documents

- 'Melbourne Metropolitan Urban Forest Strategy, Local Government Workshop, Summary Report' (10/2017)
- 'Melbourne Metropolitan Urban Forest Strategy, Multi-Stakeholder Workshop, Summary' (12/2017)
- 'Melbourne Metropolitan Urban Forest Strategy, Stakeholder Workshop' (07/2018)
- 'Living Melbourne - The Melbourne Metropolitan Urban Forest Strategy' + Technical support document -draft (10/2018)
- 'Living Melbourne - Our metropolitan urban forest + Technical support document - draft (02/2019)
- 'Living Melbourne' - Our metropolitan urban forest + Technical support document (06/2019)

Documents

- 'Metropolitan Cycling Network - Workshop #1, Summary' (09/2017)
- 'Metropolitan Cycling Network - Workshop Two, Summary' (11/2017)
- Victorian Cycling Strategy 2018-28, Increasing cycling for transport (VIC Gov)

Figure 2 Overview of data collection.

attention it gains, particularly through the 100RC network which actively promotes this action (100RC, 2019). While green infrastructure in Melbourne has been supported and initiated by several local governments, a metropolitan-wide strategy is lacking (Resilient Melbourne, 2016). This action was initiated in a partnership between the RMDO and The Nature Conservancy (TNC), a non-governmental organization (NGO) and 'platform partner' of the 100RC network. The overarching goal of this action is to develop a strategy that helps to increase tree canopy cover and overall vegetation of the city-region to tackle a range of challenges, including loss of biodiversity, climate change and related hazards such as heatwaves and flooding, and issues around physical and mental health. The underlying goal of this action is to link existing urban green infrastructure, reforestation and other environmental initiatives (Resilient Melbourne, 2016). In late 2018, the action was renamed Living Melbourne – The Metropolitan Urban Forest Strategy (Resilient Melbourne, 2019a).

Participatory architecture (coordination and structure)

The action is organized through the RMDO and TNC. These two key actors curate the network of participating actors and set the 'rules of engagement' by inviting other actors. Based on this reading, which is supported by interview insights (e.g., FOR-5), the action can be interpreted as a 'top-down'-driven process. To date, more than 60 stakeholders from public and private sectors, NGOs and academia have been involved in shaping this action (FOR-1; Resilient Melbourne, 2019a). The Resilient Melbourne initiative and its actions has established a new platform for cross-sectoral and cross-scale urban governance, but with a strong presence of public sector stakeholders. Membership to this platform is predicated on whether the respective stakeholders contributes with relevant knowledge and expertise. In particular, knowledge about related urban planning processes was brought to the table by urban planners, forestry and utility experts of local governments; representatives of state government planning authorities; and researchers from different disciplines. Compiling this knowledge was crucial to set targets, develop concrete strategies, but also to identify challenges and barriers. A wider 'opening' to the general public has not yet happened, but is planned as soon as the strategy framework is set (FOR-1). The evolution of the action's structural architecture shows it is flexible enough to cope with a growing diversity and heterogeneity of stakeholders. This includes also 'bottom-up' actors such as smaller networks of local governments, NGOs and grassroot movements. One example is the network 'Greening the West', an initiative that supports communities in Melbourne's western suburbs through the development of green infrastructure (FOR-4; Resilient Melbourne, 2019a). In addition, two external private sector actors have been involved in a more marginal role. DigitalGlobe and Trimble, also 100RC platform partners, provided satellite images which helped mapping Melbourne's green and open spaces.

Multivocal inscription (goals and understandings)

While there is clarity around the action's overarching goal in increasing Melbourne's green infrastructure to tackle a range of socio-ecological challenges, there is 'interpretative flexibility' around single aspects of the action. For example, the observed debates around definitions of canopy cover, vegetation, targets and measures, underlines the openness, flexibility and processual logics of this action (FOR-5; Resilient Melbourne, 2019a). The ongoing discussions around single definitions and goals (such as the percentage of increase of canopy cover in the city) can be seen as important drivers to facilitate ongoing articulation of different stakeholders' interests in the action. Four multistakeholder workshops, summary documents and report drafts which were open for comments, guided the development of the strategy, incorporated different stakeholder perspectives; and probably most importantly, they helped to review and adjust the strategy as it progressed (Resilient Melbourne, 2019a). The renaming of the action in late 2018 to Living Melbourne – The Melbourne Metropolitan Urban Forest Strategy also reflects how the scope of strategy was deliberately opened up beyond environmental policy to include issues of general well-being and liveability.

Distributed experimentation (processes)

In the action, experimentation is primarily enacted through ongoing debates over the last two years in stakeholder workshops and engagement through reports. The engagement in this action, particularly the participation in the workshop series, has been important to generate and exchange knowledge between local and state government authorities, the private sector, NGOs and academia. The workshops led to incremental learning about challenges, potential solutions and the experiences of others in the action. A representative of local government and expert in urban forestry highlighted that the action's processual approach helps to 'break down silos and lead to intersectoral thinking' (FOR-7). Another local council representative said this action has led to learning processes and exchange between councils that usually do not regularly cooperate, and therefore helps to understand who else is in the space' (FOR-8). Other interviewees said the action helped then to learn about the challenges of and solutions by other actors (FOR-1). Despite the long process of exchange and the released strategy document, there is a debate around how the strategy can be implemented in the next step.

The metropolitan cycling network

Cycling was identified as the second priority area in the RMS and is seen as an important way to tackle socio-ecological challenges related to traffic congestion, pressures on infrastructure, pollution and health issues (Resilient Melbourne, 2016). While some local councils within metropolitan Melbourne have played a driving role in supporting cycling and establishing cycling infrastructure, there are others lagging behind or disconnected from other local councils. Therefore, a key goal of this action is to develop cycling paths and corridors that connect the whole metropolitan Melbourne. This action, described as 'planning and coordination initiative' (Resilient Melbourne, 2016, p. 114), is closely tied to the objectives of the Victorian state government in supporting active transport and cycling commitments in Plan Melbourne, the metropolitan planning strategy that defines the future shape of the city and state over the next decades (VIC Government, 2016). As the key driver of this resilience action, Resilient Melbourne seeks to pool knowledge from academia, government agencies on different levels and cycling advocacy groups. Building on existing initiatives, the goal is to bring together key stakeholders and encourage 'local government and infrastructure agencies to build new bicycle paths' (Resilient Melbourne, 2016, p. 114).

Participatory architecture (coordination and structure)

The action is coordinated by the RMDO and relies on close collaboration between local municipalities and state government transport bodies. At the early stages of the action, in 2017, the 100RC platform partner and consultancy company Jacobs played an important role as facilitator of two kick-off workshops. Attendees of these workshops were representatives from state government agencies, each of Melbourne's six urban 'sub-regions' and advocacy groups (CYC-1, CYC-6). After Jacobs' facilitating role ended after convening the two workshops, the action is mainly driven by the action's 'steering group', a network of representatives of the public sector and advocacy groups under the lead of Resilient Melbourne (CYC-7–9). This group further seeks to open the action's structure for a growing and more heterogenous actor network (CYC-1, CYC-7). While Resilient Melbourne is seen as a novel 'advocate in raising the profile for cycling and shaping a message' (CYC-9), its limited power to influence planning directly was highlighted as a possible barrier to achieving transformative outcomes (CYC-6–9).

Multivocal inscription (goals and understandings)

As a Resilient Melbourne representative described, the goal of the overarching action is Melbourne's 'transformation to a cycling city' (CYC-10). By establishing a city-wide cycling network, the key goal is to make cycling safer and a more practical alternative to car travel (CYC-10) (Resilient Melbourne, 2016). While there was broad agreement among interviewees around the necessity of transformational change around cycling, the interviews also revealed 'interpretative flexibility' around this resilience action. Referring to similar initiatives that target metropolitanwide cycling, the outcomes and the added value of this action were partly questioned by interviewed planners from different local governments (CYC-6–9). Nevertheless, there was agreement that the action helps further to raise attention for the topic in Melbourne and might trigger further support through higher policy levels.

Distributed experimentation (processes)

Similar to The Metropolitan Urban Forest Strategy, workshops have been the main vehicles for experimentation. Initially, these were viewed positively by the participants because they brought together many stakeholders of Melbourne's cycling 'ecosystem' to discuss the challenges of transforming cycling infrastructure (CYC-3, CYC-6–10). One interviewee described how helpful these workshops were in exploring and discussing the barriers local governments face in planning and building cycling infrastructure (CYC-7). Identified was the lack of power of local governments in making planning decisions. While local governments (city councils) are responsible for the implementation of planning processes and management of infrastructure, the planning decisions are made at the state government level. Therefore, a policy level is missing that sits between the 32 local governments, which form metropolitan Melbourne, and the state government.

Over time, however, the action lost part of its momentum (CYC-6–8). Interviewees explained that it is unclear what' the action is seeking to achieve and 'how', apart from building up a larger stakeholder network. More specifically, the overlap of similar initiatives in mapping Melbourne's cycling infrastructure, was mentioned by different representatives of local councils (CYC-3, CYC-4, CYC-6–9). One council representative pointed out: We don't need a new plan, we need implementation of infrastructure' (CYC-9). The lack of common understanding and goals might be related to the complexity and the short lifetime of the action relative to the scope and scale of infrastructural change. As Albrechts (2004) explained, the challenges in finding solution to complex problems in planning depend on the 'ability to combine the creation of strategic visions ... and the development and promotion of common assets' (p. 743). All interviewees described that a major barrier to creating a common vision around cycling in Melbourne is the lack of support from state government and the general political willingness to support and quickly transform cycling infrastructure.

Discussion

The introduced framework, based on the three-fold approach (Figure 3), has demonstrated to be a valuable entry point to unpack governance experimentation in Resilient Melbourne into concrete organizational guidelines and principles for transformative change. These organizational guidelines and principles seek to lend great specificity on how to arrange purposive interventions with an explicit attempt to innovate, learn or gain experience and to reconfigure urban governance arrangements. First, it provides guidance on how to design and implement innovation and experimentation projects seeking to drive transformative change; and second, it helps to monitor and evaluate such projects for the purpose of achieving 'fuzzy' long-term programmatic objectives and to adjust such experiments over their life course. Structured and ongoing assessment is crucial for city practitioners and policy makers in order to leverage and scale up experimental actions and to generate impact beyond the direct boundaries, stakeholders and networks of a project and increase the innovation capabilities of the local government at an organizational level (for similar conclusions, see a recent Organisation for Economic Co-operation and Development (OECD), 2019, report on enhancing innovation capacity in city government).

By applying the introduced framework, our research on resilience-building actions in Melbourne has illustrated how local government can demonstrate leadership in facilitating transformative change by orchestrating innovation and cooperation within and between local governments and other urban stakeholders. More importantly, the insights have shed light on the challenges that are linked to governance experiments for transformative change. Three key aspects can arguably be highlighted.

Multi-stakeholder collaboration and boundary management

Our insights around the coordination and structure (participatory architecture) have highlighted the crucial role of and responsibility for 'boundary management' (Cash et al., 2006). To initiate, orchestrate and facilitate a functional and continuous platform for knowledge exchange and collaboration across different institutional sectors and territorial jurisdictions, a boundary management is required that marshals sufficient convening power. 'Boundary managers' operating within and across internal and external organizational silos are critical to introduce new ways of governance and to test and adjust those in order to overcome institutional gridlocks and to identify and renew institutional barriers and lock-ins. Similar roles and responsibilities are increasingly suggested in the literature with reference to 'chief innovation officers' (OECD, 2019) or 'chief exploration officers' (Acuto, 2018) within local governments and administrations. Boundary management is integral to the scope of the RMDO under the lead of its chief resilience officer and could even be seen as one of its primary organizational missions. In light of an absent metropolitan governance structure and the risk for fragmentation of urban systems, the RMDO has de facto initiated and shaped collaboration and coordination structures across different stakeholders for urban greening and cycling. Our findings suggest that there is greater legitimacy for the convening role of the RMDO in urban greening, while there is more institutional inertia in the case of cycling. This could be explained by the relative newness of urban greening and/or nature-based solutions as an area of attention and responsibility for cities and its appeal as an effective climate change adaptation solution, whereas cycling sits more firmly within the traditional portfolio of planning departments in local and state government, creating risk for competition and/or duplication of responsibilities.

The paradox of specifying the boundary object

The second challenge is that successful 'boundary management' needs a suitable 'boundary object' that allows for multivocal inscription from a diverse set of stakeholders. An open, transparent and ongoing process of identifying and delineating problems, articulating the interests of different stakeholders as well as the capabilities and resource that they can mobilize is key to drive collective capacity-building for transformational change. Through continuous dialogue, governance experiments generate the collective vocabulary to speak about the challenges at hand that result in accountability and ownership within the platforms' participants. As the action Metropolitan Urban Cycling Network illustrates, however, experiments can get stuck in vested interests and diverging understandings as a consequence of institutional path dependencies. When the problem framing of the boundary object – in this case, 'the cycling network' – is dominated by traditional institutional logics – here, transport infrastructure planning – it runs the risk of a premature closure that precludes transformative change as it allocates old solutions to new problems. This undermines the collective understanding of the boundary objects and may drive away relevant stakeholders that feel marginalized by the dominant problem framing. The urban forest case illustrates, on the contrary, how the meaning of the boundary object has evolved successfully over time. It has gradually acquired increasing numbers in terms of different stakeholders 'buying into' the concept yet retaining a sufficient degree of coherence in terms of meaning and vocabulary. This points to the challenge of specifying the boundary object sufficiently for problem-solving to occur while at the same time keeping the problem-framing sufficiently open to allow for sufficient fluidity for inscription and contestation by different stakeholders.

Learning from failure

In order to learn from experimentation, it is important to allow for risk-taking and, consequently, not to dismiss failure as necessarily a bad thing. While readily recognized as inevitable in the private sector, this is particularly challenging for local governments when public expenditure of tax-payers' money is at stake. Rather than seeking to outlaw mistakes, local governments involved in experimentation should seek to reduce the costs of mistakes by learning from them and by learning to 'fail faster'. Therefore,

	Metropolitan Urban Forest Strategy	Metropolitan Cycling Network
	Participatory architecture	
Coordination	Public-NGO partnership	Public-private partnership (initially), then public sector driven
Structure	Heterogeneous network with participants from different sectors: public, private, academia, NGO	Heterogeneous network with participants from different sectors: public, private sector, NGO
	Participatory 'rules of engagement' and inclusive	Participatory 'rules of engagement', inclusive
	Increasing numbers and interest	Stagnating number of participants and interest
	Multivocal inscription	
Goals	Increase tree canopy cover and overall vegetation	Develop cycling paths and corridors that connect all of metropolitan Melbourne
	Transforming socio-ecological systems through 'nature-based solutions'	Transforming socio-technical systems through (hard) infrastructure extension and development
Understandings	Multiple understandings of single actions aspects but general alignment	Multiple and divergent understandings of goals and responsibilities
	Distributed experimentation	
Processes	Key platform for collaboration and learning: 4 multi-stakeholder workshops	Key platform for collaboration and learning: 2 multi-stakeholder workshops
	Workshops as vehicles for guiding the strategy, including different stakeholder perspectives and reviewing the strategy as it progressed (open-ended thinking).	Workshops as initial platforms for collaboration and problem understanding
	Building on existing (local) knowledge and institutional structures	Building on existing (local) knowledge and institutional structures

Figure 3 Overview of the case study analysis.

transparency is crucial to allow for monitoring and evaluation of experiments to happen. Still, this is often seen as low-status activities which, in the case of the RMS, were not set up as an integral part of the strategy. At best, monitoring and evaluation happens for the purpose of accountability not organizational learning. However, particularly actions with sociocultural goals such as creating social cohesion are often long-term processes and difficult to assess in real time. Moreover, barriers to organizational learning in local government are manifold: silo structures, staff turnover and the lack of time devoted to learning.

Conclusions

This paper has explored how governance experimentation has been deployed in urban resilience-building in the context of metropolitan Melbourne. It elucidates three organizational design principles that characterize the RMS as governance experimentation: (1) a participatory architecture based on cross-sectoral and institutionally diverse partnerships and networking; (2) a thematic focus and platform based on multi-stakeholder engagement with boundary objects such as 'cycling network' or 'urban forest'; and (3) an emphasis on extensive deliberation in workshops and active feedback loops between strategy and actions aimed at expedited collective learning.

The case studies in the context of Resilient Melbourne show that governance experimentation can be instrumental in breaking down institutional silos and relaxing the risk of institutional lock-in in the face of wicked urban problems by providing active learning platforms for multi-stakeholder cooperation and exchange. Particularly the case study The Metropolitan Urban Forest Strategy demonstrates how important openness for unconventional ways of thinking and practice is in contemporary urban planning. Ongoing exchange and engagement with a variety of stakeholders has proven to be crucial.

At the same time, the emphasis on tentative strategies, deliberation and social enquiry exposes governance experimentation to significant vulnerability and risks for cooptation by vested interests and historically dominant institutional logics (especially in relation to urban planning and urban design as the case study 'metropolitan cycling network' has explored).

The paper sheds a light on some of the critical challenges in implementing governance experimentation. Three important insights are as follows:

- Governance experimentation needs effective and active 'boundary management'. Novel organizational entities within local governments, such as the RMDO, can fulfil this role, partly relying on the existing knowledge, capabilities and trust that local government holds with local stakeholders in the city. Organizational responsibility for boundary management in governance experimentation is however contingent on local institutional conditions and networks and could also evolve over time towards other stakeholders implied in the experimentation.

- Governance experimentation needs flexible 'boundary objects' to transform understandings of urban systems. The resilience lens recasts and opens up for considerable interpretative flexibility around traditional urban systems – such as urban forest and cycling networks – across different stakeholder groups and the way these groups offer different inscriptions in terms of objectives, meanings and challenges. Implementation of strategy can thus be seen as an ongoing negotiation and calibration of such boundary objects towards closure and a common understanding across multiple stakeholder groups.
- 'Failure' is more often the rule rather than the exception in processes of experimentation and innovation. This is politically challenging especially in institutional contexts that are organized around short time horizons and principles of cost-efficiency. Monitoring and evaluation of actions should therefore be seen as an integral part of governance experimentation, not solely due to issues of accountability but primarily to allow for transparency, learning and reflexivity.

Reflecting on the two case studies unveils the importance of process analysis of single experimental actions, in addition to the traditional focus on outcomes and impact, in order to provide meaningful policy advise. The introduced framework is a helpful tool for planners, policymakers and researchers to analyse, monitor and adjust governance experimentations such as urban resilience actions, living laboratories, urban laboratories or transition laboratories. Further research on the role of interactions between cities and regions or other spatial scales would further enrich the debate. Particularly, reflections on multilevel governance, 'scaling up' (Kythreotis, 2018; Smeds & Acuto, 2018) and the role of global city networks such as 100 Resilient Cities, C40 or ICLEI – Local Governments for Sustainability (Davidson et al., 2019) is needed.

Ultimately, driving urban transformations depends not only on the willingness by local governments to reflect on and innovate towards 'better' urban planning approaches, as SDG-11 has pointed out, but also, perhaps more critically, on building capacity for innovation in local governments. Such structural capacity-building is urgently needed to move innovation in local government beyond the obvious rhetoric of innovative and experimental action. Apart from more inclusive, reflective and long-termoriented policy practices and repertoires, this also requires actual allocation of resources and budget. Without substantial, consistent and 'patient' investments in innovation capacity, governance experimentation will lack the longevity and scope for policy learning that supports the scaling and mainstreaming of experiments. After all, this will determine whether governance experimentation amounts to transformative change or simply camouflages business as usual.

Acknowledgements

The authors thank all team members of the Resilient Melbourne Delivery Office (RMDO) for their openness and valuable insights and suggestions. Furthermore, they thank the guest editors of this special issue as well as the reviewers for helpful and constructive comments. Earlier versions of this paper were presented at the RSA Winter Conference and the Global Conference on Economic Geography, Cologne, in a session organized by Gernot Grabber and Oliver Ibert.

Disclosure statement

No potential conflict of interest was reported by the authors.

ORCID

Sebastian Fastenrath ⓘ http://orcid.org/0000-0001-5621-8082
Lars Coenen ⓘ http://orcid.org/0000-0002-5671-3988

References

100RC. (2019). *100 Resilient cities.* Retrieved February 20, 2019, from http://100resilientcities.org/building-resilience-nature-practitioners-guide-action/

Acuto, M. (2018). Why cities need chief exploration officers.Scientific *American.* Retrieved February 20, 2019, from https://blogs.scientificamerican.com/observations/why-cities-need-chief-exploration-officers/

Albrechts, L. (2004). Strategic (spatial) planning reexamined. *Environment and Planning B: Planning and Design, 31*(5), 743–758. https://doi.org/10.1068/b3065

Arup. (2019). *Arup's city resilience index.* Retrieved February 20, 2019, from https://www.arup.com/perspectives/city-resilience-index

Beilin, R., & Wilkinson, C. (2015). Introduction: Governing for urban resilience. *Urban Studies, 52*(7), 1205–1217. https://doi.org/10.1177/0042098015574955

Berkes, F. (2007). Understanding uncertainty and reducing vulnerability: Lessons from resilience thinking. *Natural Hazards, 41*(2), 283–295. https://doi.org/10.1007/sll069-006-9036-7

Berkes, F., & Folke, C. (1998). Linking social and ecological systems for resilience and sustainability. In F. Berkes, & C. Folke (Eds.), *Linking social and ecological systems: Management practices and social mechanisms for building resilience* (pp. 1–25). Cambridge University Press.

Bos, A. J. J., & Brown, R. R. (2012). Governance experimentation and factors of success in socio-technical transitions in the urban water sector. *Technological Forecasting and Social Change, 79*(7), 1340–1353. https://doi.org/10.1016/j.techfore.2012.04.006

Boschma, R. (2015). Towards an evolutionary perspective on regional resilience. *Regional Studies, 49*(5), 733–751. https://doi.org/10.1080/00343404.2014.959481

Brand, F. S., & Jax, K. (2007). Focusing the meaning(s) of resilience: Resilience as a descriptive concept and a boundary object. *Ecology and Society, 12*(1). https://doi.org/10.5751/ES-02029-120123

Bulkeley, H., & Castán Broto, V. (2013). Government by experiment? Global cities and the governing of climate change. *Transactions of the Institute of British Geographers, 38*(3), 361–375. https://doi.org/10.1111/j.1475-5661.2012.00535.x

Bulkeley, H., Castán Broto, V., & Maassen, A. (2011). Governing urban low carbon transition. In H. Bulkeley, V. Castán Broto, M. Hodson, & S. Marvin (Eds.), *Cities and low carbon transition* (pp. 29–41). Routledge.

Bulkeley, H., Castán Broto, V., & Maassen, A. (2014). Low-carbon transitions and the reconfiguration of urban infrastructure. *Urban Studies, 51*(7), 1471–1486. https://doi.org/10.1177/0042098013500089

Bulkeley, H., Marvin, S., Palgan, Y. V., McCormick, K., BreitfussLoidl, M., Mai, L., von Wirth, T., & Frantzeskaki, N. (2018). Urban living laboratories: Conducting the experimental city? *European Urban and Regional Studies*. https://doi.org/10.1177/0969776418787222

Burch, S., Shaw, A., Dale, A., & Robinson, J. (2014). Triggering transformative change: A development path approach to climate change response in communities. *Climate Policy, 14*(4), 467–487. https://doi.org/10.1080/14693062.2014.876342

Caprotti, F., & Cowley, R. (2017). Interrogating urban experiments. *Urban Geography, 38*(9), 1441–1450. https://doi.org/10.1080/02723638.2016.1265870

Cash, D. W., Adger, W., Berkes, F., Garden, P., Lebel, L., Olsson, P., Pritchard, L., & Young, O. (2006). Scale and cross-scale dynamics: Governance and information in a multilevel world. *Ecology and Society, 11*. http://www.ecologyandsociety.org/volll/iss2/art8/

Chelleri, L., Waters, J. J., Olazabal, M., & Minucci, G. (2015). Resilience trade-offs: Addressing multiple scales and temporal aspects of urban resilience. *Environment and Urbanization, 27* (1), 181–198. https://doi.org/10.1177/0956247814550780

Coaffee, J. (2013). Towards next-generation urban resilience in planning practice: From securitization to integrated place making. *Planning Practice and Research, 28*(3), 323–339. https://doi.org/10.1080/02697459.2013.787693

Coaffee, J., Therrien, M., Chelleri, L., Henstra, D., Aldrich, D. P., Mitchell, C. L., Tsenkova, S., & Rigaud, É. (2018). Urban resilience implementation: A policy challenge and research agenda for the 21st century. *Journal of Contingencies and Crisis Management, 26*(3), 403–410. https://doi.org/10.1111/1468-5973.12233

Coenen, L., Raven, R., & Verbong, G. (2010). Local niche experimentation in energy transitions: A theoretical and empirical exploration of proximity advantages and disadvantages. *Technology in Society, 32*(4), 295–302. https://doi.org/10.1016/j.techsoc.2010.10.006

Cote, M., & Nightingale, A. J. (2012). Resilience thinking meets social theory: Situating social change in socio-ecological systems (SES) research. *Progress in Human Geography, 36*(4), 475–489. https://doi.org/10.1177/0309132511425708

Cretney, R. (2014). Resilience for whom? *Emerging Critical Geographies of Socioecological Resilience. Geography Compass, 8,* 627–640. https://doi.org/10.1111/gec3.12154

Davidson, K., Coenen, L., Acuto, M., & Gleeson, B. (2019). Reconfiguring urban governance in an age of rising city networks: A research agenda. *Urban Studies, 56*(16), 3540–3555. https://doi.org/10.1177/0042098018816010

Davidson, K., & Gleeson, B. (2018). New socio-ecological Imperatives for cities: Possibilities and dilemmas for Australian metropolitan governance. *Urban Policy and Research, 36*(2), 230–241. https://doi.org/10.1080/08111146.2017.1354848

Davoudi, S., Brooks, E., & Mehmood, A. (2013). Evolutionary resilience and strategies for climate adaptation. *Planning Practice and Research, 28*(3), 307–322. https://doi.org/10.1080/02697459.2013.787695

Davoudi, S., Shaw, K., Haider, L. J., Quinlan, A. E., Peterson, G. D., Wilkinson, C., Fünfgeld, H., McEvoy, D., Porter, L., & Davoudi, S. (2012). Resilience, a bridging concept or a dead end? *Planning Theory and Practice, 13*(2), 299–307. https://doi.org/10.1080/14649357.2012.677124

Duit, A. (2016). Resilience thinking: Lessons for public administration. *Public Administration, 94*(2), 364–380. https://doi.org/10.1111/padm.12182

Duit, A., Galaz, V., Eckerberg, K., & Ebbesson, J. (2010). Governance, complexity, and resilience. *Global Environmental Change, 20*(3), 363–368. https://doi.org/10.1016/j.gloenvcha.2010.04.006

Elmqvist, T., Andersson, E., Frantzeskaki, N., McPhearson, T., Olsen, P., Gaffney, O., Takeuchi, K., & Folke, C. (2019). Sustainability and resilience for transformation in the urban century. *Nature Sustainability, 2*(4), 267–273. https://doi.org/10.1038/s41893-019-0250-1

Evans, J., Karvonen, A., & Raven, R. (Eds.). (2016). *The experimental city.* Routledge.

Fainstein, S. (2018). Resilience and justice: Planning for New York city. *Urban Geography, 39*(8), 1268–1275. https://doi.org/10.1080/02723638.2018.1448571

Fastenrath, S., Coenen, L., & Davidson, K. (2019). Urban resilience in action: The Resilient Melbourne Strategy as transformative urban innovation policy? *Sustainability, 11*(3), 693. https://doi.org/10.3390/su11030693

Ferraro, F., Etzion, D., & Gehman, J. (2015).Tackling grand challenges pragmatically: Robust action revisited. *Organization Studies, 36*(3), 363–390. https://doi.org/10.1177/0170840614563742

Flick, U. (2004). Triangulation in qualitative research. In U. Flick, E. von Kardorff, & I. Steinke (Eds.), *A companion to qualitative research* (pp. 178–183). Sage.

Folke, C. (2006). Resilience: The emergence of a perspective for social–ecological systems analyses. *Global Environmental Change, 16*(3), 253–267. https://doi.org/10.1016/j.gloenvcha.2006.04.002

Frantzeskaki, N., Castán Broto, V., Loorbach, D., & Coenen, L. (2017). *Urban sustainability transitions.* Routledge.

Fuenfschilling, L., Frantzeskaki, N., & Coenen, L. (2019). Urban experimentation & sustainability transitions. *European Planning Studies, 27*(2), 219–228. https://doi.org/10.1080/09654313.2018.1532977

Garud, R., &Karnøe, P. (2001). Path creation as a process of mindful deviation. In R. Garud, & P. Karnøe (Eds.), *Path dependence and path creation* (pp. 1–38). Lawrence Erlbaum.

Garud, R., Kumaraswamy, A., & Karn0e, P. (2010). Path dependence or path creation? *Journal of Management Studies, 47*(4), 760–774. https://doi.org/10.1111/j.1467-6486.2009.00914.x

Hay, I., & Muller, S. (2014). Questioning generosity in the golden age of philanthropy: Towards critical geographies of super-philanthropy. *Progress in Human Geography, 38*(5), 635–653. https://doi.org/10.1177/0309132513500893

Hodson, M., Geels, F. W., & McMeekin, A. (2017). Reconfiguring urban sustainability transitions, analysing multiplicity. *Sustainability, 2017, 9.*

Holling, C. S. (1973). Resilience and stability of ecological systems. *Annual Review of Ecology and Systematics, 4*(1), 1–23. https://doi.org/10.1146/annurev. es.04.110173.000245

Intergovernmental Panel on Climate Change (IPCC). (2018). *Summary for urban policy makers. What the IPCC special report on global warming of 1,5°C means for cities.* Retrieved October 12, 2019, from https://www.ipcc.ch/site/assets/uploads/ sites/2/2018/12/SPM-for-cities.pdf

Kythreotis, A. P. (2018). Reimagining the urban as a dystopic resilient space: Scalar materialities in climate knowledge, planning and politics. In K. Jonas, B. Ward, & D. W. Miller (Eds.), *The Routledge handbook on spaces of urban politics* (pp. 589–600). Routledge.

Kythreotis, A. P., & Bristow, G. I. (2017). The 'resilience trap': Exploring the practical utility of resilience for climate change adaptation in UK city-regions. *Regional Studies, 5–7*(10), 1530–1541. https://doi.org/10.1080/00343404.2016.1200719

Leitner, H., Sheppard, E., Webber, S., & Colven, E. (2018). Globalizing urban resilience. *Urban Geography, 39*(8), 1276–1284. https://doi.org/10.1080/02723638.2018. 1446870

MacKinnon, D., & Derickson, K. D. (2013). From resilience to resourcefulness: A critique of resilience policy and activism. *Progress in Human Geography, 37*(2), 253–270. https://doi.org/10.1177/0309132512454775

Martin, R., & Sunley, P. (2015). On the notion of regional economic resilience: Conceptualization and explanation. *Journal of Economic Geography, 15*(1), 1–42. https://doi.org/10.1093/jeg/lbu015

Matyas, D., & Pelling, M. (2015). Positioning resilience for 2015: The role of resistance, incremental adjustment and transformation in disaster risk management policy. *Disasters, 39*(sl), s1–s18. https://doi.org/10.1111/disa.12107

McGuirk, P., Dowling, R., Brennan, C., & Bulkeley, H. (2015). Urban carbon governance experiments. *Geographical Research, 53*(1), 39–52. https://doi. org/10.1111/1745-5871.12098

Meerow, S., & Newell, J. P. (2016). Urban resilience forwhom, what, when, where, and why? *Urban Geography.* https://doi.org/10.1080/02723638.2016.1206395

Meerow, S., Newell, J. P., & Stults, M. (2016). Defining urban resilience: A review. *Landscape and Urban Planning, 147,* 38–49. https://doi.org/10.1016/j. landurbplan.2015.11.011

Moore, T., de Haan, F., Home, R., & Gleeson, B. (2018). *Urban sustainability transitions: Australian cases –International perspectives.* Springer Singapore.

Nevens, F., Frantzeskaki, N., Gorissen, L., & Loorbach, D. (2013). Urban transition labs: Co-creating transformative action for sustainable cities. *Journal of Cleaner Production, 50,* 111–122. https://doi.org/10.1016/j.jdepro.2012.12.001

Organisation for Economic Co-operation and Development (OECD). (2019). *Enhancing innovation capacity in city government.* OECD. https://doi.org/10.1787/ fl0c96e5-en

Padgett, J., & Ansell, C. (1993). Robust action and the rise of the Medici, 1400–1434. *American Journal of Sociology, 98*(6), 1259–1319. https://doi.org/10.1086/230190

Padgett, J. F., & Powell, W. W. (2012). The problem of emergence. In J. F. Padgett, & W. W. Powell (Eds.), *The emergence of organizations and markets* (pp. 1–29). Princeton University Press.

Pelling, M., & Manuel-Navarrete, D. (2011). From resilience to transformation: The adaptive cycle in two Mexican urban centers. *Ecology and Society, 16*(2), 1–11. https://doi.org/10.5751/ES04038–160211

Porter, L., & Davoudi, S. (2012). The politics of resilience for planning: A cautionary note. *Planning Theory and Practice, 13,* 329–333.

Raven, R., Sengers, F., Spaeth, P., Xie, L., Cheshmehzangi, A., & de Jong, M. (2019). Urban experimentation and institutional arrangements. *European Planning Studies, 27*(2), 258–281. https://doi.org/10.1080/09654313.2017.1393047

Resilient Melbourne. (2016). *Resilient Melbourne Strategy.* Retrieved February 11, 2019, from https://resilientmelbourne.com.au/ strategy/

Resilient Melbourne. (2019a). *Living Melbourne.* Retrieved February 11, 2019, from https://resilientmelbourne.com.au/livingmelbourne/

Resilient Melbourne. (2019b). *Resilient Melbourne Delivery Office. Annual report 2018–19.* https://resilientmelbourne.com.au/wpcontent/uploads/2019/10/Resilient-Melbourne-Annual-Report2018–19-Full-Double-Spread-Version-Web.pdf

Rogers, P. (2015). Researching resilience: An agenda for change. *Resilience, 3*(1), 55–71. https://doi.org/10.1080/21693293.2014.988914

Schwanen, T. (2016). Rethinking resilience as capacity to endure. *City, 20*(1), 152–160. https://doi.org/10.1080/13604813.2015.1125718

Sengers, F., Berkhout, F., Wieczorek, A. J., & Raven, R. (2016). Experimenting in the city. Unpacking notions of experimentation for sustainability. In J. Evans, A. Karvonen, & R. Raven (Eds.), *The experimental city* (pp. 15–31). Routledge.

Shaw, K. (2012). 'Reframing' resilience: Challenges for planning theory and practice. *Planning Theory & Practice, 13,* 308–312. https://doi.org/10.1080/14649357. 2012.677124

Shaw, K., & Maythorne, L. (2013). Managing for local resilience: Towards a strategic approach. *Public Policy and Administration, 28*(1), 43–65. https://doi.org/10.1177/0952076711432578

Simmie, J., & Martin, R. (2010). The economic resilience of regions: Towards an evolutionary approach. *Cambridge Journal of Regions, Economy and Society, 3*(1), 27–43. https://doi.org/10.1093/cjres/rsp029

Smeds, E., & Acuto, M. (2018). Networking cities after Paris: Weighing the ambition urban climate change experimentation. *Global Policy, 9*(4), 549–559. https://doi.org/10.1111/17585899.12587

Turnheim, B., Kivimaa, P., & Berkhout, F. (2018). Beyond experiments. In B. Turnheim, P. Kivimaa, & F. Berkhout (Eds.), *Innovating climate governance: Moving beyond experiments* (pp. 1–26). Cambridge University Press.

United Nations. (2015). *Transforming our world: The 2030 Agenda for Sustainable Development.* Retrieved February 20, 2019, from http://www.un.org/ga/searcn/ view_doc.asp?symbol=A/RES/70/ l&Lang=E

VIC Government. (2016). *State government of Victoria. Plan Melbourne.* Retrieved February 20, 2019, from https://www.planmelbourne.vic.gov.au/the-plan

Webb, R., Bai, X., Smith, M. S., Costanza, R., Griggs, D., Moglia, M., Neuman, M., Newman, P., Newton, P., Norman, B., Ryan, C., & handl, H., Steffen, W., Tapper, N., & Thomson, G. (2018). Sustainable urban systems: Co-design and framing for transformation. *Ambio, 47*(1), 57–77. https://doi.org/10.1007/s13280-017-0934–6

Welsh, M. (2014). Resilience and responsibility. *Geographical Journal, 180*(1), 15–26. https://doi.org/10.1111/geoj.12012

Yin, R. K. (2014). *Case study research design and methods* (5th ed.). Sage.

The new normative: synergistic scenario planning for carbon-neutral cities and regions

Joe Ravetz⬤, Aleksi Neuvonen and
Raine Mäntysalo ⬤

Introduction

Transformative changes in transportation networks, energy systems, commercial centres, neighbourhoods and even governance practices are essential to meeting the challenge of cutting greenhouse gas emissions at least 80% by 2050' (Carbon Neutral Cities Alliance, 2016, p. iv). The imperative of cutting carbon emissions to 'net zero' or 'neutrality' in just one generation calls for a rapid expansion in the scope of urban and regional planning. System level socio-technical transformations are needed in the energy, transport, industry and buildings sectors, far beyond the normal spatial or economic planning remit. The transformation imperative constitutes the 'new normative' for urban-regional planning – but as yet the implications are unclear and contested.

The carbon-neutral goal (also termed 'net zero') is defined by the Carbon Neutral Cities Alliance (CNCA), as a city or region where the net greenhouse gas emissions 'associated' with that territory, are zero or less (Plastrik & Cleveland, 2019). In technical terms this can be achieved either by changing the energy mix (supply or demand) within the boundary, generating excess renewable energy ('energy positive'), or by purchase or management of carbon offsets elsewhere. The concept links to the Greenhouse Gas Reporting Protocol (2016), which includes Scope 1 emissions (within the boundary), Scope 2 emissions from electricity generated elsewhere and Scope 3 emissions 'embedded' in goods and services. In engineering terms the way forward seems quite feasible: decarbonize fuel sources and power generation on the supply side, increase efficiency on the demand side, while managing land use, waste and other greenhouse gas sources. But in reality, each system and subsystem is complex and conflicted, a multilevel array of social, technical, economic and political challenges and uncertainties. The different carbon-neutrality options and emissions 'scopes', with typical agendas for urban-regional stakeholders, are summed up in Table 1. The

Table 1. Carbon neutrality and urban-regional planning agendas.

Institutional agendas	Public sector policy and planning	Private sector/ partnership	Wider public and civic society
Carbon neutrality (a): via positive (exported) renewable energy	Local energy resource planning	Incentives and standards for energy firms	Bio-regional resource stewardship
Carbon neutrality (b): via carbon offsets/ sequestration/other	Local land-use management and finance for offsets	Incentives and standards for energy firms and carbon markets	Integrated landscape stewardship
Emissions scope			
SCOPE 1: On-site direct emissions	Building regulation and transport planning	Building standards and transport technology	Integrated urban form & infrastructure
SCOPE 2: Indirect emissions via off-site electricity generation	Energy system local regulation	Energy system quotas and incentives	Energy system stewardship
SCOPE 3: Indirect emissions via traded products and services	Supply chain incentives and standards	Public procurement, innovation incentives	Supply chain and value chain stewardship

Sources: Authors based on CNCA (2016) and Greenhouse Gas Protocol (2016).

implication is that the targets of the CNCA, C40, Covenant of Mayors and similar groups may be aspirational but problematic, lacking clear definitions and responsibilities (Bansard et al, 2017). Apparently simple decarbonization programmes have to engage with large complex infrastructures, macroeconomic forces, real estate markets, sector supply chains, professional institutions and lifestyle patterns. Meanwhile, the 'ghost at the table', the 'Scope 3' indirect emissions from international trade, is a reality check on the direct carbon neutrality. For instance, the UK has now exported most of its former heavy industry, so its Scope 1–2 emissions show rapid improvement, while its Scope 3 account shows rapid growth in imports with higher carbon intensities (Department for Environment, Food and Rural Affairs (Defra), 2019).

Moreover, it seems that policy is often ambiguous between a linear approach to 'problem solving', and a more complex socio-technical systems transformation. At the global level, the targets for emissions budgets call for extremely challenging rates of change, estimated by some at 15% emissions reductions/year (Anderson, 2015). At the local level, many cities around the UK and European Union are (as of 2019) declaring 'climate emergencies', where aspirations are strong, but local powers and resources are weak. Most carbon studies focus on energy technology and economics, and tend to assume that policy levers can be pulled, or that coordination can be achieved. Some look more systematically at the policy challenges, for instance, the Association for Conservation of Energy (Guerder & Rosenow, 2016), but as yet few address the scale of transformation needed.

Aims, scope and methods

In that context, this paper aims first to contribute to the theoretical-methodological side with a framework which can help both practitioners and academics to respond to the 'new normative'. Second, we demonstrate this with a single case study, which allows some detail and realitychecking. Thus, our theoretical-methodological contribution helps to map complex systems, and the opportunities of the 'new normative' transformation. Our practical contribution should help cities and regions to achieve carbon-neutral targets by means of a rational and transparent approach to system transformation, here tided 'synergistic scenario planning' (SSP).

The case material has been gathered through a long series of collaborative research-policy projects (see policy references in the next section). Documentary evidence from stakeholder dialogue was used for methodological development in three main phases. First, the Sustainable City Region programme (1993–2000) developed an urban metabolism/integrated policy model (Ravetz, 2000). More detailed resource modelling and supply/value chain analysis then followed (Ravetz, 2006, 2010). A third phase (2010–20) explored the cognitive side of policy learning, sociotechnical transition, urban-regional foresight and collective intelligence (Ravetz, 2020; Ravetz & Miles, 2016). Meanwhile the three main components of the SSP framework have been developed over some years by each co-author, and the combination is presented here for the first time.

With that in mind, the paper is structured as follows. Following this introduction is a brief review of 'debates and tensions' in the literature around the new normative challenge. A third section oudines the case study of Greater Manchester (GM) and its many phases of climate/carbon policy. The central section then sets out the SSP framework in three main parts: futurity, alignment and transformation. The fifth section applies the framework to the case study for insight on both problems and forward opportunities. Finally, we highlight some implications for theory and practice on urban-regional futures to help on the journey towards the 'new normative'.

Carbon-neutral planning: a landscape of tensions

Here we sketch some topical debates and tensions in the field, as context to the SSP framework detailed in the next section. In summary, the SSP framework contains three key dimensions: *futurity* and the practice of scenario planning; *alignment* of wider communities of interest; and *transformation* or structural socio-technical change. This conceptual three-dimensional space then locates around it three key debates and conceptual tensions, as pictured in Figure 1: 'institutional tension', 'experimental tension' and 'systemic tension'.

Institutional tension? Territorial planning versus systemic

The perennial tension of spatial/territorial planning versus non-territorial political economy comes to a carbon-neutral head – should the unit of analysis and governance be cities and regions, or global supply chains and corporations? Many critique idealized models of strategic planning that bypass institutional/political realities, and this is highlighted by carbon-neutral goals that shift from rigid statutory frameworks with outdated zoning tools towards networked 'soft' space governance (Mäntysalo et al., 2019; Steele & Ruming, 2012; Van den Broeck, 2013).

As Newman (2008) has noted, existing forms of strategic planning are 'not just a convenient contrast to the ideal form ... but the origin and residue of previous institutional designs that generate constraints and forms of path dependence' (p. 1374). Where carbon-neutral policy calls for both a legalistic spatial planning, alongside an entrepreneurial approach to supply chains and technologies, the coexistence of such parallel systems raises many ambiguities (Castan Broto & Bulkeley, 2013). The barriers to institutional change are then a major concern, even more so with headline carbon targets

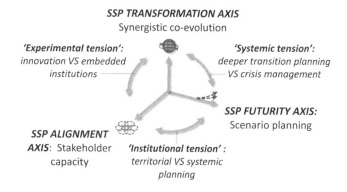

Figure 1 Synergistic scenario planning (SSP): framework and tensions.
Note: VS, versus.

that highlight gaps and mismatches all around (Granqvist & Mäntysalo, 2020). While 'soft space' approaches raise both opportunities and ambiguities (Allmendinger ScHaughton, 2010; Backhand et al., 2018; Mantysalo et al., 2015), new concepts of collaborative 'co-governance' with hybrid organizations are equally relevant to the carbon-neutral agenda (Johanson & Vakkuri, 2018; Ravetz, 2020, pp. 225–237).

Experimental tension? Between innovation and vested interests

A second tension arises between the goals of transition/ transformation and the realities of incumbent institutions. Luque-Ayala et al. (2018) suggest that traditional forms of urban-regional policy are not (yet) capable of the structural changes implied by carbon neutrality. With the focus on networked infrastructure (energy, transport, construction supply chains etc.), transitions in such large and complex systems call for new forms of governance, with new forms of engagement of multiple stakeholders, through 'triple helix' or similar models of engagement (Bulkeley et al., 2013; Etzkowitz & Leydesdorff, 2000).

This opens a wider agenda, one of complexity, emergence and collective learning in urban and regional analysis (Komninos, 2015; Uyarra & Flanagan, 2010). Looking beyond evolutionary thinking on path dependencies and spillovers, co-evolutionary thinking now explores 'pathinterdependencies' and 'transversalities' (Cooke, 2012), with 'platforms for industrial interaction' and wider public–private–civic–academic ecosystems (Asheim, 2018). As for starting points, one is urban experimentation, as an enabler of institutional collaborations across the public–private–civic divide (Luque-Ayala et al., 2018). The 'experimental city' of small-scale Living Labs and embedded innovations also highlights the granularity of change and transition in large complex systems (Evans et al., 2017; Hodson et al., 2019). It also renews interest in learning for organizational change, now applied to strategic planning as 'extended co-production' (Albrechts, 2012; Argyris & Schön, 1996). Strategic or higher order learning can prepare and empower stakeholders for future-oriented action (Neuvonen & Ache, 2017; Quist et al., 2011), and mobilization around strategic frames (Healey, 2009). However on the ground many tensions arise, where such experimental/learning zones are seen as risky or vulnerable to special interests, with open questions on the 'transformative capacity' of cities and regions (Wolfram, 2016).

Systemic tension: transition planning versus crisis management?

A third tension is on the mismatch between longer term transition planning, and short-term crisis management (in this case, 'climate emergency'). Transition theory and practice has also spawned a new approach to 'system innovation', not only in niche technologies or business models but also in the wider system architecture (Organisation for Economic Co-operation and

Development (OECD), 2015; Schot & Steinmueller, 2018). In reality this is the beginning of a dialogue, which for carbon-neutral policy includes many stakeholders: finance, infrastructure, regulators, construction, labour, households, digital providers and public services, to name a few (Borras & Edler, 2020; Weber & Truffer, 2017). And while such engagement can look good on paper, the reality is often one of disconnected policy, market hurdles and split incentives, for example, in housing retrofit (see the next section) (Guertier & Rosenow, 2016; Webber et al., 2015). A strategic response would aim to enhance the 'collective anticipatory intelligence' via urban-regional foresight, but this faces a typical reality of under-resourced and disempowered local government (Ravetz & Miles, 2016).

Parallel thinking also comes up for the energy sector itself, with some similarity to SSP, which contrasts a linear problem-solving approach to evolutionary innovation, to strategic systems transformation (Grubb et al., 2014). But again, even the most simple carbon targets conceal a jungle of organizational conflicts (Lippert, 2012), and the gap grows between the nuances of planning theory (Alexander, 2010; Watson, 2008), and the urgency of the climate crisis (cf. Phdungsilp, 2011). The rapid emergence of Extinction Rebellion in 2019 is a stark reminder of the possible tipping points in global systems, with unquantifiable risks of catastrophic impacts on many cities and regions (Fischer et al., 2018).

Overall, a picture emerges of many tensions in theory and in practice, between different transformation agendas, different future horizons, and different policy frames and institutions. Some results on the ground are demonstrated by the 'Long road to low-carbon' case study that follows.

'A long road to low carbon': the case of Greater Manchester

GM is the UK's second city-region after London, a hub of investment and innovation, and a global destination for young people, culture and sport. It is also a sink of unemployment and deprivation, poor housing and low productivity, costing around £5 billion/year in net public expenditure. GM also considers itself a showcase for urban renewal and regeneration, devolution and publicprivate partnerships, and its climate/carbon targets are framed in that context. Several phases of strategic spatial planning have emerged in GM, in parallel with climate/ carbon policy (Hodson et al., 2018). This shows scenario planning in both 'explicit' forms (technical modelling and social deliberation on alternative futures): and more typically, 'implicit' forms, where scenario-type thinking is part of a wider policy process.

Carbon as an environmental agenda

Climate change and carbon awareness in GM emerged in 1992, and practical action took shape following the 1997 Kyoto protocols, building on evidence from the Town & Country Planning Association's (TCPA) Sustainable

City-Region project (Ravetz, 2000). The UK then took the lead as the first nation with a mandatory carbon budget, in the Climate Change Act 2008 and the Low Carbon Transition Plan (Department of Energy and Climate Change (DECC), 2009). In parallel, the (then) regional development agencies each produced a climate change strategy to meet the new national target for 80% carbon reductions, with support from the 'Regional EconomyEnvironment Input-Output' scenario model (Ravetz, 2010). Meanwhile, the Manchester Independent Economic Review set up a city-region version of the global Stern Report, the GM 'Mini-Stern' (McKillop et al., 2009). With scenario modelling for the urban-regional economy and energy system, this report provided a longlasting 'boundary object' (as defined in the next section), a common reference point between different sectors.

However, progress was not straightforward. In 2008, a public referendum was held on a proposed congestion charge and public transport plan for the whole inner urban area, which aimed to contribute to the carbon targets (Sherriff, 2013), and the scenario modelling showed a clear carbon benefit of 10–15% of all local transport emissions. However, the proposals were framed by a free-market opposition as an attack on civil liberties and low-income motorists, and after a heated campaign, the proposals were rejected by a large majority. With growing uncertainty on the GM low-carbon strategy in the face of public and media scepticism, the 2008 financial crisis displaced much long-term thinking, followed in 2010 by the coalition government, committed to cutting 'red tape' and 'rolling back' the public sector. The general effect was to keep carbon targets on the policy agenda, but to sideline most of the practical actions: for instance, both regional innovation clusters and the national Code for Sustainable Homes were abolished, with little to replace them.

Meanwhile, the newly established Greater Manchester Combined Authority (GMCA) set up an #, later renamed the GM Low Carbon Hub, with a multi-sector partnership (www.ontheplatform.org.uk). The GM Climate Change Strategy (GMCA, 2013) then aimed at a short-term carbon reduction of 48% (1990–2020). With a range of scenario model results, the strategy acknowledged that the 'easy wins' since 1990 had been made already, including the national shift from coal to gas for power generation, improvements in vehicle technology, and export of heavy industry to the developing world.

Carbon as an economic agenda

Meanwhile, the moves towards city-region devolution were gathering pace. Regional development agencies were replaced by a patchwork of local enterprise partnerships: the 'Northern Powerhouse' was in many ways a rebranded interregional strategy, and critiqued by some as a 'Northern Poorhouse' (Moran & Williams, 2015). Shortly after, the 'Devo-Manc' experiment in devolution was set up in 2014, with enhanced powers including housing, transport, skills and infrastructure (Haughton et al., 2016). In parallel, the GM Spatial Framework was launched in 2016, with three scenarios/options for growth, ranging from 152,000 to 336,000 new dwellings over 20 years; in parallel was a modest target of 60% carbon reduction (1990–2035), but with few specific actions (Deas, 2014; GMCA, 2015).

One headline policy was the national Green Deal, promoted as the 'world leader' for energy retrofit in housing, but on the ground a near total failure, GM being the only city which enrolled more than a few households (Webber et al., 2015). Currently the UK lacks any programmes beyond the most basic (at the time of writing) for energy efficiency in housing or commercial buildings or the fuel poverty which still afflicts 15% of GM households.

As for 'explicit' scenario planning and foresight, various methods were tried with mixed results. An interactive 'sustainable eco-region' model was tested with stakeholders (Ravetz, 2010). The DECC 'Pathways' programme put up an interactive online energy model, with stakeholder workshops to debate the implications (http://2050calculator-tool.decc.gov.uk/#/guide). Another strand came via the UK Foresight on Future of Cities, which in GM this demonstrated some advanced foresight methods (including a forerunner of 'synergistic scenario planning'), to inform energy, transport and housing strategies. However, at that time it seemed that exploration of the 'future' was overshadowed by the 'Devo-Manc' agenda of the 'present' (Ravetz & Miles, 2016).

Carbon as 'climate emergency'

Against a turbulent context, the incoming GM mayor set up a Green Summit 2018 which put new carbon targets at the centre of a new five-year Environment Plan (GMCA, 2019). The calculations were based on the energy/emissions model SCATTER (Setting City and Area Targets and Trajectories for Emission Reduction), with detailed energy/carbon scenarios and priorities for action, backed up by sectoral studies such as 'retrofit regeneration' (UKGBC, 2017). The key graph (Figure 2a) shows that carbon neutrality is possible under Scenario 4, but this 'recommended budget will be challenging to achieve and represents a much greater level of ambition than is embedded in current national policy' (Kuriakose et al., 2018, p. 23).

The carbon-budgeting method translates global commitments and national multi-year budgets into tangible goals for the city-region (Anderson & Bows, 2011). The recommendations are for GM to make its 'fair' contribution, with immediate and drastic action for emissions reduction at 15%/year (and for aviation, to stabilize emissions by 2030 and then reduce to zero by 2075). However, the detailed action plans show many leaps of optimism with, for instance, a proposed 'retrofit accelerator' innovation hub, or 'national fiscal policies to be identified'. There is an overarching sense of near-impossible aspiration, which fits with the GM self-image of bold innovation and creative action: and so the technical carbon targets are as pieces in a larger game or discourse, or as we explore below, boundary objects in a wider 'trading zone'.

A synergistic scenario-planning framework

The GM story shows how the transformations of buildings, transport, industry, land use, energy and waste systems cross between sectors, challenge policy structures and change the power relations between stakeholders. It seems evident that new theoretical-methodological frameworks and practical tools are needed (1) to understand the implications of the 'new normative' and (2) to apply this in practice.

The analytical framework we propose addresses three key challenges: how to link future goals with present day actions, how to bring stakeholders into alignment, and how to look beyond problem-fixing towards system transformation. The first is about the 'longer' horizons of scenario planning which we link particularly to the back-casting approach. The second concerns the *'deeper/wider* interconnections between knowledge and value between different groups, and the alignment or coordination between them, drawing on the insights of *boundary objects and trading zones.* The third challenge concerns the *'further* agenda of system transformation, which we tackle with the synergistic approach. Interestingly, a current handbook on carbonneutral cities follows quite similar principles, that is, innovation culture, ecological 'abundance', social 'sharing' and future-oriented adaptive governance (Plastrik & Cleveland, 2019). In this section we first introduce these three components and then combine them into an integrated framework, with visual mapping methods shown in Figure 2 and the analytical fields in Table 2.

Scenario planning and back-casting

The simplicity of carbon targets and the possible complexity of responses suggests the use of 'scenario planning with back-casting'. Such methods emerged in the 1970s for sustainability transitions such as food, energy, water and climate change (Quist, 2007). Back-casting scenarios are formed by defining normative criteria for desirable futures (e.g., sustainable level of carbon emissions), and then building a feasible, rational pathway towards them (Börjeson et al., 2006). In other words, back-casting (1) assumes a normative frame to the future, in addition to the descriptive, and (2) explores the human intentions and strategy to achieve the goals (Dreborg, 1996).

Carbon-neutrality targets are an interesting case for scenario planning: the more ambitious the target, the larger the 'aspiration-reality gap' that can undermine their credibility as practical policy tools. In this context the overall purpose of normative back-casting scenarios is to expand the scope of future options, and thus find ways around gaps and barriers to systems change (Höjer & Mattsson, 2000; Zegras & Rayle, 2012).

Scenario planning in practice often uses the medium of narratives or stories, sharing 'rich' information in a simplified format (Harris, 2016; Mäntysalo et al., 2020). Some examples from GM (next section) have resonance as stories, even where technical evidence may be lacking, for instance 'Transition Towns' or 'Incredible Edible' (Figure 3d), using an 'implicit' scenario approach, which describes positive visions in contrast to 'business-as-usual' dystopias.

Back-casting scenario methods have been applied in urban-regional planning in various ways, from generalized visioning' to specific policy development (e.g., Phdungsilp, 2011; Viguié et al., 2014). Most urban-regional plans are developed with a narrow range of demographic, traffic, and economic forecasts and scenarios based on technical modelling (Chakraborty et al., 2011; Myers & Kitsuse, 2000), leaving the transformative agenda to fuzzy aspirations such as 'sustainable', 'smart' or 'liveable'. Some cities and regions have followed the integrated foresight approach, where scenario studies are integrated to capacity-building and roadmapping/strategy development (Phaal et al., 2007; Ravetz & Miles, 2016). Figure 2(a) shows a narrow functional version of back-casting, while Figure 2(b) shows there is a synergistic version with a wider and deeper scope.

Boundary objects and trading zones

The concept of *'boundary object'* was coined by Star and Griesemer (1989) to explain the boundary-crossing capacities of coordinated action, involving multiple actors from different 'social worlds'. A simple carbon target can be considered a boundary object of a sort, but one with weak connections to the agencies and interests of its stakeholders, whereas an elaborated carbon strategy, which connects visions to actions, could be much stronger (e.g., carbon policy with specifics on urban greenspace or public transport). This suggests the role of multiple interconnected boundary objects in a cognitive chain where the carbon object is connected to other more tangible or 'material' objects, for example, carbon policy/public transport/clean air/quality of life.

Such chains may then grow into locally or regionally grounded *trading zones* between many stakeholders in which boundary objects can emerge (Galison, 1997, 2010). The concept of 'trading zone' refers to hybrid platforms where information and services are 'traded' between different actors, with different problem framings or value systems, but where there is scope for alignment, by trading in boundary objects 'enabled by the *thinness* of interpretation rather than the thickness of consensus' (Galison, 2010, p. 36). Boundary objects and trading zones, and their implications for social learning and policy innovation, have also been examined in the strategic planning context (e.g., Bälducci & Mäntysalo, 2013; Fuller, 2006; Mäntysalo & Jarenko, 2014). Figure 2(c) shows a typical *'nexus'* of climate policy syndromes, gaps, barriers or conflicts between the values and objectives of different domains. Meanwhile Figure 2(d) shows some typical interconnecting synergies, agendas, narratives and discourses, linking between multiple domains of value and rationality.

Synergistic thinking, methods and tools

'*Synergistic* methods and tools then bring together the '*longer* scenario perspective, and the '*deeper/wider* trading zone approach, to look 'further' beyond functional problem fixing towards system transformation (Ravetz, 2015, 2020). With a combination of visual thinking (Figure 2) and analytic matrices (Table 2), the method helps to map complex problems and explore forward pathways.

A typical 'functional' scenario-planning process is shown in Figure 2(a): the carbon scenario modelling outputs show a range of options from

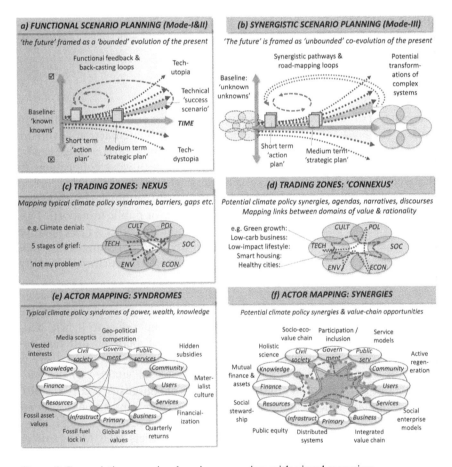

Figure 2 Synergistic scenario planning: overview with visual mapping.

'business as usual' to 'aspirational'. Intermediate options can be debated as a balance of risk, innovation, social change, policy effort and financial cost. For example, the Intergovernmental Panel on Climate Change (IPCC) reports and United Nations Framework Convention on Climate Change (UNFCCC) protocols provide the aspiration of a '1.5 degree world', with an agreed target for a '2 degree world', which contrasts to current trend projections for a '3–4 degree world' (Tyndall Centre, 2018).

A more realistic picture shown in Figure 2(b): here the baseline axis includes for complex realities, and future scenarios are more about system-wide transformation, involving many stakeholders with many domains of value, summed up with the flexible menu known as 'STEEPC' (social, technological, economic, ecological, political, cultural) (Loveridge, 2008). As in Figure 2(d), for system transformation the many actors will need to coordinate and collaborate, via supply chains, markets, finance, regulations, skills, procurements and so on, within and between the various trading zones. In each there is a process of collaborative value chain development,

Table 2 Synergistic scenario planning: a combined framework.

	Synergistic transformation		
	Mode-I linear	Mode-II evolutionary	Mode-III co-evolutionary
Targets/ boundary objects	(Functional complexity)	(Emergent complexity)	(Deeper complexity)
Low-carbon overall targets	e.g., CO_2 total emissions	CO_2 as adaptive target	CO_2 footprint as a proxy for global responsibility
Low-carbon economy	CO_2/GVA (gross value-added)	CO_2 as market opportunity	CO_2 as a proxy for economic transformation
Low-carbon society, etc.	CO_2/person or household	CO_2 as product/ service (CO_2 per unit of 'benefit')	CO_2 as a proxy for social transformation
Scenario-planning processes			
Systems (relational thinking)	'Known knowns': material functional systems	'Unknown knowns': incentives, enterprise	'Unknown unknowns' with cognitive complexity
Scenarios (divergent thinking)	Tangible trends, projections, forecasts	Evolutionary trends/scenarios	Co-evolutionary transformation
Synergies (emergent thinking)	Functional problem solving	Innovation and problem insight	Societal co-creation and co-design
Strategies (convergent thinking)	Specific actions/ responses	Entrepreneurial strategy and roadmapping	Transformation via collective intelligence

which rests on collective ('co-') learning, cocreation or co-production, that is, the components of an overall collective intelligence for carbon policy, or a *'collective carbon intelligence'*. Such intelligence can then work in different 'modes' of systems complexity (Ravetz, 2015, 2020):

- *Mode-I* or 'linear' complexity: functional energy/carbon systems, which can be framed as bounded problem-solving with 'known knowns'.
- *Mode-II* or 'evolutionary' complexity, for adaptive/optimizing energy/carbon markets or enterprises, framed as partially bounded problems of innovation or competition (Modes-I and -II are shown together on the left sides of Figures 2 and 3).
- *Mode-III* or 'co-evolutionary' energy/carbon systems (shown on the right sides of Figures 2 and 3): framed as collective learning, thinking, co-creating and co-production.

Similar frameworks for co-evolutionary systems have emerged in various fields, such as energy/climate economics (Grubb et al., 2014), organizational learning (Argyris & Schön, 1996), and the widely shared aspiration for 'new forms of government which are adaptive, responsive, participative and deliberative' (Revi et al., 2014, p. 28).

By comparing the concept mappings for Modes-II and -III, we can explore the opportunities in the trading zone behind the single-issue carbon targets, for both value systems and real stakeholders. In Figure 2(e) we see a typical set of stakeholders ('actors') in the energy/carbon system, with typical syndromes, gaps, barriers, split incentives, moral hazards or 'lost in translation', where the 'new normative' targets are difficult or impossible to achieve.

A positive alternative then emerges in Figure 2(f), with many potential synergies and value-chain opportunities in various trading zones. For example, a low-carbon supplychain depends on synergy between finance, designers, builders, citizens and municipalities: or a low-carbon finance model can work on the synergies between ecostewardship, public procurement and green municipal bonds. Here the extended trading zones, shown in Figure 2(d), enable stakeholders to make shared commitments or investments (economic, political, technological). Likewise, the boundary object concept helps to realize the practical applications of the carbon targets: so that 'carbon per unit of GVA' is an environment–economic object for firms or sectors, or 'carbon per household' is a socioenvironmental object, as in Table 2.

Synergistic process model

Overall, synergistic thinking can enable collaborative learning, thinking, co-creation and co-production, in other words, the components of a *collective intelligence*. It also helps to integrate scenario planning with the mapping of trading zones, often opaque and compromised in practice. In response, the synergistic method helps to map and manage a more systematic cycle of

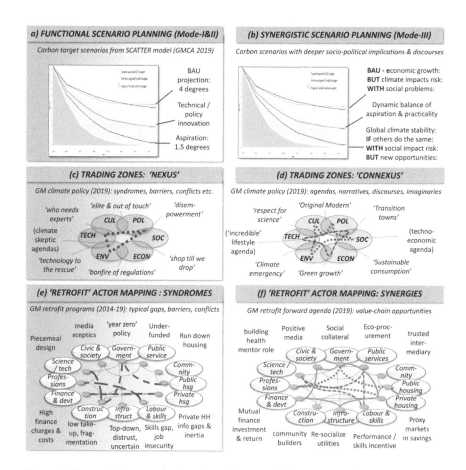

Figure 3 Synergistic scenario planning: the case of Greater Manchester.
Sources: GMCA (2019); Tyndall Centre (2018); Ravetz and Miles (2016).

knowledge flows and cognitive learning, linking present and future, with a process model for different modes of thinking, from 'relational to divergent, emergent and convergent' (Ratcliffe & Krawczyk, 2011). The synergistic cycle then includes four stages:

- *Baselines*: problems, challenges and the underlying systems in the present; ('relational thinking' which explores the trading zones with actor mapping).
- *Scenarios*: forces of change, uncertainty and alternatives in the future ('divergent thinking', centred on the back-casting process).
- *Synergies*: visions, opportunities, innovations and interconnections for the future ('emergent thinking', for transformation and the *collective intelligence* to enable it).

- *Strategies*: pathways and road-mapping for action, which link the future back to the present ('convergent thinking', and the strategic planning and management to implement it).

Further detail on these stages is available as the 'synergistic toolkit' (Ravetz, 2020).

Towards a combined framework

These three conceptual approaches (back-casting scenario planning, boundary objects and trading zones, and synergistic thinking) can then be combined into the SSP framework, summed up with a simple matrix as shown in Table 2:

- 'New normative' carbon targets, elaborated into interconnected boundary objects and trading zone platforms.
- Back-casting scenario-planning processes, linking future goals with present-day actions.
- Systems transformation: with synergistic mapping from linear (Mode-I) and evolutionary (Mode-II) to co-evolutionary (Mode-III).

The matrix analysis, in combination with visual thinking, can help to analyse a case such as GM, with typical gaps and mismatches between problems, targets, pathways and solutions.

Application to the case study

The case of GM shows how apparently simple carbon targets raise many challenges in the transformation of a major city-region. Here we explore some of the nuances and implications, using the SSP approach, with both matrix and visual mapping techniques.

From scenario planning to action planning

The carbon scenario modelling from the SCATTER programme forms the key diagram in the GM Environment Strategy (GMCA, 2019) (Figure 3a). This shows a typical range from the 'aspirational' (targets for 1.5°C of global warming *if* replicated around the world), the 'desirable' (rapid policy innovation, technology rollout and social change), the 'probable', with less ambitious change, and the 'do nothing' option which points towards a 4°C rise. Some key policy discourses are then interpolated from the strategy and supporting documents (Figure 3b). Either economic growth continues but with growing climate risks: or, global climate stability could result *if* others do the same, but at risk of societal impacts, and so on.

Looking more closely at the *nexus* of syndromes, many climate-sceptical patterns in GM surfaced around the 2008 Congestion Charge episode, and continue in various forms. Some, such as the *'bonfire of regulations'* or *'who needs experts'* are from national politicians, others are more apparent in popular media.

In contrast is a mapping of a 'connexus' of synergies, in Figure 2(d), with key 'trading zones' in the strategy (these are interpolated and not always explicit). We can track the 'climate emergency' rhetoric in the technical-environment trading zone, 'green growth' in the environmenteconomy zone, 'sustainable consumption' in the economy-society zone, and 'liveable city' in the urbanenvironment zone. Each of these in various ways combines political discourses, lifestyle trends, media narratives or policy agendas: each also represents various shades of ambiguity or managed tension. Mapping of underlying layers may reveal deeper assumptions or archetypes, such as *'trust in policy-makers'* or *'respect for science'* which are often contested in public life (Inayatullah, 2011). The implication of such multilayer mapping is that successful climate/carbon policy will focus on key trading zones, systematically shifting negative syndromes towards positive synergies, as identified in the right hand column of Table 3.

Sector examples

The housing energy retrofit agenda is very topical in GM, with its stock of older less efficient dwellings (Ravetz, 2008). This is a challenge that appears technically simple and cost-effective, but where syndromes, gaps and barriers of every kind seem to block progress (Guertier & Rosenow, 2016). The stakeholder/actor mapping in Figure 2(e) shows many gaps, myopias, perverse incentives, 'moral hazards', 'landlord traps' and other barriers around the table (Ravetz, 2020).

Learning from the failure of the national Green Deal programme, as above, GM is developing a new policy model for a 'retrofit accelerator' (at the time of writing). Therefore, Figure 3(f) shows an alternative mapping of the same actors, now co-creating new 'synergies' and value-chains, with various pathways to mobilize them. The policy model looks for synergies between procurement and sector innovation, finance and home ownership, poverty alleviation and area regeneration, warm homes and public health benefits, retrofit and skills training, and so on (UKGBC, 2017). Some pathways are focused on finance or technology, some more social and lifestyle related, and others are more ethical and cultural. Each of these and more are currently debated in an ongoing programme of forums, 'listening events', business breakfasts, citizens' assemblies and online consultations, and then assembled into policies and road-maps.

On the social and cultural side, Carbon Literacy is an award-winning programme, born in GM and now working internationally, providing training in basic climate change knowledge, and capacity-building for organizations and institutions (https://carbonliteracy.com/). Carbon Literacy works in the 'baseline' area of the matrix, to create a Mode-I type systems understanding, and also in the Mode-III 'synergy' area, where it enables creative interactions between a wider circle of stakeholders. This programme emerged from a previous venture of 2005–09, 'Manchester is My Planet', which asked organizations and individuals to make a 'pledge' to reduce their emissions.

On the sectoral supply chain agenda, green public procurement is in principle a good place to start a low-carbon innovation ecosystem and supply chain transformation. However, the current reality in the UK is one of scarce funds and skills, low tolerance of risk, and fragmentation of local government and public services (Georghiou et al., 2014). The boundary objects/targets on the right of the matrix help to identify the potential role and scope, not just as procurement of low-carbon products which may be higher cost and risk, but as strategic leadership of a fast growing economic sector, in collaboration with other public bodies, with social co-learning all around.

Green or low-carbon finance is a complex and controversial agenda in the UK: the Green Investment Bank was reduced and sold, and capital controls on local authorities restrict the scope of long-term green finance (ING Bank, 2015). However, in GM there are interesting developments under the heading of natural capital (ecosystems and their services), and the current investment plan aims to bring together *'wider'* stakeholders, with *'deeper'* layers of value, to collaborate on *'further'* social-eco-business models, all in the zone of Mode-III thinking (Eftec et al., 2019). Work is now in progress on specific low-carbon policies as part of the national Transforming Cities Fund and Brownfield Fund.

Process analysis

Overall, some key challenges and potentials of SSP for a carbon-neutral GM are summed in the matrix in Table 3. The 'carbon targets' here are framed as boundary objects linking different sectors and domains: economy-environment, socioeconomic, eco-technical and so on. The 'process' views the scenario planning methods in their context of the four-stage process model presented above, that is, 'systems, scenarios, synergies and strategies'. Table 3 then shows different levels of system complexity, from the Mode-I 'functional' and Mode-II evolutionary, to a Mode-III co-evolutionary transformation. The experience in GM shows how policy typically puts up material carbon targets, supported by energy-emissions modelling in the background (functional Mode-I type thinking); and to achieve the targets relies on markets, innovations and incentives for other actors beyond its direct control (Mode-II thinking). However, making such incentives work in reality calls for mutual learning and collaboration in a wider community, which then calls for new forms of 'associative and deliberative' governance

Table 3 Greater Manchester case: 'synergistic scenario planning' analysis.

Targets / boundary objects	Mode-I linear	Mode-II evolutionary	Mode-III co-evolutionary
Low-carbon targets: annual emissions/multi-year budget/base year change	e.g., CO_2 direct emissions in tonnes	CO_2 as an indicator of change and development	Carbon neutral as civic responsibility, ethical stewardship
Low-carbon economy: 'green growth'/'circular economy'/ eco-business	CO_2/GVA (gross value-added) indicators, total or sectoral	CO_2 reduction as market opportunities, supply chain innovations	Carbon neutral as economic and livelihood transformation
Low-carbon society: 'sustainable consumption'/ 'clean inclusive growth'	CO_2/person, household	CO_2/person for social incentives, peer pressure, performance benchmarks	Carbon neutral as social and civic transformation
Low-carbon city: liveable cities/ accessible neighbourhoods	CO_2/community, town or other settlement	CO_2/community for benchmarks, peer learning etc.	Carbon neutral as liveable and healthy urban future

Processes

Systems	Greater Manchester data: 2.75 million persons: £56 bn GVA: 10.3 mt CO_2/year (2019)	'CO_2 economy'/ energy efficiency and low-carbon transition in firms, sectors, markets	Innovation on cognitive side, e.g., carbon literacy, pledges, extended corporate social responsibility (CSR)
Scenarios	'SCATTER' model scenarios: BAU (business as usual)/policy push/1.50 outcome	Some economic modelling, but lacking sector-level scenarios	Transformation scenarios are implicit in political discourses
Synergies	Current opportunities in 'devolution'	Incentives in efficiency, market opportunity, business model innovation	Alternative ventures, e.g., 'Transition Towns', 'Incredible Edible', 'Beyond Carbon' etc.
Strategies	Five-year strategies, technically correct but vulnerable to 'unforeseens'	Sector strategies dependent on firm/stakeholder/ national government support	Emerging models for 'accelerator' or 'Collaboratorium' (work in progress)

(Mode-III thinking). There are also ongoing tensions between mainstream policy and a 'wider' range of actors who argue for 'deeper' economic or political transformation. The synergistic process model also provides another perspective on current gaps in GM and any further potentials:

- *Systems/baselines* ('relational thinking'): despite a multi-year programme of evidence-building there is no overall inventory and little wider understanding of the city-region carbon system or metabolism. The Carbon Literacy programme above has spread basic awareness, but this needs to multiply up into every sector at every level.
- *Scenarios* ('divergent thinking'): there is some explicit scenario planning in the previous and current GM climate/carbon strategies: and various 'implicit' scenario methods in the background to many policies: here the previous insights on ambiguities help to explain the viable scope of scenario planning (Mäntysalo & Grišakov, 2017).
- *Synergies* ('emergent thinking'): GM is clearly fertile ground for the co-creation of synergies and innovations. However, there is critique of an inner circle of 'usual suspects' working in a neoliberal framework, lacking an open 'trading zone platform' which could involve wider communities (Hendriks, 2014). And to accelerate the transformation up to 15% carbon reduction/year, the synergy formation process is even more critical, and the spaces/resources/skills more urgent.
- *Strategies/pathways* (with 'convergent thinking'): in principle the road-mapping of actions (short, medium and long term) should follow logically from the synergy formation, and mobilize action from all stakeholders concerned. In practice nothing is simple: the public sector is underfunded and overstretched, the business sector focused on survival or growth, and the academic sector often disconnected from local needs. However, with an exceptional stakeholder community, GM continues to work on carbon-neutral pathways. The policy agenda includes (at the time of writing) low-carbon supply chain initiatives, energy up-skilling, micro-generation and carbon finance: public sector eco-stewardship and natural capital finance: next-generation smart transport and waste systems. Meanwhile, civil society is designing countless experiments, social innovations, living laboratories, fab-labs, carbon coops and similar spaces for collective learning, thinking, co-creation and co-production.

Discussion: challenges and ways forward

Cities and regions around the world are planning their pathways towards climate neutrality and the 'new normative'. But the chances of success are small if they lack the most effective methods and tools, together with the theory behind them. In this paper, 'synergistic scenario planning' is proposed both to understand the challenge of systems transformation and to facilitate practical pathways towards it. This final section sketches (1) the implications and transferability of the GM case study and (2) the relation to broader planning debates. It then points to (3) beyond the state of the art and (4) implications for urban-regional planning practice.

Practical implications and transferability

The GM case shows by experience three key challenges for synergistic scenario planning: how to link future goals with present actions, how to bring stakeholders into alignment and how to design a system transformation. GM over 25 years has seen many versions of climate policy, scenario methods and experiments in stakeholder alignment and capacity-building. The goals of system transformation are often contentious, but arguably there is more awareness of the challenge now than in previous decades.

For transferability, the GM experience is in many ways typical of a post-industrial secondary city-region. However, in contrast to others, GM sees ongoing experiments in devolution of powers (while the UK remains one of the most centralized of all developed nations). The urban infrastructure of energy and transport is largely privatized in terms set by national government and so calls for special efforts for alignment and synergy at the city-region level. The growth agenda of gross domestic product (GDP) and urban expansion, as seen in many countries, in GM is quite constrained. Meanwhile there is a culture of active innovation in GM which is not easy to replicate: all the more reason for GM to lead the way with its many experiments in deliberative democracy, action learning sets, citizens' assemblies and crowd-sourced forums.

Broader planning debates

For our first challenge of 'futurity', strategic urban-regional planning has often been slow to adopt the principles and practices of scenario planning (Chakraborty et al., 2011). Basic economic or population scenarios are often used for vision documents' that serve multiple jurisdictions, and then the 'central estimate' is applied for technical land-use or economic policies; but such documents are often opaque and disconnected from the main policy process (Myers & Kitsuse, 2000). In response, the scenario back-casting approach aims to be more explicit and transparent in both technical modelling and participative envisioning. Here the urban-regional scenarios are contested zones of vision, aspiration, imaginaries and discourses, ripe for deliberation and negotiation, as boundary objects themselves (Zegras & Rayle, 2012). Climate/carbon scenarios are particularly topical, combining simple headline targets with the complexities of responses.

For the second challenge of 'alignment', the concepts of trading zones and boundary objects help with mapping a complex territory to identify potential synergies between different actors (Mantysalo et al., 2020). Some of the most crucial trading zones lie between future scenarios, physical maps/ plans and wider stakeholder engagement, but such links are often missing in practice (Petrov et al., 2011), and this calls for skills and methods to enable such links (Freestone, 2012). And for the wider urbanregional community, the principles of 'collaborative co-production' can be more explicit and effective by the SSP approach (Albrechts, 2012; Healey, 2009).

Third, for the challenge of 'system transformation', SSP provides practical methods and tools. It addresses the perceived gaps and common shortcomings in exploring multiple futures, engaging diverse stakeholders and linking scenarios to practical strategic planning (Bartholomew, 2007; Zapata & Kaza, 2015).

For the 'institutional tensions' above, of spatial versus economic planning, the mapping of trading zones may help to resolve and move forward. The experimental tensions may be addressed through the mapping of actors/stakeholders and their value chain opportunities: and for the 'systemic tensions' of transition versus crisis management, the mapping of co-evolutionary change helps to see the overlaps and differences.

Beyond state of the art?

The 'new normative' points towards 'beyond state of the art' in planning for urban-regional futures. The urban-regional as a unit of governance is under pressure from all sides: the political economy of (carbon-related) infrastructure is increasingly globalized, while many displaced communities are seeking a new kind of local identity and empowerment (Goodhart, 2017). More workplaces and social networks are global, while the physical impacts of climate change are stubbornly local. All this calls for a new generation of planning theory and practice to rationalize and enable and mobilize, with longer time horizons, wider communities, deeper values and *further* levels of transformation. The SSP proposed here is one contribution, which fits alongside other emerging initiatives, such as, bio-regional participative planning (Robinson et al., 2011); stakeholder deliberation forums (Mulgan, 2016); and 'urban living labs' for grassroots innovation (Evans et al., 2017). All this suggests an update of the current communicative paradigm of planning theory, responding to the implications of the new normative, with new insights on co-evolutionary 'Mode III' governance for system transformation.

Implications for urban-regional planning

This paper proposes the SSP concepts and tools for carbon-neutral planning: meanwhile the mainstream continues in very different situations around the world, calling for comparative research on the international context of carbon-neutral cities and regions. Many of the CNCA members (Melbourne, London, Stockholm etc.), it seems, are affluent well-organized metropolitan areas, resting on a post-colonial legacy, and highly dependent on global trade, technology and finance. Vancouver for one prides itself on its Zero Emission Building Plan, electric vehicles and reforestation of its hinterland, all building on abundant hydroelectric power resources. However, just over its city boundary are other municipalities in the wider metropolis, which are (at the time of writing) set on a trajectory of intensive fossil-fuel mobility and globalized consumption (Robinson et al., 2011). Meanwhile, there is a sense of urgency and looming catastrophe. Many cities and regions set off on a 'climate emergency' with high aspirations and simple carbon targets, then find themselves entangled in energy economics, infrastructure renewal, real estate markets, fossil-fuel lobbies, supply chain inertia and, not least, public resistance. There is an urgent need for a new generation of 'futureproof urban-regional planning to respond, for which the SSP aims to contribute. This paper takes a first step on that journey, with a mapping of the challenges, review of a major case study, outline of the Synergistic Scenario Planning approach and wider implications. We aim for this to stimulate further advances in theory, and urgently needed practice, for the 'New Normative'.

Acknowledgements

The authors acknowledge many years of advice and dialogue with the Greater Manchester Combined Authority and its Low Carbon Hub.

Disclosure statement

No potential conflict of interest was reported by the authors.

ORCID

Joe Ravetz ⓘ http://orcid.org/0000-0003-4288-2200
Raine Mäntysalo ⓘ http://orcid.org/0000-0002-91094764

References

Albrechts, L. (2012). Refraining strategic spatial planning by using a coproduction perspective. *Planning Theory, 12*(1), 46–63. doi:10.1177/1473095212452722
Alexander, E. (2010). Introduction: Does planning theory affect practice, and if so, how? *Planning Theory, 9*(2), 99–107. doi:10.1177/1473095209357862
Allmendinger, P., & Haughton, G. (2010). Spatial planning, devolution, and new planning spaces. *Environment and Planning C: Government and Policy, 28*(5), 803–818. doi:10.1068/c09163
Anderson, K. (2015, December). Duality in climate science. *Nature Geosdence, 8*(12), 898–900. doi:10.1038/ngeo2559
Anderson, K., & Bows, A. (2011). Beyond 'dangerous' climate change: Emission scenarios for a new world. *Philosophical Transactions of the Royal Society A: Mathematical, Physical and Engineering Sciences, 369*(1934), 20–44. doi:10.1098/rsta.2010.0290

Argyris, C., & Schön, D. A. (1996). *Organizational learning II: Theory, method, and practice.* Addison-Wesley.

Asheim, B. T. (2018). Smart Specialisation, innovation policy and regional innovation systems: What about new path development in less innovative regions? *Innovation: European Journal of Social Science Research, 32,* 8–25. https://doi.org/10.1080/13511610.2018.1491001.

Bäcklund, P., Häikiö, L., Leino, H., & Kanninen, V. (2018). Bypassing publicity and transparency for getting things done: Between informal and formal planning practices in Finland. *Planning Practice and Research, 33*(3), 309–325. https://doi.org/10.1080/02697459.2017.1378978

Balducci, A., & Mäntysalo, R. (Eds.). (2013). *Urban planning as a trading zone* Urban and Landscape Perspectives, Vol. 13. Springer.

Bansard, J. S., Pattberg, P., & Widerberg, O. (2017). Cities to the rescue? Assessing the performance of transnational municipal networks in global climate governance. *International Environmental Agreements, 17*(2), 229–246. doi:10.1007/s10784-016-9318-9

Bartholomew, K. (2007). Land use–transportation scenario planning: Promise and reality. *Transportation, 34*(4), 397–412. doi:10.1007/slll6-006-9108-2

Börjeson, L., Hojer, M., Dreborg, K.-H., Ekvall, T., & Finnveden, G. (2006). Scenario types and techniques: Towards a user's guide. *Futures, 38*(7), 723–739. doi:10.1016/j.futures.2005.12.002

Borrás, S., & Edler, J. (2020). The roles of the state in the governance of sociotechnical systems' transformation. *Research Policy, 49*(5), 1–9. doi:10.1016/j.respol.2020.103971

Bulkeley, H., Castán Broto, V., & Maassen, A. (2013). Governing urban low carbon transitions. In H. Bulkeley, V. Castán Broto, M. Hodson, & S. Marvin (Eds.), *Cities and low carbon transitions* (pp. 29–41). Routledge.

Carbon Neutral Cities Alliance. (2016). *Framework for long-term deep carbon reduction planning.* Innovation Network for Communities. Retrieved from https://carbonneutralcities.org/initiatives/ resources-and-reports/

Castan Broto, V., & Bulkeley, H. (2013). A survey of urban climate change experiments in 100 cities. *Global Environmental Change, 23*(1), 92–102. doi:10.1016/j.gloenvcha.2012.07.005

Chakraborty, A., Kaza, N., Knaap, G., & Deal, B. (2011). Robust plans and contingent plans. *Journal of the American Planning Association,* 77(3), 251–266. doi:10.1080/01944363.2011.582394

Cooke, P. (2012). *Complex adaptive innovation systems: Relatedness and transversality in the evolving region.* Routledge.

Deas, I. (2014). The search for territorial fixes in subnational governance: City-regions and the disputed emergence of post-political consensus in Manchester, England. *Urban Studies, 51*(11), 2285–2314. doi:10.1177/0042098013510956

Department for Environment, Food and Rural Affairs (Defra). (2019). *UK's carbon footprint 1997–2015.* Defra.

Department of Energy and Climate Change (DECC). (2009). *Low carbon transition plan for the UK.* DECC.

Dreborg, L. (1996). Essence of backcasting. *Futures, 28*(9), 813–828. doi:10.1016/S0016-3287(96)00044-4

Eftec, Environmental Finance and Countryscape. (2019). *Greater Manchester natural capital investment plan.* GMCA.

Etzkowitz, H., & Leydesdorff, L. (2000). The dynamics of innovation: From national systems and 'mode 2' to a triple helix of university–industry–government relations. *Research Policy, 29*(2), 109–123. doi:10.1016/S0048-7333(99)00055-4

Evans, J., Karvonen, A., & Raven, R. (Eds.). (2017). *The experimental city.* Routledge.

Fischer, H., Meissner, K. J., Mix, A. C., Abram, N. J., Austermann, J., Brovkin, V., Capron, E., Colombaroli, D., Daniau, A.-L., Dyez, K. A., Felis, T., Finkelstein, S. A., Jaccard, S. L., McClymont, E. L., Rovere, A., Sutler, J., Wolff, E. W., Affolter, S., Bakker, P., ... Zhou, L. (2018). Palaeoclimate constraints on the impact of 2°C anthropogenic warming and beyond. *Nature Geoscience, 11,* 474–485. https://doi.org/10.1038/s41561-018-0146-0

Freestone, R. (2012). Futures thinking in planning education and research. *Journal for Education in the Built Environment, 7*(1), 8–38. doi:10.11120/jebe.2012.07010008

Fuller, B. (2006). *Trading zones: Cooperating for water resource and ecosystem management when stakeholders have apparently irreconcilable differences.* MIT Press.

Galison, P. (1997). *Image and logic: A material culture of microphysics.* University of Chicago Press.

Galison, P. (2010). Trading with the enemy. In M. E. Gorman (Ed.), *Trading zones and interactional expertise: Creating new kinds of collaboration* (pp. 25–52). MIT Press.

Georghiou, L., Edler, J., Uyarra, E., & Jillian Yeow, J. (2014). Policy instruments for public procurement of innovation: Choice, design and assessment. *Technological Forecasting and Social Change, 86,* 1–12. doi:10.1016/j.techfore.2013.09.018

Goodhart, D. (2017). *The road to somewhere: The populist revolt and the future of politics.* Hurst.

Granqvist, K., & Mäntysalo, R. (2020). The strategic turn in planning and the role of institutional innovation. In A. Hagen, & U. Higdem (Eds.), *Innovation in public planning. Calculate, communicate and innovate* (pp. 73–90). Palgrave Macmillan.

Greater Manchester Combined Authority (GMCA). (2013). *GM climate change strategy.* GMCA.

Greater Manchester Combined Authority (GMCA). (2015). *GM spatial framework: Strategic options.* GMCA.

Greater Manchester Combined Authority (GMCA). (2019). *5-Year environment plan.* GMCA.

Greenhouse Gas Protocol. (2016). *FAQ \ Greenhouse Gas Protocol.* Retrieved from www.ghgprotocol.org

Grubb, M., with Hourcade, J.-C., & Neuhoff, K. (2014). *Planetary economics: Energy, climate change and the three domains of sustain*able development. Routledge.

Guertler, P., & Rosenow, J. (2016). *Buildings and the 5th carbon budget.* Association for Conservation of Energy.

Harris, T. M. (2016). From PGIS to participatory deep mapping and spatial storytelling: An evolving trajectory in community knowledge representation in GIS. *Cartographic Journal, 53*(4), 318–325. doi:10.1080/00087041.2016.1243864

Haughton, G., Deas, L, Hincks, S., & Ward, K. (2016). Mythic Manchester: Devo Mane, the Northern Powerhouse and rebalancing the English economy. *Cambridge Journal of Regions, Economy and Society, 9,* 355–370. doi:10.1093/cjres/rsw004.

Healey, P. (2009). In search of the 'strategic' in spatial strategy-making. *Planning Theory and Practice, 10*(4), 439–457. doi:10.1080/14649350903417191

Hendriks, F. (2014). Understanding good urban governance: Essentials, shifts, and values. *Urban Affairs Review, 50*(4), 553–576. doi:10.1177/1078087413511782

Hodson, M., Marvin, S., & McMeekin, A. (2018). The amenable city-region: The symbolic rise and the relative decline of Greater Manchester's low carbon commitments, 2006–17. In A. Luque-Ayala, S. Marvin, & H. Bulkeley (Eds.), *Rethinking urban transitions: Politics in the low carbon city* (pp. 73–88). Routledge.

Hodson, M., McMeekin, A., Froud, J., & Moran, M. (2019). Staterescaling and re-designing the material city-region: Tensions of disruption and continuity in articulating the future of Greater Manchester. *Urban Studies, 57*(1), 198–217. doi:10.1177/0042098018820181.

Höjer, M., & Mattsson, L.-G. (2000). Determinism and backcasting in future studies. *Futures, 32*(7), 613–634. doi:10.1016/S00163287(00)00012-4

Inayatullah, S. (2011). City futures in transformation: Emerging issues and case studies. *Futures, 43*(7), 654–661. doi:10.1016/j.futures.2011.05.006

ING Bank. (2015). *Rethinkingfinance in a circular economy: Financial implications of circular business models.* ING Bank.

Johanson, J.-E., & Vakkuri, J. (2018). *Governing hybrid organizations: Exploring diversity of institutional life.* Routledge.

Komninos, N. (2015). *The age of intelligent cities: Smart environments and innovation-for-all strategies.* Routledge.

Kuriakose, J., Anderson, K., Broderick, J., & McLachlan, C. (2018). *Quantifying the implications of the Paris Agreement for Greater Manchester.* Tyndall Centre.

Lippert, I. (2012). Carbon classified? Unpacking heterogeneous relations inscribed into corporate carbon emissions. *Ephemera, 12*(1/2), 138–161.

Loveridge, D. (2008). *Foresight: The art and science of anticipating the future.* Taylor & Francis.

Luque-Ayala, A., Marvin, S., & Bulkeley, H. (2018). Introduction. In A. Luque-Ayala, S. Marvin, & H. Bulkeley (Eds.), *Rethinking urban transitions: Politics in the low carbon city* (pp. 1–12). Routledge.

Mäntysalo, R., & Grišakov, K. (2017). Framing 'evidence' and scenario stories in strategic spatial planning. In L. Albrechts, A. Balducci, & J. Hillier (Eds.), *Situated practices of strategic planning. An international perspective* (pp. 348–361). Routledge.

Mäntysalo, R., & Jarenko, K. (2014). Communicative planning theory following deliberative democracy theory: Critical pragmatism and the trading zone concept. *International Journal of e-Planning Research,* (1), 38–50. doi:10.4018/ijepr.2014010104

Mäntysalo, R., Jarenko, K., Nilsson, K. L., & Saglie, I.-L. (2015). Legitimacy of informal strategic urban planning – Observations from Finland, Sweden and Norway. *European Planning Studies, 23*(2), 349–366. doi:10.1080/09654313.2013.861808

Mäntysalo, R., Olesen, K., & Granqvist, K. (2020). 'Artefactual anchoring' of strategic spatial planning as persuasive storytelling. *Planning Theory, 19*(3), 285–305. doi:10.1177/1473095219893002

Mäntysalo, R., Tuomisaari, J., Granqvist, K., & Kanninen, V. (2019). The strategic Incrementalism of Lahti master planning: Three lessons. *Planning Theory and Practice, 20*(4), 555–572. doi:10.1080/14649357.2019.1652336

McKillop, T., O'Neill, J., Glaeser, E., Coyle, D., & Kestenbaum, J. (2009). *Manchester independent economic review.* AGMA.

Moran, M., & Williams, K. (2015). *'Devo Mane': 'Northern* Powerhouse' or 'Northern Poorhouse'? Retrieved from http://speri.dept.shef.ac.uk/2015/04/07/devo-manc-northern-powerhouse-northern-poorhouse/

Mulgan, G. (2016). *Big mind: How collective intelligence can change our world.* Princeton University Press.

Myers, D., & Kitsuse, A. (2000). Constructing the future in planning: A survey of theories and tools. *Journal of Planning Education and Research, 19*(3), 221–231. doi:10.1177/0739456X0001900301

Neuvonen, A., & Ache, P. (2017). Metropolitan vision making–Using backcasting as a strategic learning process to shape metropolitan futures. *Futures, 86,* 73–83. doi:10.1016/j.futures.2016.10.003

Newman, P. (2008). Strategic spatial planning: Collective action and moments of opportunity. *European Planning Studies, 16*(10),1371–1383. doi:10.1080/09654310802420078

Organisation for Economic Co-operation and Development (OECD). (2015). *System innovation: Synthesis report.* Directorate of Science, Technology and Innovation.

Petrov, L. O., Shahumyan, H., Williams, B., & Convery, S. (2011). Scenarios and indicators supporting urban regional planning. *Procedia – Social and Behavioral Sciences, 21,* 243–252. doi:10.1016/j.sbspro.2011.07.012

Phaal, R., Farrukh, C. J. P., & Probert, D. R. (2007). Strategic roadmapping: A workshop-based approach for identifying and exploring innovation issues and opportunities. *Engineering Management Journal, 19*(1), 16–24. doi:10.1080/10429247.2007.11431716

Phdungsilp, A. (2011). Futures studies' backcasting method used for strategic sustainable city planning. *Futures, 43*(7), 707–714. doi:10.1016/j.futures.2011.05.012

Plastrik, P., & Cleveland, J. (2019). *Life after carbon: The next global* transformation of cities. Island.

Quist, J. (2007). *Backcasting for a sustainable future: The impact after 10 years.* Eburon.

Quist, J., Thissen, W., & Vergragt, P. J. (2011). The impact and spin-off of participatory backcasting: From vision to niche. *Technological Forecasting and Social Change, 78*(5), 883–897. doi:10.1016/j.techfore.2011.01.011

Ratcliffe, J., & Krawczyk, E. (2011). Imagineering city futures: The use of prospective through scenarios in urban planning. *Futures, 43*(7), 642–653. doi:10.1016/j.futures.2011.05.005

Ravetz, J. (2000). *City-Region 2020: Integrated planning for a sustainable environment.* Earthscan with the Town & Country Planning Association.

Ravetz, J. (2006). Regional innovation & resource productivity – New approaches to analysis and communication. In S. Randies, & K. Green (Eds.), *Industrial ecology & spaces of innovation* (pp. 63–81). Ashgate.

Ravetz, J. (2008). State of the stock: What do we know about existing buildings and their future prospects. *Energy Policy, 36*(12), 4462–4470. doi:10.1016/j.enpoL2008.09.026

Ravetz, J. (2010). Rethinking low-carbon strategy in the regions: Applications of the territorial principle in a networked landscape. In *Regions and the environment* (pp. 136–142). Regional Studies Association (RSA).

Ravetz, J. (2015). *The future of the urban environment & ecosystem services in the UK* (Report to the Government Foresight on Future of Cities). Government Office of Science.

Ravetz, J. (2020). *Deeper city; Collective intelligence and the pathways from smart to wise.* Routledge.

Ravetz, J., & Miles, I. D. (2016). Foresight in cities: On the possibility of a 'strategic urban intelligence'. *Foresight, 18*(5), 469– 490. doi:10.1108/FS-06–2015–0037

Revi, A., Satterthwaite, D., Aragón-Durand, F., Corfee-Morlot, J., Kiunsi, R. B. R., Felling, M., Roberts, D., Solecki, W., Gajjar, S. P., & Sverdlik, A. (2014). Towards transformative adaptation in cities: The IPCC's Fifth Assessment. *Environment and Urbanization, 26*(1), 11–28. doi:10.1177/0956247814523539

Robinson, J., Burch, S., Talwar, S., O'Shea, M., & Walsh, M. (2011). Envisioning sustainability: Recent progress in the use of participatory backcasting approaches for sustainability research. *Technological Forecasting and Social Change, 78*(5), 756–768. doi:10.1016/j.techfore.2010.12.006

Schot, J., & Steinmueller, W. E. (2018). Three frames for innovation policy: R&D, systems of innovation and transformative change. *Research Policy, 47*(9), 1554-1156. doi:10.1016/j.respol.2018.08.011

Sherriff, G. (2013). From burden to asset – The political ecology of sustainable transport. *Town and Country Planning, 82*(10), 431–434.

Star, S. L., & Griesemer, J. (1989). Institutional ecology, 'translations' and boundary objects: Amateurs and professionals in Berkeley's Museum of Vertebrate Zoology, 1907–39. *Social Studies of Science, 19*(3), 387–420. doi:10.1177/030631289019003001

Steele, W., & Ruming, K. J. (2012). Flexibility versus certainty: Unsettling the land-use planning shibboleth in Australia. *Planning Practice and Research, 27*(2), 155–176. doi:10.1080/02697459.2012.662670

Tyndall Centre. (2018). *The implications of global warming of 1.5°C and 2°C: WP 164.* Tyndall Centre.

UKGBC. (2017). *Regeneration and retrofit: Task group report.* UKGBC.

Uyarra, E., & Flanagan, K. (2010). From regional systems of innovation to regions as innovation policy spaces. *Environment and Planning C, 28*(4), 681–695. doi:10.1068/c0961

Van den Broeck, J. (2013). Balancing strategic and institutional planning: The search for a pro-active planning instrument. *disP, 49*(3), 43–47. https://doi.org/10.1080/02513625.2013.859007

Viguié, V, Hallegatte, S., & Rozenberg, J. (2014). Downscaling long term socio-economic scenarios at city scale: A case study on Paris. *Technological Forecasting and Social Change, 87,* 305–324. doi:10.1016/j.techfore.2013.12.028

Watson, V. (2008). Down to Earth: Linking planning theory and practice in the 'metropole' and beyond. *International Planning Studies, 13*(3), 223–237. doi:10.1080/13563470802521408

Webber, P., Gouldson, A., & Kerr, N. (2015). The impacts of household retrofit and domestic energy efficiency schemes: A large scale, ex post evaluation. *Energy Policy, 84,* 35–43. doi:10.1016/ j.enpol.2015.04.020

Weber, M., & Truffer, B. (2017). Moving innovation systems research to the next level: Towards an integrative agenda. *Oxford Review of Economic Policy, 33*(1), 101–121. doi:10.1093/oxrep/grx002

Wolfram, M. (2016). Conceptualizing urban transformative capacity: A framework for research and policy. *Cities, 51,* 121–130. doi:10.1016/j.cities.2015.11.011

Zapata, M. A., & Kaza, N. (2015). Radical uncertainty: Scenario planning for futures. *Environment and Planning B: Planning and Design, 42*(4), 754–770. doi:10.1068/b39059

Zegras, C., & Rayle, L. (2012). Testing the rhetoric: An approach to assess scenario planning's role as a catalyst for urban policy integration. *Futures, 44*(4), 303–318. doi:10.1016/j.futures.2011.10.013

Index

Note: **Bold** page numbers refer to tables; *italic* page numbers refer to figures and page numbers followed by "n" denote endnotes.

Abercrombie, P. 24
action planning 302
actors 15, 26, 59–60, 113, 121–122, 126, 130–132, 140, 152, 155–156, 164–166, 225, 266, 270–271, 273–274, 299–300, 303–304, 306–307
Addie, J. P. 133
Addis Ababa Declaration 86
Africa 45, 48, 56–57, 60–62, 67, 75, 79
African Development Bank (AfDB) 84, 86
African urban futures 60
Agnew, J. 102
Agyemang, F. 45
Albrechts, L. 222, 238, 278
alignment 25, 100, 111–112, 204, 290–291, 296–297, 307
Allen, J. 126
Allmendinger, P. 137
Alonso, W. 174
alternative-substitute place-making 53, 64–69
Amedzro, K. 45
American Planning Association 28
Anderson, B. 102
Andersson, M. 175
anti-urban ideology 153
Asian Infrastructure Investment Bank (AIIB) 85, 88
asset assessment 24

balanced regional growth 77–78, 84, 153
Baldwin, R. 91
Barnett, C. 36
Beauregard, R. 24

Bel, G. 210
Béland, D. 197, 213
Belt and Road Initiative (BRI) 76, 84, 86–89
Berry, B. J. L. 115n3
Bishop, P. 175–176
Blache, Vidal de la 249
Boria, E. 155
Born, B. 42
boundary management 279, 281
boundary objects 266, 270–271, 279–282, 294, 296–297, 302, 307
Branford, Victor 254
Brenner, N. 100–101, 106

Canada 128, 130–132, 136, 141
capitalism 101, 257–258
carbon: as 'climate emergency' 295; as economic agenda 294; as environmental agenda 293
carbon-neutral cities 288, 308; synergistic scenario planning for 288–309
Carbon Neutral Cities Alliance (CNCA) 288
carbon-neutral goals 288, 291
carbon neutrality 292, 295
carbon-neutral planning 291, 308
carbon targets 294, 296, 300, 304
cartographic representations 155–156, 163, 166
Cash, D. W. 271
Castoriadis, C. 102, 114
Catalan governments 205, 208, 210
Catalonia 194, 198, 201–202, 205, 208–210, 213–215

Cervero, R. 174
Chen, Y. 180
Chicago 105, 173, 179–180, 187, 189
Chicago Metropolitan Planning Agency
    (CMAP) 173, 177, 182–183, 187–188
Chicago Regional Econometric Input-
    Output Model (CREIM) 177
chronic stresses 267, 272
city-regional/city-regionalism 40,
    104, 122, 141, 155; agglomeration
    economies 108; imaginaries 99–113;
    imaginary 100, 103, 105–106, 108,
    111–114; relationships 99; space 104,
    106, 108–109, 113
city-regionalization 104–105, 108, 111
city-regional scales 104, 107, 111, 113,
    122, 127, 140; institutionalization of
    111–112
city-regions 5, 34–45, 47–49, 57, 65,
    99–100, 104–114, 123, 152, 293, 295;
    approach 42, 45; concept 35, 45–46,
    48; functions 56, 68; level 46, 307; in
    NUA 47–48; plans 37, 46
classic planning theory 224
climate change 19–20, 37, 208, 265, 267,
    272, 274, 294, 296, 299, 308
coalitions 112–113, 126–127, 137, 139,
    144, 193, 201, 203, 208, 210–211,
    213–214
Cochrane, A. 41
Coenen, L. 6, 271
coherent regional economy 121, 143
collective action 124, 126–127, 164, 225,
    231, 269
communication 25–26, 66, 87, 89, 127,
    195, 197, 253, 258
competitive megaregions 152,
    154, 157
competitive regionalisms 122
competitive regions 122, 128, 141–142
complexity 14, 54, 57, 62, 67, 110, 123,
    223, 225, 235, 265
comprehensive rational approach 224
comprehensive reform 154
connectivity 17, 58, 84, 88, 91, 180,
    185, 187
Connell, R. 35
contradictory regional imaginaries
    122, 143
Coombes, M. 110
core cities 109–110, 128, 141
Cox, K. R. 143
crisis management 227, 267, 292, 308
cultural criticism 244, 247–261

Dados, N. 35
Davoudi, S. 38, 268
Deal, B. 180
debt crisis 79
decentralization 48, 81, 90, 154, 167,
    193, 195, 198, 201, 212
developmental outcomes 77, 91–92
developmental state 257, 259
development planning 160, 222, 258
development policy 76, 79, 83
De Vries, J. 214
discourses 99, 102–103, 107, 110, 152,
    155, 194, 198, 202–203, 296, 298
disjointed incrementalism 224
Distributed experimentation 270–271,
    276–277
Dühr, S. 155
Duranton, G. 182

early market reform 153
economic-and city-centric (ECC) space
    100
economic development 46, 107, 123,
    130, 159, 165, 188–189, 194, 198, 204,
    257–258
economic geography 100, 128
economic planning 187, 227, 308
economy 36, 43, 49, 57, 76, 81, 83, 89,
    108, 204, 210
Edward, Glaeser 188
effective strategic planning 221,
    223, 228
Ellis, Clough Williams 253
Ellison, Echoing 188
employment growth 177, 180, 183, 185,
    187–189
England 82, 88, 100, 104–105, 107,
    110–112, 201, 203–205, 213, 222,
    226–227
Etherington, J. 196
experimental tensions 291–292, 308
extrospective regionalism 141

Fawcett, C. B. 109, 249
Fenneman, Nevin 249
Ferraro, F. 267, 270–271
financial crisis 83–84, 92, 294
Five-Year Plan 77, 153–155, 160
Flanders 194, 197–198, 201–202,
    210–214, 239
Flick, U. 273
foreign direct investment (FDI) 81
formal planning 4, 54–56, 59–62, 64–65,
    67, 69

Friedmann, J. 78, 246, 258
Fujita, M. 174
functional economic area (FEA) 109–113, 233, 288, 296
future-proof cities 265, 267, 269, 271, 275, 277, 279

Geddes, P. 38, 109, 254
geographies 41, 103, 110, 127–128, 133, 136, 143, 160, 162, 248, 253, 256–257
Glaeser, E. L. 174–176, 189
global city-regions 41, 81, 107
globalization 40, 42, 45, 47, 76, 89, 101, 107–108, 152, 260
global Marshall Plan 76
Global North 12, 15, 35, 39, 41–43, 47–48, 55, 58
Global South 34–35, 41–43, 45, 48–49, 53–55, 57–58, 60–61, 68–69, 76, 80, 87, 91
good governance agenda 80
governance 20, 22, 37, 41, 43–45, 48, 126, 149, 151, 223, 226, 291–292, 308
governance experimentation/experiments 6, 265–267, 269–272, 275, 277–279, 281–282
Gras, N. S. B. 109
Greater Manchester Combined Authority (GMCA) 294–295, 302
Greenhouse Gas Reporting Protocol 288
green infrastructure 183, 274–275
Griesemer, J. 297
Gripaios, P. 175–176
growth model 184–185, 187

Hall, P. G. 53, 151, 231
hallmarks 5, 11, 167
Hanlon, W. W. 175–176
Harrison, J. 110, 260
Harvey, D. 101, 124
Haughton, G. 137
Healey, P. 39, 41
Heley, J. 110
Henderson, V. 175
Herbertson, Frank 249
heterogeneous spatial production externalities 174, 188–189
Hewings, G. 175, 180
Horak, M. 131
Howard, Ebenezer 251

inclusive planning 59
informality 4, 12, 56, 62

informal settlements 53, 56, 58–62, 65, 67
infrastructure-led development 75–77, 82–83, **82**, 86–88, 90–92
infrastructure planning 195, 227
infrastructure projects 85–87, 89–90, 236
innovation corridor 122, 138, 141–144
institutionalized regional planning 3, 5–6, 11, 16, 26
institutional tensions 291, 308
insurgent planning 58, 66
integration 19, 25, 47, 75–76, 85, 134, 220, 251, 256
Integration of the Regional Infrastructure of South America (IIRSA) 82, 89
interwar regional planning 247–251
interwar regional thinkers 6, 244
investments 64–65, 68, 78, 80, 83–84, 87–89, 91, 124–125, 144, 151, 293, 300

Jessop, B. 40–42, 126
Jin, Y. 175
Jonas, A. E. G. 41, 152, 155
Jones, M. 107
Jones, R. 204

Kaiser, R. 107
Katz, C. 59
Keil, R. 133
Kenya 54–55, 60–62, 64–68, 90
Kim, J. H. 172, 189
Kitchener-Waterloo 121, 128, 131–132, 139, 141
knowledge 20, 26, 43, 100, 103–104, 106, 237, 269–270, 272, 275, 281
Krugman, P. R. 174

Lamu Port-South Sudan-Ethiopia-Transport Corridor 90
land 43, 56, 81, 125, 130, 194, 196, 205, 213–215, 253, 256
land-use planning 156, 172–176, 183, 188–189, 194, 201, 211–212
Larsson, J. P. 175
Lecours, A. 197, 213
Leys, C. 79
Li, Y. 45–46
London 6, 75, 142, 228–233, 235–236, 293, 308
Lucas, R. E. 189
Luo, X. 46

Luque-Ayala, A. 292
Luukkonen, J. 108

MacKaye, B. 38, 246, 248, 250
Marcus, G. E. 102
market-driven growth versus plan
    183–185, 187
markets 12, 16, 76, 79–80, 85, 88, 222,
    226, 232, 299, 304
Marx, Leo 251
McCann, E. 141
McGuirk, P. 40
mediation 25
megalopolis 148, 150–151, 167
megaregionalism 150, 153, 155–157,
    162, 164
megaregionalization 152, 162
megaregional planning 5, 150, 159, 163,
    165–166
megaregional spaces 149, 154
megaregions 148–152, 154–157, 159–167;
    concept 149–150, 155, 164; formation
    148–151, 155, 163, 166; geographies
    of 151–152, 160, 166; planning 150,
    163–166; scale 21, 154, 161, 163–164,
    166–167
methodological territorialism 41
metropolitan cycling network 272,
    276, 281
Metropolitan Urban Forest Strategy
    272–274, 277, 281
Mills, C. W. 102
Miscio, A. 175–176
mobilized spatial planning 194, 197, 202
Moisio, S. 41, 152, 155
Moore, A. 111
multi-stakeholder collaboration 279
multivocal inscription 270–271, 275,
    277, 279
Mumford, L. 38, 246, 248–249

National Development Reform
    Commission (NDRC) 157, 159–160
national identity 196–197, 209
nationalism 193–198, 203, 205, 209, 211,
    213–215, 253
national-level megaregions 154–155,
    157–158
national main functional area planning
    156, 159
national new urbanization 160
national planning systems 195, 212
national urban system planning 155–159

neoclassical economics 83
neoliberal policies 78
neoliberal reforms 15, 76, 78–79, 81, 85
neoliberal scalar strategy 104
network-centrism 40
networked cities 153–154
networks 35, 39–41, 57, 86, 88, 152, 157,
    272, 274–275, 277–278, 281
Newman, P. 291
new regionalism 39–40, 81, 107, 122,
    125, 130
Nieuw-Vlaamse Alliantie (N-VA)
    210–211, 213
Nikiforova, N. 107
normality 62
North American Industry Classification
    System (NAICS) 177

Offe, C. 124

Painter, J. 40
Pan, H. 175, 180, 185–186
parallel thinking 293
Parnell, S. 36
participatory architecture 270, 274, 276,
    279, 281
Peck, J. 78, 141
permanent impermanence 55, 59–62,
    64–65, 69
Pfeiffer, U. 53
phasing 25, 236
place-making 2, 4, 54–57, 60–61, 64–67,
    69, 266
planners 2, 4, 6–7, 10–11, 13, 18, 21,
    23–24, 26, 28–29, 61–62, 64–67, 173,
    220–222, 226
planning and place-making approach
    (PPA) 55, 60, 63, 69
planning regional futures 2–7, 10–11,
    16–17, 23–24, 26–29, 54, 58, 60,
    68–69, 114
planning skills 23–25, 28
planning theory 43, 220–222, 224, 251,
    293, 308
planning tools 166, 174
policies 12, 62, 64–67, 69, 78–79, 114,
    149, 165, 197, 210, 213, 215,
    303–304, 306
political astuteness 24
politics 99–114, 122, 152, 155–156, 162,
    193, 202, 212, 222, 230, 245–247
population dynamics 3, 229, 233–234
post-reform economic transition 153

power 78–79, 103, 110–111, 113–114, 193, 195, 201, 205, 208, 210, 222, 253, 256, 277, 279
process analysis 282, 304
productive ambiguity 122, 127, 134
Purcell, M. 42

Reagan, Ronald 78
regionalism 39–41, 81, 107, 121–128, 130–131, 133–134, 136–141, 143–144, 150, 153, 155–157, 164, 244–247, 253–255, 258–259; change 16, 19, 24–26, 35; collective action 122–126, 138–139, 141; development 34, 49, 107, 125, 150–152, 154, 255, 259; economic development 39; economy 125, 132, 138, 172, 176; entrepreneurs 122, 127, 134, 139, 141, 144; imaginaries 121, 123, 126–127, 130–131, 133, 137, 139–141, 143–144; institutions 20, 104–105, 112, 134; logics of 121, 123, 125–128, 130–131, 133–134, 139–141, 143; multiplication of *129*; plans 13, 17–18, 20–21, 46, 228, 235; studies 2–3, 5–7, 10–11, 13, 26, 28, 42, 107, 124, 126, 244–246
regionalization 104–105, 107–108, 111
regional planning 2–7, 10–25, 27–29, 38, 77–78, 81, 148, 156, 164–166, 239, 244–261; definition of 247, 249–250, 257; emergence of 17, 38; evolution of 246; future of 3, 244; hallmark of 5, 13, 17, 28; history of 246; philosophy of 250; purpose of 14, 28, 249
regulations 11, 22, 49, 58, 62, 64, 80, 173, 183, 194, 197
relational thinking 301, 306
resilience 13, 265–269, 271; actions 266, 269, 276–277
Resilient Melbourne Strategy (RMS) 265, 267, 272, 276, 281
resources 23, 28, 35, 56, 61–62, 193, 196, 225–226, 229, 250, 266, 279, 282
responsibilities 12, 22, 67, 140, 149, 156, 228, 232, 234, 279, 289
robustness check 181, 185
Ross, A. 204
Rossi-Hansberg, E. 189
Roy, A. 43

Said, E. W. 103, 110
Salet, W. 221, 238
Salman, Mohammed bin 75

Sandercock, L. 58
scalar fixing 100, 103–104, 110–113
scalar imaginaries 100, 103–105, 107, 112–114, 143
scenario planning 25, 291, 293, 296, 300, 302, 306–307
Schon, D. A. 226
Scotland 194, 197–198, 202–205, 213
Scott, A. 40, 43
Scottish National Party (SNP) 201–205
Seton-Watson, H. 113
shadow placemaking 58
Shen, J. 46
short-term crisis management 292
Silva, E. 45
Sirvio, H. 108
Slater, D. 67
smart cities 2
Smith, A. D. 196–197
Smith, J. Russell 249
Smith, N. 101
social actors 44, 124–125, 214–215
southern Ontario 128, 130, 134, 141–142
spatial economic model 173
spatial imaginaries 13, 102–103, 110–111, 127, 148, 224
spatial planning 36, 38, 83–86, 90, 92, 151, 164, 166, 193–195, 197–198, 201–205, 209, 211–215; politics of 164, 166; role of 38, 214
spatial production externalities 172–175, 183, 185–190
Star, S. L. 297
state government 156–157, 277–279
state-led planning 48–49
state socialism 153
Storper, M. 40, 43
strategic planning 6, 18, 110, 154, 221–223, 225–226, 229–232, 234–235, 237–239, 291–292, 302
strategic regional planning 220–221, 223, 228, 235–236
strategic spatial planning 6, 198, 201, 214, 221, 226, 293
structural adjustment loans (SALs) 79
structured coherence 4, 124–128, 143
substate nationalist agendas 202
systemic tensions 291–292, 308
system transformation 290, 296, 298–299, 302, 306–308

Taylor, Charles 107
temporalities 4, 25, 59, 65–66

temporary urbanisms 53–55, 57–62, 65, 67, 69
territorial alliances 121, 123–125, 143
territorial planning 36–38, 81, 195, 291
territorial politics 46, 166, 193–194
Thatcher, Margaret 78
Tickell, A. 78, 141
Tonkiss, F. 67
Tooze, A. 84
Toronto-Waterloo Innovation Corridor (TWIC) 121–144
Tory, Mayor 133
trading zones 296–297, 299–303, 307–308
traditional regional planning process 23
transformation 56, 67–68, 91, 113, 244, 288, 290–292, 296, 301–302, 306, 308
transition planning 292
transport 48, 53, 64, 105, 194–195, 204, 208–209, 272, 288, 292, 295–296
Turner, M. A. 182

UN-Habitat 5, 16, 34, 36–38, 43–44, 48, 61–62, 77
United Nations Human Settlements Programme (UNHSP) 45
urban economic futures 172
urban economic growth 173, 188
urban forest strategy 273
urban governance experimentation 269, 271
urban planning 209, 281
urban-regional planning 288, 297, 308–309

urban resilience 267–269
urban systems, future 155

values, of planning 3, 11, 17
Van Westen, G. 42, 44
Venables, A. J. 174
Volksunie 210
Von Hippel, E. 66

Wachsmuth, D. 4, 123, 127, 133
Wannop, U. 227
Ward, K. 41
Waterloo Region 131, 133, 138, 142
Watkins, J. 103
Weaver, C. 78, 246, 258
Weber, E. 195
Wernberg, J. 175
wicked regional problems 3–4
Wiesenthal, H. 124
Williams, C. H. 196–197
Wolch, J. R. 59
work 44–45, 57, 59, 85, 103–104, 110, 112, 140, 142–143, 244, 246–248, 251–252, 256, 260, 300
World Bank 76–77, 79–81, 83–86
world development report 79–80, 83
World Economic Forum (WEF) 84
Wray, I. 7
Wu, F. 45–46, 153

Yang, T. 175, 180, 185–186

Zoomers, A. 42, 44

For Product Safety Concerns and Information please contact our EU

representative GPSR@taylorandfrancis.com Taylor & Francis Verlag GmbH,

Kaufingerstraße 24, 80331 München, Germany

Printed and bound by CPI Group (UK) Ltd, Croydon, CR0 4YY

08/05/2025

01864358-0006